READING THE NEW NIETZSCHE

READING THE
NEW
NIETZSCHE

The Birth of Tragedy, The Gay Science,
Thus Spoke Zarathustra, and
On the Genealogy of Morals

David B. Allison

ROWMAN & LITTLEFIELD PUBLISHERS, INC.
Lanham • Boulder • New York • Oxford

ROWMAN & LITTLEFIELD PUBLISHERS, INC.

Published in the United States of America
by Rowman & Littlefield Publishers, Inc.
4720 Boston Way, Lanham, Maryland 20706
http://www.rowmanlittlefield.com

12 Hid's Copse Road
Cumnor Hill, Oxford OX2 9JJ, England

British Library Cataloguing in Publication Information Available

Library of Congress Cataloging-in-Publication Data

Allison, David B.
    Reading the new Nietzsche : The birth of tragedy, The gay science, Thus spoke
Zarathustra, and On the genealogy of morals / David B. Allison.
       p.   cm.
    Includes bibliographical references and index.
    ISBN 0-8476-8979-4 (alk. paper)—ISBN 0-8476-8980-8 (pbk. : alk. paper)
    1. Nietzsche, Friedrich Wilhelm, 1844–1900.   I. Title.

B3317.A42   2001
193—dc21   00-057584

Printed in the United States of America

♾ ™ The paper used in this publication meets the minimum requirements of
American National Standard for Information Sciences—Permanence of Paper for
Printed Library Materials, ANSI/NISO Z39.48–1992.

CONTENTS

PREFACE

Perhaps more than any other philosopher who readily comes to mind, Nietzsche writes exclusively for *you*. Not at you, but for you. For you, the reader. Only you. At least this is the feeling one often has when reading him. Like a friend, he seems to share your every concern—and your aversions and suspicions as well. Like a true friend, he rarely tells you what you ought to do—that would be too presumptuous, immodest, authoritarian. And friends don't moralize, either. They share secrets and encourage you—to enjoy, to travel, to try something new, to get out of your skin for a while. As for the "others," he can be paralyzingly critical, lacerating in his acerbic wit and humor. But he won't betray you, of that you can be certain. You have earned his trust. You have both been there, on the oblique and pretty far down at times, really, but now you can laugh—at the pettiness, the stupid mistakes, at all you had to go through to be where you are. No great revelations, no absolute knowledge, no timeless, leaden certainties—but things do look a bit different now, and one gets a better perspective on things, new perspectives, a nuanced appreciation. One is more tolerant of everything ambiguous and is far better disposed to oneself and to others. One begins to spare oneself the small annoyances, the sense of regret or shame, at the way things were supposed to be. And things take on a richer patina in turn, a sensuous immediacy, the way one feels after a long illness, when rediscovering the simple fact that sunlight is itself a medium of pleasure, or when warm voices and laughter once again drift up from the evening boulevards below.

Nietzsche lends a remarkable historical and philosophical resonance to the wide variety of subject matter he writes about. Tacitus, Themistocles, Aeschylus, Emerson, Pindar, Homer, Plato, Aristotle, Goethe, Empedocles, Schiller, Schopenhauer, Herodotus, and Heraclitus infuse his reflections as effortlessly as a returned gesture of welcome. In part, it is due to the fascinating wealth of material he draws upon, his great knowledge of traditional thought and faith, his concern to communicate through an effective literary style, and his remarkable control of rhetoric that enable his works to become so successfully personalized by the attentive reader. Of course, this is part of the problem as well; namely, the paradoxical fact that everyone seems to find a different Nietzsche, that he is continually being reinvented and reappropriated, precisely because his work so readily lends itself to the plethora of interpretations that have arisen in response to it. The interpretations vary from the naive to the sublime, from the desire to have his thought serve a quite narrow, particular interest, to reduce and simplify it to a caricature of itself, or to positively exclude it from the company of civil discussion altogether—effectively, to interpret Nietzsche's work right out of all plausible existence. Nietzsche himself recognized that given the personal, intellectual, and historical specificity of the particular reader, any text would be necessarily factored by the agendas—the pretexts, concerns, and prejudices—of the audience it chanced upon. And to write in such a way as to foster this diversity of interpretation is a signal mark of generosity by an author, a quality rarely found in traditional philosophers.

Nonetheless, Nietzsche's writings are far from rudderless, nor are they merely capricious exercises for the endless improvisations of the reader's imagination. Rather, Nietzsche writes for a particular audience, a particular reader. And in the same way one has to work to cultivate and to maintain a friendship, Nietzsche desperately sought to cultivate an audience—one he would come to call his "Good Europeans." What motivated Nietzsche to assiduously pursue such an audience was his deep conviction that he, perhaps more than anyone else at the time, was in possession of a newly emergent truth—one he experienced and internalized as a veritable trauma—namely, that the world was on the brink of a completely unfathomable disruption and dislocation. It was his recognition that the very foundations of Western culture were being withdrawn: the God of the West, who for millennia on end had served humanity as the font of traditional faith, as the creative source of all being, truth, and moral value, was no longer credible to the scientifically educated classes of late nineteenth-century Europe.

If the "death of God" is perhaps the foremost central concern in Nietzsche's work, it is precisely his response to this "greatest event in history" that governs the detailed analyses of his more general reflection. Specifically, two broad motifs organize Nietzsche's painful attempts to achieve some livable, thinkable, harmonious resolution to this situation: the first, on the brighter side, is what he terms the "newly redeemed" innocence of becoming. And this is already and palpably given to us as a de-deified world of nature and human nature, one that must be felt and experienced by all in the absence of the angry old God. Not only is this a universe of vibrant sensuous immediacy, but it also bears the enormous legacy of the classical civilizations, of European Renaissance humanism, and the Enlightenment project of modernity itself—an effulgent natural world of superabundant beauty and historical depth, whose very accomplishment subtends our every value, choice, and action. But, the second side is darker—Nietzsche's horrified apprehension that the old God had become ideologically resurrected as a savage form of modern nationalism, with its hydra-head of xenophobia, anti-Semitism, plutocratic greed, and class hatred—all hardened avatars of the old, universal church, only this time, emboldened by the prosperity of modern science and fueled by a mighty industrial revolution.

The shadows materialized early on for Nietzsche through his firsthand experience of the highly mechanized and industrial-scale hostilities of the Franco-Prussian War, one Nietzsche knew could only be the Bismarckian herald of the unspeakable century to come. All the personal bitterness and pietistic *ressentiment* that had been developing for two millennia—now bereft of their stabilizing, if not fundamentally mendacious, ontotheological grounds—would be recast blindly and hatefully into the armed legions of so many divisive European nation-states. This will to destruction, nihilism, weariness, decadence, the all-so-many interconnected notions that Nietzsche struggled with in this domain, notions that would lead straight to despair and ruination—or, what he would simply call "woe" in *Zarathustra*—had to be thought through, anticipated, and countered on new grounds. It would have to be overcome by a willed unity of Good Europeans, and perhaps this might even have to come at an enormous human expense. But nonetheless, these concerns crystallized into Nietzsche's oft-repeated "task," progressively elaborated throughout his principal texts and correspondence. This task, framed against a volatile Europe of discredited value-formations, reeling into a thoughtless future, would prove to be the armature of Nietzsche's lifework, one that positively begged for completion against all odds. Ultimately, he knew, however, that the larger task would be Europe's own. Nietzsche's personal task would be to articulate it, even if this sometimes entailed a tone of desperation or stridency in his writing. Given the urgency of his task—most simply stated, "I would like to *take away* from human existence some of its heartbreaking and cruel character"—Nietzsche would attempt to induce a commensurate feeling and intellectual awareness in his audience. Writing to the heart as to the mind, he would draw upon every artistic and stylistic device from antique poetry and tragedy, from Aristotle right through contemporary opera, invoking a wide range of rhetorical and figurative usage: the employment of hyperbole, of striking imagery, the frequent use of aphorisms and apothegms, of analogy and metaphor, as well as elements of musicality, psychological association and projection, of personal reminiscence, and more. Nietzsche would employ all these stylistic devices to induce the reader to come to an understanding of his philosophical works, his reflections, indeed, of his very temperament and character. It is an extremely difficult thing to do well, especially for one who claimed to have written in blood.

The four works that are focused upon in the present volume—*The Birth of Tragedy, The Gay Science, Thus Spoke Zarathustra*, and *On the Genealogy of Morals*—are surely Nietzsche's most celebrated and widely read texts. While they each express many of Nietzsche's central concerns and teachings, their style of composition differs significantly. *The Birth of Tragedy* (1872) was written when Nietzsche was a professor of classical philology at the University of Basel and it is projected as a relatively straightforward scholarly analysis of the evolution and decline of classical Greek tragic drama. But rather than deal with the textual provenance and derivation of the tragedies themselves, as would a more conventional philologist (careful to note interpolations or emendations in the text through later transcriptions, differing word usages, stylistic or grammatical inconsistencies, etc.), Nietzsche examines the broader culture, whose richness and creativity gave rise to these stunning accomplishments— dramatic tragedies that Nietzsche saw as the highest artistic achievement of classical Greek culture. In seeking to uncover the deep cultural dynamics of the classical period, Nietzsche hoped to present a model by which his contemporary audience could come to better understand the often obscure underpinnings of their own—modern—European condition and to prepare themselves in turn for the enormously difficult problems he foresaw emerging in the coming century.

Nietzsche attributed the decline of classical Greek culture, at least in part, to the progressively lessened importance given to its rich mythological heritage, and he struck a similar theme in *The Gay Science*, with his pronouncement that God is dead and that European morality itself was spiritually and intellectually bereft of any higher legitimacy than inertia and simple habit. In striking contradistinction to the scholarly organization of *The Birth of Tragedy*— twenty-five closely linked sections detailing the historical emergence of the Greek myths, the evolution of epic, lyric, and dithyrambic poetry into the tragic drama, and its demise by Socratic rationalism—*The Gay Science* (1882, with a fifth chapter added in the second edition of 1886) is a collection of some 383 aphorisms, each varying in length from a few lines to several pages, with little overall sense of organization, thematic development, or extended philosophical argument. Having left the university because of his poor health, and being bitterly disappointed by the complete lack of any professional recognition for his *Birth of Tragedy*, Nietzsche would turn to a far more poetic form of expression in *The Gay Science*, one in fact influenced by the medieval Provençal troubadour tradition of song and lyric poetry. Indeed, *The Gay Science* included a "Prelude" of some sixty-three poems and an appendix of fourteen songs. Nietzsche expressly abandoned the style of the scholarly treatise for one of a far more personalized appeal. Seeking a broader audience for his urgent concerns, he hoped that the rhetorically and poetically charged aphorism would be precisely the kind of expression with which his readers would have to actively and seriously engage themselves—by personally interpreting the aphorism (with its rhetorical reliance on metaphor, simile, analogy, and so forth), and thereby contextually situating themselves in responding to the dramatic issues raised by *The Gay Science*. It was the existential effect of having to think through the prospect of a world with no moral absolutes, no transcendent authority, no higher purpose than the conservation of energy, and to come to some resolution of all this in one's own person that Nietzsche sought to achieve. Since such concerns were expressed in a largely figurative manner in *The Gay Science*, one would have to come to one's own conclusions regarding their significance, and hence the attitudes provoked by their resolution would dramatically affect one's own lived experience, one's self-conscious situation in a world whose very values were at stake.

The general lack of organization to *The Gay Science*—the disconnected series of short aphorisms, the long intervals separating Nietzsche's discussion of the same subject matter (often from a markedly different viewpoint or context), the later statements that seem to contradict earlier ones, the lack of a guiding narrative structure and argument, and so forth—in fact serves to assist the reader in coming to his or her own conclusions as to the importance and relevance of the issues initially raised by the author. It is much as when, in a series of conversations with one's various friends and chance acquaintances, one invariably encounters a problem from a variety of perspectives—some consistent, some inconsistent, some paradoxical and refractory—and in the end arrives at one's own studied solution.

Due in part to poor distribution by the publisher and in part to the fact that

The Gay Science proved difficult indeed to understand (precisely because its nondirective character was so problematic for his readers), Nietzsche finally admitted to his friend Erwin Rohde that, effectively, he had written the book for himself. Frustrated in not receiving the audience he wished for, Nietzsche recast the principal themes of *The Gay Science* in a far more programmatic way, this time in the dramatized narrative of *Thus Spoke Zarathustra* (1883–85). His concerns would appear as the "teachings" of the rebaptized founder of Zoroastrianism—Zoroaster, or Zarathustra—and would be progressively explicated in dialogue form. This would take place through Zarathustra's encounters with a broad variety of characters: village folk, a tightrope walker, his followers, the Higher Men, dancing girls, the old pope, a shepherd, a hunchback, the saint in the forest, a magician, even a series of animals. Zarathustra's "teachings" would include the death of God, the Overman, the Eternal Return, Will to Power, his critique of traditional morality, and the difficulties of self overcoming one's own limitations. All these would be delivered in a highly oracular fashion by drawing on such classic literary models as the New Testament Gospels, the Platonic dialogues, the prose of Goethe and Schiller, and even the stylized prose of Luther's sermons and biblical translations—the very source of literacy itself for his German-speaking audience. Hence, in what Nietzsche himself thought to be his most fully accomplished literary work, one that expressed his entire philosophy, he would at once articulate and lend precision to his intellectual concerns and also find the complex stylistic vehicle he thought most appropriate to his long-sought-for audience.

Once again, however, Nietzsche's efforts seemed to be markedly out of step with his contemporary audience: *Zarathustra* was far too "untimely," or as he would more frequently remark during this period, his reputation would be a "posthumous" one. The elevated tone of *Zarathustra*'s prose appeared pretentious to his readers, and the complexity of Nietzsche's historical allusions and symbolism bordered on the encyclopedic, if not apoplectic. Indeed, the great psychoanalyst and renowned symbol-scavenger Carl Jung devoted a continuous seminar of five years to analyzing *Zarathustra*, producing a two-volume work of more than 1,500 pages—and he missed an abundance in the process!

What compounded the complexity of *Zarathustra*, and this is not at all evident on the surface, is that the book also served as the vehicle for Nietzsche's working through his personal problems at the time. These problems included his growing exasperation with his own inability to communicate his concerns and his doubts about his capacity to do so, given what he saw as the magnitude of his task. Also deeply troubling to Nietzsche was his sense of growing isolation following the end of his university career, the loss of his only real love, Lou Salomé, his sense of personal betrayal by Paul Rée—who left with Lou for Berlin—and his humiliating break with Wagner and the Wagner circle at Bayreuth. During this period Nietzsche suffered an increasingly painful and severe set of attacks of ill health—migraine headaches for weeks on end, a near-total blindness, agonizing bouts of neuralgia, an inability to sleep, and severe digestive cramps, all exacerbated by the increasingly strong doses of medication he took to alleviate the pain. What had been conceived then as a great literary and philosophical work, modeled on the very classics of the public domain, resulted in a highly complex and intensely personal testimony. By summer's end, in 1886, he would write a friend, "My _Zarathustra_ . . . is an _unintelligible_ book, because it is based on experiences which I share with nobody. . . . The parts of _Zarathustra_ have sold sixty or seventy copies, and so on, and so on."[1]

Following _Zarathustra_, Nietzsche would write a series of prefaces for the second editions of his earlier works and begin to articulate his understanding and criticism of the traditional value system in _Beyond Good and Evil_ (1886). While this work would address the broad range of concerns he engaged in _Zarathustra_, its style was once again aphoristic in nature, but it was divided into nine well-developed chapters. Highly encouraged by an extremely positive review of _Beyond Good and Evil_ in the Bern journal _Der Bund_, Nietzsche was once again disappointed by the public reception of the difficult work: "Everybody has complained that I am 'not understood,' and the approximately one hundred copies which have been sold have made it quite obvious to me _that_ I am not understood. . . . No honorarium has been paid me, of course—and . . . no German publisher _wants_ me (even if I do not claim an honorarium)."[2] Determined to reach the audience he felt he deserved, Nietzsche would make every attempt to attain the clarity of exposition his task required. Summing up his situation at the time, in a letter to Franz Overbeck, Nietzsche would remark,"Ah, everything in my life is so uncertain and shaky, and always this horrible health of mine! On the other hand, there is the hundredweight of this need pressing upon me—to create a coherent structure of thought during the next few years."[3] In view of focusing his concerns on the problematic nature of traditionally received value, and in anticipation that a more coherent, well-defined approach that would finally draw his elusive readers to his earlier works, Nietzsche would compose _On the Genealogy of Morals_ (1887) in the form of three straightforwardly written and clearly argued essays.

Nietzsche would draw upon chapter 1 of _Beyond Good and Evil_, "On the Prejudices of Philosophers," which explored the underlying linguistic con-

straints and motivational assumptions involved in the very vocabulary of philosophical practice, to structure the project of *On the Genealogy of Morals*.
Specifically, this would be a metacritique of our inherited system of moral
values, and it would raise as its principal question, What is the value of these
values themselves? Such a critique would proceed in the first essay of the *Genealogy* to analyze the origins, that is, the historical derivation, of the various
central terms in the vocabulary of moral evaluation: the origin of the terms
"good" and "bad" and their inversion by "slave" or "herd" morality into the
value terms "good" and "evil." Nietzsche would once again draw upon his
training as a classical philologist to note that terms of moral value, in earlier
societies—and in a variety of ancient languages—were originally framed according to distinctions of social status. Thus, positive moral terms would be
derived from the higher social class and would reflect the positive attributes
associated with that class. Negative terms would be applied, likewise, by the
ascendant class to the characteristic qualities and social status of the lower
classes. These value terms, like historical surnames, could thus be traced by a
historical-linguistic, "genealogical" descent, or provenance. Nietzsche went on
to argue that these traditional "aristocratic" values became "inverted" or "revalued" with the ascendancy of the Judeo-Christian tradition and its characteristic psychological motivation of resentment—or, as he uses the French term,
for the insistence of this feeling, *ressentiment*—against the ruling class.

The second essay of the *Genealogy* pursues Nietzsche's concerns with the
role played in moral evaluation by the individual's "conscience" as well as the
cultural evolution of conscience into the psychological state of "bad conscience" (i.e., "guilt"). Initially, he argues, "conscience" arose out of early humanity's need to structure contractual dealings involving trade and barter. To
ensure the stability of economic commerce, one had to cultivate a trained
memory and a sense of responsibility. At the basis of these two considerations
was the fear of what the debtor would incur if he failed to fulfill the terms
of his obligations: ultimately, cruel punishment at the hands of the creditor.
Culturally, Nietzsche went on to argue, this debtor-creditor relationship would
be transformed on the level of civil society into a generalized sense of obligation to the society's ancient founders. What complicates this obligation is that
with entry into a primitive—and punitive—civil society, the individual could
no longer freely express his instinctual nature, his affects, such as anger and
emotional frustration, at will, as he could in a more primitive state. To avoid
the risk of disturbing civil tranquility and social order, the individual must repress and internalize these potentially dangerous outbursts, or face punish-

ment—indeed, expulsion—from society. And this repression of instinct results in a greatly increased suffering for the individual, Nietzsche would argue—anticipating Freud's later analysis of the topic. Nietzsche would go on to explain that this increased suffering brought about through the repression of instinct in civil society would come to be interpreted as "punishment" brought about by the displeasure caused the ancestors—transformed into gods—by violation of their traditional and divine laws. In the Judeo-Christian tradition, where the ancestors and deities had become fused and melded into the monotheistic creator god, to whom one is indebted for the universe at large, this sense of guilt or transgression would become sin. This would be an impossible burden, rendered even more extreme in the Christian formulation, due to guilt that accrues from Christ's suffering the crucifixion out of a freely given love.

It would be the effects of this guilt upon various individuals, and the pangs of suffering they would undergo in atoning for this guilt through ascetic practices that Nietzsche would develop in the third essay, "What Is the Meaning of Ascetic Ideals?" There, he would explore the complex set of relations among sin, guilt, suffering, discipline, cruelty, and self-cruelty, as well as the various meanings attributed to them, under the title of "the ascetic ideal." Nietzsche would himself conclude that all these ascetic practices were themselves fraudulent fictions, products of what he termed "the religious neurosis"; nevertheless, the increased human suffering they entailed was all too real. What the "ascetic ideal" provided was a humanly intelligible meaning to the individual's suffering: one suffers because one is guilty, sinful. Ultimately, the ascetic ideal is the *unity of interpretation* that the tradition of moral metaphysics has imposed upon the world of human concerns. This tradition stems from Platonic metaphysics and continues through the modern Judeo-Christian religious and moral teaching. The tradition posits a divine transcendent source for all intelligibility, value, and truth. In the human need to find meaning in the world and in one's own life, the ascetic ideal provides that meaning. If this is ultimately poisonous to the human condition, nonetheless Nietzsche finds a paradoxical virtue to it. It is not so much suffering itself that is a threat to humanity, but rather the meaninglessness of suffering. In giving meaning to human suffering, humanity was possibly spared a suicidal extinction, a nihilistic exhaustion. It was by redirecting the flow of *ressentiment* back upon themselves in the form of atonement for guilt and expiation of their sins, all the while increasing their suffering and exhausting themselves in the process, that humanity was preserved and human lives found meaning. Work would become a virtue, and the state would be less vulnerable to sedition, with the help of the ascetic ideal.

The coherence of argument and the clarity of expression of *On the Genealogy of Morals*—even its quite polemical tone—would prove successful. The *Genealogy* was accessible to a broad audience, and, through it, all the author's works would find a wide and influential readership. Unfortunately, his health deteriorated swiftly in January 1889, and when he died in 1900, at only fifty-five years of age, he did not realize that the accomplishment of his lifelong task was within his reach. Only eight days into the conception and composition of the *Genealogy*, Nietzsche wrote to Peter Gast, "Perhaps this small polemical pamphlet will help to sell a few copies of my older writings (honestly, it always hurts me when I think of poor Fritzsch [i.e., Nietzsche's printer], who is now carrying the whole burden). I hope my publishers will benefit from it; for myself I know only too well that I shall *have no benefit* when people begin to understand me."[4]

INTRODUCTION

THE FACTS IN THE STRANGE CASE OF MR. NIETZSCHE

We often consider it a mark of ability or distinction in a thinker that a certain reputation should precede him, but in Nietzsche's case the situation is altogether unique. Few modern thinkers have evoked such intense and widely differing responses as Nietzsche. In fact, the very mention of his name is usually enough to awaken strong opinion.[1] Thus, Nietzsche almost inevitably comes to our attention by way of reputation: our first encounter is usually secondhand, and it is not surprising to find that we are already predisposed toward or against him, even before having read a single one of his texts.

Nietzsche's reputation is especially problematic, however, in that it so rarely has any substantial bearing upon the content of his work. For the most part his general reputation derives from an overly curious fascination with Nietzsche's personal life, his physical and mental health, his associations with such figures as Richard Wagner, his alleged attitudes toward women, religion, culture, politics, and morality. More often than not, the opinions formed on such issues as these have gradually hardened to become interpretive registers, each contributing to the reputation of Nietzsche, each precluding a relatively unbiased— much less, generous—analysis of his writings.

Of all the misplaced and unwarranted prejudices to envelop Nietzsche, however, surely the most baleful is his association in the popular mind with the extremist politics of national socialism. We now know, definitively, that the association concerned his sister, Elisabeth, rather than Nietzsche himself, but this unfortunate prejudice persists, and it continues to operate at a distance, even upon his most well-intentioned reader.[2] To address and, thus, to dispense with this most disquieting issue at the start, it should be enough to set forth the circumstances that gave rise to it.

It is well known that his sister professed a great devotion to Nietzsche, and that she often came to assist him in the management of his domestic affairs, particularly during his early years as a professor in Basel (1869–79). But despite her oftentimes practical help, she incessantly meddled in his personal and intellectual life, much to the detriment of his own interests. An early instance of her intrusive and thoroughly deceitful behavior resulted in driving away one of Nietzsche's closest admirers, Lou Salomé, an extremely gifted and cultivated young woman, one of the few whose affection and companionship Nietzsche actively sought (later, after her marriage to Friedrich Andreas, Lou Andreas-Salomé would become an intimate friend of Rainer Maria Rilke, Sigmund Freud, and Alfred Adler).

Even more distressing to Nietzsche, though, was Elisabeth's marriage to Bernhard Förster, an anti-Semitic propagandist who devoted the sum of his energies to founding a German emigrant colony abroad, in Paraguay, in the hope of revitalizing the racial and cultural "purity" of the Germanic peoples. While Nietzsche never really reciprocated Elisabeth's affection to the extent she had imagined, her marriage to Förster and her support of his extremist projects quickly brought the prospect of any fond relations with her brother to an end.[3] When Förster died in 1889, Elisabeth returned to Germany, her modest inheritance lost in the support of her husband's bankrupt "Nueva Germania" colony. By this time, however, Nietzsche himself had fallen ill and was hospitalized, a helpless, mentally incompetent invalid.

With no source of income and with her brother's fame quickly growing, despite his complete debilitation, Elisabeth promptly obtained a court order and changed her name from Förster to Förster-Nietzsche, thereby asserting at least nominal support to the claim of being her brother's closest collaborator. She then threatened to sue her mother for administrative control of her brother's estate, which consisted almost entirely of unpublished manuscript material, as well as the copyrights and royalties from his already published work. In the face of a public lawsuit filed by her own daughter, Frau Nietzsche relinquished control of the entire estate to Elisabeth. With her brother's manuscripts in hand, Elisabeth set up a Nietzsche Archive and presided over the editing and publishing of the material. Having complete control of Nietzsche's writings, Elisabeth saw fit to publish only the material she thought highly of, and she deleted a considerable volume of work in which Nietzsche was highly critical of German nationalism, with its emphasis on racial purity, ethnic identity, and cultural genius. She also ignored extensive material in which Nietzsche expressed toleration, even praise, of racial or ethnic equality, political internationalism, and cultural diversity. To buttress the import of the writings she was then beginning to put out, she forged several letters in her brother's name and altered many others, thus making it appear as if she had been entrusted with the task she so shamelessly assumed, as if Nietzsche himself had appointed her to be his chosen successor and interpreter.[4]

After she allied herself with various groups in support of defending and propagating a strictly Germanic culture (the *Kulturkampf* movement), especially with the Wagner circle of Bayreuth, Elisabeth's fortunes grew apace with the rise of extremist German nationalism. Seeking and receiving financial support from both the Hindenburg government and the National Socialist Party, she was particularly encouraged by the latter. Indeed, because of her marriage to Förster, she was elevated by the Nazi Party to the status of a far-seeing prophetess. With the political and financial support of that party, she and her cousin Max Oehler continued to direct the publication of the unpublished manuscripts.[5] Under the personal sanction of Elisabeth Förster-Nietzsche, the title of *The Will to Power* was placed on a mass of Nietzsche's posthumous notes and drafts, and after several variant editions, it was heralded as the official philosophy of national socialism. Only with the aftermath of the Second World War was it finally established that Nietzsche's thought had been distorted beyond recognition to serve the personal, financial, and political interests of his sister and to lend intellectual "support" to the desperate aims of a totalitarian government. But by then, almost fifty years after Nietzsche's death, the damage had been done. A large part of two generations of educated Europeans would come to regard Nietzsche as the prophet of an unspeakable tyranny.[6]

NIETZSCHE'S LIFE

While the public reception of Nietzsche's work and, thereby, his reputation, were seriously compromised by his sister's manipulating activities, his own life by contrast was relatively modest. Born on October 15, 1844, in the village of Röken in Prussian Saxony, Friedrich Wilhelm Nietzsche was the first of three children, the only boy to survive, his younger brother, Joseph, having died in infancy. His father, Karl Ludwig, was a Lutheran clergyman as were, traditionally, both sides of the family. By 1848, Karl Ludwig's health began to fail, the result of what was then diagnosed as "brain softening" (i.e., a series of convulsive states compounded by extreme depression and paralysis); later, Elisabeth would attribute her father's illness to a severe fall. The responsibility thus passed to Nietzsche's mother, Franziska, to look after the ailing Karl, to care for his two spinster sisters, as well as her mother-in-law, and to raise two young children. This became an increasingly burdensome task, especially following the death of Nietzsche's father in 1849. Having been provided with only a small pension upon her husband's death, Frau Nietzsche was obliged to leave the parsonage at Röken and to install the entire family in a small apartment in the nearby town of Naumburg. After nine years, she managed to purchase a village home, occasionally taking in boarders to help meet household expenses.

A gifted child, Nietzsche was first instructed by his mother, and to a lesser extent, by his maternal grandfather, David Oehler (who served as the Lutheran pastor for the village of Pobles). In Naumburg, he briefly attended the local elementary school and was then transferred to a preparatory school for three years, after which he entered the Naumburg gymnasium. By the age of fourteen, he had won a scholarship to the prestigious boarding school of Pforta, just outside Naumburg. He pursued a traditional and rigorous course of studies at Schulpforta (as had Fichte, Novalis, Ranke, and other celebrated figures before him), where he showed exceptional abilities in classical studies and languages. A particularly good student, he also participated in many activities—chorus, theater, hiking, swimming—and formed several lasting friendships there both with his fellow students and with his teachers.

If anything troubled him at Schulpforta, aside from the strictures of boarding school life itself, it was perhaps the school authorities' assumption that he had somewhat fragile health. The medical records at the school recalled the diagnosis of Nietzsche's father and gave instructions that young Friedrich was to be discouraged from any exhausting activity. His letters from this period, however, seem to attest to good health, save for some occasional remarks about "rheumatism" and, even then, persistent migraine headaches.

It was expected of Nietzsche that, like his father and for generations of his family before him, he would enter the clergy. In preparation for this seeming eventuality, Nietzsche enrolled as a student of theology and philology at the University of Bonn in the fall of 1864. His interests at Bonn proved to be more philological than theological, however, and he chose to devote himself to the lectures of two of Germany's most prominent classical philologists, Otto Jahn and Friedrich Ritschl. When Ritschl moved to the University of Leipzig the next year, Nietzsche followed him.[7] The decision to abandon his theological studies to pursue philology provoked a family crisis of sorts, one that would never be entirely put to rest. A series of bitter exchanges over this decision took place at the Nietzsche home during the Easter vacation of 1865. Besides provoking his mother's great disillusion with the young Nietzsche, the outburst led to a lengthy and somewhat disagreeable correspondence with his sister, which has since become famous.

Reproaching her brother for his recent course of action, Elisabeth claimed that he was being both unthinking and spiritually indolent, that it was far more difficult to believe in the traditional doctrines of the Christian faith and to pursue them than not. Indeed, she argued, the very difficulty of faith no doubt attested to its truth. Nietzsche's response to Elisabeth (of June 11, 1865) illustrates the kind of personal decision he finally arrived at, not only about changing his prospective vocation, but about the pursuit of conventional matters generally. His strongest objection would be against the theological concerns that had dominated his family for so long:

As for your principle, that the truth is always on the more difficult side, I concede this to you in part. Nonetheless, it is difficult to understand that two times two does not equal four; but does that make it any the more true? On the other hand, is it really so difficult simply to accept everything in which one has been brought up, which has gradually become deeply rooted in oneself, which holds true among relatives and among many good people, which does moreover really comfort and elevate man? Is that more difficult than to take new paths, struggling against habituation, uncertain of one's independent course, amid frequent vacillations of the heart, and even of the conscience, often comfortless, but always pursuing the eternal goal of the true, the beautiful, the good?

Is it then a matter of acquiring the view of God, world, and atonement in which one can feel most comfortable? Is it not, rather, that for the true researcher [*Forscher*], the result of his research [*Forschung*] is of no account at all? Do we, in our investigations, search for tranquility, peace, happiness? No—only for the truth, even if it were to be frightening and ugly.

One last remaining question. If we had believed since youth that all salvation came not from Jesus but from another—say, from Mohammed—is it not certain that we would have enjoyed the same blessings? To be sure, faith alone gives blessings, not the objective which stands behind the faith. I write this to you, dear Lisbeth, only in order to counter the most usual proofs of believing people, who invoke the evidence of their experiences and deduce from it the infallibility of their faith. Every true faith is indeed infallible; it performs what the believing person hopes to find in it, but it does not offer the least support for the establishing of an objective truth.

Here the ways of men divide. If you want to achieve peace of mind and happiness, then have faith; if you want to be a disciple of truth, then search [*so forsche*].

Between, there are many halfway positions. But it all depends on the principal aim.[8]

It was thus with a certain spirit of independence that he resumed his philological studies in Leipzig. Encouraged by Ritschl, Nietzsche founded the Leipzig Philological Society in December 1865, together with Erwin Rohde, who, like Nietzsche, had recently left Bonn. Ritschl was so impressed by Nietzsche's first address to the Leipzig Society (on the ancient Greek poet Theognis of Megara) that he implored Nietzsche to publish it in the prestigious review *Rheinische Museum für Philologie*. As he continued to enjoy Ritschl's strong confidence and support, Nietzsche's philological studies quickly prospered. Before long, he had published several other monographs for the *Rheinische Museum* and the *Litterarische Centralblatt*, on such classical figures as Diogenes Laertius, Hesiod, and Homer.[9]

In October 1867, Nietzsche was called away from Leipzig to serve his required year of military duty with the Prussian army. But, since the brief Austro-Prussian War of 1866 had already ended by the time of his induction, he saw no combat. Nietzsche did sustain a severe chest injury, however, in a riding accident (while on duty with his mounted artillery unit) and was hospitalized for a month. After several months further convalescence in Naumburg, he returned to Leipzig in October 1868. Three months later, Ritschl notified him that he was recommending him for the vacant chair of classical philology at the University of Basel in Switzerland. It took the university authorities only a month to confirm Nietzsche's appointment, despite the fact that he had neither completed his doctoral studies nor received his degree. Confronted with this astonishing appointment, and in view of his already published work, the University of Leipzig quickly conferred the doctoral degree on Nietzsche in March 1869 without even pausing for the formality of an examination or defense.

That such an appointment and degree were granted to a virtually unknown youth of twenty-four testifies at least as much to the eminence of Ritschl as to Nietzsche's own abilities. But it is clear that Ritschl did think most highly of Nietzsche's abilities. His recommendation to the Basel authorities is an exuberant paean to the young scholar:

However many young talents I have seen develop under my eyes for thirty-nine years now, *never yet* have I known a young man, or tried to help one along in my field as best I could, who was so mature as early and as young as this Nietzsche. His *Museum* articles he wrote in the second and third year of his *triennium*. He is the first from whom I have ever accepted any contribution at all while he was still a student. If—God grant—he lives long enough, I prophesy that he will one day stand in the front rank of German philology. . . . He is the idol and, without wishing it, the leader of the whole younger generation of philologists here in Leipzig who—and they are rather numerous—cannot wait to hear him as a lecturer. You will say, I describe a phenomenon. Well, that is just what he is—and at the same time pleasant and modest. Also a gifted musician, which is irrelevant here. . . . What more am I to say? His studies so far have been weighted toward the history of Greek literature (of course, including critical and exegetical treatment of the authors), with special emphasis, it seems to me, on the history of Greek philosophy. But I have not the least doubt that, if confronted by a practical demand, with his great gifts he will work in other fields with the best of success. He will simply be able to do anything he wants to do.[10]

Nietzsche began teaching at Basel in the summer semester of 1869 and within a year he was promoted to full professor (*Professor Ordinarius*), an unheard of accomplishment for someone only twenty-five years of age. It was also at Basel that Nietzsche made the acquaintance of Franz Overbeck and Jakob Burckhardt, both of whom would remain close friends and confidants for the rest of his active years. Overbeck was perhaps Nietzsche's closest friend, and the somber task would later fall to him of bringing Nietzsche back from Turin, where in 1889 he had his final breakdown. While Overbeck was Nietzsche's senior by seven years, they enjoyed a common enthusiasm for music, especially that of Wagner, and shared much the same critical disposition toward Overbeck's own field of study, church history. The fruits of these discussions with Overbeck would emerge later, with the appearance of *On the Genealogy of Morals* in 1887 (especially part 3, devoted to the ascetic extremism of the early Patristic period of Christianity). Nietzsche's relation to Jacob Burckhardt, however, had a more immediately evident impact. Best known for *The Civilization of the Renaissance in Italy* (1860), Burckhardt was lecturing on classical Greek history during this period, lectures that Nietzsche attended as regularly as possible and that they often discussed afterward at great length.[11]

These conversations with Burckhardt tended to confirm Nietzsche's own reading of classical Greece, an interpretation that saw such elements as conflict, pessimism, and the continual danger of decadence as inner, guiding principles for the evolution of Greek culture. Burckhardt had himself been influenced by the German philosopher Arthur Schopenhauer, particularly by the latter's doctrines of cultural pessimism and personal resignation, attitudes Schopenhauer viewed as survival strategies, given that the human condition was basically one of necessary confrontation with a world of implacable and antagonistic metaphysical forces. Burckhardt's successful use of these doctrines in devising a realistic analysis of historical development was a great encouragement to Nietzsche at the time; with this firm example in mind, Nietzsche would hasten to complete the difficult work he then had in progress, *The Birth of Tragedy*.

Certainly the most notable friendship Nietzsche enjoyed during his Basel years was that with the famous composer Richard Wagner. Nietzsche had previously met Wagner in Leipzig, on November 8, 1868, at a gathering arranged by the wife of his teacher, Ritschl. Already familiar with Wagner's music, Nietzsche was immediately enthralled by the man himself. Indeed, the day after his first encounter with Wagner, Nietzsche wrote to Rohde:

> Now I shall briefly tell you what this evening offered: truly enjoyments of such peculiar piquancy that I am today not quite my old self and can do nothing better than talk to you, my dear friend, and tell you "passing wondrous tales." Before and after dinner Wagner played all the important parts of the *Meistersinger*, imitating each voice and with great exuberance. He is, indeed, a fabulously lively and fiery man who speaks very rapidly, is very witty, and makes a very private party like this one an extremely gay affair. In between, I had a longish conversation with him about Schopenhauer; you will understand how much I enjoyed hearing him speak of Schopenhauer with indescribable warmth, what he owed to him, how he is the only philosopher who has understood the essence of music; then he asked how the academics nowadays regarded him, laughed heartily about the Philosophic Congress in Prague, and spoke of the "vassals of philosophy." Afterward, he read an extract from his biography, which he is now writing, an utterly delightful scene from his Leipzig student days, of which he still cannot think without laughing; he writes too with extraordinary skill and intelligence. Finally, when we were both getting ready to leave, he warmly shook my hand and invited me with great friendliness to visit him, in order to make music and talk philosophy; also, he entrusted to me the task of familiarizing his sister and his kinsmen with his music, which I have now solemnly undertaken to do. You will hear more when I can see this evening somewhat more objectively and from a distance.[12]

Nietzsche responded to the invitation as soon as he arrived in Basel by promptly visiting Wagner at his estate, Tribschen, only fifty miles away on Lake Lucerne. Indeed, some historians claim Wagner's proximity was a major consideration for Nietzsche in deciding to teach at Basel in the first place. Nietzsche's repeated visits to Tribschen soon resulted in his being accepted, quite literally, as a part of the family. His friendship with Wagner and Cosima von Bülow (who would become Wagner's wife in the summer of 1870) grew to such an extent that Nietzsche offered his own services as secretary to Wagner and as a fund-raiser for his various projects, notably for the construction of the Bayreuth Festival Theater, which was to be used exclusively for the performance of Wagnerian opera. Wagner's interest in classical tragic drama and Schopenhauer, his theories of total art, and a music of the future all helped to develop Nietzsche's own concepts and to deepen the relationship between the two men. Nietzsche in fact saw Wagner as the embodiment of artistic genius, an individual who might well initiate a profound cultural renewal of Europe. In view of his admiration and respect for Wagner, Nietzsche would dedicate his first book, *The Birth of Tragedy*, to him in 1871.

Within a year of his installation in Basel, Nietzsche asked for and received a leave of absence to serve as a medical orderly in the Franco-Prussian War of 1870. While Nietzsche felt duty-bound to serve his native Prussia in time of war, the conditions of Swiss citizenship forbade active military participation in foreign armies. His duties as an orderly with the Prussian forces were themselves quickly terminated for medical reasons; after a month of service, Nietzsche contracted a severe case of diphtheria compounded by dysentery. During this period in which his health suffered a major reversal, his attitudes toward Prussia's increasing military and political hegemony would also undergo a complete change; sobered by his experiences at the battlefront, he would henceforth become extremely critical of Prussia's strident nationalism and aggressive foreign policy. Following a brief period of convalescence, first in a military hospital, then at his family home in Naumburg, he resumed his teaching duties in Basel. This respite was to be short-lived, however. By February 1871, his health had once again deteriorated, and he took a medical leave of absence for the rest of the year. He suffered from increasingly painful migraine headaches, severe depression, dizziness, temporary losses of vision, and convulsive digestive disorders, symptoms that, it is now fairly well agreed upon, characterize the tertiary phase of a cerebral syphilis.[13]

Despite his poor health, Nietzsche finished his *Birth of Tragedy* by the end of December 1871. Its reception was, to say the least, mixed. Wagner and his circle of admirers (including Bernhard Förster) admired it immensely. Critically, the response was far less favorable. Ritschl, to whom Nietzsche sent one of the first copies, was extremely disappointed by it. Only after repeated prodding by Nietzsche did Ritschl even deign to acknowledge its receipt. In a now famous pamphlet, the German classical scholar Ulrich von Wilamowitz-Moellendorf denounced the text in terms that can only be called vituperative; among other remarks, he characterized it as "a nest of imbecilities," unworthy of serious philological attention.[14] The aftereffects of the recently published work were felt even in Basel. After Wilamowitz's broadside, Nietzsche found that his students practically abandoned him. Indeed, he wrote to Wagner in November 1872:

> I have no students at all! . . . The fact is, indeed, so easy to explain—I have suddenly acquired such a bad name in my field that our small university suffers from it! This agonizes me. . . . A professor of classical philology at Bonn, whom I highly regard, has simply told his students that the book is "sheer nonsense" and is quite useless; a person who writes such things is dead to scholarship. . . . Of course I can make good use of this winter semester, because my only assignment now as a simple schoolmaster is the Pädagogium.[15]

In a letter of the same month, he wrote to Malwida von Meysenbug, "My *Birth of Tragedy* has made of me the most offensive philologist of the present day. . . . Everyone is of a mind to condemn me."[16]

Difficult times, indeed, for the young Nietzsche. Of his friends and colleagues, Rohde alone publicly defended Nietzsche's work on professional grounds—a defense that, it should be added, Nietzsche himself helped orchestrate. Even though, in later years, Nietzsche came to hold the work in somewhat more measured esteem, at the time of its composition he was most enthusiastic about it and felt it to be his first truly philosophical writing. Of course this was precisely part of the problem: *The Birth of Tragedy* did mark Nietzsche's turn away from strictly philological concerns to those of a more philosophical interest. Its poor reception by Nietzsche's colleagues, then, is understandable; it was *not* conceived as a rigorous and exclusively philological exercise, it was quite obviously indebted to the philosophy of Schopenhauer, and it was, by their measure, overly effusive in its praise of Wagner's aesthetic theories.

Nietzsche did write an essay explicitly devoted to Wagner during this period, "Richard Wagner in Bayreuth" (to commemorate the long-awaited opening of the Bayreuth Festival Theater), but aside from this last piece, his interests became decidedly directed elsewhere. He began to lecture more extensively on Greek philosophy and to write polemical essays on Schopenhauer and David Strauss (a contemporary literary figure). He also completed an extended reflection on historiography, titled *History in the Service and Disservice of Life*. Four of these pieces would be combined and republished as his second major work, *Unmodern Observations* (1876).

By the fall of 1876, Nietzsche's growing disenchantment with Wagner finally ran its course. His response to the lavish pomposity of the first Bayreuth Festival, from which he promptly fled, was complete revulsion. Nietzsche now perceived a completely transformed and unrecognizable Wagner; no longer the admired genius of classical taste and visionary talent but a cult figure, an exhibitionist personality surrounded by a philistine public of fawning claques and sycophants. What artistic and creative virtue Wagner formerly possessed now seemed hopelessly squandered, transformed into what Nietzsche came to see as a risible spectacle of mysticism and self-indulgence. Wagner himself became extremely arrogant and abusive toward Nietzsche, even to the extent of publicly ridiculing his many practical attempts to assist in the planning and fund-raising for the Bayreuth project.

Having so obligated himself to Wagner and his grandiose schemes, Nietzsche now saw this to be a lamentable mistake. As a result of his overly enthusiastic support, he had suffered professional ostracism, now personal abuse, and finally his own contempt for what he felt Wagner had come to represent: the cult of personality, the abandonment of intellectual integrity, the mystique of petty nationalism, and a savage anti-Semitism.

At the time of his break with Wagner, Nietzsche's own health progressively deteriorated. He was once again obliged to take a leave of absence from the University of Basel. In hopes of recuperation, he traveled first to the Swiss resort of Bex, then to Geneva and Genoa, and on to Sorrento, where he stayed at the villa of Malwida von Meysenbug until May 1877.

Recovering his health somewhat, Nietzsche was able to resume teaching in the fall of 1877 and to complete the first volume of *Human, All Too Human*. Yet, within two years of his return to Basel and despite the efforts of his sister Elisabeth and the help of his friend, composer Peter Gast (who served as his secretary and almost constant companion during this period), Nietzsche's health once again collapsed and he submitted his resignation to the university. His resignation accepted on June 14, 1879, Nietzsche, at the age of thirty-five, was released from all teaching duties and given a modest pension for some six years, which was subsequently renewed.

For the next ten years of his life, Nietzsche traveled extensively, always seeking at least a climatic reprieve from his continuing physical ailments. Like Goethe before him, Nietzsche was continually drawn to Italy, to the south, and

to the warmth of the Mediterranean. In the summer, he regularly sought the
dry and elevated mountain valleys of the Bernese Oberland and the Upper
Engadine in Switzerland. Despite the ever more frequent and severe attacks of
his illness, Nietzsche nonetheless managed to work prodigiously, all the while
exhausting his failing health and precipitating his eventual breakdown. In a
period of less than ten years, traveling from village to village, living in furnished
rooms and pensions, Nietzsche would write *The Wanderer and His Shadow*,
Dawn, *The Gay Science*, *Thus Spoke Zarathustra*, *Beyond Good and Evil*, *On
the Genealogy of Morals*, *The Case of Wagner*, *Twilight of the Idols*, *Nietzsche
contra Wagner*, *The Antichrist*, and *Ecce Homo* in addition to several volumes
of notes and drafts (much of this subsequently assembled to make *The Will to
Power*) and an extensive correspondence.

On January 3, 1889, Nietzsche's health finally abandoned him altogether;
during the course of a morning walk in Turin, he was overtaken by a seizure
and collapsed unconscious on the Plaza Carlo Alberto. Overbeck was quickly
summoned and, within a week, he brought Nietzsche back to Basel for clinical
examination by a Swiss psychiatrist, Professor Ludwig Wille. His condition was
diagnosed as a progressive paralytic state and his mother authorized institutional care at the Jena psychiatric clinic. Despite the attention given him by
the clinic's eminent director, Otto Binswanger, the prognosis was poor. Nietzsche was released in his mother's custody, and on May 13, 1890, they returned
together to Naumburg. When Nietzsche's sister, Elisabeth, returned from her
ill-fated colonial adventures, she established an archive at the Naumburg
home, where she installed the by-then hopelessly invalid Nietzsche in an up-
stairs room, such that he might be observed by her visitors, yet remain seques-
tered and relatively comfortable. Upon obtaining control of his estate and
following the death of Nietzsche's mother in 1897, Elisabeth transported the
disabled Nietzsche to Weimar, where she had already reestablished the Nietzsche Archive in the Villa Silberblick. Nietzsche would die there, on August 25,
1900, in total and uncomprehending silence.

THE BIRTH OF TRAGEDY

Friedrich Nietzsche completed *The Birth of Tragedy* in 1871, two years after his arrival in Basel, where he was then teaching classical philology. He began work on the text in the fall of 1869 in the form of several preparatory studies, some to be given as lectures at the University of Basel. Four of these studies deserve brief mention, not only because they closely anticipate the final subject matter of *The Birth of Tragedy*, but because they indicate his breadth of interests at the time and show that this first book was already the work of extensive research: "The Greek Musical Drama" was presented as a lecture on January 18, 1870, "Socrates and Tragedy" was delivered two weeks later on February 1, and "The Dionysian Worldview" was written during June and July of the same year. The latter would be expanded into an essay titled "The Birth of Tragic Thought" and would serve as the textual basis for the early chapters of *The Birth of Tragedy*. A final study, "Socrates and Greek Tragedy," printed privately in June 1871, in part borrowed from these earlier works and further investigated the important relationships between music and language (particularly the section that has since come to be known as "On Music and Words").[1]

By October 1871, Nietzsche had decided upon the title *The Birth of Tragedy: Out of the Spirit of Music*. It first appeared in January 1872 and underwent two subsequent editions in his lifetime: one with minor revisions in 1874 (which was withheld from distribution for four years due to financial difficulties with his publisher, E. W. Fritsch of Leipzig), and the final version of 1886, which bore the somewhat different title, *The Birth of Tragedy; or, Hellenism and Pessimism*, as well as a completely new preface, titled "Attempt at a Self-Criticism." The two later editions also retained the brief dedicatory preface to Richard Wagner.

In the later preface of 1886, Nietzsche reproached himself for having fallen so shamelessly under Wagner's influence during the period in which he wrote *The Birth of Tragedy*. His earlier association with Wagner had since soured and had become a source of painful embarrassment to him. No doubt this sentiment tempered the accuracy of his self-portrait: in retrospect, he made it seem as if he had been the youthful innocent, helplessly seduced by Wagner's brilliance and, surely, by his growing celebrity in European cultural circles as one of the century's greatest composers.[2] But in fact, Nietzsche was twenty-seven years old at the time, well-schooled and well-traveled, and was quite aware, even then, of the dangers that a too-close association with Wagner might hold. In what proved to be a prophetic letter to Erwin Rohde (December 21, 1871), Nietzsche expressed clear forebodings about the last part of his just-completed book, the section that practically propagandizes Wagnerian opera:

> I have only a little more to correct, and the introduction. The whole last part, which you do not know, will certainly astonish you; I have been very daring . . . for which reason I am very pleased with the book and am not disturbed by the chance that it may cause as much offense as may be and that from some quarters there may be raised a "cry of outrage" when it is published.[3]

In anticipation of such a reception, Nietzsche completely rewrote the dedication to Wagner and abridged it by several pages, transforming it from a wildly enthusiastic testimonial to a more modest statement of admiration.[4] Nonetheless, a "cry of outrage" was exactly the kind of welcome the book met from Nietzsche's professional colleagues, the classical Greek scholars. Ulrich von Wilamowitz-Moellendorf denounced the work, Friedrich Ritschl ridiculed it, and others saw it as Nietzsche's professional death warrant. It was judged an entirely unprofessional work at best—the philological journals would not even review it—and an exercise in Wagnerian pamphleteering at worst.[5] The book was speculative, enthusiastic, and totally outside the conventional bounds of philological scholarship. As Wilamowitz-Moellendorf chided, if this was an example of philological research, then it surely must be some "philology of the future," just as Wagner's operas were called "music of the future," in which case it deserved no respect in present philological circles.[6]

Despite his suspicions about how the book might be received, Nietzsche was nonetheless stunned and personally wounded by the vehemence of the criticism. To make matters worse, he was professionally ostracized the moment the book appeared. Like so many of Nietzsche's subsequent works, *The Birth of Tragedy* was highly polemical: it was an attack against the practically unquestioned interpretation of classical Greek culture and thought, its art, drama, and institutions. Moreover, the book championed a contemporary aesthetic (i.e., Wagner's theory of the opera) as a means of achieving, if not surpassing, the brilliance and variety of Hellenic culture. In short, *The Birth of Tragedy* was *not* the kind of work expected by nineteenth-century classical scholarship. To aggravate matters, Nietzsche continually made parallels between classical culture and that of his own society—not to grasp the latter as a fall from some remote and idyllic period of halcyon grace, but rather to make Hellenic Greece and the breadth of its achievements intelligible, and thus accessible, to a modern age. Only then would it be possible to bring about a cultural and political transformation of an age Nietzsche saw as becoming ever more nihilistic, ever more abandoned to mediocrity, divisiveness, and self-annihilation.

PREFACE TO *THE BIRTH OF TRAGEDY*: "ATTEMPT AT A SELF-CRITICISM"

The preface of 1886 served the purpose of placing *The Birth of Tragedy* in perspective, then, at least for its author. Reviewing the book some sixteen years after its conception, Nietzsche found its style at best overly flamboyant:

> To say it once more: today I find it an impossible book: I consider it badly written, ponderous, embarrassing, image-mad and image-confused, sentimental, in places saccharine to the point of effeminacy, uneven in tempo, without the will to logical cleanliness, very convinced and therefore disdainful of proof, mistrustful even of the propriety of proof, a book for initiates . . . an arrogant and rhapsodic book.[7]

Nietzsche acknowledged that the excesses of the work were due in large part to inexperience, or as he said, to "youthfulness," particularly because he did not yet have the confidence of his own vocabulary and personal style of expression. Rather, he borrowed the then fashionable language of German idealist philosophy, and for his readers, this seemed to commit him to the philosophical doctrines of such thinkers as Immanuel Kant and Arthur Schopenhauer. But despite his admittedly borrowed vocabulary, Nietzsche's own concerns were neither Kantian nor Schopenhauerian. On the one hand, Kant's formulations seemed to lead to the extremes of speculative excess: his "three most important questions" concerning metaphysics—What can I know? What ought I to do? What may I hope for?—were, for Nietzsche, hopelessly naive and optimistic. The immodest pretense that such kinds of questions were even legitimate, much less that they could be resolved by human reason alone, was, for Nietzsche, doomed from the start. Indeed, Kant's excessive optimism inevitably provoked the extreme opposite response—the metaphysical pessimism of Schopenhauer. By Schopenhauer's own admission, "Life can never give real satisfaction, and hence it is *not worthy* of our affection . . . it leads to resignation."[8]

While *The Birth of Tragedy* supported neither Kant nor Schopenhauer on these matters, Nietzsche would go further in the 1886 preface and explicitly criticize both thinkers, claiming that his own work, with the values it expressed, was at basic odds with both. Ultimately, Nietzsche came to see Kant and Schopenhauer as typically romantic thinkers whose concerns stemmed from a fundamental misunderstanding of human existence. As Nietzsche would claim time and again throughout his later writings, romanticism could well assume the guise of optimism or pessimism; but in either case, it expressed an essentially hostile attitude toward the very conditions of life. This hostility might appear as the shattered hopes for salvation and redemption—or, as the intense longings of human aspiration, bred from personal incapacity and unfulfillment. In any case, the romantic interpretation fears a complex world of human capabilities and dangers, and thus retreats from the world of human concerns, which is, after all, the *only* world.

Due to its basic hostility, Nietzsche would explain, the romantic attitude forever seeks some form of escape or flight into another world—an ideal world before the fall, in the sabbath of myth, or a world after the fall, in the serene and blissful twilight of the gods. Only in such an ideal world could peace, the cessation of all strife, be hoped for (as, for example, in Schopenhauer's concept of "nirvana," born from the "absence of all willing"); here alone could beauty itself be finally cherished (in what Kant called "the sublime"). Nietzsche viewed these concepts as pessimistic in the extreme and decadent, since they demanded a virtual withdrawal from life for their very possibility. Guided by this kind of thinking, the individual would desperately come to *need* redemption. Indeed, this was one of the most frequent criticisms Nietzsche made of Wagner, especially in his later work, *The Case of Wagner* (1888). There, Nietzsche argued that the entire corpus of Wagner's opera was obsessed with these issues, centering precisely on the problem of redemption: innocence as the redemption of sin (the case of *Tannhäuser*), marriage as the redemption of passion, aspiration, and ultimately of all personal integrity (*The Flying Dutchman*), chastity as the power to redeem corruption (*Parsifal*), beauty redeemed by chivalry (*Die Meistersinger*), and so forth. In light of these observations, Nietzsche would conclude, in *The Case of Wagner*, "The need for redemption,

the quintessence of all Christian needs . . . is the most honest expression of
decadence, it is the most convinced, most painful affirmation of decadence in
the form of sublime symbols and practices. The Christian wants to be *rid* of
himself. The ego is always hateful."⁹

In reacting to the world it perceives, the romantic view founders upon its
own *moral interpretation* of reality: it indicts reality and finds it guilty for the
individual's painful shortcomings. Moreover, that Nietzsche came to associate
the teachings of idealist philosophy and romanticism with Christian moral doctrine was no accident. The latter, for Nietzsche, was merely "the most prodigal
elaboration of the moral theme to which humanity has ever been subjected."[10]
It is in this sense that he characterized *The Birth of Tragedy* as an "antimoral"
work: "Nothing could be more opposed to the purely aesthetic interpretation
and justification of the world which are taught in this book than the Christian
teaching."[11]

Among other things, then, what was at stake in the 1886 preface was to
show the independence of his own formulations and to distinguish his views
from those of his idealist predecessors, with whom he was often confused. It
was also important to show how the independence and success of his formulations could be judged by their *distinctively affirmative* response to an issue that
underlies every particular analysis of aesthetics, culture, social institutions, or
morality—as a *response* to what he called "the question mark" concerning the
meaning and value of existence. Only when this question about the fundamental value of life itself is raised do the subsequent interpretations of pessimism,
romanticism, Christian morality, or their alternative formulations, such as Hellenism, even arise. Perhaps this is why Nietzsche went so far as to change the
very title of *The Birth of Tragedy* in 1886. Its earlier subtitle, "Out of the Spirit
of Music," was replaced by "Hellenism and Pessimism," so as to lessen the
impression that the book dealt merely with a historical observation about the
evolution of tragedy. Rather, the new title would better reflect the much
broader claim of offering a comprehensive evaluation of tragic Greek culture
itself. By the same token, the new title would also give some indication as to
how Greek culture came to understand and, thus, to resolve, this "question
mark" of existence.

Nietzsche's initial remarks about tragic culture, in section 5 of the preface,
were meant to stress how radically different its outlook was from that of the
Christian-moral variety. As for the latter, and in what amounts to a veritable
manifesto, he would charge:

Behind this mode of thought and valuation, which must be hostile to art if it is at
all genuine, I never failed to sense a *hostility to life*—a furious, vengeful antipathy
to life itself. . . . Christianity was from the beginning, essentially and fundamentally, life's nausea and disgust with life, merely concealed behind, masked by,
dressed up as, faith in "another" or "better" life. Hatred of "the world," condem-
nations of the passions, fear of beauty and sensuality, a beyond invented the
better to slander this life, at bottom a craving for the nothing, for the end, for
respite, for "the sabbath of sabbaths"—all this always struck me, no less than the
unconditional will of Christianity to recognize *only* moral values, as the most
dangerous and uncanny form of all possible forms of a "will to decline"—at the
very least, a sign of abysmal sickness, weariness, discouragement, exhaustion, and
the impoverishment of life. For, confronted with morality . . . life *must* continually and inevitably be in the wrong because life *is* something essentially amoral—
and eventually, crushed by the weight of contempt and the eternal No, life *must*
then be felt to be unworthy of desire and altogether worthless.[12]

Alternatively, the culture of classical Greece responded to "the question
mark concerning the value of existence" by affirming life in an entirely antimoral, that is, in what Nietzsche termed an "anti-Christian," sense: it understood itself according to the image of a Greek artist-god, Dionysus.

When Nietzsche mentions Dionysus in the 1886 preface, we should note
that his own use of this term has changed somewhat during the course of the
fifteen years since the initial appearance of *The Birth of Tragedy*. In brief, *The
Birth of Tragedy* attempts to portray two quite distinct psychological attitudes
or dispositions that helped to determine classical Greek culture, especially insofar as these attitudes were expressed in art and myth. The attitudes were
traditionally symbolized in Greek culture by two different deities, Apollo and
Dionysus. While the significance of these two figures exceeded what might be
called a strictly artistic function (e.g., Apollo and Dionysus had an important,
if not preeminent, place in the religious and civil life of ancient Greece, in its
communal festivals, mythology, politics, etc.), Nietzsche claimed that they
served as the patron deities for artistic inspiration and practice.[13] In this wider
sense, as Nietzsche understood it, Apollo came to stand for order, measure,
form, clarity, and individuality of creation as well as uniqueness and singularity.
Apollo was traditionally associated with epic poetry (especially that of Homer)
and the plastic arts (sculpture, painting, and to a lesser degree, architecture),
since these best exemplified the delimited, well-formed, and precisely exe-
cuted work of art; discrete artistic forms were creatively imposed upon the
unformed or chaotic raw materials of nature. Implicit in Apollonian art was

the concept of restraint, of balance or limitation, qualities that required the intervention of human reflection and rationality for the proper execution of the artwork.

Dionysus, by contrast, represented the instinctual elements in human expression: the sometimes violent drives of intense emotion, sensuality, intoxication, of frenzy and madness. Dionysus was traditionally associated with lyric and dithyrambic poetry, music, and drama, which were principally performed at public spectacles (most notably, the Greek *Dionysia* festivals), often requiring the active participation of an audience. Unlike Apollo, Dionysus was thought to inspire collective outbursts of ecstatic celebration, wherein the individual insensibly lost possession of himself and became part of a larger whole through chants, recitation, music, and song.[14] In their ritual form, these celebrations were usually accompanied by the consumption of great quantities of wine (Dionysus was also the god of wine), sometimes of narcotic and hallucinogenic drugs, and they often resulted in orgiastic displays of mystical and sexual frenzy. Dionysus thereby stood for the explosive powers of generation, growth, and abundance, the luxuriance of vegetation and harvest, of drunkenness and libidinal discharge, in short, for those awesome, joyful, and occasionally fear-inspiring expenditures of energy and eroticism that transgress the general rules, norms, and codes of individual and social existence.

In *The Birth of Tragedy*, Nietzsche maintained that both the Dionysian and Apollonian attitudes, far from being random or infrequent states of mind, were specific responses to "the question mark concerning the value of existence." By adopting one attitude or the other in varying degrees, one thereby chose to establish a basic set of valuations within existence (i.e., for one's own life, and, as the orientation for a culture at large). Each attitude, therefore, signified an interpretive stance toward the whole of existence, toward an existence that was itself essentially amoral, or, as Nietzsche said in the 1886 preface, one "beyond good and evil." In the end, he argued, the magnificence of classical Greece was due in large part to the frank recognition and acceptance of both attitudes and to the acknowledgment that both attitudes were *necessary* for the highest state of classical Greek art, tragic drama.

Classical tragedy thus achieved a balance of the Dionysian and Apollonian attitudes as a response that mirrored the complexities of human existence, never simply sacrificing one attitude for the other. For Nietzsche the tragic spirit consecrated both the human passions and the intellect, neither abandoning the mystery of what was unknown nor the intelligibility of what was understood. In doing so it created an open space for individual action and performance, and this was not at all thought to be at the expense of social or political cohesion. The greatness of Hellenic culture required a complex but commanding unity of belief, purpose, and aspiration, and the tragic spirit provided it. It gave to Greece what Nietzsche called "the grand style."[15]

In the years that followed the appearance of *The Birth of Tragedy*, Nietzsche came more and more to use the term Dionysian to represent the fusion of the two attitudes, which he thought was expressed in the tragic spirit of the Greek classical age. It is this progressively developed sense of the Dionysian that Nietzsche would continually oppose, not to the Apollonian, but to the asceticism of Christian moral doctrine. In section 5 of the 1886 preface, he explicitly identified the term Dionysian with what he called the "purely artistic and anti-Christian" valuation of life: "As a philologist and man of words I baptized it, not without taking some liberty—for who could claim to know the rightful name of the Antichrist?—in the name of a Greek god: I called it Dionysian."[16]

Some two years later, in *Twilight of the Idols* (1888), Nietzsche claimed that this Dionysian valuation of life was the "basic fact of the Hellenic instinct," and that it found its truest affirmation in the veneration of sexuality, whereby:

> The Hellene guaranteed himself . . . eternal life, the eternal return of life . . . true life as the over-all continuation of life through procreation, through the mysteries of sexuality. For the Greeks the sexual symbol was therefore the venerable symbol par excellence, the real profundity in the whole of ancient piety. Every single element in the act of procreation, of pregnancy, and of birth aroused the highest and most solemn feelings. . . . Here the most profound instinct of life, that directed toward the future of life, is experienced religiously—and the way to life, procreation, as the *holy* way. It was Christianity, with its *ressentiment* against life at the bottom of its heart, which first made something unclean of sexuality; it threw filth on the origin, on the presupposition of life.[17]

Unlike the developed Dionysian attitude, which effectively "spiritualized" the passions (i.e., retained them, venerated them, and sublimated them to an order of beauty and deification), the ascetic or antisensualist practice of Christian moral doctrine was simply to *excise* the passions. Its "cure," Nietzsche remarked, is "castratism," and this means nothing other than "an attack on the roots of life: the practice of the church is hostile to life."[18]

THE TRADITIONAL MYTHOLOGY OF DIONYSUS AND APOLLO

Two of the most popular and important deities in ancient Greece, Dionysus and Apollo enjoyed innumerable cults, drew throngs of followers, and had temples erected for their worship and festival celebration everywhere throughout Greece—indeed, everywhere Greek influence was felt in the ancient world.

It is generally thought that the worship of Dionysus first originated in the regions beyond Greece proper, most likely in Phrygia or Thrace, possibly in Lydia or Crete, even though many places in ancient Greece itself were claimed as his birthplace (e.g., Naxos, Prasiae, Thebes, Dracanum). Not only are his geographical origins somewhat indistinct, but the etymology of his very name adds to the obscurity surrounding him. Dionysus is traditionally derived from Nysus, the name of the mountain on which Dionysus was said to have been raised. What complicates matters is that no one is at all sure where this mountain is located. It has been assigned to Libya, Africa, Thrace, Asia Minor, and even to India by various sources, and many writers feel that the etymological identification with Mt. Nysus was simply an afterthought—an attempt to secure an entirely mythical residence for this far-traveling god so as to distribute his importance and make him less of a regional deity. To make matters worse, Dionysus was often called by various names: Diounsis (the Phrygian term), Zagreus (of Orphic tradition), Bacchus (a name the Romans later adopted, often identifying him with their god, Liber), Iaccus (the god of the Eleusinian mysteries), Bromius (the thunderer), Lenaëus (of the wine-press), Lyaeüs (he who frees), and Dendrites (of the trees).[19]

The variant names and the diversity of locales in which he was worshiped indicate that, in the earliest times, Dionysus was held to be a god of fertility, probably by rural agrarian peoples, concerned as they would be with the seasonal rebirth of their crops and vegetation. That he was also a god of wine testifies both to his likely alien origins and to his liberating capacities—he was held responsible for inducing madness as well as for curing it. Through the drinking of wine and by orgiastic rites the followers of Dionysus would become *dispossessed* of themselves and feel identified, ecstatically united, with the god himself. This veritable madness brought on by wine and sexual license was held intolerable by the austere nomadic Greeks of the Homeric period, and the practice of Dionysian cults was doubtless initially repressed by the native populations.[20]

The hostile reaction to Dionysus and his followers (who were called Satyrs, Sileni, and Maenads) is strikingly contained within the Dionysian myths themselves. In one case, Dionysus and his followers were driven out of Thrace by Lycurgus (king of the Edonians) after they introduced the cultivation of wine to the region. In another instance, which took place in the city of Thebes, the sisters of Dionysus's mother, Semele, resolutely refused to acknowledge his divinity, and the king attempted to imprison Dionysus. In still another, when Dionysus arrived in Attica and taught Icarius and his daughter Erigone the art of wine making, the outraged citizens immediately killed Icarius and forced his daughter to hang herself. In each of these cases, however, we are told that Dionysus quickly dispensed his own vengeance and drove Lycurgus mad, who in his crazed attempt to cut down the newly planted vineyards, chopped his own wife and son to bits. For good measure, Dionysus promptly rendered the land sterile. In the second case, which Euripides portrayed in *The Bacchae*, Dionysus drove the women of Thebes mad and made his aunt Agave tear her only son (the Theban king Pentheus) to pieces. After this Dionysian-inspired carnage, she returned to Thebes in procession, with Pentheus's head on a thrysus (the Dionysian phallic staff, carried in ritual celebrations), not knowing the gravity of her crime until the madness passed. When she did recover, Dionysus promptly exiled her and turned her parents into serpents. Answering the third rebuke, Dionysus rendered the women of Attica insane, to the point where they commenced hanging themselves.

These myths surely betray an extraordinary fear of the advancing Dionysian cults. On the one hand, the cults had immense *popular* appeal, since the lowest peasant or serf could at least briefly exchange his or her grinding poverty and tedium for the blissful feeling of a divine existence. Furthermore, the ecstatic celebrations constituted a real danger to the already established social order, and extended periods of intoxication and sexual frenzy could seriously threaten the fabric of family life and the political order itself. Indeed, by the sixth century, several Greek tyrants (most notably Pisistratus) were able to garner great political support from the lower classes by establishing temples and sanctuaries for the practice of just these rites.[21] Finally, the Dionysian cults tended to exacerbate the differences between the sexes, with the followers of Dionysus most often being women, who were called maenads (literally, "mad women"). Due to deep social and economic inequalities between the sexes, the Dionysian cults offered women (especially women from the cities and villages, where role differences would tend to be exaggerated) a strong means of compensation for their restricted social and sexual status. Indeed, wherever social or sexual prohibitions were strongly enforced in the ancient world, one could usually find some means of transgressing them.

The Dionysian votaries certainly pursued their transgression with a terrifying maenadic fury. Ancient writers (e.g., Hesiod, Hyginus, Nonnos, Apollodorus, Euripides, and Pausanius) hastened to describe, in quite lurid detail, the outrages allegedly performed by these maddened hordes: bulls, lions, cows,

Eucharist

goats, deer, children, men, and women were claimed to have been torn to pieces in the course of the Dionysian rites. In their fury to dismember and actually eat these sacrificial victims (the practice is called omophagia), the cult ritually reenacted one of the principal myths of Dionysus's rebirth: the Orphic account wherein Dionysus himself was torn to pieces by the Titans (at the instigation of Hera, who was the wife of Zeus, king of the Olympian gods) and *reborn* through the agency of Zeus. According to this account, Zeus swallowed the dismembered heart of Dionysus and quickly proceeded to impregnate the mortal Semele (daughter of Cadmus, king of Thebes), thus transferring Dionysus to her womb—an early instance of transubstantiation, as it were. Avoiding Hera's "ever-searching wrath," the reborn Dionysus immediately transformed himself in appearance and was raised as a young girl.

Other versions of the myth also contributed certain elements to the Dionysian ritual, although perhaps somewhat less dramatically. One non-Orphic variant begins with Zeus's seduction of Semele. Angered by the seduction, the perpetually jealous Hera conspired to bring about Semele's death by Zeus's own hand. She had Zeus visit Semele once again, but this time in the form of a divine thunderbolt—which proved to be altogether too lethal for the mortal Semele. At the moment of her death, however, Zeus rescued the unborn child from Semele's womb and sewed it inside his own thigh, whereupon *he* later gave birth to Dionysus. According to this account, Dionysus once again escaped Hera, this time by transforming himself into a goat kid. However differing, both accounts labor to stress the double birth of Dionysus, the pursuit by Hera, and his subsequent transformation—dynamic and regenerative elements Nietzsche would emphasize when he later argued for his own "Dionysian" interpretation of Greek culture.

Despite the apparently severe aspect of these received myths, Dionysus himself was rarely thought of as altogether vicious. On the contrary, he was often called "the gentle god" and was held to give the highest pleasures to his followers, not the least of which were the joys of fertility and wine. As a god of the earth and of the underworld (a "chthonian" deity), he fully understood both regions and was capable of the extreme kinds of behavior usually associated with them. His mythical genealogy, as related by Hesiod in *The Theogony*, attested to the diversity of character traits such a figure might be expected to inherit. As the offspring of divine Zeus and the mortal Semele (whose name in Greek means "seed" or "germ"), Dionysus would *become* a god. Thus, at the outset, he would enjoy both human and divine attributes and be blessed with earthly and divine wisdom. His mother, Semele, was herself descended, through the goddess Harmonia ("harmony"), from Ares (god of war) and Aphrodite (goddess of love), two of the most powerful deities on Olympus, and for the ancient Greek, the two gods who perhaps best represented the most primal claims on the mortal spirit.

Like Dionysus, Apollo was also counted as a son of Zeus, the offspring in this case of the titaness Leto. Once again, Hera sought to avenge Zeus's rather frequent infidelities by sending a serpent to kill Leto. Nonetheless, Leto did give birth to Apollo on the island of Delos, and he was subsequently raised by the goddess Themis (yet another of Zeus's consorts; Themis represented order throughout the universe and lawful conduct in the affairs of mankind), who nourished him on a diet of divine nectar and ambrosia. After what is doubtless one of the shortest periods of childhood dependence ever recorded—it was said that he fully matured in four days—Apollo then traveled to Delphi and slew the serpent Hera had earlier dispatched against Leto. The serpent itself was said to have protected an ancient oracle, belonging to the primal earth goddess Gaia. In any case, after having killed the serpent, Apollo installed his own oracle and named the first priestess Pythia, or "pythoness," after the serpent.

Gaining the oracle at Delphi, Apollo came to be known as the god of prophecy and visions, and the oracle acquired immense power and influence throughout the Greek world. Besides being known for the often enigmatic wisdom of his oracle, Apollo was also regarded as a divine healer (he was the father of Asclepius, god of medicine) and, as a patron of music (which Nietzsche does not stress, so as to emphasize the opposition with Dionysus), he was often depicted as leading the Muses in song. His instrument was traditionally the lyre, which was thought to produce the most melodic and harmonious music, and he was said to have invented the cithara, or lyre.

Apollo's dealings with mankind were universally held to be just. When honored and venerated, he was profuse in dispensing rewards: to King Admetus he brought twofold prosperity and, against the very fates, he was able to extend Admetus's life. Like Dionysus, his revenge could be awe-inspiring as well: he killed the giant Tityus, who attempted to ravish his mother, Leto, and he systematically exterminated the children of the Theban queen Niobe, who regrettably boasted a family even more beautiful than that of Leto.

Apollo was traditionally held forth as a model of classical Greek beauty, and as Hesiod claimed in *The Theogony*, of all the children descended from Father Sky (Uranos), those of Leto were the loveliest. These several aspects of Apollo tended to associate him with the source of all beauty and light, the sun. He came to be known as Phoebus Apollo, the god of light, sun, beauty, order, health, and harmony. Indeed, his two most common names were Phoebus ("the bright one") and Lyceius ("light god"), and he was sometimes identified with the ancient sun god Helius.

Once again, like Dionysus, Apollo was most likely introduced into Greece from the regions of the East, although this probably occurred much earlier than the introduction of Dionysus. His name is not mentioned in Linear B tablets (i.e., late Bronze Age Greek, ca. 14th–12th century B.C.), but traditional sources held him to be among the most ancient, and most distinctively Greek, gods. One indication of his foreign provenance, however, was the necessity of his having to attack and defeat an earlier, preexisting oracle (i.e., the python at Delphi). Another indication of this is the etymology of his title "Lyceius," which might once have simply designated an origin in Lycia, a southeastern region of Asia Minor. Finally, the very name Apollo might well have evolved from that of the earlier Hittite god Apulunas.

CONCERNS OF *THE BIRTH OF TRAGEDY*

With the conjunction of the Dionysian and Apollonian attitudes, tragic Greek culture was able to provide itself with the resources of what Nietzsche saw as an extraordinary health. For Nietzsche, this would be a culture imbued with a generous understanding of and toleration for the whole of human experience, with a strength to survive in the face of personal and political adversity, a culture that would admit a wide latitude in the pursuit of individual creativity, coupled with a deep-seated feeling of social and political identity.

Historically, Nietzsche argued, the decline of the classical period—or, what he saw more specifically as its greatest moment, "the tragic age"—began with the rise of Athenian military and economic superiority, following the defeat of the Persian fleet at Salamis (480 B.C.).[22] This period of unheralded prosperity quickly bred divisiveness and internal turmoil; Athens became militarily aggressive, and immense fortunes were made. Vested military and economic forces further contributed to social and economic disparity, to an abandonment of the fully integrated life of the Greek city-state—with its requirements of communal religious, military, and political obligations on the part of its citizens. The deep sentiment of a public belonging, of a common heritage, and of shared beliefs quickly fractured in an environment that became wolfishly individualistic and aggressive. It was only in such a period of traditional decay, of decadence, that the relatively modern concept of "the individual" could emerge with a vengeance in the form of ever more severe political tyrants, military adventurers, skeptics, and iconoclasts, all of whom removed themselves from the culture that made their rise possible in the first place. What was taking place in Athens during this inception of decline was, to Nietzsche's mind, symbolized nowhere more pointedly than in the person of Socrates.

While Nietzsche was of two minds concerning Socrates—in many respects he admired Socrates immensely and often chose Socrates as a model of personal integrity—he nonetheless saw the distinctive features of cultural decadence forcefully at work in him: the extremist individual, the fanatical moralist, the fanatical rationalist, the calumniator of art, the apolitical corruptor of Athenian culture (and of its youth).[23] With his analysis of Socrates, Nietzsche brought his examination of tragic culture to a close. That tragic culture should abruptly conclude with the figure of Socrates, however, was not merely due to the appearance of an exceptional individual. Rather, for Nietzsche, the end seemed to be prefigured long in advance by the very terms of the culture itself, each given component struggling for ascendancy. Socrates (or, better, "the Socratic type") represented just one case of the Apollonian attitude: its most exaggerated extreme. No longer moderated by its Dionysian complement, the Apollonian temper came full circle, finally exhausting itself, as it were, by means of its own resources. The danger and divisiveness posed by this Apollonian limit case would continue to remain an extremely important insight for Nietzsche. In his very last work (*Ecce Homo*, 1888), he remarked that besides his analysis of the Dionysian, the most decisive innovation of *The Birth of Tragedy* was his understanding of Socrates: "Socrates is recognized for the first time as an instrument of Greek disintegration, as a typical decadent. 'Rationality' against instinct. 'Rationality' at any price as a dangerous force that undermines life."[24]

In sketching this portrait of ancient Greece, Nietzsche thereby drew painful attention to the conditions of decline within the Europe of his own time, one characterized by a surfeit of extremist attitudes and practices. As with Greece, so now with Europe.[25] It was all too clear, for Nietzsche, that the process of erosion and decline was once again at work, further debilitating an already fragile European health and greatness. For a modern age, this signaled the inevitable advent of nihilism—the abandonment of all values, beliefs, and ideals, the recourse to desperate ideologies to stem the flow, to serve as reactive countermeasures—which, Nietzsche sadly knew, would only intensify the rate and severity of the decline itself.[26]

on nihilism

With his analysis in *The Birth of Tragedy*, Nietzsche claimed to have presented an interpretation of historical fact, not unlike the analyses of Thucyd-
ides, Machiavelli, Gibbon, or Burckhardt. Nietzsche himself, however, held out
the possibility of alternative developments within European culture, and to this
end he examined the promise of emergent formulations, particularly those of
Wagner, or what he termed a new "artist's metaphysics," a modern "tragic
wisdom." While he was to be quickly disappointed by the train of events surrounding Wagner himself, Nietzsche never ceased to explore the resources
needed for such a new age of human achievement. Realistically, he understood
that if such an age were possible, it would have to be purchased at great expense.

> A tremendous hope speaks out of this essay *The Birth of Tragedy*. In the end I
> lack all reason to renounce the hope for a Dionysian future of music. Let us look
> ahead a century; let us suppose that my attempt to assassinate two millennia of
> antinature and desecration of man were to succeed. That new party of life which
> would tackle the greatest of all tasks, the attempt to raise humanity higher, in-
> cluding the relentless destruction of everything that was degenerating and para-
> sitical, would again make possible that excess of life on earth from which the
> Dionysian state, too, would have to awaken. I promise a tragic age: the highest
> art in saying Yes to life, tragedy, will be reborn when humanity has weathered
> the consequences of the hardest but most necessary wars *without suffering from
> it*.[27]

Nietzsche had already termed this task "the revaluation of all values" by then
and, in retrospect, he saw *The Birth of Tragedy* as his own first step for carrying
it out.[28]

On many later occasions, Nietzsche remarked that perhaps the single greatest discovery of *The Birth of Tragedy* was its insight into the psychology of
pain.[29] This would be one of his most penetrating and enduring perceptions,
and he would develop it at length, under various headings, throughout the
course of his subsequent work, especially in *On the Genealogy of Morals, Thus
Spoke Zarathustra, Beyond Good and Evil*, and *Twilight of the Idols*.[30] What
Nietzsche attempted to gain in these extended analyses was not merely a psychological understanding of the particular individual, of his personal motivations or individual contributions to the culture (e.g., by analyzing a particular
work of art, a single dramatic presentation, or a philosophical work). Rather,
by turning to the distinctive features of an entire culture, he attempted to
discern its underlying and more general patterns of motivation. Thus, Nietz-

sche would come to find certain "typical" responses to frequently recurring problems encountered by the culture in question. These responses would often serve as models of cultural adaptation, as solutions or resolutions to the presence of one kind or another of threat or danger—whether the dangers were of a political kind or of a social, economic, religious, or even natural variety.

In the course of time, the patterns of adaptive behavior may become relatively explicit to the members of a culture, and indeed, may appear in institutional or codified form, as civil laws, as religious practices, as conventional rules of social conduct, or as explicit norms of ethical or moral judgment.[31] Alternatively, they may be so taken for granted that they pass unnoticed, just as in language, where the rules of grammar determine how to speak properly, even though the speaker may be ignorant or quite unaware of them while speaking. Collectively, such patterns determine what we mean by a general style or type of culture—they lend it structure, coherency, and content and, in the end, they determine the specific evolution of its very institutions. By the same token, however, it is on the basis of this already established and generally unquestioned style of *cultural* configuration that the *individual* acts in turn. Likewise, it is on this basis of tradition that the individual comes to understand, interpret, and judge him- or herself and his or her contributions and relations to that culture. That is, the individual attains self-understanding in terms of his or her broader cultural resources; the person *sees* things and events according to *its* perspective.

It was this insight into the general motivational patterns of a culture that established Nietzsche as a distinctively modern thinker, in the company of Marx and Freud.[32] What Nietzsche grasped, as did Marx and Freud, was the complex and systematic set of preconditions that underlies both individual and collective behavior, which determines the nature and aspirations of the society as a whole. While Nietzsche later termed his method of analysis "genealogical"—and here one should read, especially, his introduction to *On the Genealogy of Morals*—its importance in *The Birth of Tragedy* was that it enabled him to perform an in-depth analysis of classical Greek culture according to registers that were ignored or simply not understood by the writers of his day; namely, the entire motivational context within Athenian society, especially in its historical and psychological dimensions. Precisely this "lack of historical understanding" and "psychological ignorance" were the epithets Nietzsche directed most unsparingly against his contemporaries. Moreover, he saw that the presence of one misunderstanding tended to indicate that of the other: for failure to understand the deep, long-protracted struggles through which Greek culture evolved; for failure to grasp the historical impact of the earliest Doric invasions, the continual incursions of predatory armies, the frequent periods of climatic change, with their attendant economic and social perils; for failure to take into account the various Mycenaean, Cretan, and Egyptian influences, the successive introduction of innumerable religious sects, together with their competing beliefs and practices—in short, the failure to understand the extremely long and complex train of historical influences upon the development of classical Greece—all resulted in the failure to grasp the often brutal, strident, and aggressive character of the Greek spirit. Likewise, by not understanding the psychological and emotional resources of the Greeks, one is entirely perplexed to explain the kind of adaptive responses Greek society made in the course of its own evolution, much less to understand how it managed to remain intact and to flourish.

The failure to appreciate these two dimensions of Greek life resulted in an extraordinarily naive and idealized view of the Greeks, one propagated even today in the popular and professional mind.[33] This entirely commonplace notion is of a timeless Greece, radiant in the splendor of its benign gods, its noble and beautiful souls—a Greece that appeared to emerge miraculously, spontaneously, out of a long-forgotten barbarism—in short, the notion of an idyllic society, serene in its own confidence and prosperity, acutely sensitive to the truly civilized life of art, beauty, and intellect.[34]

Of course, this idyll was the Greece of European romantics and it had less to say about the Greeks themselves than about the envious longings of a politically unstable Europe hell-bent on a path of ruthless industrialization. The idealized conception of Greece tended to minimize conflict, both individual and social, and as a result, there seemed to be little dynamism to the classical period, save for the appearance of particularly striking or heroic individuals. Understandably, such individuals would seem far larger than in life and would be entirely removed from any usual orientation within a society. This distortion in turn only served the cause of a more intense form of idealization, the determined tendency to find great-souled men of genius and heroism at every juncture. The consequence of such romantic exaggeration was to elevate Greek culture right out of all plausible existence: romanticized Greece thus served as an "ideal" model of social and political order and a veritable utopia for nineteenth-century thought. In the end, since any attempt at self-understanding is ultimately indebted to its cultural and historical resources, such views as the romantic conception of classical Greece did far more than a disservice. For Nietzsche, they were dangerous in the extreme, for they denied a real understanding of our own long-forming historical presence and the future it extends before us. Indeed, it would be precisely such views as the romantic conception that Nietzsche would criticize at length in the work he explicitly devoted to the study of historiography, *History in the Service and Disservice of Life* (1874).[35]

That the Greeks *had* a remarkably developed civilization in the period with which Nietzsche was concerned, the sixth and especially, the fifth centuries B.C., was an article of faith for him, as it was for classicists in general. Quite simply, classical Greece was gifted with a prodigal creative genius. But the question that intrigued Nietzsche was *how* such a society was *possible*. To understand classical art, sculpture, drama, and philosophy as a kind of *vision* is what romanticism did, and to some extent, this was correct. More than anything else, however, what differentiated Nietzsche's approach from that of the classical-romantic school, was that the latter simply took the vision at face value. Thus, its value as a vision, as a visionary reality, or as a kind of regulative illusion was simply lost to nineteenth-century thought. By not asking what the tragic vision or illusion stood for, what it represented to the Greek mind, and why the Greeks saw fit to produce this kind of vision, the classicists created a total misunderstanding of Greek culture and civilization.

It was with these considerations in mind that Nietzsche's "genealogical" analysis pursued a double path: (1) Out of what did the highest art form of classical Greece (i.e., Greek tragic drama) evolve? (2) What motivated this evolution of tragic drama (i.e., to what needs, to what instinct or understanding in the Greek mind, did this evolution of tragic drama testify)? Nietzsche's response to these questions was complex, and to say the least, arduous, but it can be briefly anticipated.

In answer to the first question, Nietzsche claimed that the tragic drama evolved out of dithyrambic poetry and Greek liturgical music (specifically, the choral music of Dionysian religious cults), together with elements from conventional drama (the introduction of several actors, character analysis, and a refined plot development). This was in large part a historical question, and it was dealt with at some length by Aristotle, in his *Poetics* (1449 a 20–1459 a 16), and again by Cicero. Modern scholarship has generally tended to agree with Nietzsche and to confirm this derivation.[36]

The deep psychological motivation of tragic drama, and its significance for Greek culture, is of course closely involved with this same historical derivation. Nietzsche interpreted the tragic spirit as a fusion or coalescence of the two dispositions mentioned previously, the Dionysian and Apollonian. Insofar as they were embodied in the particular dramatic work, the Dionysian attitudes were best expressed by the music and chants of the chorus, the Apollonian attitudes by the recitative (i.e., by the speeches and dialogues of the actors, who represented distinct characters, served to enact the original myth, and performed it according to the scripted text of the dramatist). By separating out the formal elements of the tragic drama and by claiming different motivations for the derivation of each, Nietzsche raised the subsequent question, What gave rise to the Dionysian and Apollonian attitudes in the first place?—and this, for Nietzsche, was the central question of *The Birth of Tragedy*. Both the Dionysian and Apollonian attitudes were, as Nietzsche interpreted them, basic types of responses to the issues the Greeks found most vital, the problems of ordinary and extraordinary human existence.

[margin note: central question]

"HOMER'S CONTEST": APOLLO

Whatever obscurities are contained in the mythical accounts of Apollo and Dionysus—and they are not inconsiderable—these two gods were sufficiently distinguished in the mind of the classical Greek to serve as separate deities of artistic inspiration and be endowed with quite distinctive attributes.[37] Nietzsche's concern in *The Birth of Tragedy* was to understand these figures, not so much in their mythological roles, but insofar as they symbolized two fundamentally different kinds of attitudes that found expression everywhere throughout Greek culture of the classical period. As mentioned earlier, his intention was to analyze the motivations behind these attitudes and to see them essentially as attitudes taken in response to the issues and difficulties of human existence. Moreover, as typical kinds of response, the two attitudes could best be explored on the general level of distinctive cultural configurations (e.g., in terms of characteristically Greek social rites and practices, institutions, politics, and art).

If the terms Apollonian and Dionysian thus served as categories to designate two basic kinds of cultural attitudes, and these attitudes were thought of as responses Greek culture typically adopted to ensure its own survival in the face of adverse conditions, then we can understand why Nietzsche's use of them was so exceedingly broad: for the most part, Apollonian and Dionysian were used as descriptive terms, but often—and this is important to his analysis—he employed them as prescriptive terms as well. His argument was not simply so that we, the modern reader, could understand the period of classical Greece by our judicious use of two descriptive categories. Rather, he claimed that by

[margin note: descriptive vs. prescriptive]

analyzing these attitudes as they were characteristically expressed, we could to a large extent understand how and why Greek culture responded as it did to the various problems it faced. By extrapolation, the question moves from Greek culture per se to that of any other: what must a culture do, what responses must that culture prescribe to itself, to ensure its continuation, when confronted by human and natural threats to its very existence? It is in this prescriptive sense that Nietzsche often spoke of the "health," "exuberance," "sustenance," or "decline" of a culture—about its strength to survive and to adapt itself to changing conditions, or, about its weakness, its inability to adapt to change in such a way as to preserve its most esteemed features, its values, institutions, traditions, and so forth.[38]

From the start, then, Nietzsche's understanding of classical Greek culture was to stress its dynamic properties: each stage in its developing evolution was a response to the aggravated conditions of natural human existence, with its ever-attendant dangers. Each stage thus appeared as a provisional "victory," an "overcoming," or "resolution" to a set of oftentimes hostile provocations. In this sense, the continuing development of a culture appears, dynamically, as an ongoing contest. It was precisely in these terms that Nietzsche described the painful emergence of a distinctively Greek culture: "Homer's Contest." The initial resolution for what comes to be known as Greek culture was the Homeric victory over the earlier period of barbarism, a period of violence and unremitting chaos.[39]

In his essay of 1872, entitled "Homer's Contest," Nietzsche characterized this pre-Homeric age (i.e., the early archaic period, which was marked by the Mycenaean and Doric invasions) and suggested what this period must have meant to the Greeks of the Homeric period:

> Where do we look when we are no longer led and protected by the hand of Homer, striding back into the pre-Homeric world? Only into night and horror, into the products of an imagination accustomed to the horrible. What kind of earthly existence is reflected in these repulsively terrible theogonic myths: a life over which alone the *children of Night* rule, Strife, Lustful Greed, Deception, Old Age, and Death [among Night's other children, Hesiod includes Doom, Deceit and Love, Sleep, Blame, Sad Distress, and Nemesis: *Theogony*, 211–31] . . . let us mix this thick Boeotian air with the dark voluptuousness of the Etruscan; then such a reality would *extort* from us a world of myths in which Uranos, Kronos, and Zeus and the fighting Titans must appear as a relief. . . . And in truth, just as the concept of Greek law developed from *murder* and the expiation of murder, so too, the nobler culture takes its first victory wreath from the altar

of the expiation of murder. Following that bloody age a furrowing wave cuts deeply into Hellenic history.[40]

Particularly central to Nietzsche's account were the consequences of such a desperate pre-Homeric worldview. On the one hand, the Greek world of warfare and cruelty—an "abyss of horrible savagery"—gave rise to "the disgust with existence, toward the interpretation of this existence as a punishment and atonement."[41] But by taking this interpretation one step further and asking what this bloody world of fighting and occasional triumph could possibly mean, the response would serve as the first resolution of a distinctively Greek culture. To understand the precise nature of this resolution, Nietzsche observed, "We must first assume that the Greek genius once found value in the existence of such a terrible drive and thought it *justified*. . . . Fighting and the lust for victory were acknowledged: and nothing separates the Greek world from ours as much as the *coloring*, derived hence, of individual ethical concepts, for example, of *eris* [strife] and *envy*."[42]

Finally, Nietzsche went on to argue in the same essay that it was by internalizing or incorporating this resolution—to admit and to justify the necessity of strife—that Greek culture at large found a means of preserving itself and ensuring its prosperity. Thus, the struggle, contest, or competition (what the Greeks called the *agon*) would itself prove to be the very salvation of Greek culture. In the form of warfare, the *agon* would emerge as the passion for victory at all costs.[43] In peace, it would appear as the intense desire to excel in art, politics, athletic competition, or in thought. By incorporating the *agon* as a principle of cultural definition, the Greeks in turn cultivated a people who were capable of developing their natural endowments to an as yet unheard-of extent. The resolution required that the contest as such continue unabated: one victory stimulates another in an ongoing process, whereby the society as a whole can take pride in the enhancement of its collective glory and achievement. To stand outside the human contest, or to bring it to an end, was to revert to barbarism. Even worse, it was to pretend to divinity, to the infinite—at which point one's opponents would be the jealous gods themselves, who would unhesitatingly crush any such mortal presumption.

Nietzsche speculated that the importance of the contest itself, and not the particular, individual victory, was what initially led to the widespread practice of ostracism, or enforced exile: when a subject placed himself beyond the arena (i.e., outside of the culture that sustained the *agon*), he would become a danger to society as a whole—since it was the *agon* that ultimately made the culture viable and served as its very foundation. Such a person would either discourage the possibility of the contest, since no one else could hope to achieve his own end, or he would place himself beyond the laws of the society and human commerce to become a tyrant, thence to indulge his basest instincts without restraint. The result in both cases would be dangerous to the society as a whole. The vestigial sense of this situation, whereby an individual—by his very *superiority*—stands *beyond* competition (beyond, and thus, as a *discouragement* to actual or possible future competition), is retained in the French phrase, common to English usage, "hors de concours," that is, beyond reasonable competition.

Homer and Hesiod were the founders of this uniquely Greek, agonistic culture. They idealized the eristic qualities of their legendary heroes and Olympian gods, and they presented these figures in epic form to the citizens of eighth-century B.C. Greece as a model for human existence. This model in turn served as a creative response to the pervading sense of doom that seemed to characterize the earlier, pre-Homeric age. In *The Birth of Tragedy*, Nietzsche described this first stage in the consolidation of classical Greek culture as the initial victory of the Apollonian vision.

THE APOLLONIAN VISION

The vision of Apollonian art found specific expression in epic poetry—*The Iliad*, *The Odyssey*, *The Homeric Poems*, the *Theogony*, and the *Works and Days*—and as Nietzsche described it, this vision was an artistic interpretation of human reality. While it was indeed poetically presented in these several epic works, the vision was not limited only to them, nor was it limited to the production of other specific art works either. Rather, the Apollonian vision was a kind of *illusion* by which or through which the Greek came to understand his or her world. More precisely, Nietzsche claimed that the Apollonian vision could best be described in terms of a pointed analogy: it stood as a *dream* in comparison to ordinary waking life.

As a dream, the Apollonian vision was illusory and it was produced by the dreamer. In this sense, it was within everyone's capacity to become a visionary and give rise to a singular artistic creation. Moreover, the dream was in fact intelligible, and its images served both an interpretive and a prophetic function (for which reason Apollo himself was regarded as the god of augury and divination). With this in mind, Nietzsche recalled that the significance of the dream vision often arose in striking relief against the waking background of confusion and detail. Thus, not only might the dream experience have been pleasurable in itself, but the apparent clarity of the dream brought with it a respite from troubled concerns, a delight in what appeared to be a deeper understanding of things. More important, perhaps, the respite and delight were fundamentally healing, they brought joy and meaning to life; in short, they helped the dreamer to abide or to survive in the face of a personally disquieting existence. No matter that the dream itself be recognized *as* a dream, since one rarely *confuses* the dream with empirical reality. Indeed, for the Apollonian vision, it was precisely the contrary: one dreamt a vision that "transfigured" empirical reality *so that* it could acquire a different, higher significance, one that beckoned the dreamer onward, one that made existence itself seem estimable and fully worthy of being lived.

From the standpoint of the dream, the newly envisioned world appeared calm, modulated, moderated. The dream world evolved what Nietzsche called "a plastic logic of forms," and it was free from the raucous turbulence and strife in which everyday life was so often embroiled. Thus, despite the immense fluidity of dream life, Nietzsche argued that it was basically tempered, that it was condensed into a particular series of images, bounded by the logic of its own concerns, and—what would at first seem to be contradictory—that it was consequently *less deceptive* than waking life. Ultimately, the very nature of the dream vision lent its determinations to the figure of Apollo, and in doing so, the value of the vision was made manifest. It gave delight in the beauty of its images, it provided a focused intelligibility to human concerns, and it extended a state of "calm repose" to the individual.

In section 3 of *The Birth of Tragedy*, Nietzsche advanced one such vision of Apollonian culture by drawing upon the epic content of Homer and Hesiod. Once again, the description centered on a specific analogy. In this case, he compared the Apollonian culture to an accomplished architectural structure or temple edifice:

> We see the glorious *Olympian* figures of the gods, standing on the gables of this structure. Their deeds, pictured in brilliant reliefs, adorn its friezes. . . . Whoever approaches these Olympians with another religion in his heart, searching among them for moral elevation, even for sanctity, for discarnate spirituality, for charity and benevolence, will soon be forced to turn his back on them, discouraged and disappointed. For there is nothing here that suggests asceticism, spirituality, or duty. We hear nothing but the accounts of an exuberant, triumphant life in which all things, whether good or evil, are deified. And so the spectator may stand quite

bewildered before this fantastic excess of life, asking himself by virtue of what magic potion these high-spirited men could have found life so enjoyable that, wherever they turned, their eyes beheld the smile of Helen, the ideal picture of their own existence, "floating in sweet sensuality." . . . Existence under the bright sunshine of such gods is regarded as desirable in itself, and the real pain of Homeric men is caused by parting from it, especially by early parting. . . . Do not forget the lament of the short-lived Achilles, mourning the leaflike change and vicissitudes of the race of men and the decline of the heroic age. It is not unworthy of the greatest hero to long for a continuation of life, even though he live as a day laborer. At the Apollonian stage of development, the Will longs so vehemently for this existence, the Homeric man feels himself so completely at one with it, that lamentation itself becomes a song of praise.[44]

This Apollonian vision appeared as the *creation* of a divine and exuberant world, a visionary world of Olympian beauty that would, in turn, serve as a model for one's own life. Such a world was first revealed to the Apollonian Greeks through the religion of their gods and the mythology of their exploits; it was thereby "surrounded with a higher glory" and was in all ways exemplary.

The same impulse which calls art into being, as the complement and consummation of existence, seducing one to a continuation of life, was also the cause of the Olympian world which the Hellenic "will" made use of as a transfiguring mirror. Thus do the gods justify the life of man: they themselves live it—the only satisfactory theodicy![45]

If the Apollonian vision was such a "transfiguring mirror," Nietzsche was quick to note that, in order for us to better understand it, the emphasis should perhaps be placed on the transfigurative aspect of the mirror, and especially on the motivations that gave rise to it in the first place. While the unrestrained barbarism of the pre-Homeric age had abated to some extent by the advent of the classical period, nonetheless warfare, the threat of famine, civil unrest, and natural catastrophes were forever present. It is for this reason that Nietzsche began to discuss the Apollonian vision by way of an analogy drawn from architecture: the uppermost gables and parapets of the Apollonian Parthenon celebrated the Olympian gods, and these gods were themselves the "transfiguring mirror" that arose out of the heroic deeds and splendid scenes of the frieze. By the same logic, the pillars or columns of such a temple were the very artists who constructed it (e.g., Homer, Hesiod, Phidias), and in this sense they performed a Herculean task. But finally, and what is in question for the completion of this analogy, is the foundation upon which the Apollonian edifice was erected, namely, the frank realization by the Greeks of the inevitability of human suffering, of ever-present danger, chaos, and impending disaster, the realization that human existence is itself a fragile, painful, and forever imperiled state. But, as Nietzsche observed, if the foundations upon which Apollonian culture stood were perpetually insecure, this testified all the more to the power and persuasion of the vision itself. If the Olympian world of Apollo was able to transfigure the Greek and lend him a beatific vision for the glorification of his own life, this was only possible to the extent that he was driven to elaborate such a world in the first place. Thus, Nietzsche asked the important question, What terrific need was it that could produce such an illustrious company of Olympian beings? His response was equally succinct:

> The Greek knew and felt the terror and horror of existence. That he might endure this terror at all, he had to interpose between himself and life the radiant dream-birth of the Olympian. That overwhelming dismay in the face of the Titanic powers of nature, the fates enthroned inexorably over all knowledge, the vulture of that great lover of mankind, Prometheus, the terrible fate of the wise Oedipus, the family curse of the Atriadae which drove Orestes to matricide. . . . All this was again and again overcome by the Greeks with the aid of the Olympian *middle world* of art; or at any rate it was veiled and withdrawn from sight. It was in order to be able to live that the Greeks had to create these gods from a most profound need.[46]

That the Greeks were haunted by their suffering an all too obtrusive reality was repeatedly affirmed by their epic legends and mythology. At these moments of recognition, Nietzsche argued, the veil of Apollonian illusion parted, precisely to disclose the reality of an existence that was at bottom necessarily painful. By this disclosure, the Apollonian illusion revealed a second truth, namely, that the heretofore redeeming illusion of Apollo was exactly that: an illusion. Perhaps the most striking case of this acknowledged infirmity of the Apollonian vision occurs in the mythological account of Silenus and King Midas. Nietzsche discussed the Midas myth, in section 3 of *The Birth of Tragedy*, to point out the terrifying reality over which the veil of Apollonian vision was drawn. But that he should have chosen this myth—and this variant of the myth—rather than a score of other equally distressing admissions about the deeper, underlying, painful reality of life, is due to the identification within this myth between the "terrible truth" of existence and the Dionysian tradition. Since this terrible wisdom is uttered by the Dionysian votary Silenus, the contrast between the Apollonian and Dionysian attitudes appears all the more distinct. The Midas myth was widespread and well known in the ancient world, but perhaps the clearest formulation of the variant Nietzsche selected was given by Aristotle in *The Eudemian Ethics* (the fragment of this now lost work, which contains the account of Midas and Silenus, is quoted by Plutarch in his *Moralia*, 115B–E):

> Many wise men, as Crantor says, not only recently but long ago have bewailed the human lot, thinking life a punishment, and merely to be born a man the greatest of misfortunes. Aristotle says that even Silenus revealed this to Midas when caught by him. But it is better to record the philosopher's very words. He says this in the work called *Eudemus* or *On the Soul*: "Wherefore, best and most blessed of all men, not only do we think the dead happy and blessed, and think it impious to say anything untrue about them and to slander them, since they have already become better and greater—this custom is so ancient and long established among us that absolutely no one knows either the time of its origin or who first established it; it seems to have been followed continuously for endless ages—not only that, but you see the saying that has been current in the mouths of men for many years." "What is that?" said the other. And he said in answer: "Why, that not to be born is best of all and death better than life; to many a man has the heavenly voice so testified. This, they say, is what happened to the famous Midas when he had caught Silenus and asked him what is the best thing for men and the most desirable of all; Silenus at first would not say anything but maintained unbroken silence; but when at last by using every device, Midas had, with difficulty, induced him to say something, he said under compulsion: 'Shortlived seed of a toilsome spirit and of a hard fate, why do you force me to say what is better for you not to know? The most painless life is that lived in ignorance of one's own ills. To men it is quite impossible for the best thing of all to happen, nor can they share in the nature of the best (for it is best for all men and women not to be born), but the next best, and the best achievable for men, is, having been born, to die as soon as may be.' It is clear by this he meant that the time spent in death is better than that spent in life."[47]

It was precisely this baleful philosophy—this "folk wisdom," as Nietzsche described it—which established the grounds of the divine Olympian realm, the Apollonian vision. To express the relation between the beatific dream vision and the painful reality of human existence, Nietzsche once again turned to an analogy: the former is related to the latter in the same way "as the rapturous vision of the tortured martyr is to his suffering."

If Homer's contest resulted in the victory of the Apollonian vision, the foundations for this achievement were acknowledged by the Greeks to be tenuous at best. But to understand what was at stake in this tentative resolution, we must again see the *agon* in a broader perspective: ultimately, Nietzsche argued, the artistic resolution achieved by the Apollonian vision—its "victory"—was a necessary *supplement* to natural existence. Nature requires the supplement of art in order that its own creatures may continue to exist. Thus, by enlarging the perspective of the Apollonian artist, Nietzsche introduced a theory of art, an aesthetics, which at the same time he extended to a theory of nature. During the period in which he composed *The Birth of Tragedy*, he termed this "an artist's metaphysics"; later, he came to see it under the more general formulation, "the will to power."[48] In any case, it was with this broader theme in mind that Nietzsche closed his initial discussion of the Apollonian worldview: "The complete victory of Apollonian illusion . . . is one of those illusions which nature so frequently employs to achieve her own ends. The true goal is veiled by a phantasm: and while we stretch out our hands for the latter, nature attains the former by means of our illusion."[49]

DIONYSIAN INTENSITIES: DISPOSSESSION

If the Apollonian vision stood as a dream world to waking life, then the Dionysian attitude appeared as the most extreme intensification of life. Or, as Nietzsche concisely expressed it, the Dionysian is life's intoxication with itself. Nietzsche's discussion of the Dionysian impulse—like his discussion of the Apollonian—thus begins with another *physiological* analogy; in this case, the state of "intoxication." It is important to note, then, that the Dionysian impulse is not simply the natural or base term, with regard to which the Apollonian would appear as a refracted and distorted image, however edifying and redeeming the latter might well be.[50] Both the Apollonian and Dionysian attitudes are "natural" in that they are equally the expression of natural impulses. They are both creative responses to the conditions imposed by nature on the human order. So far as the human order is itself natural, these two attitudes or impulses may be seen, at least aesthetically, in view of the economy of nature as a whole.

What distinguishes the Dionysian tendency at first sight is its contrast, in origin and ends, with the Apollonian disposition. Whereas the latter stems from the individual's desire to render existence stable by means of a personally redeeming vision—a dream vision of beauty, order, and measure, one that sustains him and offers a divine spectacle for his emulation—the Dionysian state has nothing to do with the individual per se: it concerns neither his production of the particular dream image nor his individuated (i.e., personally isolated) existence. Thus, Nietzsche claimed that the Dionysian state is more *primal* because it underlies or subtends personal individuation. In the Dionysian state of intense excitement and agitation, one is dispossessed—removed—of one's own individuality, of all that renders the individual a singular and distinctive creature in the first place—the specific constitution of his character, personality, tastes, fears, expectations, reflections, and values. The Apollonian tendency, on the contrary, begins right here, with the specific ordering, selection, and elevation of certain dispositions, with the idealization of particular values and judgments. The Apollonian inclination unifies these selected elements and casts them forth as exemplary images for the purpose of defining and preserving the individual as a *discrete* individual. By contrast, the Dionysian attitude consists in the effective *removal* of precisely these individuating features. Ultimately, if the Apollonian dream state corresponds to the idealized elements of a prescriptive code—a code that both constitutes the individual *as* an individual and preserves him as such within a society—then the Dionysian state corresponds to a *decodification* of these elements, a suspension of individual and socially sanctioned codes. 51 To borrow the analogy once again, it corresponds to the state of intoxication, within which there is no longer any concern with individual goals or specific aims. Rather, with the Dionysian state of intoxication—of frenzy and rapture—we witness the dispossession of personal identity, the suspension of discrete intention and prescription, the loss of a singular purpose: in short, we see the abrogation of ego identity, of personal singularity or uniqueness itself. The essential point of distinction between the Apollonian and Dionysian attitudes centers on individuation or its absence. As an individual, I am distressingly alone (*solus ipse*) and must contract the entirety of my resources to defend my sole possession, my self, my preservation, my very being as an individual. Only the clairvoyant image of my dreamlike Apollonian vision can suffice to redeem my person and its singular desires.

What seems to motivate the *Apollonian* state, then, is a kind of lack, the recognition of scarcity, want, or insufficiency. The saving virtue of the Apollonian vision is that it extends an image of existence by which one could rectify that insufficiency (i.e., one's own indigence and impotence). The image extended for this compensation is one of a longed-for peace, essentially static, timeless, and radiant in its enduring permanence, the image of the god Apollo. In this sense alone, the individuated state is initially one of pain, struggle, and suffering, a state of ever-watchful readiness and defense. The victory claimed by this Apollonian state is, as Nietzsche continually reminded us, a dream: the vision of a fabled and heroic Ilium, one that is admittedly precarious in the face of waking life.

The *Dionysian* state, on the contrary, should be conceived as the absence of this kind of necessity, this needful defense of the singular individual, with his discrete desires, ordered codes, and personal visions of redemption. As dispossessed—as *intoxicated*—one is no longer the singular personality with its particular attributes and goals. Rather, one has lost the specific forms of these individuating qualities, these defining characteristics that serve to delimit and direct—qualities that in the end testify to one's deeply felt paucity and need.

No longer individuated, the Dionysian state lends itself to total identification with the world beyond the individual that underlies the individual, which is the scene for his segregation, his isolation or individuation, in the first place. Thus, if Nietzsche's language suggests that the Dionysian state is in fact *more natural*, this must be understood only in the sense that nature as a whole is more extensive than the individuating and possessive dream image would have us believe. By the same token, the Dionysian state of intoxication is held to be more *primal* than the Apollonian vision, since it is essentially polymorphous, undirected, and nonspecific. It has to do with that undiminished state of existence upon which forms are enacted, codes imposed, and specific goals wrought.

The Dionysian state is thus one of abundance, plenitude, and excess.[52] And having once attained this state, one's impulses—one's drives and affects of every variety—find immediate discharge, they invest themselves with unrestrained intensity in every object thrust before them. Uninhibited and decodified, the cauldron of Dionysian forces bring the body into contact with a world of immediacy, a universe of proximate surfaces. The entire world of waking reality is thus brought forth in its sentient extreme as the recipient and nourishment of these Dionysian intensities. Explosive discharges of Dionysian forces increase and augment themselves in the absence of any restraint and of all social and civil codes. With nothing to protect, with no one to preserve, the Dionysian sensibility couples with all things: everything enters its ken, everything presents itself as a further source of satisfaction to the vertiginous spiral of libidinal excess. Each gratification appears as a stage of increasingly extensive and intensive pleasure, until the Dionysian state of heightened excitation temporarily shudders and collapses out of delighted exhaustion—only to be replenished and intensified in turn.

Dispossessed of all individuality, all specificity, the Dionysian celebrant fully experiences an orgiastic delight in his satisfaction and immediate identification with the whole, with every object of sensibility and sensuality. In this intoxicated state of dispossession, pain is indeed borne, but it is no longer suffered. The intensities sustained may well be lacerating in their frenzy, but they in turn render their host a universal agent and patient, through which existence itself seems to revel in its own excess. For Nietzsche, the Dionysian votary found his home in just such a world; indeed, he experienced himself *as* that world. Through his dispossessing intensity and by his deeply felt identification with that world, the world itself suddenly became perfectly clear, pellucid: its every object and event became his own rapture, his own meaning and life. Such a Dionysian world of superabundance postulated no other world, no prescriptive antidote to compensate for personal loss, for human frailty or indigence, since for the state of Dionysian intensity, there can be no incompletion or failed possibilities. Rather, it is a state of incandescence, fulguration, and rapture—a sovereign state of exultant strength and vitality wherein existence redeems and validates itself at every moment. Hence, there is no longer any need for the redeeming vision of Apollonian beauty, the dream image of a near-forgotten Ilium, for the nostalgic hope of a long-lost kingdom before the fall, nor for submission to the restrictive and tiresome codes of a social order.

It is easily understandable that the advent of primitive Dionysian religious cults was felt as a veritable shockwave by the Apollonian culture of the early classical period. Dionysian behavior was, for the Apollonian Greek, the very definition of barbarity itself; its practice threatened the conditions of social and political stability, and it was unhesitatingly described, even by later generations, as a kind of epidemic madness, as an alien disease that seemed to transgress all rational and social codes in the name of wanton abandon and excess.[53] In discussing this earliest and most intense form of the Dionysian impulse—the festival transgression of the "Dionysian barbarian"—there is no question that Nietzsche fully shared the apprehensions of the Apollonian Greek:

> In nearly every case these festivals centered in extravagant sexual licentiousness, whose waves overwhelmed all family life and its venerable traditions; the most savage natural instincts were unleashed, including even that horrible mixture of sensuality and cruelty which has always seemed to me to be the real "witches brew."[54]

Nietzsche himself claimed to experience the profound intensity of Dionysian transport on many occasions; indeed, he would dramatically portray these intensities throughout the four books of *Zarathustra*. But neither would the remarks he made about these states in his letters nor their portrayal in *Zarathustra* or elsewhere ever quite approach comparison with, for example, the

fury Euripides sought to express in his Bacchae. There, Euripides presented
the dreadful extreme of Dionysian barbarity in the figure of Agave. It was
Agave who, with the help of her equally blinded sisters Ino and Autonoe, mur-
dered her own son (and would-be future king), Pentheus. In a brief passage,
Euripides' messenger describes the Maenadic frenzy of this most vicious of all
murders to the attending chorus:

> But she, with foaming at the mouth and rolling eyes
> In frenzy, thinking as a mind should never think,
> Was held by Bacchus; his [Pentheus's] entreaty touched her not.
> She took his wrist, the left one, in her hands and stood
> With her feet pressing on his ribs, poor helpless man,
> And wrenched his shoulder from its socket—not by strength,
> But the god gave it to her hands an easy prey.
> The other side was Ino, finishing the work,
> Tearing his flesh asunder and Autonoe
> With all the Bacchic horde attacked: there was a cry,
> One sound from all together; Pentheus, while he breathed,
> Groaned, but the others cheered. A fore-arm one had got,
> The feet another, with the shoes; his ribs were stripped
> Piece-meal; those women, every one, with bloody hands
> Joined in a ball-game, using bits of Pentheus' flesh.
>   The body lies in different places, part below
> Sharp rocks and part in thickets deep in undergrowth,
> Not easy to discover, but the wretched head
> His mother chanced on and she took it in her hands
> And fixed it on her thrysis, thinking it to be
> A mountain lion's—through Cithaeron this she bears,
> Leaving her sisters in the Maenad choruses.
> Inside these walls, rejoicing in her luckless prey,
> She comes, acclaiming as her comrade in the hunt
> Bacchus, participator with her in the kill.
> The glorious victor—victory to her of tears.[55]

THE TRAGIC RESOLUTION

There could be no simple victory or conclusion to the opposition represented by Apollo and Dionysus. As Nietzsche observed in section 4 of *The
Birth of Tragedy*, if the primitive

Dionysian . . . seemed "titanic" and "barbaric" to the Apollonian Greek . . . at the same time he could not conceal from himself that he, too, was inwardly related to these overthrown Titans and heroes. Indeed, he had to recognize even more than this: despite all its beauty and moderation, his entire existence rested on a hidden substratum of suffering and of knowledge, revealed to him by the Dionysian. And behold: Apollo could not live without Dionysus! The "titanic" and the "barbaric" were in the last analysis as necessary as the Apollonian.[56]

Taken by itself, as we have seen, the Apollonian order is based on an illusion (the dream image). It operates through and is understood according to the elaboration of exhaustive codes, and it serves to maintain the construction of complete individuation. Individuation is thus accomplished by social, civic, and cultural encoding.[57] The Apollonian individual would thus exist apart from the whole of the underlying Dionysian reality only by repressing it or any knowledge he might have of it. For Nietzsche, the Apollonian world of "mere appearance and moderation" persisted precisely to the extent that it was "artificially dammed up." Likewise, the unrestrained excesses of the Dionysian order pointed to chaos and suffering at every register. While its intoxicating liberation brought ecstatic joy through the feeling of dispossession, this seemed to entail the collapse of social and institutional life per se. In its own way, then, the Dionysian state stood as *the* proscribed seduction. Not only would the forbidden excess of every passion and sensibility stand as an inducement to the staid Apollonian, but it brought with it a second danger, the claim of a monstrous truth: the recognition of excess, contradiction, pain, and apoplexy to be found "at the very heart of nature." In short, once the redeeming and protective image of Apollo is withdrawn, nature reveals itself in its plenitude as a meaningless and amoral plethora of conflicting impulses, struggles, and dynamic forces. The "truth" of the Dionysian—which is also the "wisdom" of Silenus—is a world unbounded by moderation, direction, purpose, or the hope of redemption. It is a truth whose object is existence in general; namely, the world in its fullest extension (and not its modulation or restriction in the form of a discrete "image"), the world as presented in its greatest intensity (so far as the world is everywhere experienced immediately, without restraint, proportion, or prescription).

Faced with such a yawning chaos, mankind could not long endure itself or existence. In the end, the terrible wisdom of Silenus corresponds to a reality that is simply anarchic, to the aimless and childlike "play" of Heraclitus's gods. Understandably, such a tragic wisdom might quickly crush the defenseless individual, who is himself fully and helplessly embroiled in the divine chaos.

The *accommodation* of these conflicting impulses occurs in one way or another, as the characteristically Greek resolution to the question mark of existence. Nietzsche argued that this accommodation was never final, nor was it ever fully stable for any length of time. But whether one turns to Greek civil and political life, to its intellectual traditions, or to the various arts practiced in Greek culture, the opposition between the Dionysian and the Apollonian, together with their "mysterious union," is everywhere to be found. Perhaps Nietzsche's single strongest claim in *The Birth of Tragedy* was to have understood the nature of this opposition and its tentative, provisional resolution, in a single form of art, tragic drama, which Nietzsche, following an entire tradition since Aristotle, saw as the highest, most developed art form. Not only did the example of tragic drama offer a relatively well-documented history by which it could be understood, but its very evolution testified to a wealth of elements, each contributing to the complex nature of the resolution. Furthermore, tragic drama manifested the contrast between its component elements at the very moment of its performance, its actual presentation. Thus, the dynamic tension and the specific resolution produced within the drama could be vital and immediately experienced elements, rather than, for example, merely abstract or formal properties. The case of tragic drama thus stands as a privileged text for interpreting classical Greek culture at large, and Nietzsche's analysis of the Apollonian and Dionysian elements constitutes a veritable inventory of Greek existence, extending from the world of epic and lyrical poetry, through the nature of language and myth, to the political consequences of the Socratic teaching.

While the period of Doric culture and art was "a permanent military encampment of the Apollonian . . . an art so defiantly prim and so encompassed with bulwarks," that "only incessant resistance to the titanic-barbaric nature of the Dionysian could account for the long survival" it enjoyed, the case was different for the development of the Attic and Ionian traditions.[58] For the latter, Dionysus was represented by a temple at Delphi as early as the Homeric period (co-residing with the temple of Apollo), and the origins of specifically Dionysian art found concrete expression with the likewise ancient tradition of lyrical poetry.

Not surprisingly, then, Nietzsche's historical analysis of tragic drama begins with the traditionally acknowledged founder of lyric poetry, Archilochus, a seventh-century B.C. Ionian who was reputed to be of a singularly Dionysian cast. Fragments of his work indicate not only that he led and composed Dionysian songs but that his work was unique for the intensity and variety of its passion,

especially for its extremely coarse eroticism. All of which suggests that his ancient critics were correct when they denounced his strikingly un-Homeric qualities. Heraclitus, Critias, and Pindar in particular excoriated him for his
rejection of the aristocratic-Homeric ideals: ideals Archilochus himself sarcastically ridiculed as vainglory and pride—more interesting perhaps for those who
preferred to die pointlessly in battle than for those, like himself, who enjoyed
the delights of a vital and sensuous existence. Nonetheless, Nietzsche observed, this bastard son of a Parian slave woman—ever-intoxicated and often
savage—was, for the Greeks, given a status equal to that of the Apollonian
Homer:

> The ancients . . . place the faces of Homer and Archilochus, as the forefathers
> and torchbearers of Greek poetry, side by side on gems, sculptures, etc., with a
> sure feeling that consideration should be given only to these two, equally com-
> pletely original, from whom a stream of fire flows over the whole of later Greek
> history.[59]

Why this should have been the case, however, is problematic. If tradition generally saw Archilochus as merely a "subjective" writer, why should this one
individual's rather sordid testimony be of any consequence at all? Nietzsche's
interpretation of this view is crucial: in analyzing the nature of lyrical poetry
(especially with regard to its conventional identification with music), and that
of Archilochus in particular, Nietzsche argued that the important consideration
was not so much the communication of a personal or *subjective* experience as
such—however intriguing that may have been—but rather, that the lyrical poet
was able to create a "musical mood." The term Nietzsche used for "mood" is
the German *Stimmung*, and this is rich in its associations: at once, it means
"mood," "tone," or "attunement." In section 5 of *The Birth of Tragedy*, Nietzsche noted that he borrowed the insight about the complex character of mood
from Schiller: namely, that *Stimmung* is not simply the objective representation
of an internal mental state. If it were only this, the musical mood would merely
be a particular image, produced by the individual poet. In that case, the mood
character of ancient lyric poetry, which is itself, quite literally, tonal and musical, would be but another example of Apollonian "objective" art, the art of
discrete representational images and concepts.

But if the "musical mood" of lyrical poetry was neither Apollonian (as the
objective image series of epic poetry) nor simply a subjective personal testimony, what then was it, and why should it have been capable of igniting the
world of tragic drama? Once mood is understood *relationally* as the emotional

or affective "attunement" or "disposition" one has with the entirety of one's surrounding environment, rather than as an internal, self-enclosed mental image of the individuated subject, it follows that the mood state is all-pervasive for one's experience: "The sphere of poetry does not lie outside the world as a fantastic impossibility spawned by a poet's brain."[60] The emotionally charged mood state is neither within nor without, neither subjective nor objective in the strict sense. Rather, it is experienced as all-permeating and suffusive. The mood lends an emotional or affective "tonality" to all things, including the lyrical poet himself. Thus, the lyrical experience and the lyrical re-creation of the mood, was something ecstatic, and as such it dispossessed the poet of his "own" subjectivity, his own "I" or ego. What was given to and by the lyric poet, then, was precisely this Dionysian state of disindividuation. As Nietzsche observed, "The artist has already surrendered his subjectivity in the Dionysian process," and he now feels an "identity with the heart of the world"—he experiences the world as his "primordial home" (*Urheimat*).

How was it possible, then, for the lyric poet to communicate such a mood, this state of dispossession and attunement with the "heart of the world"? Here, Nietzsche drew upon his own intense experience of music and reasoned that both the mood of lyric poetry and its means of expression were congruent, that they could be understood and made possible only through the medium of music. Music alone, he argued, is capable of expressing the infinitely polymorphous character of a dynamic world, a world capable of every tension, transformation, stress, intensity, and pulsion. It does this not by representing one single state, a static "image" of the world as the language of concepts does, but by manifesting the very nature, essence, or idea (*Idee*) of its general dynamic properties—in short, what Nietzsche calls its *dissonance*: "This primordial phenomenon of Dionysian art is difficult to grasp, and there is only one direct way to make it intelligible and grasp it immediately: through the wonderful significance of musical dissonance."[61]

Nietzsche thus postulated a structural identity among the dynamic properties of the world, "the Dionysian ground," "the heart of all things," and the dynamic properties of music (i.e., music taken in its most extensive and essential sense, its dissonance: that creative reservoir of tonal elements that sustains every variation in sonority, rhythm, tempo, harmony, measure, melody, polyphony, etc.).

That music has an expressive privilege over conventional language, then, is clear—at least for Nietzsche. Music is the "language" of Dionysian dispossession; as such, it expresses what is felt to be the "primal reality," the "heart of all things." By contrast, the language of images and concepts belongs to the Apollonian state of discrete form, order, and the particular appearance. The opposition between music and language (or, rather, Nietzsche's elevation of the former over the latter) appears to rest, finally, on the nature of the "world" each claims to express. But, if this "world" often seems to be *two* quite distinctive worlds, this confusion is due in no small measure to Nietzsche's reliance on the idealist vocabulary of Schopenhauer and Kant. Nonetheless, and despite the perplexities caused by this borrowed terminology, Nietzsche's analysis was his own—a fact he continually reminded us of in the 1886 preface and in *Ecce Homo*. Had, for example, he maintained the strict Kantian distinction between a noumenal and phenomenal world (or, the somewhat less exact Schopenhauerian distinction between a world-will, as "the Dionysian," and its representation, as "the Apollonian"), Nietzsche's account would have lapsed into the very paradoxes he sought to escape: music would then have been the simple expression of a "world-will" closed in upon itself—a world "in itself"—and conventional language would only have represented a world of "appearances," a deficient world of merely "phenomenal" reality. What emerges from the latter formulation (which is most often attributed to Nietzsche) is the following: music is "true" but its truth can never be experienced or communicated. But, *precisely this* is in striking contradistinction to the fact of the intensely felt musical *mood* carried by the experience of the musical performance. Furthermore, if the reality that music testified to was the Dionysian world—as noumenal—then that, too, could never be subject to human experience. The contrary case would follow for conventional language and the Apollonian world.

To correct this traditional, but understandable, impression, we should note that the entire argumentation for the privileged status of music stands or falls precisely on the listener's capacity to be effectively moved, transformed, by it (i.e., to actually experience a state of relative disindividuation). Once the listener acknowledges the *ecstatic* state brought on by music—by the musical mood or the aesthetic state—with its attendant disindividuation, then Nietzsche's arguments for the "universal" and "primal" character of musical expression seem far more plausible and far less dependent on the rather tortured metaphysics of Schopenhauer and Kant.

> I must not appeal to those who use the images of what happens on the stage, the words and emotions of the acting persons, in order to approach their help with the musical feeling; for these people do not speak music as their mother tongue

and, in spite of this help, never get beyond the entrance halls of musical perception. . . . I must appeal only to those who, immediately related to music, have in
it, as it were, their motherly womb, and are related to things almost exclusively
through unconscious musical relations. . . . Let the attentive friend imagine the
effect of a true musical tragedy purely and simply, as he knows it from experience. . . . It is as if his visual faculty were no longer merely a surface faculty but
capable of penetrating into the interior, and as if he now saw before him, with
the aid of music, the waves of the will, the conflict of motives, and the swelling
flood of the passions, sensuously visible, as it were, like a multitude of vividly
moving lines and figures; and he felt he could dip into the most delicate secrets
of unconscious emotions.[62]

Strikingly, the kind of "world" given to the ecstatic musical mood—the only
world—remained basically unchanged in its description throughout the subsequent course of Nietzsche's writings. In a passage from a fragment dated 1885,
this Dionysian world of disindividuation would be explicitly repeated, but by
then, in a vocabulary that was distinctively Nietzsche's own: that of the "eternal
return" and the "will to power"—terms that more successfully, perhaps, conveyed the sense of dynamism and dissonance at the very "heart" of all things.

And do you know what "the world" is to me? Shall I show it to you in my mirror?
This world: a monster of energy, without beginning, without end . . . as force
throughout, as a play of forces and waves of forces, at the same time one and
many, increasing here and at the same time decreasing there; a sea of forces
flowing and rushing together, eternally changing, eternally flooding back, with
tremendous years of recurrence, with an ebb and a flood of its forms; out of the
simplest forms striving toward the most complex, out of the stillest, most rigid,
coldest forms toward the hottest, most turbulent, most self-contradictory, and
then again returning home to the simple out of this abundance, out of this play
of contradictions back to the joy of concord, still affirming itself in this uniformity
of its courses and years, blessing itself as that which must return eternally . . .
this, my Dionysian world of the eternally self-creating, the eternally self-destroy-
ing, this mystery world of the twofold voluptuous delight. . . . *This world is the
will to power—and nothing else!*[63]

As the prototype of the lyric poet, Archilochus represents a development
over the Dionysian musician per se. Whereas the latter submerged himself in
the ecstasy of dispossession, totally identifying himself with—and thus losing
himself in—the "primal unity," the "heart of all things," the lyric poet focused
the musical mood on certain exemplary images, on specific symbols. That the
lyric poet employed poetic images at all pointed to a second influence, the

inspiration of Apollo. But what distinguished the lyric poet from the purely
Apollonian epic poet was the fact that the images or symbols of the lyric poet
were fully charged with a Dionysian frenzy and intoxication, which is to say,
they were images or examples of his own dispossession, his identification with
the whole, and they were in no way illusions or dreams, which would serve to
shield or protect him. These exemplary states of dispossession were, Nietzsche
claimed, "image sparks" that testified to the poet's "Dionysian-musical enchantment." It was for this reason that the lyrical poetry of Archilochus *seemed*
simply subjective to the Apollonian observer. But in fact, what occurred was a
second-order symbolization—a concretely poetic representation—of the Dionysian self-abandonment the poet himself had already undergone. It was the
lyrical representation of an ecstatic "attunement" with the whole, which is precisely why Nietzsche described Archilochus as a "world-poet" and not as a
"subjective" poet.

If lyrical poetry attempted to express the ecstatic musical mood of the lyrist,
this was no less true for other primitive forms of versification, such as the
folksong. In fact, for Nietzsche, the strophic forms of lyrical poetry, the folksong, and the dithyramb testified to the more original melodic and rhythmic
character of music itself. With the advent of the dithyramb, however, two elements intervened to lend further complexity to the process out of which tragic
drama evolved: on the one hand, ritual imagery was introduced precisely to
celebrate the god Dionysus. Second, the dithyramb was chanted by a chorus
of participants in the ritual celebration, namely, in a series of choral exchanges
by the Dionysian votaries called *satyrs* or *sileni*.

The dithyramb, with its newly added ritual content, thence became the symbolic expression of Dionysian wisdom itself, a kind of terrible knowledge about
the disindividuated, unjust, dissonant "nature" of natural existence. Moreover,
this wisdom was effectively convincing due to the dithyramb's very musicality
(i.e., due to the ecstatic music of the dithyrambic chants and to the intensely
rhythmic and tonal language of the accompanying instrumentation of flutes,
pipes, drums, etc.).[64]

It was the frenzy released by the chorus's chants that first appeared to the
observer as the most intense and perhaps shocking aspect of the dithyramb.
For the rather staid Apollonian Greek, this spectacle constituted an indictment,
if not a denial, of the very propriety of social and political life. Writing, once
again, about the mood conveyed by the frenzied Dionysian chorus, Nietzsche
was compelled to remark:

One feels in every case in which Dionysian excitement gains any significant extent, how the Dionysian liberation from the fetters of the individual finds expression first of all in a diminution of, in indifference to, indeed, in hostility to, the political instincts. Just as certainly, Apollo who forms states is also the genius of the *principium individuationis* [the principle of individuation], and state and patriotism cannot live without an affirmation of the individual personality. But from orgies a people can take one path only, the path to Indian Buddhism . . . [i.e.,] ecstatic states with their elevation above space, time, and the individual.[65]

But, Nietzsche argued, insofar as the Dionysian dithyramb finally evolved to the state of tragic drama, it would ultimately fall to one of its own ingredients—the chorus—to reawaken the possibility of a social and political community. This could only occur when the frenzied disindividuation of the Dionysian celebrant yielded and submitted to modification, when it became transformed, at the urging of the chorus, into a collective embrace, an impassioned identification by the audience with the spectacle of a common mythology, history, and destiny. All this would occur immediately on the very stage set before them. To arrive at this conclusion, however, Nietzsche first had to give extensive consideration to the history and composition of the chorus.

The evolution of the Dionysian satyr chorus into the conventional chorus of tragic drama parallels the development of tragic drama as such. Initially, according to Nietzsche, the ritual celebration of Dionysus was performed and attended by the chorus alone; thus, the participants or actors themselves constituted the audience. Ultimately, "The chorus is the dramatic proto-phenomenon," since its members fully undergo and express the ritual of Dionysian disindividuation. "In the dithyramb we confront a community of unconscious actors who consider themselves and one another transformed. Such magic transformation is the presupposition of all dramatic art. In this magic transformation the Dionysian reveler sees himself as a satyr."[66]

Insofar as it is a specific ritual, the Dionysian transformation entails a modification of the ecstatic process. One "loses" oneself and becomes an *other*, but only according to a certain image of deep ritual significance. The follower of Dionysus ritually reenacts a precise mythological role (i.e., he ritually invokes a specific image or vision according to which he becomes other than himself). In this case, it is the privileged role of the satyr. But, as Nietzsche remarked, to invoke a specific image or role at all, in the ecstasy of transformation, is already to draw upon the further resources of Apollo—even if this does result in the ritual incarnation of Dionysus himself: "As a satyr, in turn, he sees the god, which means that in his metamorphosis he beholds another vision outside himself, as the Apollonian complement of his own state. With this new vision the drama is complete."[67] By this complex stage of development, according to Nietzsche, the specific resolution between Dionysus and Apollo, which constitutes the drama itself, will already have been established.

> In the light of this insight we must understand Greek tragedy as the Dionysian chorus which ever anew discharges itself in an Apollonian world of images. Thus the choral parts with which tragedy is interlaced are, as it were, the womb that gave birth to the whole of the so-called dialogue, that is, the entire world of the stage, the real drama.[68]

Once the ritual dithyramb was brought to the stage as a public spectacle, the actor intervened and assumed the part of what was until then the visionary state of the satyr chorus.[69] Wearing the ritual mask, the actor became the figure of Dionysus himself, or that of his surrogate, the tragic hero. Nietzsche explained that "drama in the narrower sense" began here, with the introduction of the actor, since it implied a forceful distinction between the chorus and audience.[70] The chorus itself did not require the real representation of Dionysus, since it already held Dionysus before itself as a visionary state. Representation was required only for the audience, not for the chorus. Accordingly, the function of the chorus changed radically:

> Now the dithyrambic chorus was assigned the task of exciting the mood [*Stimmung*] of the listeners to such a Dionysian degree that, when the tragic hero appeared on the stage, they did not see the awkwardly masked human being but rather a visionary figure, born as it were from their own rapture.[71]

Nietzsche went on to argue that the representation of the god or hero was made fully convincing to the audience by the double process of transference and condensation. Initially, the audience transferred its own rapturous vision of Dionysus onto the specific representation (the actor), thereby transforming the concrete actor into the god Dionysus (or into the tragic hero, who was himself one ritual image of Dionysus): "He transferred the whole magic image of the god that was trembling before his soul to that masked figure and, as it were, dissolved its reality into the unreality of spirits."[72] Once the transfer was made, the process of transformation could be completed by a second stage—a kind of image intensification—and this was brought about by the actor himself.

Ecstatically charged by both the chorus and audience to a heightened state of divinity, divine presence, and authority, the actor then took it upon himself to condense this fevered excitement into the most economical form of expression: the epic pronouncement, the precise statement of Dionysian wisdom, which until the moment of his speech had been everywhere only felt. Viewed as this trembling figure, and sustained by the rapture of the chorus and the transported audience, "Dionysus no longer speaks through forces but as an epic hero, almost in the language of Homer."[73] He now appeared dreamlike and spoke through the clairvoyant language of images. The forces struggling for expression—the frenzied music and dance, the disindividuated states of excess, joy, suffering, and abandon—all found their voice, but now in the language of Apollo.

It was Sophocles and Aeschylus who intervened and invested the ritual dithyramb with the more extensive mythological content of the epic tradition. And by doing this, Nietzsche maintained, not only did they save these myths from the inevitable fate of becoming mere historical curiosities, but they gave them their highest achievement: they infused the myths with the profound significance of Dionysian wisdom. The already fading world of Homeric myth henceforth became reanimated by a far deeper and more penetrating worldview: "Dionysian truth takes over the entire domain of myth as the symbolism of its knowledge which it makes known partly in the public cult of tragedy and partly in the secret celebrations of dramatic mysteries, but always in the old mythical garb."[74]

Under the hand of Sophocles and Aeschylus, the old myths were retained and became strengthened; they became vehicles of Dionysian wisdom, which taught that all human suffering comes from individuation, whether this be of the individual who confronts the laws of nature, society, the gods, or fate. For this tragic individual (e.g., Oedipus, Prometheus, etc.), noble in the magnitude of his tasks,

> The misfortune in the nature of things . . . the contradiction at the heart of the world reveals itself to him as a clash of different worlds, e.g., of a divine and human one, in which each, taken as an individual, has right on his side, but nevertheless has to suffer for its individuation, being merely a single one beside another. In the heroic effort of the individual to attain universality, in the attempt to transcend the curse of individuation and to become the one world-being, he suffers in his own person, the primordial contradiction that is concealed in things, which means that he commits sacrilege and suffers.[75]

Expressing the Dionysian wisdom in the clarity of epic terms, precisely by drawing upon the long-venerated tradition of Greek mythology, resulted in what Nietzsche termed a new "optical phenomenon." We see all too clearly what is at once a human and natural struggle in the fate of the tragic hero. Across every register, both the fact of Dionysian wisdom and the tragedy of the hero who attempts to act upon this wisdom is strikingly clear: "He who by means of his knowledge plunges nature into the abyss of destruction must also suffer the dissolution of nature in his own person."[76]

The tragic hero who, like Dionysus, seeks a final reconciliation of things—ultimately, to put an end to pain, injustice, alienation, individuation, ostracism, and so forth—*inevitably* comes to grief. While he acts out of tragic or Dionysian wisdom, he nonetheless does so as an individual; and as an individual, he stands as *nothing* to that Dionysian ground of all things. Hence the "optical illusion" brought about by tragic drama: the audience is spared the fate of the tragic hero precisely by *understanding* the necessity of his annihilation. In this sense, the tragic drama serves to remedy that which it testifies so convincingly about: we see the effects of that abyss that subtends every human activity—whether such activity be vain, inglorious, or on the contrary, heroic—and we are consequently spared the pain of looking too deeply into that abyss. Rather, tragic drama presents the audience with an intense and profoundly felt ritual spectacle, a symbolic image of the deeper reality.

Nietzsche's analysis of tragedy guides us one step further, however, in our attempt to comprehend this spectacle. If tragedy were simply a means of absorbing human emotions and anxiety, thereby draining off one's emotional affects, such an understanding of tragedy would differ little from that of other dramatic forms, and Nietzsche's explanation would largely repeat that of Aristotle. In a note from 1888, Nietzsche expressly criticized the artificial character of Aristotle's concept of tragedy as an emotional "catharsis" or purgation:

> *What is tragic?* On repeated occasions I have laid my finger on Aristotle's great misunderstanding in believing the tragic affects to be two *depressive* affects, terror and pity. If he were right, tragedy would be an art dangerous to life; one would have to warn against it as notorious and a public danger. . . . One can refute his theory in the most cold-blooded way: namely, by measuring the effects of a tragic emotion with a dynamometer. And one would discover as a result what ultimately only the absolute mendaciousness of a systematizer could misunderstand—that tragedy is a *tonic*.[77]

Far from being a simple palliative or anesthetic, tragedy has a quite different function: its tonic effects bring about the greatest joy to an audience, a strong confidence and exuberant health in the face of the most intense human sufferings. Indeed, if the content of tragic drama consists in the endless repetition of human sufferings, in the "most antagonizing oppositions of motives, in short, the exemplification of this wisdom of Silenus," Nietzsche could well ask, "Surely a higher pleasure must be perceived in all this."[78]

What is perceived in tragic drama is the unerring recognition that suffering, too, is overcome and transfigured—out of joy: tragic drama is a "metaphysical supplement to the reality of nature, placed beside it for its overcoming." If, as Nietzsche repeatedly claimed, "the world seems justified only as an aesthetic phenomenon," this is because it is only a stage—or one scene in an endless drama—on which the enormity of Dionysian reality casts itself forth in discrete, individuated images. Through its process of transference and condensation, tragic drama enacts this world-struggle of individuation as a dramatic representation, for the sole delight of its audience. At once this is a spectacle of tragic beauty and a ritual sacrifice for the audience who, all the while, find their home and joy in the Dionysian world of disindividuation—of which the particular tragic myth or drama is itself but a brief and fleeting part.

In the degree to which the ecstatic state is maintained by the frenzied chorus and musical "dissonance," so will the most tortuous and fear-inspiring images of the drama be intensely experienced and overcome. Such images will stand as *appearances* to be transfigured in turn, in what Nietzsche called "the playful construction and destruction of the individual world, as the overflow of a primordial delight." Upon such a Dionysian ground of "play," the most terrible image of reality would "fade away charmingly," offered up as it is for no reason at all, moral or otherwise. Hence the necessity for tragic drama itself—as an antidote to such a world, as a "saving illusion," as a kind of "redemption" for that world. Or, once again, as a "metaphysical supplement" to that world, a supplement that is at the same time entirely natural and fully experienced—as drama and intoxication. What is aimed at through the tragic supplementation of nature is the Dionysian identification with the whole, a state of being that Nietzsche termed a "metaphysical joy" or "comfort" wherein the individual profoundly feels that, for once, he too belongs to the deeper reality behind all phenomena, prior to all individuation, and despite all annihilation:

> The metaphysical joy in the tragic is a translation of the instinctive unconscious Dionysian wisdom into the language of images: the hero, the highest manifestation of the will, is negated for our pleasure, because he is only phenomenon, and because the eternal life of the will is not affected by his annihilation. "We believe in eternal life," exclaims tragedy. . . . In Dionysian art and its tragic symbolism the same nature cries to us with its true, undissembled voice: "Be as I am! Amid

the ceaseless flux of phenomena I am the eternally creative primordial mother, eternally impelling to existence, eternally finding satisfaction in this change of phenomena!"[79]

That the Greek of the classical period could experience such a world, despite the enormity of his suffering, and find in it the highest degree of human joy and belonging—with no desire to flee or to escape that world—prompted Nietzsche to conclude his discussion of tragedy in a tone of utter amazement and admiration:

> Walking under lofty Ionic colonnades, looking up toward a horizon that was cut off by pure and noble lines, finding reflections of his transfigured shape in the shining marble at his side, and all around him solemnly striding or delicately moving human beings, speaking with harmonious voices and in a rhythmic language of gestures—in view of this continual influx of beauty, would he not have to exclaim, raising his hand to Apollo: "Blessed people of Hellas! How great must Dionysus be among you if the god of Delos considers such magic necessary to heal your dithyrambic madness!" To a man in such a mood, however, an old Athenian, looking up at him with the sublime eyes of Aeschylus, might reply: "But say this, too, curious stranger: how much did this people have to suffer to be able to become so beautiful! But now follow me to witness a tragedy, and sacrifice with me in the temple of both deities!"[80]

In the end, the tragic vision of the world was exuberant and vital, as well as pessimistic, and its strength was such that it could sustain both extremes—and Greek culture along with it. Drawing upon the wisdom of the Dionysian worldview and the healing power of Apollo, tragic drama "may really be symbolized by a fraternal union of the two deities: Dionysus speaks the language of Apollo: and Apollo, finally the language of Dionysus."[81] The possibility of the union, however, ultimately derives from the power of Dionysian reality to compel the Apollonian production of visionary states. As such, the union is neither static nor one of simple equality:

> In the total effect of tragedy, the Dionysian predominates once again. Tragedy closes with a sound which could never come from the realm of Apollonian art. And thus the Apollonian illusion reveals itself as what it really is—the veiling during the performance of the tragedy of the real Dionysian effect; but the latter is so powerful that it ends by forcing the Apollonian drama itself into a sphere where it begins to speak with Dionysian wisdom and even denies itself and its Apollonian visibility.[82]

It is for this reason that while the audience "comprehends" the tragic resolution—"deep down," as Nietzsche said—the significance of the tragic vision was never made strictly intelligible through the language of images or concepts. The "shepherd's dance of metaphysics" could never be simply thought or spoken, and every attempt to understand it cognitively only resulted in a continuous series of symbolizations, which but weakly attested to the "magical" properties of Dionysian transfiguration. Since these properties owed their force to music and the myth that was charged by music and condensed into images, the tragic drama appeared at once overdetermined and miraculous: "Myth is a concentrated image of the world that, as a condensation of phenomena, cannot dispense with miracles." Understandably, then, Nietzsche made the somewhat immodest claim:

> The meaning of tragic myth set forth above never became clear in transparent concepts to the Greek poets, not to speak of the Greek philosophers: their heroes speak, as it were, more superficially than they act; the myth does not at all obtain adequate objectification in the spoken word. The structure of the scenes and the visual images reveal a deeper wisdom than the poet himself can put into words.[83]

This was also why the Dionysian voice, which spoke through tragic drama, was perhaps more of a cry, a lament, a song of joy or praise, than a discourse—properly speaking. Consequently, it was never simply true, nor was it ever simply opposed to a "false" discourse of Apollo.

THE DEATH OF TRAGEDY

If the vitality of tragic drama (as well as its lack of discursive intelligibility) testified to its profoundly mythopoeic character, the *death* of tragedy is explained easily enough. Nietzsche located its demise in the lessened importance given to the musically charged myth: specifically, this followed upon the progressively diminished role of the chorus, the introduction of dramatic naturalism, and the use of the rationally explanatory prologue in the developing Greek drama. In short, Nietzsche pointed to the figure of Euripides, and he attributed the decline of tragic drama to Euripides' introduction and elevation of these elements, elements through which he sought to reform tragic drama and—once and for all—to make it fully articulate and intelligible. For Nietzsche, this was precisely Euripides' problem: that tragic drama, traditionally, had *not* attained to the logical clarity of rational exposition, of sensible motives, and of intelligible design.

With all the brightness and dexterity of his critical thinking, Euripides had sat in
the theater and striven to recognize in the masterpieces of his great predecessors,
as in paintings that have become dark, feature after feature, line after line. And
here he had experienced something which should not surprise anyone initiated
into the deeper secrets of Aeschylean tragedy. He observed something incommensurable in every feature and in every line, a certain deceptive distinctness
and at the same time an enigmatic depth, indeed an infinitude, in the background. . . . Twilight shrouded the structure of the drama, especially the significance of the chorus. And how dubious the solution of the ethical problems
remained to him! How questionable the treatment of the myths! How unequal
the distribution of good and bad fortune! . . . So he sat in the theater, pondering
uneasily, and *as a spectator he confessed to himself that he did not understand
his great predecessors*. But if the understanding was for him the real root of all
enjoyment and creation, he had to inquire and look around to see whether no
one else had the same opinion and also felt this incommensurability. . . . And in
this state of torment he found *that other spectator* who did not comprehend
tragedy and therefore did not esteem it. . . . Socrates . . . was that *second spectator*.[84]

Euripides' reform of tragic drama was thus motivated by an entirely new
impulse: "The deity that spoke through him was neither Dionysus nor Apollo,
but an altogether newborn demon, called *Socrates*. This is the new opposition:
the Dionysian and the Socratic—and the art of Greek tragedy was wrecked on
this."[85]

In an extended analysis of Socrates' influence on Euripides—strikingly reminiscent of Aristophanes' view[86]—Nietzsche charged that Euripides elevated
the Socratic moral teaching (that knowledge is virtue) to the inappropriate
domain of aesthetics. He thus gave rise to a kind of *"aesthetic Socratism* whose
supreme law reads roughly as follows: 'to be beautiful everything must be intelligible.' " With this maxim in view, Euripides transformed tragic drama into
what Nietzsche saw as a merely dramatized tale or narrative (i.e., a species of
dramatically embellished poetry). As such, the Dionysian resources of music
and myth were largely forsaken, as was the Apollonian power of illusion and
redemption. What remained to be expressed by this hybrid product were the
rather sober pronouncements of natural language and the perfectly conventional portrayal of emotions. Since these were things to which no one was
entirely immune, Euripides certainly enjoyed a large measure of success. In
the absence of its traditionally tragic content, the drama became more and
more a fully conscious vehicle of rational strategy and intelligent characteriza-

tion, finally evolving into what Nietzsche described as "that drama which re-sembles a game of chess," the new Attic comedy.

For Nietzsche, however, the Socratic aesthetic was perhaps best character-ized by its naively optimistic reliance upon the powers of rational knowledge and dialectic. What for Sophocles and Aeschylus were the tragic concerns of the individual and his heroic accommodation to a world of strife beyond his control, a world that embraced the human and divine orders, now became diminished to the field of dialectical argumentation, "which celebrates a tri-umph with every conclusion and can breathe only in cool clarity and conscious-ness." Moreover,

> The optimistic element which, having once penetrated tragedy, must gradually overgrow its Dionysian regions and impel it necessarily to self-destruction—to the death-leap into the bourgeois drama. Consider the consequences of the So-cratic maxims: "Virtue is knowledge; man sins only from ignorance; he who is virtuous is happy." In these three basic forms of optimism lies the death of tragedy.[87]

With the death of tragedy went the abandonment of its vital resources. The distinctive character of the chorus was lost when the chorus came to be identi-fied with the actors themselves to better serve the new task of "character repre-sentation." With Euripides, this representational process was brought to such a state of "anatomical" refinement and precision "that the spectator is in gen-eral no longer conscious of the *myth*, but of the vigorous truth to nature and the artist's imitative power."[88] Ultimately, the chorus came to be seen as "some-thing accidental, a dispensable vestige of the origin of tragedy." Music, like-wise, was evicted from its foundational role by the abstract force of the logical syllogism. In replacing music with dialectical argumentation, "the essence of tragedy" was destroyed, "since this can be interpreted only as a manifestation and projection into images of Dionysian states, as the visual symbolizing of music, as the dream-world of Dionysian intoxication."[89]

Because the death of tragedy was at the same time "the demise of myth," this event signaled no less than the possibility of modernity itself; namely, the emergence of a secular world armed with the new resources of theoretical knowledge. At the close of the classical period, this new world was nowhere more strikingly symbolized than by the person of Socrates: "It is enough to recognize in him a type of existence unheard of before him: the type of the *theoretical man*." As for Nietzsche, although the wisdom possessed by the the-oretical man was more often than not naive and optimistic—due as it was to the belief that reason alone is fully capable of understanding, indeed, of rectifying, the "deepest abysses of being"—it had nonetheless inaugurated a universal domain, the exclusively secular world of scientific explanation. In this sense, Nietzsche rightfully described Socrates as "the one turning point and vortex of so-called world history."[90]

Positively, and thanks to the Socratic teaching, the cultural energy and faith invested in the universal quest for knowledge have doubtless spared humanity from a tragic extinction, perhaps from some unforeseen result of a "practical pessimism" taken to its extreme. But despite the success and universality of the Socratic legacy, Nietzsche argued that in its very essence, this new teaching remains illusory: its faith in its own capacities is itself an instinct, a powerful and protective illusion which, inevitably, forces the scientific enterprise to acknowledge its own limits. At its limits, the logic which impels the Socratic project finds no ground save its own compulsion, one that quite lacks all logical justification. At such a point in its development, the Socratic project must appeal to its *other*, namely to myth, an appeal that, indeed, occurred often enough in the works of the Platonic Socrates to effectively subvert the proper or rational account, the *logos* (e.g., recall Socrates' almost embarrassed reliance upon the figurative "myths" of Gyges, Er, or the charioteer, or upon the "images," the "icons," of the divided line, the sun, or the cave, and so forth).[91]

Most important for Nietzsche's interpretation, however, the Socratic teaching of logic and dialectics had already, and effectively, killed tragic myth for the declining period of classical culture. Hence, there could be no appeal by Socrates or his surrogates to retrieve the healing powers of myth. It was by then too late to arrest the Socratic teaching, and thereby, too late to prevent the dismemberment of Apollo and Dionysus. In the end, Nietzsche claimed, it was too late to preserve tragic culture itself. The mythical heritage that sustained its social and political basis had been irretrievably destroyed: "What did you want, sacrilegious Euripides, when you sought to compel this dying myth to serve you once more? It died under your violent hands."[92]

THE RESOLUTION OF SOME FURTHER ISSUES

Generally speaking, three elements—the *agon*, the Apollonian "divine realm" of Olympian myth, and the Dionysian-inspired musical drama—come together to constitute what Nietzsche understood to be the tragic wisdom of classical Greek culture. The agonistic spirit recognizes that existence is meaningless, that it is doom-laden and a scene of unremitting violence. Under such circumstances, life would be—following Thomas Hobbes's celebrated observation—"poor, nasty, brutish, and short." Just as Dionysus was torn apart by the Titans, so human existence is, by nature, lacerating, painful, insufferable. Only through cultivating the survival strategies of competition in every domain, by employing the strife-bred skills learned in warfare, in athletic competitions, and in the arts does one survive and prosper. Pessimism in the face of a relentless natural order is thus overcome by a skillfully developed and arduously cultivated capacity of human action. To encourage these skills (and the prosperity they yielded, born of desperation), the traditional poets—Homer and Hesiod—enshrined them in the creation of their acropolis of the gods and by immortalizing their courageous and clever heroes in epic myth. In this, Nietzsche observed, they effectively "aestheticized" existence according to the Apollonian model. By the sixth century B.C., he went on to argue, these life-conserving and life-enhancing "illusions" were beginning to fade in their cultural significance, and hence in their utility for life, ever-threatened as it is by warfare, plague, famine, and natural and civil peril.

The Dionysian-inspired Greek musical drama reanimated this mythic tradition with a passion and intensity that was overwhelming. Hence the Dionysian state of intoxication and ecstasy was effectively a further intensification of an already aestheticized culture, but this time, blending the dreamlike beatitude of Apollonian beauty with the transfiguring mood and excitement brought on by the tragic drama—with its chanting chorus and accompanying musical instrumentation. In such a mood, the individual was reunited in a feeling of totality—not as an individual, but as continuous with the world of Dionysian-ecstatic union. Religiously, this was experienced as Dionysus's own reunification—his scattered pieces fused in joy, being reborn by divine agency. Politically and culturally, the Greek citizen likewise felt at one with the great traditions of the past, the community of venerable ancestors, as well as with the institutions and customs of the present. Again, all this was shared and experienced as a common delight in the public performance of the tragic drama.

Nietzsche would later characterize this accomplished position of the Dionysian spirit as a "tragic pessimism," a "pessimism of strength," in his preface of 1886. These phrases were surely intended to articulate a distance between his own analysis in *The Birth of Tragedy* and that of Schopenhauer. As discussed earlier, due to Nietzsche's oftentimes borrowed vocabulary and his frequent citations from Schopenhauer, in retrospect it seemed that *The Birth of Tragedy* was simply all-too-Schopenhauerian in outlook. Two principal impressions had to be changed to correct this misunderstanding. The first impression was largely nominal, since by calling the teaching of tragic wisdom a "pessimism of strength," Nietzsche clearly alluded to the fact that the Greek pessimism, once tempered by Apollo, led the Greeks to *action*—indeed, to the prodigal creativity of the classical age, to glorious military victory in war, and to an almost timeless cultural superiority—and not to *resignation*, as Schopenhauer had argued.[93] On the other hand, the impassioned joy of the Dionysian state intensifies one's own existence to such a heightened state that the tragic individual fully, and willfully, embraces the whole of this existence. Indeed, in the last section of the work, Nietzsche claims that precisely the Dionysian intensity in congruence with the Apollonian appearance of beauty are what "make life worth living at all and prompt the desire to live on in order to experience the next moment."[94] Thus, far from following Schopenhauer's admonition that life is not worth living and that only through a disinterested, will-less aesthetic contemplation may one even hope to persist in this baleful human existence, the tragic "pessimism of strength" issues in rapturous embrace "of this foundation of all existence—the Dionysian basic ground of the world."[95] To be generous to Nietzsche, his readers should have easily grasped such a divergence of attitude and intent between a "tragic pessimism," as Nietzsche expressed it in the text itself, and that pessimism of the dour, Schopenhauerian variety.

The more difficult impression Nietzsche tried to address was the metaphysical vocabulary of Schopenhauerian idealism he so frequently employed. On the one hand, he commends Kant and Schopenhauer for their "critical" philosophy, which restricts any knowledge claim about reality to the level of ordinary, phenomenal experience (i.e., to the empirical order of objects in space and time, subject to the laws of causality). Following Kant and Schopenhauer, his motivation was to limit—to place a "critique" upon—the speculative excess of knowledge claims that optimistically "believed that all the riddles of the universe could be known and fathomed."[96] Specifically, this charge is directed against the "Socratic type," "the theoretical optimist who, with his faith that the nature of things can be fathomed, ascribes to knowledge and insight the power of a panacea, while understanding error as the evil *par excellence*."[97] Nietzsche clearly specifies the kind of knowledge claimed by the "Socratic type," or, more generally, the nature of knowledge as claimed by the modern science of his day.[98] Such a knowledge is reason, and its basis is essentially a "faith" in reason, in logical argumentation.

> The unshakeable faith that thought, using the thread of logic, can penetrate the deepest abysses of being, and that thought is capable not only of knowing being

but even of *correcting* it. This sublime metaphysical illusion accompanies science as an instinct and leads science again and again to its limits. . . . And since Socrates, this mechanism of concepts, judgments and inference has been esteemed as the highest occupation and the most admirable gift of nature, above all other capacities.[99]

In the context of *The Birth of Tragedy*, what is important to this statement about the Socratic claim to knowledge and its rational means as the instrument for all knowledge claims is what it *excludes*. For Nietzsche, Socratic—and by extension, scientific—knowledge excludes precisely what is *not* circumscribed by logic and by objective, formal analysis: namely, the entire domain of the cultural, mythical, and religious heritage that gives meaning and value to one's life and lends direction and purpose to society as a whole.

> Socratism condemns existing art as well as existing ethics. Wherever Socratism turns its searching eyes it sees lack of insight and the power of illusion; and from this lack it infers the essential perversity and reprehensibility of what exists. Basing himself on this point, Socrates conceives it to be his duty to correct existence: all alone, with an expression of irreverence and superiority, as the precursor of an altogether different culture, art, and morality, he enters a world, to touch whose very hem would give us the greatest happiness.
>
> This is what strikes us as so tremendously problematic whenever we consider Socrates, and again and again we are tempted to fathom the meaning and purpose of this most questionable phenomenon of antiquity. Who is it that may dare single-handed to negate the Greek genius that, as Homer, Pindar, and Aeschylus, as Phidias, as Pericles, as Pythia and Dionysus, as the deepest abyss and the highest height, is sure of our astonished veneration? What demonic power is this that dares to spill this magic potion into dust?[100]

What is rejected by the Socratic teaching, then, is the entire dimension of tragic culture, and this is based, ultimately, on "the Dionysian ground of all things."

While Nietzsche's discussion of this Dionysian "ground," in *The Birth of Tragedy*, seems to be "the metaphysical" basis that would "underlie" the order of experience, or as he says "the order of appearances," he was deeply suspicious of this position even as he resorted to a conventional metaphysical vocabulary. What aroused his suspicions is precisely what attracted Nietzsche to the "critical" aspects of Kant's and Schopenhauer's philosophy in the first place, namely, that a metaphysical "ground" would, by definition, escape all experience. Any such metaphysical element of a thing-in-itself, a "noumenon," as Kant used the term, or the "World Will," as Schopenhauer employed it, could only apply to something beyond the order of space and time, empirical causality, and conceptual identification. It would be accessible neither to our sensible intuition nor to our intellectual comprehension—since these constitute the "critical" limits of human understanding. Ultimately, it was the virtue of "critical" philosophy to prevent any such "metaphysical" speculations about what could not be humanly experienced.⁽¹⁰¹⁾ *N.B.*

What troubles Nietzsche's explanation of the Dionysian is the patent fact that he himself "experienced" such a dizzying state of transfiguring ecstasy on frequent occasions. Hence, with the last two sections of *The Birth of Tragedy*, sections 24 and 25, Nietzsche once again addresses "the Dionysian," not so much in metaphysical terms (although the vocabulary accompanies his analysis), but rather in psychological terms.⁽¹⁰²⁾ Instead of addressing the "objective" status of the metaphysical ground, he turns to his own subjective experience of the Dionysian state, namely, his often rapturous experience of music. More specifically, he addresses the experienced sense of *dissonance*, and claims this psychologically joyful experience of musical dissonance to be at the very origin of the Dionysian.

> But this primordial phenomenon of Dionysian art is difficult to grasp, and there is only one direct way to make it intelligible and grasp it immediately: through the wonderful significance of *musical dissonance*. Quite generally, only music, placed beside the world, can give us an idea of what is meant by the justification of the world as an aesthetic phenomenon. The joy aroused by the tragic myth has the same origin as the joyous sensation of dissonance in music. The Dionysian, with its primordial joy experienced even in pain, is the common source of music and myth.[103]

What is experienced psychologically, then, is said to be a "joyous sensation" (*lustvolle Empfindung*) of the "phenomenon" of "musical dissonance," and, again, this is the Dionysian state of ecstasy.

It should be said that recent analysis of ecstatic states suggests that two components are involved: what were formerly held to be the *objects* or *causes* of ecstatic rapture (e.g., the Passion of Jesus, communion with the gods or with angels, and so forth) are now considered as psychologically causative "triggers" (i.e., certain occasions or events that seem to be associated with the onset of ecstatic states).[104] Some triggers are termed *inducing triggers* and others are called *inserted triggers*, the latter of which are said to be the set of intense qualities that correspond to the lived or experienced sense of ecstasy. Inducing triggers include nature, sexual love, exercise, religion, art, poetic knowledge, recollection, and beauty. Inserted triggers include experiences described in "up-words" and phrases such as experiences associated with sensations of flying, weightlessness, floating, or rising up, as well as by "contact words," namely, experiences that include claims of union, presence, mingling, identification with totality, god, nature, spirits, peace, timelessness, perfection, eternity, knowledge, and bliss. Such feelings include loss of self, time, place, limitation, and language. One likewise feels a gain of eternity, a feeling of release, a new life, another world, joy, satisfaction, salvation, perfection, mystical knowledge, and enhanced mental capacity.[105] ∿.⊙.

In attempting to understand the psychological dynamics of these ecstatic states, Nietzsche undertook an analysis of them in an unpublished essay known as "On Music and Words" that he was working on at the time he was composing the later sections of *The Birth of Tragedy*.[106] In this early essay of 1871, Nietzsche comes to realize the very simple truth that it is the subjective states of our experience of music that provokes our ecstatic response. Again, this is now termed its "trigger" effect, and because our ecstatic response is of such a nature that we feel positively transfigured by an experience characterized by loss of ego and a suspension of ordinary object-relations, the very distinction between subject and object becomes blurred, attenuated, if not entirely suspended. The distinction, which supports ordinary intentional experience, between the objective and subjective genitive simply does not obtain in the ecstatic state.

In addressing exactly what the object of music is (i.e., the theoretical model of its subject matter), Nietzsche realizes that its object (*Gegenstand*) is given to us as the content (*Inhalt*) of our own intensely undergone aesthetic experience, our ecstatic states of dispossession. This musically charged state of ecstatic dispossession is precisely what he terms "the Dionysian state," and such a state is effectively the entire *field* of experience, shorn of simple subject-object relations. Earlier, we said that Schiller had termed this state one of intense "mood" or "disposition," specifically a "musical mood" (*musikalische Stimmung*), and this had been discussed by Schopenhauer, but it is Nietzsche who really analyzes it in detail.[107]

To explain the nature of this state, Nietzsche argues that this intense, musically ecstatic mood cannot take place on the level of discrete feelings or sensations, since they are still bound with specific object representations: the simple feeling of sympathy, for example, is always "for" a particular person. Likewise, the particular sensation is always "of" some thing—of the hard stone, of the glaring light, of the loud horn. Rather, what occurs in this state of Dionysian

See Ricoeur on metaphor

musical enchantment is an emotional dissociation or detachment of affective states from specific object relations. It will be this new distinction between feelings (*Gefühle*) and emotions or affects (*Affekte*) that will begin to emerge as an explanation for the broader phenomenon. The former do not have the power to generate the Dionysian state of dispossession because they retain their fixed association with representations.[108] It is on the level of affect or emotion that the dissociation begins to take place. The excitement provoked by musical tonality is experienced as a fluidity of affect, in that intense emotional states lose their conventional associations and tend toward reinvesting their objects of pleasure with more immediate, hallucinatory cathexes and such states involve an extreme intensification of psychic discharge, resulting in a heightened increase of satisfaction. But to the extent to which further intensification of psychic discharge is provoked and occurs, with its concomitant increase in pleasure, so do the states of emotion or affect become progressively freed from their associative connections altogether, their regular accompanying object representations, until the point of frenzy (*Rauch*) is attained, in which case the underlying drives (*Triebe*) become completely free-flowing, anarchic, and unbound.[109] These deeper instinctual drives will ultimately constitute the power (*Kraft*) or force (*Macht*) that drives the emotions themselves—and for the intense, musically aesthetic experience, they will constitute what he calls the very "sanctuary of music."[110]

Nietzsche often speaks of these states of Dionysian excess and frenzy as states of "drunkenness," "the horrible 'witches brew' of sensuality," "intoxication," or "wanton abandon," and indeed, by the time he composed *The Birth of Tragedy*, he begins to explain the Dionysian drives themselves by appeal to these most natural and extreme states of intoxication and frenzy. This is, of course, opposed to the other natural term by which he addresses the Apollonian drive—as the state of dreaming.[111] This experienced state of intense emotional intensity and dissociation, when one's drives themselves are no longer bound—what Freud would later describe as the psychological level of primary process formation—is precisely the Dionysian state of disindividuation or dispossession. Thus, Nietzsche would write, in a draft as early as 1869, that music is "through and through symbolic of the drives [*der Triebe*]" and is thus "more general than any particular action."[112] Since the drives—the instinctual expressions of psychic energy—are themselves unconscious or sublimated, their subjective translation occurs to us as intense emotional states. The musical effect (*musikalische Wirkung*) thus occurs on the deeper level of drives and is in turn quickly discharged or depotentialized to become an emotional affect (*Affektw-*

irkung). According to a strikingly similar Freudian vocabulary, all drives are expressed in terms of emotion and representation, and emotion—or affect—is, for Freud, the qualitative expression of the quantity of instinctual energy, or drive. That these affective states can be transformed, for example, through conversion, displacement, and transformation of affect, as we have seen, constitutes the very dynamics of tragic drama in *The Birth of Tragedy*.

That Nietzsche chose to focus on dissonance as "the primordial phenomenon of Dionysian art" was prescient. Dissonance presupposes the entire creative reservoir of musical elements within the tonal system—arguably, within any tonal system: tone, sonority, beat, rhythm, tempo, harmony, measure, melody, polyphony, progression, and so forth. Modern cognitive science shows that, much like the visual field, which we continually stabilize and model according to a relatively small number of visual foci, the auditory field anticipates tonal progression, chord development, and harmonic resolution—according to the cultural norms that govern the tonal scale.[113] On the twelve-tone scale, resolution usually occurs within the diatonic frame (i.e., the first ten tones), offset by the chromatic or "dissonant" tones above that, as well as by certain minor keys. We know from his early essays that Nietzsche was familiar with Helmholtz's important work on tone sensation, which experimentally demonstrated that pleasure tends to accompany the listener's resolution of musical dissonance into consonance. Effectively, music sets up anticipations and then satisfies them. As Robert Jourdain has described, the anticipation is of temporally developing patterns in tone, melody, harmony, rhythm, tempo, phrasing, and form. Music, he says, is basically "a construction of a continual temporal flux, orchestrated according to precise proportions in which the listener's anticipation of tonal movement and proportion are gracefully integrated and resolved."[114] To the extent that the musical composition can continually reshape and heighten anticipation—by withholding resolution, by temporarily violating and delaying resolution—and then satisfy the more complex anticipation with a crescendo of resolution, music becomes far more "expressive" and more richly satisfying. In short, it yields great emotional satisfaction—where our experience is heightened to exceed the fulfillment of ordinary satisfaction (i.e., of built up tension and its satisfying, pleasure-giving release).[115]

Recent work in musical psychoacoustics shows that with the auditory resolution of dissonance, within the neural routings of the primary and secondary auditory cortex in the brain, the entire kinesthetic muscular system becomes subsequently engaged to help "score" or "model" or "map" these complex tonal progressions and structures onto the body itself, as a kind of sensory-motor register, so as to supplement the auditory system in attaining resolution, completion, and thereby, satisfaction. It is with this supplement of kinesthetic modeling (effectively, a ~~somatic~~ <u>encoding</u>), whereby the body is moved to mimic beat, rhythm, harmony, and melody through muscular flex and contraction (i.e., through bodily gesture, movement, and dance), that the higher-order neural networks in the somatosensory and motor cortex areas of the brain begin to produce endorphins. This production of endorphins raises what was largely an automatic, relatively homeostatic response to auditory stimuli into an intensely pleasurable experience of ecstasy.¹¹⁶ As Nietzsche expressed this in 1869, the power of musical experience operates upon our instinctual drives so as to provoke their discharge into highly excited emotional states, characterized by fluidity of affect and ego loss—states seemingly beyond space and time, and where causality itself becomes magical—that is to say, dispossession, disindividuation.

Doubtless, it was one of Nietzsche's most striking and compassionate achievements to have understood that the death of myth laid nothing at all to rest, save perhaps that which was most meaningful and valuable, for only after its effective demise does a culture begin to feel "the deep sense of an immense void," what Nietzsche would later describe in *The Gay Science* as the breath of empty space, the ever colder and darker night, which attends the death of the old God.¹¹⁷ Only in retrospect and with the lament bred from an unspeakable loss can one finally understand "how necessary and close the fundamental connections are between art and the people, myth and custom, tragedy and the state."¹¹⁸ For the Greeks, this understanding came entirely too late to avert their decline into Alexandrine culture and political vassalage. For a period of more than five centuries, the myths that had infused tragic drama and had brought classical culture to its highest development were hardly less than the very lifeblood of Greek social and political existence. If the individual of classical Greece felt himself to be far more than an isolated subject, through his enjoyment of tragic drama, his sense of belonging was likewise acutely political. Having become who he was through the vital resources of myth and the significance it conferred upon him, the individual fully assumed a political being at the same time: he shared the values, aspirations, beliefs, and concerns of those with whom he lived. Not only did he thereby find his home and familiarity in this condition, but he felt this to be more primary and praiseworthy than reason itself, a sentiment that even provoked the usually inquisitive Aristotle to exclaim, "there is no need to ask why this [civic sentiment] is so."¹¹⁹

Nietzsche ended *The Birth of Tragedy* with the hope that a specifically modern culture could somehow retrieve the significance of its all-but-forgotten mythical heritage and fuse this with the immense resources that yet remain to be developed in music. That he once so positively located this hope for an awakened culture in the person of Richard Wagner, Nietzsche quickly came to regret. But in his subsequent works Nietzsche himself would assume this task and devise his own responses to the abstract and mythless state of the modern distress.[120] By way of a new and joyful wisdom, the myth of the eternal return, and the prospect of a higher humanity, ennobled and united by the grand style, Nietzsche would time and again attempt to answer Zarathustra's bewildered exclamation, "How many new gods are yet possible?"

THE GAY SCIENCE

Of all of Nietzsche's texts, *The Gay Science* (or *Joyful Wisdom* [*Die fröhliche Wissenschaft*]) is probably his most important. Nietzsche not only came to think of it in later years as his most congenial and personal work, but he often referred to it as his "most *medial* book," the one that stood at the midpoint of his life and served as a fulcrum for his subsequent thought. Indeed, shortly after completing the first edition in 1882 (an additional chapter would be added in 1887, together with a preface and an appendix of poems), Nietzsche stressed the crucial importance of the work in a letter to Franz Overbeck, perhaps his closest friend at the time:

> If you have read the "Sanctus Januarius" [i.e., book 4], you will have remarked that I have crossed a tropic. Everything that lies before me is new, and it will not be long before I catch sight also of the terrifying face of my more distant life task. . . . This whole interim state between what was and what will be, I call "in media vita."[1]

"*In media vita*" (in midlife) is the title of a section near the end of book 4, and the "interim state" it implies aptly described the author's own frame of mind. Furthermore, the section indicates how Nietzsche came to achieve this state, and in its exuberance, it echoes the tone of the book and reproduces the entire range of the book's subject matter:

> In Media Vita.—No! Life has not disappointed me! On the contrary, I find it truer, more desirable and mysterious every year—ever since the day when the great liberator came to me: the idea that life could be an experiment of the seeker for knowledge—and not a duty, not a calamity, not trickery.—And knowledge itself: let it be something else for others; for example, a bed to rest on, or the way

to such a bed, or a diversion, or a form of leisure—for me it is a world of dangers and victories in which heroic feelings, too, find places to dance and play. "*Life as a means to knowledge*"—with this principle in one's heart, one can live not only boldly but even gaily, and laugh gaily, too.[2]   324

For Nietzsche, this medial book was both intensely personal and all-pervasive in its import: personal, since Nietzsche claimed that, through having written it, he was able to formulate the means for his own liberation, that is, to devise a "Gay Science," or "Joyful Wisdom."[3] The text was all-pervasive in the import of its subject matter, since his liberation was a direct response to what he discussed throughout the book as the greatest single event in world history, the event that inaugurated modernity itself: the "death of God." Thus moved, Nietzsche recognized that the life of the individual could no longer be believed, bound by, or even be understood in terms of the demands of an absolute moral order, one that had its basis in the authority of a transcendent God. Since it was through the authority of just such a transcendent, divine order that the *human* world was traditionally thought to have any meaning or value at all— that existence itself was believed to have a purpose or destiny—the passing away of that divine authority would, as Nietzsche suggested, be "terrifying" indeed. In fact, the death of God would itself bring about an "interim state" par excellence—the point between a comprehensible moral world order and something else: perhaps, a world of unexampled chaos and nihilism. What remained in the balance and what the middle position thus implied, therefore, far outweighed any consideration of one individual's personal disposition. Rather, what was announced by the death of God—and Nietzsche hardly hesitated to dramatize this (e.g., in section 125)—was an irrevocable age in human history, one to be measured in eons. "It is not inconceivable that I am the first philosopher of the age, perhaps even a little more, something decisive and doom-laden standing *between* two millennia."[4]

One could easily say that the main concern of *The Gay Science* is precisely to understand and to address the problem of the "between": to focus on the medial state, to question the position and significance of human existence within an age that no longer seemed to have a discernible center. Thus, by emphasizing the all-too-apparent loss of this center (i.e., what traditionally served as a supreme—and divinely sanctioned—source of meaning, value, and purpose), Nietzsche commenced his task of establishing a "joyful wisdom." He claimed to do this by investing human existence with the active desire to desire itself, to serve itself in its own name—to joyfully legislate its own human values,

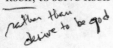
rather than desire to be god

vocations, and ends. With this in view, Nietzsche set out to formulate a proposal for an entirely immanent human future, one he conceived under the enigmatic title "the eternal recurrence." The medial state of *The Gay Science* thus unfolded, as he pointed out in his letter to Overbeck, from what was to what would be: from his initial analysis of the so-called "purposive existence" to his concluding remarks on the doctrine of eternal recurrence.

Five years would separate the publication of the last section of *The Gay Science*, book 5, from the earlier chapters. During the intervening years, Nietzsche continued to explore the consequences of the "death of God" and his conception of the "eternal return"—most notably, in the dramatic prose of *Thus Spoke Zarathustra* (1883–85). In the following work of 1886, *Beyond Good and Evil*, he would draw upon the methodological insights he achieved in *The Gay Science* to further examine the deeper origins and underlying motivations—psychological, cultural, social, philosophical—that found expression in the traditional metaphysical worldview, together with its accompanying moral system. He would explicitly focus on the origins and dynamics of morality as the main concern of his next work, *On the Genealogy of Morals*, in 1887. Nonetheless, he had already raised these closely intertwined issues, at the very beginning of book 1 in *The Gay Science*—section 1, "The Teachers of the Purpose of Existence."

The first five sections in book 5 strongly reassert the major themes of the earlier chapters, and they point to his growing concern with how the deeply rooted, traditional religious values serve to limit the individual's freedom and autonomy and to weaken, if not destroy, the individual's sense of self-worth. In such circumstances, all of human pain and suffering is interpreted in religious terms, under the form of sin and guilt, and this burden results in even more suffering for the individual: it creates an impossible situation of humiliation and shame, a state of impoverished despair—wherein the individual comes to despise himself and is driven to exact revenge upon the very conditions of human existence as psychological compensation for this suffering.[5] By the time Nietzsche completed book 5 and the introduction to the second edition, he would address this complex problem of suffering, guilt, and shame—he considered it a pathology—analyzing the means by which it is induced, as well as perpetuated. He would then go on to propose how it could be overcome: through the cultivation of a critical awareness, through a sense of generosity and self-respect, and by learning how to become well-disposed to oneself. Looking back on *The Gay Science* in 1888 in the brief section devoted to it in

Ecce Homo, he would point to the "granite words in which a destiny finds for the first time a formula for itself"[6] in the last three aphorisms of book 3:

> *Whom do you call bad?*—Those who always want to put to shame.
> *What do you consider most humane?*—To spare someone shame.
> *What is the seal of liberation?*—No longer being ashamed in front of oneself.

This would correspond, at least in part, to what Nietzsche wrote to Heinrich von Stein, concerning "what I have never yet revealed to anyone—the task which confronts me, my life's task": namely, that "I would like to *take away* from human existence some of its heartbreaking and cruel character."

Oddly, there is no mention of the "eternal return" in book 5 nor in the introduction. When Nietzsche developed this theme at length in *Zarathustra*, he cast it under the aura of a myth, hoping to find in the resources of myth an antidote to the metaphysical doctrines of religious belief. While such an approach served him well in *The Birth of Tragedy*, it seems Nietzsche felt these resources—myth, music, drama, and so forth—had become by now inappropriate and inadequate to the task.

STYLISTIC CONCERNS IN NIETZSCHE'S WORKS

It is hardly an overstatement to say that Nietzsche writes with a certain extravagance of style, even with hyperbole and excess—or, as he says, "in blood." His thought issues forth in what seems to be almost an abandonment of conventional philosophical form and constraint. That the style of the book was meant to be poetic in nature is indicated by its very subtitle, "La Gaya Scienza," which refers to the tradition of chivalric poetry of the French Provençal courts, dating back to the early Middle Ages. Indeed, Nietzsche's style of composition is profuse in the variety of expressive and rhetorical techniques it draws upon, and this tends to render his thought extremely resistant to systematic elaboration, even by his most generous reader. As he would say in *Zarathustra*, "It is not easily possible to understand the blood of another."[8]

To begin to examine this unsystematic character of expression and the difficulties this entails for understanding, much less interpreting, the text of *The Gay Science*, the reader must first attend to Nietzsche's peculiar style of thought and to his complex style of writing. While Nietzsche often claimed many literary and philosophical antecedents, it is arguable whether one could find a stronger single example of a thinker from the Western tradition whose distinctive style of expression so forcefully reflects the content of his concerns. What he says and how he says it are so much the same: both his own style and the world he writes about confront us as a dynamic play of multiple and continually changing appearances. It is precisely this dynamic play of successively experienced events, a world understood as the active insurgence of all process and change, that he would later term "the will to power." He conceives this to be the expression—the self-articulation—of all force, energy, life: of nature itself as a dynamic process of teeming and recurrent metamorphosis. To see the confluence of Nietzsche's style and the content it so forcefully expresses, we look at paragraph 310, where he explicitly addresses this dynamic "will to power." The image or metaphor he uses to describe it is the *wave*. Not only does he explicitly identify *himself* with the wave, with its surging foam and thunder, its infinite capacity to transform itself and to recur, once again, bearing its emerald crest of elemental nature, but he also *writes* in waves— investing a rhythmic and pulsatile flow to the very composition of his prose. Read, or better still, speak aloud, the following passage:

> How greedily this wave approaches . . . but already another wave is approaching, still more greedily and savagely than the first, and its soul, too, seems to be full of secrets and the lust to dig up treasures. Thus live waves—thus live we who will. . . . Carry on as you like, roaring with overweening pleasure and malice—or dive again, pouring your emeralds down into the deepest depths, and throw your infinite white mane of foam and spray over them: everything suits me, for everything suits you so well, and I am so well-disposed toward you for everything; how could I think of betraying you? For—mark my word!—I know you and your secret, I know your kind! You and I—are we not of one kind? You and I—do we not have one secret?[10]

The vibrant expressiveness of Nietzsche's prose, the fertility and suggestiveness of its content, refuse to be systematized; it resists the imposition of static categories, of rule governance—whether logical or linguistic. The dynamic flow of the experienced events he evokes cannot be easily articulated: it bears no simple definition, it claims no essence or distinctive form. In this respect, Nietzsche's discourse declines reliance upon strict definition, upon the single, unchanging, univocal meaning of a term, upon the rigorous logical argument, and most forcefully, upon the principle of identity, which certifies that one thing is only one thing—and nothing else. Nietzsche turns away from all this, on the level of *style*, toward the more poetic, *figurative* use of language: the aphorism, the apothegm, the image, the simile, the metaphor, all of which are essentially unstable, imbalanced means of expression. For the predominant tradition of Western thought, these figures of language have been rigorously set apart from philosophic expression proper, figurative (i.e., nonliteral) language having been deemed imprecise, and worthy only for "art" or rhetorical "distortion," for the "impure" domain of poetic obscurity, confusion, and nonsense.

Nietzsche's use of the aphorism or apothegm is fully crucial to his dynamic engagement of style and content of thought and the world it bespeaks. In fact, it is surely one of his most distinctive features of expression.[11] The aphorism—the short, terse, witty, and incisive remark that expresses a far wider truth than the strict meaning of the terms it employs—is itself alive, animate: that is to say, open-ended in its possible significance. It *responds* to the genius and inspiration of a critical mind, an inquisitive reader, but it resists formalism and catechism. In this regard, it is a "turn" or "trope" of phrase and thought, a *movement* of expression, that by means of its distinctive agency, directs us beyond a fixed idea, beyond a simple corresponding meaning or referent in a static system of rules or definitions. The aphorism destroys the possibility of such a fixed, literal system because it is essentially *incomplete* in its significance. It demands that an interpretive operation be performed upon it by the reader for its very intelligibility. The aphorism demands that the reader give it meaning, for it does not possess a single, discrete meaning *in itself*. You, the reader, are immediately involved, enamored, intertwined with the aphorism, with the proverb or parable. You invest it with meaning by *interpreting* it, by inserting it into ever-new contexts, by directing its words to ever-new occasions, associations, events—and what follows? The aphorism itself changes, it assumes a new reference, situation, context, appropriateness, valence—and hence, a *new* meaning. This dynamic property of expressiveness renders the aphorism essentially *metaphorical*: as such, it induces the reader to gather resemblances, to cull differences, to collect similarities, to compare and contrast markedly different cases, and to assemble all these, however briefly, and to thereby exhibit, to make manifest, the very movement of thought. In this sense, the metaphor is an instrument *for* thinking and not an end-point or terminus of thought. The term metaphor itself comes from the Greek *meta-pherein*, to carry or to transport across a distance. So understood, the metaphor is neither static nor complete. Rather, it brings together scattered semantic elements of meaning in a movement of thought, in a shifting process of displacement and transference.[12]

Active, incomplete, manifold, and alive, the metaphor not only characterizes a movement of thought, it also stands as an analogy, or an analogue, for what exists. The very structure of the metaphor serves as an analogical expression for the dynamic flow of appearances themselves, for the constant motion, mutation, and change of objects, events, situations—what we earlier saw Nietzsche come to call "the will to power." For Nietzsche, the metaphor enjoys a very real privilege, in fact the metaphor serves to structure cognitive and semantic processes and at the same time it is the most apt means of expressing reality itself. How we think, therefore, is basically understood by Nietzsche to be a metaphorical process. The meanings of those things we in fact experience or think about likewise result from these metaphorical processes. Finally, the fact that the world itself is mobile, dynamic, fluid, changeable—understood as shifting arrangements, as constellations, or as factored groupings of force or energy—demands a dynamically conceived means of expression, of representation, of language, to adequately portray it. For Nietzsche, the metaphor is the most appropriate means.

With this admission, however, we come to a most crucial point for understanding Nietzsche. According to his account, the *real* is no longer what tradition formerly held it to be. That is, Nietzsche no longer conceives reality according to the model of a stable, essentially static, or even law-governed, order. Nor does he claim that the real is itself rational or logical, much less that the natural order is reasonable or purposive. For Nietzsche, there is no enduring, fixed, absolutely stable form of reality either outside ourselves, in the world, outside our own thought, or even within the confines of our thought. Neither is there a stabilizing logic to reality itself, nor is there an absolutely governing form of reason naturally inherent or ingredient in our own thought that would strictly conform to the real.

Approaching Nietzsche's texts—especially those written after *The Birth of Tragedy*—we seem to encounter a dramatically new frame of reference. Here is indeed a world, but one of "appearances" only, of insubstantial pulsions of energy, or what Nietzsche often terms "will"—again, in the sense of "force"—a perplexingly chaotic state that seems to reflect the anarchic world of the pre-Olympian gods—before creation—a state of primordial strife, warfare, and force, whose only reality is the dynamics of its appearance, of its perpetual conflict and mutation. The world *is* as it presents itself to us: motile, dynamic, in flux, in constant metamorphosis and change.

Against this newly conceived, dynamic frame of reference, the stable notions of logic itself seem weak and inadequate. Nietzsche, for example, denies the heretofore unquestioned authority of the very first principle of logic, that is, the simple principle of identity that *A* is *A*. For the employment of language or thought, therefore, Nietzsche's account charges that there is no strictly identi-

cal word, thought, or meaning—that strict self-identity could never, in principle or in fact, occur to human experience.[13] Words, terms, meanings,
propositions, and concepts, for Nietzsche, are generalized constructs of human
invention—they merely serve as momentarily agreed-upon fabrications, as the
conventional fictions of a given culture and its language. In no way are they
taken to be simple, single, and unchanging definitions, forms, or essences. In
the absence of a strict sense of logical identity, the subsequent issue of contradiction fails to arise, since there is, literally, nothing to contradict. For Nietzsche, then, logical contradiction itself gives way to frenzy, identity to chaos. As
he would say in his essay of 1873, "On Truth and Lie in an Extra-Moral Sense":

> Every word immediately becomes a concept inasmuch as it is *not* intended to
> serve as a reminder of the unique and wholly individualized original experience
> to which it owes its birth, but must at the same time fit innumerable, *more or
> less* similar cases—which means, strictly speaking, *never* equal—in other words,
> a lot of unequal cases. Every concept originates through *our* equating what is
> *unequal*. No leaf ever wholly equals another, and the *concept* "leaf" is formed
> through an arbitrary *abstraction* from these individual differences, through for-
> getting the distinctions. . . . What, then, is *truth*? A mobile army of metaphors,
> metonyms, and anthropomorphisms—in short, a sum of human relations, which
> have been enhanced, transposed, and embellished poetically and rhetorically, and
> which after long use seem firm, canonical, and obligatory to a people: *truths are
> illusions* about which one has forgotten that this is what they are; metaphors
> which are worn out and without sensuous power . . . to be truthful means using
> the customary metaphors—in moral terms: the obligation to *lie* according to a
> fixed convention, to lie herd-like in a style obligatory for all.[14]

Given this warning as to the impossibility of precise logical expressiveness
and the impossibility of any strictly truthful content, Nietzsche nonetheless
goes on to write some sixteen major works. Precisely for whom, though, is
not immediately evident. Nonetheless, that he does seem to have a particular
audience in mind is strongly suggested by his employment of a stylistic device
well known to the philosophic and rhetorical tradition: namely, the use of what
is often termed "hidden" or "concealed" writing. According to the concerns of
such a tradition, an author, for a variety of reasons, may choose to employ some
stylistic element of indirection, of silence, of a low-profile sort of encoding a
message, which provides certain "clues" or gives a certain nonapparent "consistency" to the text that would enable sympathetic readers to properly grasp his
message. While what the author intends to say to his own select audience is
thereby "concealed" or "hidden" to a more general, and perhaps unsympa-

thetic, audience, the latter will grasp the text on a surface or manifest level, which to all general appearances, is simply a straightforward exposition or narrative. The author quite literally presents two faces of himself, each of which answers to a specific objective and is addressed to a different audience. The objectives and different audiences, in turn, warrant the author's use of different stylistic strategies and tactics, such that he might ensure the effective concealment of one message (i.e., the restriction of what is important and what must be said to those who can understand it), to conceal that important message from the other, inappropriate, audience.

Why an author should choose to compose his text in such a fashion is, of course, an extremely complex issue. The author may be subject to popular disapproval or persecution for his views. He may wish not to upset or to needlessly offend an otherwise well-disposed general public. He may wish not to provoke public opinion over issues he considers to be important, but which are necessarily restricted to a particular, selected audience of like-minded readers, of sympathizers and intellectual collaborators, whose identity might be better kept secret, or discretely hidden from view.[15] Alternatively, the author may well wish to provoke a negative or emotional response in the wider audience, precisely to deter those individuals from examining his text too closely, and thus, to prevent them from being unduly influenced, and perhaps harmed, by his text. Stylistic and rhetorical excess, in this case, can well serve a prophylactic function. In some cases, then, the author may well wish to close the reader's ears beforehand, precisely in deference to their own best interests.[16] Nietzsche discusses this distinction of audience in section 381 of *The Gay Science*, the section entitled "On the Question of Being Understandable":

> One does not only wish to be understood when one writes; one wishes just as surely *not* to be understood. It is not by any means necessarily an objection to a book when anyone finds it impossible to understand: perhaps that was part of the author's intention—he did not want to be understood by just "anybody." All the nobler spirits and tastes select their audience when they wish to communicate; and choosing that, one at the same time erects barriers against "the others." All the more subtle laws of any style have their origin at this point: they at the same time keep away, create a distance, forbid "entrance," understanding, as said above—while they open the ears of those whose ears are related to ours.[17]

Elsewhere, in a letter to one of his friends, Malwida von Meysenbug,[18] Nietzsche elaborates this distinction of audience and shows how he will use certain parts of the text (e.g., the preface) to communicate different messages and to provoke different responses, accordingly:

The long prefaces which I have found necessary for the new edition of my complete works tell with a ruthless honesty some curious things about myself. With these I'll ward off "the many" once and for all. . . . I've thrown out my hook to "the few" instead, and even with them I'm prepared to be patient. For my ideas are so indescribably strange and dangerous that only much later (surely not before 1901) will anybody be ready for them.[19]

Finally, and again from *The Gay Science*, paragraph 381, Nietzsche offers us an explanation as to *why*, at least in the case of the present work, he chose to maintain this clear distinction of audience:

Being an immoralist, one has to take steps against corrupting innocents—I mean, asses and old maids of both sexes whom life offers nothing but their innocence. Even more, my writings should inspire, elevate, and encourage them to be virtuous. I cannot imagine anything on earth that would be a merrier sight than inspired old asses and maids.

Even granting the distinction of audience—and the correlative observation that a text may be *understood* in quite different ways, that one text may sustain markedly different interpretations and, thus, markedly different meanings—once we commence reading such a work as *The Gay Science*, particularly when we read what Nietzsche has to say about the subject of ethics and morality, we are struck by the excess, the hyperbole, and the evocative force of his pronouncements. What, one is tempted to ask, could conceivably account for the apparent extremism of his views? How does one plausibly accept, for example, his assertions that Eastern religion dwells on rice and indolence? Or, that the founding fathers, the Patristic saints, of the Christian church are "holy epileptics"? That Judeo-Christian values are merely "slave values," that they foster a "slave mentality"? That what is important to a statement of knowledge or belief is not so much its "truth" but, rather, that it is a "coherent" pattern of lies? That the German spirit has been ruined by a diet composed entirely of beer, newspapers, and Wagnerian music? That human pride and national patriotism are but simple forms of obstinacy and ignorance?

These seemingly intemperate remarks are not just random assertions, scattered and ill-humored passing observations, however. We have already suggested how the reader might better view the style and purpose of Nietzsche; that is, he must be read properly, the mechanics of the metaphor and aphorism must always be kept in mind and taken seriously. A properly responsive thought, then, must be alive and attentive to the nuances and provocations of his style. This is done, at least in part, by being *impatient*, by refusing to stop with a simple definition, some fixed term or meaning, or with a purportedly "complete" explanation; by never ceasing to be incited by the ruse or play of the text, by its emotionally charged solicitation of the reader, even if at first sight this appeal seems unusual or excessive or dramatically exaggerated. All these considerations point to the fact that Nietzsche writes to the heart as well as to the mind. He wants to draw upon all the resources through which we come to understand, value, and feel things. The complexity—and often enough, the audacity—of his style is thus attuned to the fullest range of our cognitive and affective capabilities.

Just as importantly, Nietzsche repeatedly insists that the reader exercise his own independence and generosity and that the reader recognize that a stated position, viewpoint, or claim is in fact merely the statement of its author—that it is partial, provisional, and limited to the concerns of its author, as well as to the circumstances of its utterance. In this sense, Nietzsche would claim that his writings were "perspectival," that they assumed the meaning or significance they did by virtue of occupying a certain *perspective* and by having a particular context. Each statement, then, occupies a position with regard to other statements, to a particular set of references and concerns, to the author's stated or implied intentions, to the nature of their rhetorical formulation, and to the specific place, time, history, and culture that subtends them—all this multiplied and factored by the respective context of the reader who interprets them, in short, with regard to the equally particular interlocutor, who constitutes but one of many possible audiences, each with its own unique and distinctive formation.[20] Doubtless, these considerations are complex, and they tend to make any claim upon Nietzsche's final judgments equally complex.

What the reader should keep in mind to aid in sorting out these complicating factors of interpretation is the predominant concern Nietzsche has with ethics and morals, understood in the broad sense as the Greek *ethos* (character) and as the Latin *mores* (customs and manners), which is to say, ethics and morals seen as those conventional patterns of action, judgment, value, and behavior that govern the life of an individual and structure the society within which the individual lives.

It should be noted that Nietzsche generally writes *against* the prevailing tradition, and in doing so he is fully sensitive to the properties or principles that define the tradition *as* a coherent system. For this reason, Nietzsche will often *employ* the most traditional oppositions within the reservoir of its significant codes, to question, criticize, contradict, and *fracture* the coherence of the system itself—and thereby, also, the hold, the constrictive purchase, that the traditional system exercises upon both the individual and his or her culture. Nietzsche would later thematize this task, and, in an ironic turn of phrase, lend its name as a subtitle to his work of 1888—*Twilight of the Idols; or, How to Do Philosophy with a Hammer.*[21] Furthermore, and we should keep this on the horizon, such a task will raise the strongest question—for Nietzsche and for a tradition—the question of totality, the very possibility of an exhaustive, totalizing understanding of human and natural existence.[22]

Let us anticipate the kind of subject matter Nietzsche wished to criticize in traditional ethics and moral theory by constructing a brief grid or taxonomy, a system of classification for identifying the possible content of these ethical and moral systems. In doing so, we want to see the outlines and contours of the various concepts that form a set of oppositions—oppositions of meanings, terms, and concepts—within *any* reflection on human activity, individual or social. This shall serve as a key or guide to a reading of *The Gay Science* and as an aid in recognizing the broad themes that will emerge from it. What are these basic, foundational oppositions of meanings and concepts? One risks embarrassment in mentioning them, since they constitute the very vocabulary of our own speech; without them, little makes sense. Nonetheless, when the terms of these oppositions are directed back against themselves, back against similarly paired oppositions in the system of our reflection on ethical and moral concepts, they can assume a terrifying agency of critique. Gilles Deleuze, for example, likens Kafka's use of his adopted language (i.e., from Yiddish to German) to Nietzsche's critical employment of these defining categories of thought and action: "To confound all codes is not easy, even on the simplest level of writing and thought. The only parallel I can find here [i.e., to Nietzsche] is with Kafka, in what he does to German, working within the language of Prague Jewry; he constructs a battering ram out of German and turns it against itself."[23]

Among the many consenting pairs of concepts which, together and systematically, fuse to form the general subject matter of ethical and moral reflection, at least the following should be noted:

absolute / relative	gain / loss
action / reaction	give / receive
body / soul	good / evil
cause / effect	immanent / transcendent
conscious / unconscious	intent / deed
faith / knowledge	life / death

male / female	strength /weakness
nature / culture	subject / predicate
origin / goal	substance / accident
pleasure / pain	success / failure
positive / negative	theory / practice
pretended / actual	time / eternity
public / private	true / false
rational / irrational	utility / truth
sensible / immaterial	

If one adds to these terms all the conceptual and logical oppositions formed by the prefixes a-, un-, im-, in-, non-, super-, supra-, infra-, para-, meta-, and so on, much less those oppositions governed by such grammatical concerns as gender, tense, case, voice, and so forth, one begins to sense the enormous scope of such an underlying, systematic character to human reflection. This inventory or vocabulary of opposed concepts will constitute what Nietzsche termed the unconscious "grammar" of thought, and it serves as the very code, the very system, of philosophical intelligibility.[24] As such, it is by the involution, the recursive function of the code (i.e., when he turns certain elements of the code back upon the whole system of ethics and morality) that Nietzsche first starts his own distinctive analysis. By means of this code, we can understand the major themes or motifs in any system of ethics—we can view the stresses and predominant structures that inhabit any such system. By criticizing one set of oppositions from the standpoint of another and by analyzing the result from the perspective of a third or fourth set, we can begin to ask the kinds of questions that Nietzsche typically poses and begin to see the organic character claimed by, or implicit in, any particular system.[25]

One can demand of a particular assertion or judgment, drawn from a particular ethical system, that it answer as to its stated origin, as to its pretended or actual origin. One can continue to locate the effective agency of such issues in the conscious intentions of that doctrine's founder, or, on the contrary, in the subconscious habits of its quotidian propagators, its followers, and adherents. What purpose or good, for example, does the particular ethical or moral position serve? What are its organizing principles? Who, in fact or in principle, derives benefit from the particular ethical code in question? Does it largely serve to benefit its followers?—the public at large?—the founder of the religious sect or of the political party?—its priests and agents?—the secular rulers?—the prince?—anyone?

It may be objected that many of Nietzsche's analyses thus stated are psychological, if not even pathological, in origin, in that they tend to stress the motivational patterns of concept formation or of ethical justification. In this sense, it is often said that Nietzsche defends those conditions that serve to establish a position rather than the validity of the claim or the truth of the position itself. Nietzsche's counter? That veracity—truth itself—is *also* motivated, as is consistency, as are the very norms of verification and justification themselves.[26] Moreover, they, too, constitute part of the systematic coherency claimed by the larger code. Each presumed "ground" or "origin" or "final account" or "in the beginning" or "original intent" testifies to a vertiginous spiral of presuppositions, prejudices, and agendas beneath it, prior to it—caves behind caves, as he would say in *Zarathustra*.

Such a tendency to stress the deep motivational aspects of statements or positions acknowledges a mechanics of action and reaction on the level of the individual and the group. A set of oppositions like the one Nietzsche proposes seeks in many cases to explain the deeper, underlying system of *needs* that gives rise to the construction and elaboration of particular ethical or moral codes, which would in turn govern the course of our action. Such deep-seated origins clearly result in more than a particular set of rules. Unconscious and unstated drives also incline the individual to interpret his culture and his world in congruence with his needs or desires, and this in turn gives rise to particular evaluations of reality—and these evaluations (i.e., ethical and moral values) are subsequently reflected in the higher-order constructions of literature, mythology, religion, philosophy, politics, and the sciences.[27] That this tendency may often lend itself to the informal fallacy of ad hominem argumentation does not seem to be one of Nietzsche's principal concerns. In fact, he seems to welcome its "supplementary" value: "I'm not afraid to cite *names*: one illustrates one's point of view very quickly when, here or there, one argues *ad hominem*. For me, all this enhances clarity."[28]

NIETZSCHE'S PSYCHOHISTORICAL ACCOUNT OF MORALITY AND RELIGION

Perhaps more strikingly than any other determining factor, morality finds its distant origins in *fear*, that is, in human weakness and despair, in a terrible sickness of the will—at least, this is one of Nietzsche's most frequently stated hypotheses, throughout the entire span of his writings.[29] Of course, Nietzsche was not alone in this view; the English philosopher of the seventeenth century Thomas Hobbes, for example, saw this general human fear as the condition for a social contract, for the origin of the civil state, the state he called the ugly beast Leviathan. Hobbes postulated that the state was initially constructed by means of a majority consent or contract, namely, a mutual agreement, a covenant, that would serve to combine the several weak and dispersed agencies of the many in order to combat the excesses of the powerful few. The majority of individuals, each on his own, might well desire to take charge of his own life, possessions, and situation and to conquer his opponents by force of arms. Unfortunately, as individuals, they are effectively powerless to do so in the face of those few *other* individuals who are naturally strong. The solution to such a state of natural inequality—a natural state of war, as Hobbes expressed it—was for the weak to gather themselves together for their mutual security and to construct a political state so as to collectively safeguard what little they did possess, rather than to lose all of it to the rapacity of those few individuals who were readily capable of violent conquest.[30]

In very general terms, Nietzsche's account of the origin of religion may be said to be constructed by analogy to Hobbes's account of the state.[31] For Nietzsche, religion especially begins in fear of the gods. In fact, Nietzsche maintains that man himself *invented* the gods out of a more primordial fear. The initial fear of an unbridled and destructive nature gave rise to the invention of the gods as a controlling force and countermeasure. Such a presumed divine omnipotence, however, gave rise to a second fear, namely, a fear of the gods themselves. This in turn resulted in mankind's voluntary submission to the divine, that is, in the formation of religions. Nietzsche's account of the origin of religion and the system of ethics and morality it entails, may thus be briefly summarized: awestruck by the force and violence of nature, by the cataclysmic upheavals of the world that are far beyond man's effective control, early man postulated a *unifying cause and origin* to them, one that was *also* beyond his control. He did this, Nietzsche argues, by a rather rude analogy, by supposing there was some kind of *will or intention behind* these natural events:

> Every thoughtless person supposes that will alone is effective. . . . The will is for him a magically effective force; the faith in the will as the cause of effects is the faith in magically effective forces. Now man believed originally that wherever he saw something happen, a will had to be at work in the background as a cause, and a personal, willing being. Any notion of mechanics was far from his mind. But since man believed, for immense periods of time, only in persons . . . the faith in cause and effect became for him the basic faith that he applies wherever anything happens . . . it is an atavism of the most ancient origin.[32]

In the same way that primitive man demanded gratification from his immediate family or from his own community and subjected them to abuse when
they failed to please his slightest whims, so he postulated that there was, likewise, a *higher* cause beyond these *natural* events, some *cause* behind these
natural *effects*, these terrifying spectacles of nature—volcanic eruptions and
earth-rending quakes, frightfully destructive hurricanes and ravaging floods,
lightning-generated firestorms, uncontrollable outbursts of disease and
plague—in short, some cause or intention that *also*, like man himself, seemed
to demand a kind of gratification or appeasement, a particular duty or obligation, some praise or pleasure from mankind, and, it should be added, at mankind's expense. Primitive peoples thus initially invented the divine and
continued to live in fear of its wrath. By analogy, the primitive ancestor projected his own rancorous spirit upon the whole of nature and supposed that
there was a far more powerful agent who exercised a similarly perverse will
upon the world at large and upon humanity in particular. Not only, then, is
there held to be a god, but it is a god whose motives and intentions dramatically
reflect man's own weak and impotent psyche: a god who demands obeisance,
fear, and capitulation—or, as Judaism and Christianity will say, a jealous god, a
vengeful god.

> The Christian presupposes a powerful, overpowering being who enjoys revenge.
> His power is so great that nobody could possibly harm him, except for his honor.
> Every sin is a slight to his honor, a *crimen laesae majestatis divinae*—and no
> more. Contrition, degradation, rolling in the dust—all this is the first and last
> condition of his grace: in sum, the restoration of his divine honor. Whether the
> sin has done any other harm, whether it has set in motion some profound calam-
> ity that will grow and seize one person after another like a disease and strangle
> them—this honor-craving Oriental in heaven could not care less! Sin is an offense
> against him, not against humanity. Those who are granted his grace are also
> granted this carelessness regarding the natural consequences of sin. God and
> humanity are separated so completely that a sin against humanity is really un-
> thinkable: every deed is to be considered *solely with respect to its supernatural
> consequences*, without regard for its natural consequences.[33]

God, who is invented *by* man, thus appears (through retrospective inference, Nietzsche would say) as the very cause and ordering principle of natural
existence.[34] Moreover, a god so conceived demands a particular course of action
and behavior from his subjects, in accordance with his purposefully crafted
universe. This is the origin of what Western religion and philosophy will call
natural law, the order and rule within the design of God's universe. In further

agreement with human pride, Nietzsche notes, it is supposed, in Europe and the West at least, that the universe is rational, logical, because this trait reflects the highest capacity of human nature. It is this human nature, or self, that is now *projected to godhead*: man differs from the brutes, the "lesser" animals, in that he possesses speech, reason, and logic. That is, mankind displays its very essence—rationality—in its thoughts and actions. Cherishing this distinctive possession of rationality out of overweening pride, because, after all, it is the only property that truly elevates humanity above the beasts, mankind then projects it onto the divine. With this projection, God henceforth becomes understood as the *source* of rationality, the overbounding source of rational order—as is manifest in turn, throughout the created world. The ordered seasons, the regular growth of plants and animals, the ordered movements of the heavenly spheres themselves, all have been traditional testimony to a universe of divine, rational creation.[35]

According to the traditional account, people have come to understand themselves as products of this grand creation. For millennia of Western thought, the rational individual occupied a unique and privileged place in what Arthur Lovejoy has termed "the great chain of being"—a rationally ordered universe that extends from the godhead and the angelic natures down to the lowliest organism, down to the dust itself. By the same token, mankind is also subject to an absolute *morality*, a system of absolute commandments that are promulgated by the creator god. The authority of this divine lawgiver is absolute, and so is its extent. As payment, as compensation, for our dutiful travail of obedience to the divinely ordained moral law, it is supposed, or at least hoped, that we will be rewarded with an afterlife—an eternal life in heaven—in this *otherworldly* region we only get intimations of in our dreams, the one area *outside* of life, where our impoverished wishes and hopes are to be fulfilled, once and for all, where our tedium with *this* human life of suffering will be miraculously relieved and our sore afflictions remedied. In this sense, the afterlife, as conceived in the religions of the West, serves as a longed-for escape *from* pain and dissatisfaction, a desperate flight from this world. The afterworld, the otherworld—heaven itself—thus stands as an anesthetic balm of Gilead for our all-too-real existence in this world.

After this whole progression of the argument, Nietzsche goes one step further to point out the moment of greatest deceit: like the civil servant or the corporate executive who attains recognition and self-respect according to his position in the managerial hierarchy, our own personal existence *now*, for the *first time*, is understood to be objectively meaningful.[36] We now *belong* to the

well-ordered universe and become what we are, who we are, precisely in function of the divine order. *We* are rational because *he* is. We properly and religiously guide ourselves by universal, rational principles. Our destructive
passions are guided and channeled by our so-called "higher faculties," and all
this reflects and enhances the glory that is the divine.[37]

But more and more, the whole system of religious conviction and practice
evolves into habit and passive belief in the system. This order of universal
purpose and meaning has, for millennia, been so thoroughly invested into our
very psyches and societies that personal understanding, self-respect, and esteem become wholly dependent upon the explanations of religion or, what for
Nietzsche is the same thing, frightened superstition. We continually crave that
our existence be rendered objectively meaningful and morally justified by the
Almighty—that it be reaffirmed and approved time and again—but, for Nietzsche, when *God dies* and a *secular* age begins, our long-held religious beliefs
and the needs that have been so deeply formed by those beliefs will *still* have
to be fulfilled and reaffirmed. For a secular age, however, such fulfillment will
be henceforth performed through *another* agency, whether this be politics,
science, moral causes, or something else in turn.

Given the history and provenance of this entire epoch, Nietzsche effectively
poses the subsequent questions: "Why maintain *this* system? Why not another?"[38] Perhaps we should experiment with an infinitude of possible systems
to find a morality that does not inculcate shame, guilt, impotence, fear, and
superstition in its adherents—not to speak of suppressed rage and boundless
greed. Aren't all the conflicting moralities, not only within the traditions of the
West but throughout history and worldwide, themselves readily *explained* by
observation, by hypothesis and empirical verification? Perhaps the ancient
Greek religious poet Hesiod simply *drank* too much and merely conjured up
the Olympian gods. Perhaps Abraham and St. Paul were themselves victimized
early on in life, bereft of love and instruction—stranger things have been
known to happen. Can't we easily see how the ideals of a society are themselves
generated from its work habits, its expectations, anticipations, and dreams?[39]
Isn't the Viking Valhalla different from the Elysian Fields of Greek bucolic
poets? Isn't the corporate banker's god different from that of the Central
European peasant, or of mountain tribesmen in Persia, or of the Eritrean
mystic?

Nietzsche's response to these issues is relatively succinct. By inventing—by
constructing—this world of God's design and rational order, mankind has quite
simply made two mistakes: First, overvaluing his own worth and projecting this

to the status of creative godhead, and second, taking his own thought too seriously, overvaluing his own rationality. Nature, therefore, becomes fixed on the model of man himself: it becomes *anthropomorphized*, cast in the form of man—and rationalized. In truth, it is quite independent of man (and of God) and indifferent to any human order. Mankind *imputes* purpose and causality to something that is inherently *indifferent* to reason, morality, or motivation. He imputes unity and order when in fact there is only relative chaos and complete lack of rationality. As Nietzsche would say at the very beginning of his 1873 essay, "On Truth and Lie in an Extra-Moral Sense,"

> In some remote corner of the universe, poured out and glittering in innumerable solar systems, there once was a star on which clever animals invented knowledge. That was the haughtiest and most mendacious minute of "world history," yet only a minute. After nature had drawn a few breaths the star grew cold, and the clever animals had to die. . . . There is nothing in nature so despicable or insignificant that it cannot be blown up like a bag by the slightest breath of this power of [human] knowledge; and just as every porter wants an admirer, the proudest human being, the philosopher, thinks that he sees the eyes of the universe telescopically focused from all sides on his actions and thoughts.[40]

These are fundamental errors for Nietzsche. But, at the same time, they are necessary errors, necessary illusions. They are human abstractions or fictions that are nonetheless useful for life: we impute concepts such as strict causality, moral purposiveness, rational order, and logical unity when there are none. Across the teeming profusion of particulate and subparticulate activity, we very grossly impute the fictions of unity, enduring substance, and names that point to a supposedly identical thing. In fact, there is largely confusion and difference.[41]

Our identifying, unifying, and expressing a *verbal* similarity are only a convenient fiction imposed from without, and we do this out of biological necessity: we *need* to describe, categorize, and identify if we are to find and cultivate food, exchange information, and provide for the necessities of human life. It is the necessary function of the intellect to lie, and therefore to abstract, generalize, idealize, conceptualize. The whole conceptual order, the whole religious order, the whole conventional moral, ethical, and religious, not to mention philosophical, order is precisely a fabric of lies. What is important is not so much the truth of these concepts, but rather, the effects and beliefs that are engendered by them. Truth is a construction, an arbitrary fiction, that is agreed upon and valued, as long as it remains plausible and necessary for the continuance of life. There could be better ways.

THE GAY SCIENCE: THE DEATH OF GOD

Doubtless, the most striking theme introduced by *The Gay Science* is what Nietzsche termed "the Death of God." That, and its purported consequences, best serve to open up the broad concerns of the present work. Let us first attend to the "event" of God's death, as Nietzsche formulates it in paragraph 125, surely one of the most dramatic passages in his entire corpus:

Have you ever heard of that madman who lit a lantern in the bright morning hours, ran to the market place and cried incessantly: "I seek God! I seek God!"[42]—As many of those who did not believe in God were standing around just then, he provoked much laughter. Has he got lost? asked one. Did he lose his way like a child? asked another. Or is he hiding? Is he afraid of us? Has he gone on a voyage? emigrated?—Thus they yelled and laughed.

The madman jumped into their midst and pierced them with his eyes. "Whither is God?" he cried; "I will tell you. *We have killed him*—you and I. All of us are his murderers. But how did we do this? How could we drink up the sea? Who gave us the sponge to wipe away the entire horizon? What were we doing when we unchained this earth from its sun? Whither is it moving now? Whither are we moving? Away from all suns? Are we not plunging continually? Backward, sideward, forward, in all directions? Is there still any up or down? Are we not straying as through an infinite nothing? Do we not feel the breath of empty space? Has it not become colder? Is not night continually closing in on us? Do we not need to light lanterns in the morning? Do we hear nothing as yet of the noise of the gravediggers who are burying God? Do we smell nothing as yet of the divine decomposition? Gods, too, decompose. God is dead. God remains dead. And we have killed him.

"How shall we comfort ourselves, the murderers of all murderers? What was the holiest and mightiest of all that the world has yet owned has bled to death under our knives: who will wipe this blood off us? What water is there for us to clean ourselves? What festivals of atonement, what sacred games shall we have to invent? Is not the greatness of this deed too great for us? Must we ourselves not become gods simply to appear worthy of it? There has never been a greater deed; and whoever is born after us—for the sake of this deed he will belong to a higher history than all history hitherto."

Here the madman fell silent and looked again at his listeners; and they, too, were silent and stared at him in astonishment. At last he threw his lantern on the ground, and it broke into pieces and went out. "I have come too early," he said then; "my time is not yet. This tremendous event is still on its way, still wandering; it has not yet reached the ears of men. Lightning and thunder require time; the light of the stars requires time; deeds, though done, still require time to be seen and heard. This deed is still more distant from them than the most distant stars—*and yet they have done it themselves*."

It has been related further that on the same day the madman forced his way into several churches and there struck up his *requiem aeternam deo* [requiem for the eternal God]. Led out and called to account, he is said always to have replied nothing but: "What after all are these churches now if they are not the tombs and sepulchers of God?"[43]

An assertion of such magnitude requires at least the following clarification, in the form of a question: namely, "Who is this God?" Or, stated somewhat differently, we must first establish his divine provenance, his paternity, his origin and identity. Certainly, such a God is not merely the image or figural representation of a personally conceived deity—rendered particular by experience, faith, or doctrine. Rather, what Nietzsche is concerned with in this polemic is the God of the West, of Europe and Persia, of Rome and Athens. It is first of all the God of Being, of all that is real, all that exists: "I am He who am," the Old Testament tells us. Such a God is the creator, the source of Being and of all things. He is the first cause, the material cause, the efficient cause, the formal cause, and the final cause. This is what we have come to know as the God of Genesis.[44]

Yet such a God is also the God of *truth*, he is the neo-Platonic inspiration for St. John the Divine. In this sense, he speaks across the New Testament: "I am the *word*," the word made "flesh." Let us not be mistaken: the word in question, of course, is the *logos*, the philosophical pattern of rationality and intelligibility that theologians and philosophers, like St. Augustine, will find reflected and incarnated everywhere throughout the universe. To see nature in this fashion is literally to recognize the traces of God therein. Nature itself and human nature stand as the very signature and substance of his rational creation. It is precisely in this way that Western morality, philosophy, and theology are essentially united. The Judeo-Christian tradition repeats the founding doctrines of Plato and of Greek antiquity, and this is to be echoed at every period and from every thinker in philosophy and religion for the next two millennia—across Plotinus, Eriugena, Bonaventura, the medieval theologians to Descartes, Kant, Hegel, and right down to the present day. The study of nature and man is essentially one with that of religion. It is this totality which Martin Heidegger has called the Western tradition of ontotheology, that is, the study of being as such, of what is, or, metaphysics.[45]

The Good, the Beautiful, and the True for Plato and Greek philosophy become the Way, the Light, and the Truth for two thousand years of Western thought. The source of Being is also the source of value and truth. Our rational *concepts* ultimately find their true referent in the *mind* of God. *Being* finds its source in the *grace* of God, and *values* find their strict justification and vindication in the *will* of God.[46]

The *death* of God, then, does not just mean that a social or political revolution will simply choose to dispense with the organized practice of a particular religious faith. Rather, what is at stake—and this is why the malingerers and idlers in the marketplace do not fully comprehend the *magnitude* of God's death—is the rejection, the toppling, of metaphysics: the very demise of onto-theology. The event of God's death, therefore, signifies the passing away of religion, philosophy, and morality as we have come to know them—as we have come to know it—across the history of Western thought. What this passing away ultimately means for Nietzsche will have to be patiently assembled throughout the course of his various works. Here in *The Gay Science*, however, he says that the death of God is the "Lucifer-match," the spark that ignites the whole of our all-too-volatile tradition.

In view of Nietzsche's extraordinary assertion about the death of God, the subsequent question quickly ensues: namely, "how did God's death occur?" Even more perplexing, how is this death, even now, continuing its reverberation, its death-rattle or *rigor mortis*? Perhaps the image of a bloody murder is too strong and violent for this *deicide*. Elsewhere, Nietzsche suggests that, one day, God simply found himself locked out of the church, temple, and mosque. In this sense, we could say that God simply died of atrophy, that there was no longer felt to be a need for the old God.[47] His function as creator, confessor, balm, judge, and accountant was replaced by another agency, namely, by *science*, and by another faith—the faith and belief in an omnipotent *technology*. If fear and weakness generated the need for a God, for a divine alter ego, those original wellsprings are now far better gratified by something new, by something whose worth and efficacy are more easily demonstrable. The death of God in the narrower sense (i.e., the specifically theological and doxological office of the divine) is thus really an exchange, a substitution, of one belief system for another. The Judeo-Christian God eventually comes to be replaced by the new marvel of a universal scientific order of creation, production, and rationally consistent explanation—in which case, there is little need any more for the modern citizen to sacrifice the first-born child or to pull out his or her own hair in remonstration or atonement. Plagues and pests are more readily subdued by insecticides. Droughts and inundations are more easily calmed by dams and irrigation networks.

Not only does the rise of the new sciences, beginning with the Enlightenment, serve to kill the traditional God, but another, related, factor arises from within the development of Western theology itself to aid in this deicide. Nietzsche locates this second contributing factor to the death of God in the appearance of Martin Luther and the Protestant Reformation. What theological functions were previously performed by the Roman Catholic priest—the very real, psychological functions of confession and consolation, the absolution of sin and guilt—now become the superfluous trappings of an obsolete ecclesiastical hierarchy, due to Luther and the Reformation, and to figures such as John Calvin, John Knox, and Huldrych Zwingli.

> We Europeans confront a world of tremendous ruins. A few things are still towering, much looks decayed and uncanny. . . . The church is this city of destruction: we see the religious community of Christianity shaken to its lowest foundations; the faith in God has collapsed. . . . An edifice like Christianity that had been built so carefully over such a long period . . . naturally could not be destroyed all at once. All kinds of earthquakes had to shake it, all kinds of spirits that bore, dig, gnaw, and moisten have had to help. But what is strangest is this: Those who exerted themselves the most to preserve and conserve Christianity have become precisely its most efficient destroyers—the Germans.
>
> The Lutheran Reformation was, in its whole breadth, the indignation of simplicity against "multiplicity" or, to speak cautiously, a crude, ingenuous misunderstanding in which there is much that calls for forgiveness. One failed to understand the expression of a *triumphant* church and saw nothing but corruption. . . . Luther's . . . work, his will to restore that Roman work became, without his knowing or willing it, nothing but the beginning of a work of destruction. He unraveled, he tore up with honest wrath what the old spider had woven so carefully for such a long time. . . . He destroyed the concept of the "church" by throwing away the faith in the inspiration of the church councils; for the concept of the "church" retains its power only on condition that the inspiring spirit that founded the church still lives in it, builds in it, and continues to build its house. . . . Luther, having given the priest [sexual intercourse with] woman, had to *take* away from him auricular confession; that was right psychologically. With that development the Christian priest was, at bottom, abolished, for his most profound utility had always been that he was a holy ear, a silent well, a grave for secrets. "Everyone his own priest"—behind such formulas and their peasant cunning there was hidden in Luther the abysmal hatred against "the higher human being."[48]

All the practical and psychological functions of the priest thus became internalized under the Reformationist doctrine of a personal *conscience*: they became subject to one's *own* alter ego, which now answers *for itself*, which finds its spiritual strength within. Moral duty now becomes a function of the individual's personal thought and labor. The public spectacle of confession becomes internalized in the form of a private meditation; namely, the cultivation of a conscience through personal prayer and atonement.

Despite Nietzsche's personal distaste for Luther's "peasant revolt of the spirit," he nonetheless conceded that Luther's doctrine of a personal dialogue with the Divine—through personal prayer and atonement—was a stroke of unexampled genius. For, after all, it was the individual and the value of his or her own thought and labor that was for centuries suppressed. Luther saw that it was only under the impersonal office of an ecclesiastical institution that the church was able to impose itself as mediator, interpreter, judge, and foremost, spiritual authority. As an impersonal institution, it was responsible to no one save itself. By its own office of authority, any attempt to question theological orthodoxy was seen not as a simple difference of opinion or belief, of heterodoxy, but rather as heresy. Let us not forget that one prohibition of the Old Testament: "Thou shalt not eat of the tree of knowledge." That kind of knowledge or wisdom (Latin *scientia*) is not joyous; it will reap the whirlwinds of pain, suffering, divine wrath, and death.

The wind had nonetheless shifted by the time of the New Testament. It then blew from Athens: "*Know the truth* and the truth shall make you *free*." This is the God of Plato, the God who demands inspection and answers, for he is the source of all truth. Nietzsche asserts that *this* doctrine of seeking the *truth*, which has both moral and metaphysical dimensions of enormous proportions, was a mistake. In it lay the seeds of God's own death, a death which first becomes evident, we saw, in the rise of the New Sciences and in the Protestant Reformation. As Nietzsche would remark:

> The most fateful act of two thousand years of discipline for truth . . . in the end forbids itself the *lie* in faith in God. You see what it was that really triumphed over the Christian god: Christian morality itself, the concept of truthfulness that was understood ever more rigorously, the father confessor's refinement of the Christian conscience, translated and sublimated into a scientific conscience, into intellectual cleanliness at any price.[49]

The tension between authority and knowledge, belief and truth, or revelation and reason had, of course, been developing ever since the early church began. The problem was essentially that God is held to be the source of universal intelligibility, but he himself is *unknowable*, inscrutable. To know the world and to understand its divinely wrought order, one must first pass by the mediation of faith and belief. The how and why of things, the explanation of the meaning and purpose of nature, had thus traditionally been the exclusive province of theology.[50] Forced to explain the irrational and divine elements of the rational universe, medieval theologians such as St. Thomas Aquinas and Moses Maimonides attempted to give an account of the divine nature itself, which would ideally clarify matters—by means of *analogy*. To know the world completely we must first know God: precisely, because God is the world's rationally creative source and ordering principle of truth. But we can only know God analogically. How, then, is this analogical knowledge of God at all possible?

Aquinas formulates the analogy in the following way:

(1)		(2)
man	:	God
his products	:	his products (i.e., creation, the world)

Based on the causal "model" of the "craftsman," this is an analogy that is itself composed of two relations. It is called a four-termed analogy, or the analogy of proper proportionality, and it seeks to express a relation between relation (1) and relation (2).[51] The real problem, of course, is that we cannot know relation (2) until we know the principal term (God) that is needed to construct the relation in the first place. Analogy, in short, gets us nowhere. It only appeared to work on the assumption that the four items mentioned in the analogy belonged to the same order, the order of continuous magnitude (as Euclid used the analogy in book 2 of his *Elements*). But this is precisely the difficulty to be resolved: the relation of the finite to the infinite is not continuous; the two orders are different in kind, so the relation cannot be finitely fixed. The infinite term, God, cannot be simply extrapolated from the other three finite terms, since, by definition, the infinite—whatever it is—is precisely that which *transcends* the finite.

What fatally compromises any attempt to know the divine nature is that to know God is to reduce him to the level of human understanding and finitude. To know God is, in this sense, to kill him. In fact, it was this classic medieval debate, between realism (the *via affirmativa*: one can have a positive knowledge of God) and nominalism (the *via negativa*: one can only have a negative understanding—i.e., only in name), which generated the unsuccessful attempt at a middle way, or an analogical understanding (the *via analogia*), in the first place, namely, the possibility of an indirect knowledge of the divine nature.

Hopelessly blocked by these mutually exclusive positions, the historical figure who resolves the impasse of analogy—of direct and indirect knowledge of God—is also the figure who ushers in the humanism of the Renaissance, the shift from a God-centered universe to one that is man-centered. This figure is the fifteenth-century mystic Nicholas of Cusa.[52] Cusa (or Cusanos) reasoned in a somewhat negative way in his work of 1440, *Learned Ignorance*: if God is what exceeds our knowledge, then it is sufficient for us to apprehend the greatest possible extent of our own finite, human knowledge. Once we reach the frontier of our own, positive human knowledge, we will have, by definition, attained the *delimitation* of God. Or, as Voltaire well knew, to be at the French frontier is, at the same time, to see Switzerland. Of dramatic importance here is that the general focus of intellectual concern is, for once, directed away from the attempt to grasp the divine nature as such and is turned toward an understanding of the finite domain of human nature and human experience. What becomes important for Cusanos and for the whole of the subsequent period of Renaissance humanism, then, is human thought (*scientia*) and humanity's productive labor, its human creativity (*techné*). These two human formations, *science* and *technology*, effectively seal God's coffin.

Nicholas of Cusa opens the breach: man now becomes "man the maker"—*homo faber*—for Marsilio Ficino and the Italian Renaissance, man "the maker of politics and nations" for Niccolò Machiavelli, man "the master and possessor of nature" for Francis Bacon, René Descartes, Isaac Newton, and for a modern age. For Nietzsche, quite simply, the god of traditional theology is dead because he is useless, superfluous. He has been displaced by the products of man's own knowledge, by science and technology. Moreover, what he was can now be explained by this new science, by the universal mathematics and mechanics of Descartes and the Enlightenment, and ultimately, by Nietzsche himself: God was a fiction all along, a psychological construct and fabrication.[53] Useless and a fiction, he is left to decay—for, as Nietzsche remarked, "even Gods decompose."

CONSEQUENCES OF THE DEATH OF GOD

What does Nietzsche recognize as the consequences of God's death? Initially, we can enumerate at least four—and here we see the wider meaning Nietzsche ascribes to this event. Certainly, the *first effect of God's death is to remove the universal foundations of morality*. A dead God no longer has the power and authority to determine values. There is no longer an absolute or

transcendent ground for ethics and morality, since there is no ground of authority or justification beyond the merely human actions and habits of those
who live. All of which is to say that morality enters into history and that its
claims are strictly conditioned by that history. Religion, ethics, and morality are
merely historical and relative codes for organizing, regulating, and determining
human activity. They are evanescent configurations of a society, a culture,
which vary according to time and place. No longer, then, can one point beyond
life to determine the value of life. Likewise, there can no longer be any universal and absolute moral precepts, maxims, or laws, once the human and natural
orders are understood to be essentially historical. In a striking passage, Nietzsche remarks, "How much must collapse now that this faith has been undermined, because it was built upon this faith, propped up by it, grown into it; for
example, the whole of our European morality."[54]

A second and immediate effect is that we will continue to live under the
shadow of the dead God, we will continue to display his raiments and trappings
for some time. There will begin an age of metaphysical nostalgia that will last
for hundreds of years, a period where we shall be carried along by the mere
inertia and habit of theology and metaphysics. Thus, what powers were formerly granted to the godhead are now given over to the unbounded belief in
science. Indeed, one often speaks about the "religiosity" of scientism and the
"messianic" appeal of modern technological growth and progress. Nietzsche
even remarks about the "evangelical" character of nihilism and positivism, the
patent rejection of and opposite to Western ontotheology. Even if the Western tradition has generated and sustained a system of artificial needs and beliefs, an articulated project of weakness, to Nietzsche's mind, it is nonetheless
a system of such comprehensiveness and persistence that it continues to exercise its authority at a distance, even as the secular age has lost faith in the
foundational principles of faith.

A third consequence of God's death is that we enter an age of ambiguity
and transition, characterized precisely by that nostalgia for the earlier age. He
calls it an impending age of "breakdown, destruction, ruin, and cataclysm."
God's death, we remember, is called the greatest, the most momentous event
in history, yet one whose reverberations are just now beginning to be felt: "This
tremendous event is still on its way, still wandering; it has not yet reached
the ears of men. Lightning and thunder require time." Nietzsche goes on to
observe:

> Even we born guessers of riddles who are, as it were, waiting on the mountains,
> posted between today and tomorrow, stretched in the contradiction between

today and tomorrow, we firstlings and premature births of the coming century, to whom the shadows that must soon envelop Europe really *should* have appeared by now—why is it that even we look forward to the approaching gloom without any real sense of involvement and above all without any worry and fear for *ourselves*? Are we perhaps still too much under the impression of the *initial consequences* of this event—and these initial consequences, the consequences for *ourselves*, are quite the opposite of what one might perhaps expect: They are not at all sad and gloomy but rather like a new and scarcely describable kind of light, happiness, relief, exhilaration, encouragement, dawn. Indeed, we philosophers and "free spirits" feel, when we hear the news that "the old god is dead," as if a new dawn shone on us; our heart overflows with gratitude, amazement, premonitions, expectation. At long last the horizon appears free to us again, even if it should not be bright; at long last our ships may venture out again, venture out to face any danger; all the daring of the lover of knowledge is permitted again; the sea, *our* sea, lies open again; perhaps there has never yet been such an "open sea."[56]

The title of the section just quoted—"The Meaning of Our Cheerfulness"—is itself crucial to understanding the importance the event of God's death will have for Nietzsche and for his own doctrine of a "gay science," a "joyful wisdom." The sea, in any case, is now opened: boundless and infinite. It is upon this open sea of an infinite future that we, of an ambiguous age, are to wander. Like young Oedipus, we have each killed our father and we are condemned to leave our father's home:

> We who are homeless.—Among Europeans today there is no lack of those who are entitled to call themselves homeless in a distinctive and honorable sense; it is to them that I especially commend my secret wisdom and *gaya scienza*. For their fate is hard, their hopes are uncertain; it is quite a feat to devise some comfort for them—but to what avail? We children of the future, how *could* we be at home in this today? We feel disfavor for all ideals that might lead one to feel at home even in this fragile, broken time of transition; as for its "realities," we do not believe that they will *last*. The ice that still supports people today has become very thin; the wind that brings the thaw is blowing; we ourselves who are homeless constitute a force that breaks open ice and all other too thin "realities." We "conserve" nothing; neither do we want to return to any past periods.[57]

To answer the question posed by Schopenhauer (the philosopher who perhaps most influenced Nietzsche in his early years), the question that must now be asked—"Has existence, then, any significance at all, any meaning whatsoever?"—Nietzsche responds that the fourth consequence of God's death is the *recognition of man's birth*. Like Cusanos, without God's support, we become divine. We now become the responsible bearers of world and history. Our existence will embrace this whole, and no other, world; it will invoke no sanction or salvation outside the world. For Nietzsche, we shall embrace the thought of the "eternal return" and this will be our newly found significance, a significance that will transfigure reality, humanity, and history as we now know them. Indeed, this shall be our "gay science."

OVERCOMING AND AFFIRMATION

Let us briefly summarize our reading of *The Gay Science*. We recall that it is one of Nietzsche's most central works—he called it his "most medial [central] work"—since it contains, in varying degrees of explicitness, almost all of his major philosophical themes, his most celebrated teachings: the death of God, the eternal return, the will to power, and his general critique of morality.

We initially specified the nature of that God, which Nietzsche alleges to have died: First, He is, or was, the object of conventional worship in the West. But second, and perhaps more importantly, such an eminent divine was also the God of Being and of Truth (i.e., the god of traditional metaphysics). We made the comparison between the god of Plato and that of the Judeo-Christian tradition and found them to be essentially the same. The Platonic Unity, the supraessential One, of the Good, the Beautiful, and the True, this is also the Way, the Light, and the Truth for two millennia of Christendom. Specifically, the creative God of being is also the source of all value and truth. For the tradition, all concepts find their highest referent in the mind of God, all being is created by the grace of God, and all value finds its origin in the will of God. The realms of being, truth, and value are thus fundamentally united for our tradition, and this unity, which is our tradition, can be summarily characterized by the term *ontotheology*.

We also saw that the death, the passing, of this God was explained by the development of two historical trends, two historical events: the rise of science and technology, beginning with Renaissance humanism and extending throughout the Enlightenment; and the Protestant Reformation. It was the latter that replaced the mediating authority of the priest, the church's ecclesiastical hierarchy, with the doctrine of an internalized conscience (i.e., a moral and intellectual self-responsibility exercised by the individual). In short, the Enlightenment and the Reformation present us with the historical beginnings of a rigorous personal autonomy, of personal and practical independence. God's death, of course, is hardly a simple affair: "After Budda was dead, his shadow was still shown for centuries in a cave—a tremendous, gruesome shadow. God is dead; but given the way of men, there may still be caves for thousands of years in which his shadow will be shown.—And we—we still have to vanquish his shadow."[58]

Following God's death, we become both his executors and legatees: it remains for us to administer this—his—divine estate. We already specified four consequences of this "greatest event in history": (1) Absolute morality has passed away. (2) We shall continue to live, inertially, under the effects of the old god. His agency will be transferred, however, to a variety of substitutes: science and technology, but also moral causes, political movements, and ideologies—all having an implicit eschatological or redemptive, salvational function to them. (3) We thereby enter an age of transition and ambiguity. Nothing is sure, nothing certain, although we may desperately—nostalgically—wish something were. (4) Finally, we become only gradually, progressively, aware of the effects of our newly found freedom—in such a way that the old ontotheological beliefs are seen to belong to a past era; the belief in a divine creation, the concept of rational causation, or the belief in any universal moral purpose and destiny now appears to be simply a vestige of the old faith, the leftover shards or shrouds that still linger about the coffin of the dead god. The world no longer appears as a purposive or rational order, nor does it plausibly reflect any aspect of the divine:

> The astral order in which we live is an exception; this order and the relative duration that depends on it have again made possible an exception of exceptions: the formation of the organic. The total character of the world, however, is in all eternity chaos—in the sense not of a lack of necessity but a lack of order, arrangement, form, beauty, wisdom, and whatever other names there are for our aesthetic anthropomorphisms . . . it is neither perfect, nor beautiful, nor noble, nor does it wish to become any of these things; it does not by any means strive to imitate man. None of our aesthetic and moral judgments apply to it.[59]

Nonetheless, even *we*, whom Nietzsche terms the "firstlings and premature births of the coming century," still remain bound by these old shrouds, by these lingering shadows on the walls of the Platonic cave. We still have to *overcome* the old morality—or at least this is what Nietzsche sees as our immediate task:

> If one would like to see our European morality for once as it looks from a distance, and if one would like to measure it against other moralities, past and fu-

ture, then one has to proceed like a wanderer who wants to know how high the towers in a town are: he *leaves* the town. "Thoughts about moral prejudices," if they are not meant to be prejudices about prejudices, presuppose a position *outside* morality, some point beyond good and evil to which one has to rise, climb, or fly—and in the present case at least a point beyond *our* good and evil, a freedom from everything "European," by which I mean the sum of the imperious value judgments that have become part of our flesh and blood.[60]

As a result of such an overcoming, such a distancing from all that which constitutes our present natures, Nietzsche envisions the emergence of a transformed human subject, one who would find joy in this new prospect:

> One could conceive of such a pleasure and power of self-determination, such a *freedom* of the will that the spirit would take leave of all faith and every wish for certainty, being practiced in maintaining himself on insubstantial ropes and possibilities and dancing even near abysses. Such a spirit would be the *free spirit* par excellence.[61]

But would this appeal be merely *one more* exhortation for us to act in a particular way? Is Nietzsche simply following the structural pattern in turn— filling in the "old God" dictates, the litany of the "thou shalt"—with the precepts, rules, and moral exhortations of the "new man"? Is Nietzsche one more preacher, yet another didactic at best or authority figure at worst? Is this text meant to convey, to inspire, an evangelism for the new Calvinist elect? Is he a zealot? Another Luther or Zwingli in atheist disguise?[62] And just as Zwingli's followers threw the Bavarian Catholic emissaries out of the Prague town hall window in 1618, shall Nietzsche himself be "defenestrated" in turn, only to await the next prophet of yet another new world order?[63]

In any case, Nietzsche surely does not pose himself as one more replacement prophet: this would be to profoundly misunderstand Nietzsche's own, that is, a positive, conception of morality. His expression is not meant to gratify the fearful weak—for he urges no desultory escape from pain, from life, into a fictional world of imaginary compensation. Nor is his work simply meant to be a palliative or tonic for the confused spirit of a troubled Europe. Why, then, does he write? To surround himself with followers? Clearly not!—and if he did, he failed dramatically. Indeed, Nietzsche continually chides his readers: he asks to be criticized, not to be adulated. Nietzsche knows full well that the large majority of followers and converts bear only the resentment and helplessness that ceaselessly search out the next command, the next dictate, the next authority to whom they would willingly submit.[64] While Nietzsche does tell us that he writes as a way of "getting rid of my thoughts,"[65] this may well be an act of grace, but it is certainly not to proselytize nor to institute a new sect—in the fashion of, for example, the French positivist, Auguste Comte. He writes only *for* those who have already become matured: "We are, in one word . . . *good Europeans*, the heirs of Europe, the rich, oversupplied, but also overly obligated heirs of thousands of years of European spirit. As such, we have also outgrown Christianity, and are averse to it—precisely because we have grown out of it."[66]

As for the others, those individuals who have not yet matured, Nietzsche remarks, "What can it matter to us with what tinsel the sick may use to cover up their weaknesses? . . . We know full well the hysterical little men and women who need this present religion and morality as a cloak and adornment."[67] To these people, Nietzsche implores, one simply must be generous. Believers, he says, invariably have a profound need to believe, a need that in one way or another, testifies strikingly to their own infirmity:

> Metaphysics is still needed by some; but so is that impetuous *demand for certainty* that today discharges itself among large numbers of people in a scientific-positivistic form. The demand that one *wants* by all means that something should be firm (while on account of the ardor of this demand one is easier and more negligent about the demonstration of this certainty)—this, too, is still the demand for a support, a prop, in short, that *instinct of weakness* which, to be sure, does not create religious, metaphysical systems, and convictions of all kinds but—conserves them.[68]

In a very concrete sense, therefore, Nietzsche seems to be writing for those people who don't need to read him. His audience is calculated to be precisely those for whom the old order is already beginning to gray, and for whom such beliefs are beginning to appear as empty shells, stale fodder, lifeless conventions, whether these beliefs be of God or are directed to his modern placeholders or surrogates. That modern science is such a preeminent surrogate for Nietzsche is clear:

> We see that science also rests on a faith; there simply is no science "without presuppositions." . . . From where would science then be permitted to take its unconditional faith or conviction on which it rests, that truth is more important than any other thing, including every other conviction? . . . But you will have gathered what I am driving at, namely, that it is still a *metaphysical faith* upon which our faith in science rests—that even we seekers after knowledge today, we godless anti-metaphysicians still take our fire, too, from the flame lit by a faith

that is thousands of years old, that Christian faith which was also the faith of Plato, that God is the truth, that truth is divine.—But what if this should become more and more incredible, if nothing should prove to be divine any more unless it were error, blindness, the lie—if God himself should prove to be our most enduring lie?[69]

According to Nietzsche's analysis, then, we are prepared to confront, to appraise, and to evaluate the entire tradition. For a modern secular age, there is no longer the universally felt need to be constrained by the ancient morality of God and religion, or by its more recent surrogates—totalizing ideologies of the left or right, extremist forms of nationalism, utopian economic or moral movements, ethnic and political irredentism, and so forth.[70] *incorporate surrounding territory* If the possibility of overcoming this tradition is prepared by our newfound maturity, then Nietzsche's own agency is, indeed, but emblematic; he is only the Orpheus, the "Lucifer match." With no divine impediments or pedigrees, mankind for the first time becomes "liberated" by the awareness of "this greatest event of history," the death of God.

Where does Nietzsche suggest we commence such an undertaking? Where does one situate oneself for such an impending transformation? With the admission of a godless universe, there is no longer an opposition between human and divine, between immanent and transcendent, not to speak of the opposition between what is absolute and what is historical or relative. In a strict sense, the death of God *is* the greatest event in history: it is the beginning of a resolutely autonomous human history as such. No longer are we but a dim reflection or a "moving image" of eternity. With the death of God, we have fallen into time.

The beginning of this undertaking already lies "beyond good and evil," beyond the ancient values and the purportedly "eternal" truths. Humanity, for Nietzsche, is no longer fixed as a divinely ordained measure in the whirlpool of things. The human individual is no longer bound by his supposed divinely given essence, that of being essentially rational. Rather, humanity is now to be conceived of in purely natural terms. The individual is to be situated—and understood—on the ontological plane of nature itself. But, realize that now, for Nietzsche, nature is itself undeified: it is not a created product that finds its source elsewhere. For a modern age, nature is both created and creative: it affects itself and continually transforms itself. It is no longer conceived simply as created—much less in the divine image of an eternal and rational God.

What, then, is nature? For Nietzsche, nature is at once chaos and necessity; it is profuse, luxuriant, teeming with excess and superabundance. Yet, nature *nature* is also cold, exact, bound to its sempiternal rhythms. The natural order continually transforms itself, neither increasing nor diminishing overall. It is, in this sense, a "finite" but "open" economy. All of which is to say that Nietzsche conceives nature to be fixed in its quantity of matter, energy, or force. In this respect, nature is finite. But, by the same token, this finite nature continues to operate dynamically in an infinite time. Thus a balance of sorts is attained; with neither absolute growth nor absolute diminution, nature both conserves its energy absolutely and expends it continually in the natural processes of organic and inorganic metamorphosis. Nature never simply *is*, in the sense that it could attain a final or terminal state of fixed *Being*. Rather, it continually "changes," it continually "evolves" or "becomes." What characterizes nature's economy, then, is a vicious Malthusian rigor. Its economy demands continual reinvestment and churning: quanta of forces fuse, stress, contract, and factor out to the next series and chain of impulses, into the next self-transformation, the next metamorphosis.

This is a kind of "order" if you will, and as natural beings, we are already part and parcel of it. In the absence of any transcendent order, nature for once becomes our human dominion. Upon God's death, we become naturalized citizens. We are no longer to be thought of as Gnostic exiles from an "otherworld," since there is no eternal country of origin or reprieve. There is no resting place of the soul, either, by the still waters, nor is there even an alien substance, or counter-substance, called the *soul*, that could somehow stand by impassively, unnaturally. It is in this sense Nietzsche would assert:

> The living being, moreover, is only a species of dead being, and a very rare species at that—let us be on our guard against thinking that the world eternally creates the *new*. Moreover, there are no eternally enduring substances: matter and soul are just such errors as the God of the Eleatics. But when shall we be at an end with our foresight and precaution? When will all these shadows of God cease to obscure us? When shall we be permitted to naturalize ourselves by means of the pure, newly discovered, newly redeemed nature?[71]

Just how is this naturalization possible, then, and how do we "wanderers" become *at home*, in nature, and what is the economics of this relation between man and nature, man and world? It is misleading to think that a traditional scientific account of nature would be called for at this point, precisely because "natural" science effectively *denatures* this relationship. It interprets nature, first of all, in the light of man, in light of purely subjective abstractions.[72] The traditional view thus gives a subjective, anthropomorphic account of nature and calls this *idealizing construction*, this series of *images*, "objective."[73]

For Nietzsche, there would be a double fault: science conceives nature in terms of our quite human abstractions, generalizations, and idealizations. Nature, therefore, is seen in the image of man—just as God was, according to Nietzsche's account of the origins of religion. Second, it is claimed by science that this construction has nothing to do with subjectivity, that it is in fact the exact opposite. The scientific account, we are told, is the paradigm of objectivity. Hence, the individual human subject is necessarily pitted against the world and occupies a place that could only be termed unnatural. At best, humanity seems to occupy and rule from some sort of refugee camp.

> The whole pose of "man *against* the world," man as a "world-negating" principle, of man as the measure of the value of things, as judge of the world who in the end places existence itself upon his scales and finds it wanting—the monstrous insipidity of this pose has finally come home to us and we are sick of it. We laugh as soon as we encounter the juxtaposition of "man *and* world," separated by the sublime presumption of the little word "and."[74]

In order to *become naturalized*, in Nietzsche's sense, the individual must embrace nature, ultimately, by an act of will. He must willingly accept the natural order on its own terms. For Nietzsche, this means we must *affirm* its chaos and necessity, and, by the same token, we must *destroy* the little "and" that *separates* us from nature. Destruction, here, consists in a denial of that tradition-bound intellectual and ideological filter, that smoke-screen mediation of all the images, beliefs, projections, fictions, and shadows that are the vestiges of the "dead God," of ontotheology. Specifically, this calls for a knowing denial of the "second nature" that, over the course of millennia, had become our "first nature."[75] This task would amount to a critical deconstruction of our tradition: it would consist in a critique of those historically derived notions of causality, unity, substance, identity, divisible time, rationality, logic, truth, soul, and God. As Nietzsche would recount, *this critique of the fundamental axioms of tradition* might well entail unsuspected consequences of dramatic proportions:

> This long plenitude and sequence of breakdown, destruction, ruin, and cataclysm that is now impending—who could guess enough of it today to be compelled to play the teacher and advance proclaimer of this monstrous logic of terror, the prophet of a gloom and an eclipse of the sun whose like has probably never yet occurred on earth?[76]

This work of critique or destruction, of course, is not merely the product of one thinker. Against the commanding edifice of metaphysics, we recall, "every sort of spirit which perforates, digs, gnaws, and moulders had to assist in the work of destruction."

We must also remember that this kind of critical "destruction," or "deconstruction," is not merely negative: its results are positive, that is, it rids us of two millennia of withered pieties, of sanctimonious shrouds. Its intentions are also positive—they are not motivated by the desire to avoid pain, to seek peace and repose in the anesthetic balm of religion, or in the smug confidence and arrogance of a self-consistent logic. Rather, the motivation to destroy comes about as a gift of fullness, an expression of overflowing power that wills to create, to quicken the pace, to invoke the future—as a further contest to create and to affirm a newly understood human order.[77]

Oddly enough, the kind of nature that Nietzsche affirms is remarkably similar to an ancient, archaic Greek conception, the pre-Homeric understanding, in which nature was symbolized by the two-headed ax of fertility: nature destroys, lays waste, but also harvests. The fields are made to lie fallow such that they may in turn nurture and produce. The reaper makes way for the new crop, the new generation. To affirm such a nature is to do so totally and unreservedly, to affirm its often unpleasant consequences for us, but also to commit ourselves to its splendor, to will that our human destinies be one with nature—with no escape, no flight from nature so conceived.

Nietzsche views the affirmation of nature, of natural existence (i.e., an entirely de-deified nature, wholly amoral, without any transcending purpose, direction, or end: an "innocent" nature) as nothing less than the prospect of an entirely new and different destiny for the whole of mankind—a destiny that is at once *terrifying* and *rich* with the prospect of an infinite future. Here is a future with no possibility of transcending nature, no possibility of any human reality other than that of the natural order itself. Nietzsche expresses this concept of naturalization by the *image* or *metaphor* of what he calls the "eternal return," an image that is both terrifying and liberating to the extent that it *infinitizes* humanity and makes it aware of its newly found infinitizing destiny:

> What, if some day or night a demon were to steal after you—into your loneliest loneliness and say to you, "This life as you now live it and have lived it, you will have to live once more and *innumerable times* more; and there will be nothing new in it, but every pain and every joy and every thought and sigh and everything unutterably small or great in your life will have to *return* to you, all in the same succession and sequence—even this spider and this moonlight between the trees, and even this moment and I myself. The eternal hourglass of existence is turned upside down again and again, and you with it, speck of dust."

Would you not throw yourself down and gnash your teeth and *curse* the demon who spoke thus? Or have you *once* experienced a tremendous moment when you would have answered him, "You are a *God*, and never have I heard anything more *divine*." *If* this thought *gained possession* of you, it would *change* you as you are or perhaps *crush* you. The question in each and every thing, "*Do you desire this*, once more and innumerable *times* more?" would lie upon your actions as the greatest weight. *Or how well disposed* would you have to become *to yourself and to life* [so as] to *crave nothing more fervently* than this ultimate, eternal, confirmation and seal?[78]

This first statement of the eternal return *appears* to be another evangelical invocation. It reawakens the call of Cusanos with astonishing *psychological* force. In effect, it demands the *conditional*: it asks us, "What if?" This is an appeal to our resoluteness and steadfastness, perhaps. But it also asks *us* to be ratified in the eternal cycle.[79] Not only would *our* lives be repeated to infinity, therefore, but the very cycle of past and future—from antediluvian eons to the final cataclysm—would be ceaselessly, interminably, relived. But second, and more importantly, if we grant the finite and open economics of this natural order, we also grant the untold myriad permutations this finite order, this finite system, could endure, and our present dust-speck existence would be taken as one micro-instant of one set of atomic arrangements. This would be a system of crypto-incarnations, of insemination and dissemination of our own subparticulate matter. Like Leibniz's celebrated little monads, we would reflect a universe at all times, we would literally inhabit an infinitude of worlds. We would find our homes deep under the waves that career and smash headlong into Portofino's cliffs—and we would indeed know their secret.

Would not the *fear* of a vengeful God and the guilt-inspiring reprobation from a host of priests disappear like a sweet aftertaste in the light of such a conception, to be buried—only to rise once again—and yet again pass away, disposed, metamorphosed by another wrinkle or fold in the crystalline vaults?

Not only would this eternal return be an incentive, a psychological affirmation to strengthen our human resolve, but it would itself be the highest expression of the will to *live*. It—the eternal return itself—would be the grandest, the most complete and total expression of the *will to power*.[80] Its very conception would bring us to humanity and history. Here, it is not so much a question of projecting ourselves onto the world from without, as if we, once again, were claiming hegemony over it. Rather, it is quite the reverse; it would rather be as if nature, world, history, and humanity *became us*, became transformed and included—introjected—into *our* history, as if *they* constituted precisely what *we* are! All this unfolds itself through us. We would become the heirs and possessors of this titanic dance, which would be the blood that courses through our veins to the Dionysian strains of this Joyful Wisdom. This Gay Science, which replaces the traditional doctrines of transcendence and fearful dependence with a teaching of total immanence and a newfound autonomy, would infuse us, humanity, with a transfigured vitality, an entirely new kind of emotion and feeling, one that would enable us to identify with, and thus celebrate, the entirety of natural existence:

> This is actually one aspect of this new feeling: Anyone who manages to experience the history of humanity as *his own history*, will feel in an enormously generalized way all the grief of an invalid who thinks of health, of an old man who thinks of the dreams of his youth, of a lover deprived of his beloved, of the martyr whose ideal is perishing, of the hero on the evening after a battle that has decided nothing but brought him wounds and the loss of his friend. But if one endured, if one *could* endure this immense sum of grief of all kinds while yet being the hero, who as the second day of battle breaks, welcomes the dawn and his fortune, being a person whose horizon encompasses thousands of years past and future, being the heir of all the nobility of all past spirit—an heir with a sense of obligation, the most aristocratic of old nobles and at the same time the first of a new nobility—the like of which no age has yet seen or dreamed of; if one could burden one's soul with all of this—the oldest, the newest, losses, hopes, conquests, and the victories of humanity; if one could finally contain all this in one soul and crowd it into a single feeling—this would surely have to result in a happiness that humanity has not known so far: the happiness of a god full of power and love, full of tears and laughter, a happiness that, like the sun in the evening continually bestows its inexhaustible riches, pouring them into the sea, feeling richest, as the sun does, only when even the poorest fisherman is still rowing with golden oars! This godlike feeling would then be called—humaneness.[81]

What, then, is this cosmic vitality that eternally repeats itself—that eternally recurs, and us with it and through it? What is this "will to power"? The will to power is the will to live, the pulsions of instinct and impulse, the continually transforming and transfiguring energy of excess and superabundance that constitutes the whole of organic and inorganic existence. Seen in this way, life—vitality itself—is not mere endurance, it is not merely a question of some will to persist, to strive for mere continuation, to hope to bear the next moment, to sustain the next fetid breath. Rather, it is to create, to build, to wreak havoc doing so, possibly, but to augment and ever increase itself, out of force, youth, energy, and will—to assemble and build, to ingest, and to *overcome again*, out of surfeit, abundance, and health. As Nietzsche expressed this dynamic and affirmative conception of life:

> The wish to preserve oneself is the symptom of a condition of distress, of a limitation of the really fundamental instinct of life which aims at *the expansion of power* and, wishing for that, frequently risks and even sacrifices self-preservation. . . . But a natural scientist should come out of his human nook; and in nature it is not conditions of distress that are *dominant* but overflow and squandering, even to the point of absurdity. The struggle for existence is only an *exception*, a temporary restriction of the will to life. The great and small struggle always revolves around superiority, around growth and expansion, around power—in accordance with the will to power which is the will of life.[52]

To embrace nature and history under the image (i.e., the metaphor or myth) of the "eternal return," therefore, is to identify one's very being with the "will to power." In the absence of the infinite God, we become the infinite creators of an infinitizing future. For Nietzsche, this is at once our natural inheritance and our historical imperative.

Each moment heralds an infinite future.

Each moment recurs—again and again—in an eternal festival of transience.
  Being is thereby stamped as becoming.

Each moment is thus a contraction of the infinite past into a discrete now, which augurs an unheard of destiny.

And it is the now, this now that must be lived and filled up, complete, replete, with life—in order that there be a subsequent now.

All this happens each and every moment.

③

THUS SPOKE ZARATHUSTRA

Nietzsche wrote *Thus Spoke Zarathustra* in several bursts of extreme activity over a period of some two years, from 1883–85. It was a book he would refer to, for the rest of his life, as his most important and most intense work. In an enthusiastic letter to Carl von Gersdorff, he remarked:

> My *Zarathustra*, which will be sent to you within a few weeks, may give you a hint of how high my will has soared. Don't be put off by the mythic style of the book: my entire philosophy is behind those homey and unusual words, and I have never been more serious. It is a beginning at self-disclosure—nothing more! I know perfectly well that there is no one alive who could write anything like *Zarathustra*.[1]

In the same vein, he told Peter Gast that "it is incredibly full of detail which, because it is drawn from what I've seen and suffered, only I can understand. Some pages seem to be almost *bleeding*."[2]

Doubtless, then, *Zarathustra* was an intensely *personal* work—and due in part to this, it is often enigmatic and extremely difficult to comprehend:

> At the moment, *Zarathustra*'s value is entirely personal. . . . For everyone else, it is obscure, mysterious, and ridiculous. Heinrich von Stein (a splendid example of a man, whose company has given me real pleasure) told me candidly that of said *Zarathustra*, he understood "twelve sentences and no more." I found that very comforting.[3]

If the very title of the work—*Thus Spoke Zarathustra: A Book for Everyone and No One*[4]—suggests a profound enigma, the specific themes Nietzsche engages are at least recognizable from the start: the dynamics of the human will, the death of God, the critique of traditional Christian morality, the will to power, the eternal return, and the overman (that higher form of humanity, envisaged by Nietzsche, which has not yet been attained). Nonetheless, despite the breadth and recognizability of these often-discussed topics, there remains a deeply personal, largely hidden stratum to *Zarathustra*, wherein Nietzsche reflectively engages his own most personal, philosophical, and emotional concerns. Foremost among these personally perplexing issues were the questions about the validity and practicality of his own philosophical task, his doubts about his own capacity to effectively communicate his ideas, the stress brought on by his continually failing personal health, and the disastrous state of his personal relations during this period. His break with Wagner was virtually complete by 1877, but the tragic affair with Lou Salomé, and its hysterical exploitation by Nietzsche's sister to humiliate Lou, resulted in Nietzsche's effective banishment from the Wagner circle at Bayreuth and a near total isolation from other German and Swiss academic and cultural groups at the time. Lou was just twenty-one years old and Nietzsche thirty-seven. She had come from St. Petersburg to study in Switzerland at the University of Zurich. Much influenced by Malwida von Meysenbug's writing, she made the latter's acquaintance in Rome in the early spring of 1882. Paul Rée also was in Rome at the time, and both he and Malwida wrote Nietzsche about the remarkably intelligent and beautiful Lou. Nietzsche responded to Rée's letter with enthusiasm: "Greet this Russian for me, if that has any purpose: I lust for this species of soul. Yes I shall now look forward to plunder, and with what I have in mind for the next ten years, I will need her. An entirely different chapter would be marriage—at the most, I could agree to a two-year marriage."[5]

Arriving in Rome from Messina, Nietzsche rested for a day—due to one of his frequently violent migraine headaches—and went to Malwida's apartment in the Villa Mattéi, only to learn that both Lou and Rée were visiting St. Peter's Basilica. Rushing to St. Peter's, and on first meeting Lou, Nietzsche was transfixed. His first remark to her was: "From which stars have we fallen to meet each other here?"[6] Within a matter of hours, he proposed marriage—abruptly and clumsily. Lou declined. In a second attempt, Nietzsche asked Rée to intervene on his behalf, to encourage—indeed, to broker—a positive response from Lou. But Rée, however, had also proposed to Lou by then and had been equally rebuffed.[7] Good sense and friendship prevailed, and, by late April, the three decided to travel north to Switzerland, together with Lou's mother, who acted as a companion and chaperone. They stopped off for several days at Lake Orta, in northern Italy, where, on May 5, Nietzsche and Lou were able to go off by themselves and spend an exceptionally beautiful spring day climbing the nearby Sacro Monte.[8] This seems to have been an emotionally transfiguring afternoon for Nietzsche, who would later refer to the afternoon they spent together as "the mystery of Sacro Monte."[9] Two weeks later, on May 13, the three visited Lucerne, where Nietzsche again unsuccessfully proposed marriage to Lou—this time at the foot of the Lion Monument in the Löwengarten. Just after this third refusal, and in a seeming spirit of conciliation, Nietzsche suggested that they visit a photographer's studio, where he posed himself and Rée pulling the arms of a goat-cart, driven by Lou, who was perched behind them, holding a whip entwined with flowers (see photo).

The next day, the trio visited Tribschen, where Nietzsche, according to Lou, broke down in tears from his reminiscences over his earlier visits there with

Lake Orta near Sacro Monte, where Nietzsche traveled with Lou Salomé and her mother in 1882. (Courtesy of Andrew Mitchell.)

Lou Salomé, Paul Rée, and Friedrich Nietzsche: Lucerne, May 1882. (Courtesy of Dorothee Pfeiffer, Lou Andreas-Salomé Archive, Gottingen.)

the Wagners: "For a long, long while, he sat silent on the banks of the lake and was deeply immersed in heavy memories; then, while drawing in the moist sand with his cane, he softly spoke of those times past. And when he looked up, he cried."[10] From the end of June through the end of August, Nietzsche was in Tautenburg, in Saxony, and on August 7, he was joined by Lou and his sister, both having just visited Wagner's production of *Parsifal* in Bayreuth (to which Nietzsche was not invited!). Lou and Nietzsche spent three weeks together, their relationship oscillating between profound intellectual discussions and emotionally intense, and often trying, periods of companionship. Nietzsche's passion for philosophy and his deep love for her—as an intimate partner and disciple—were again beginning to pale for Lou, and she became reclusive, "fleeing" into a bedridden illness for several days to avoid his emotionally charged overtures.[11] Ultimately, Lou preferred to see in Nietzsche more of a friend than an intimate relation, and, perhaps even more dispiriting, she felt that Nietzsche was trying to denigrate Rée for his own sexual advantage over her. Nonetheless, the three (Lou called them "the Trinity") had often discussed the possibility of studying the natural sciences together, ever since their meeting in Rome, and had considered living in Munich, Vienna, and finally Paris— hoping to share an amicable relationship of intellectual equality and independence. On this note, Lou left Tautenburg to visit Rée's family in Stibbe, in West Prussia, and Nietzsche returned to Naumburg. In Naumburg, he had a strong falling out with his family over the "propriety" of this relationship with Lou, Nietzsche's sister ever ready to cast aspersions on Lou,[12] which provoked Nietzsche's mother to exclaim that he was a curse upon his father's grave. Fleeing his mother's home, Nietzsche joined Lou and Rée for a final time in Leipzig, once again planning for the period of study in Paris. The reunion in Leipzig was cool, however, each party recognizing their growing emotional and intellectual differences. Lou and Rée found Nietzsche's emotionalism and philosophical passion somewhat difficult to bear and increasingly distanced from their own growing interests in science. Nietzsche likewise sensed an element of distrust and cynicism on their part, their diminished interest in his own philosophical projects, as well as a chilling emotional withdrawal. By mid-November, Nietzsche would return to Basel and then go south to Genoa. Lou and Rée went back to Rée's family home in Stibbe and then settled in Berlin. Nietzsche would never see them again.[13]

Communicating his state of mind at the time, Nietzsche wrote to Overbeck from Rapallo on Christmas Day 1882:

> This last *morsel of life* was the hardest I have yet had to chew, and it is still possible that I shall *choke* on it. I have suffered from the humiliating and tormenting memories of this summer as from a bout of madness. . . . It involves a tension between opposing passions which I cannot cope with. This is to say, I am exerting every ounce of my self-mastery; but I have lived in solitude too long . . . so that I am now being broken, as no other man could be, on the wheel of my own passions. If only I could sleep!—but the strongest doses of my sedative [opium] help me as little as my six to eight hours of daily walking. Unless I discover the alchemical trick of turning this—muck into gold, I am lost. . . . My lack of confidence is now immense—everything I hear makes me feel that people despise me.[14]

ZARATHUSTRA

Some five years after the initial publication of *Zarathustra*, in another work, entitled *Ecce Homo*, Nietzsche explained that he chose to invoke the name "Zarathustra" because Zarathustra—or as he is more commonly known through the Greek derivation of his name, "Zoroaster"[15]—was the first historical thinker to pronounce the doctrine of eternal return and the first to pronounce the dualistic teaching of good and evil as separate, metaphysically governing, world principles, which Zoroaster called "Ahura Mazda" and "Ahriman," the forces of light and of darkness, respectively. Zarathustra's (or Zoroaster's) original teaching concerned man's difficult passage through life, from evil to good, by way of individual works and deeds. This life-passage was symbolized by what he called the "Chin Vat bridge," which spanned the infinitely deep chasm of fire, of adversity, and ultimately led to the Zoroastrian heaven, the "Garô-nmânem." This is, of course, one aspect of the "tightrope" metaphor that first appears in section 3 of "Zarathustra's Prologue."

In the fourth chapter of his later text, *Ecce Homo*, the section entitled "Why I Am a Destiny," Nietzsche remarked,

> I have not been asked, as I should have been asked, what the name of Zarathustra means in *my* mouth, the mouth of the first immoralist: for what constitutes the tremendous historical uniqueness of that Persian is just the opposite of this. Zarathustra was the first to consider the fight between good and evil as the very wheel in the machinery of things: the transposition of morality into the metaphysical realm, as a force, cause, and end in itself, is *his* work. But this question itself is at bottom its own answer. Zarathustra created the most calamitous error, morality; consequently, he must also be the first to recognize it. Not only has he more experience in this matter, for a longer time, than any other thinker—after all, the whole of history is the refutation by experiment of the principle of the so-called "moral world order"—what is *more* important is that Zarathustra is more *truthful* than any other thinker. His doctrine, and his alone, posits truthfulness as the highest virtue; this means the opposite of the cowardice of the "idealist" who flees from reality; Zarathustra has more intestinal fortitude than all other thinkers taken together. To speak the truth and to shoot well with arrows, that is Persian virtue.—Am I understood?—*The self-overcoming of morality, out of truthfulness*; the self-overcoming of the moralist, into his opposite—into *me*—that is what the name of Zarathustra means in my mouth.[16]

We have already seen somewhat of an anticipation of this teaching in an earlier text, *The Gay Science*. There, we saw the self-overcoming of traditional

Christian faith out of one of its own components, namely, the New Testament veneration of truth:

> You see what it was that really triumphed over the Christian god: Christian moral- —
> ity itself, the concept of truthfulness that was understood ever more rigorously,
> the father confessor's refinement of the Christian conscience, translated and sub-
> limated into a scientific conscience, into intellectual cleanliness at any price.
> Looking at nature as if it were a proof of the goodness and governance of a god;
> interpreting history in honor of some divine reason, as a continual testimony of a
> moral world order and ultimate moral purposes; interpreting one's own experi-
> ences as pious people have long enough interpreted theirs, as if everything were
> providential, a hint, designed and ordained for the sake of the salvation of the
> soul—that is *all over* now, that has man's conscience *against* it, that is considered
> indecent and dishonest by every more refined conscience—mendaciousness,
> feminism, weakness, and cowardice. In this severity, if anywhere, we are *good*
> Europeans and heirs of Europe's longest and most courageous self-overcoming.[17]

ZARATHUSTRA'S OVERMAN

Nietzsche's Zarathustra teaches the doctrine of the "overman," the *Übermen-sch*: "*I teach you the overman*. Man is something that shall be overcome."[18] From the outset, however, Zarathustra himself seems to dramatize, if not em-body, the anticipated characteristics of the overman.[19] At least in appearance. Zarathustra is presented as a strikingly singular and unique figure. He appears as a sage, a wise man, whose speech is often oracular and prophetic in nature, immediately distinguishing him rhetorically from the many—often quite un-usual—figures he encounters. The nature of his epigrammatic speeches is often patterned on, and parodies, not only Zoroaster's pronouncements in the *Zend Avesta*, but even more particularly, the accounts of Jesus in the Gospels. Some-times his lofty reflections are suggestive of the Buddha or of a Hindu sage.[20] More often, however, the philosophical content and the poetic expressiveness of Zarathustra's discourses strikingly recall such pre-Socratic thinkers as Her-aclitus, Anaxagoras, and Empedocles, as well as the Roman poet and Epicurean philosopher Lucretius, all of whom Nietzsche had studied—and taught—extensively, during his tenure at the University of Basel. Finally, Zarathustra first strikes the reader as a figure of exceptional character, generosity, and inde-pendence: full of self-esteem and at once remote and isolated, yet again com-passionate, seeking to help with a missionary zeal.[21] But what the more general and programmatic characteristics of the overman as such are purported to be—as an ideal type, as an emblematic and visionary figure of the future—will have to be deferred somewhat until we can follow Nietzsche's own progressive elaboration of them.

What complicates the attempt to positively characterize such a figure as the overman, who is dramatically announced in section 3 of "Zarathustra's Prologue," is the fact that there can really be no "essential" property to *describe* as such, precisely because there is as yet no overman to be described—nor, finally, does the overman appear even once in the whole of *Zarathustra*. Thus, it is left to the reader to fill in what the "characteristics" of the overman might be.[22] This is one of many instances of Nietzsche's using the rhetorical trope of *aposiopesis* in his writings—that is, of employing the rhetorical device of silence, or indirection, in such a way that the *reader* is forced to draw a conclusion (in this case, about the nature of the overman), one that is itself unstated by the author, but that seems implied by contextual circumstances. What lends aposiopetic rhetoric its strength is that the reader or interlocutor feels he has come to his own conclusion—quite literally—in his own terms and in function of his own judgment, thereby personalizing his understanding of what the author may, or may not, have intended.[23] Effectively, this means that each reader tends to develop a quite idiosyncratic, interpretive view (or criticism) of the celebrated "overman." Compounding this strategic use of silence, what Nietzsche's overman might be is further concealed behind his depiction of Zarathustra (i.e., behind the traditionally recognized figure of Zoroaster) the prophet and teacher, who, in addition to his teachings, left as his personal legacy three children, each of whom it was said would be born in a series of millennia to come. Indeed, by the fourth part of *Zarathustra*, the overman is mentioned but once—"God died; now *we* want the overman to live"[24]—then dropped, in favor of finding "higher men" (*höheren Menschen*) who would serve as disciples, but who clearly have a host of all-too-human imperfections. Thus, Zarathustra awaits not the overman per se at the very end of the book, nor even the higher man, but rather his own "children."

The last significant discussion of the overman is in the third part, titled "On Old and New Tablets," where Zarathustra advances his view that the sum of good and evil, all value and meaning, is man's own creation: "He who creates . . . creates man's goal and gives the earth its meaning and future."[25] Zarathustra then equates this with individual and cultural self-overcoming: man is something that must be overcome—he is a bridge and no end. Thus Zoroaster's *heaven* is forfeited, but redemption can be attained—at the moment of "noon," when one redeems what is past in man and re-creates all "it was" with a "Thus I willed it!" Absent the overman, it remains to be seen even if Zarathustra is capable of affirming, much less acting upon, such an injunction.[26]

Basically, the overman does not exist, will not exist as such, as a terminal point. Rather than pose as a stylized model, as a conflation of historical individuals, or even as an "ideal type," as most commentators conventionally argue—if that term means anything at all[27]—the notion of the overman signifies humanity's capacity for achieving a self-transformation of itself and a fully truthful understanding of the human condition. This can come about, Nietzsche argues, only when humanity is freed from the bitterness, resentment, guilt, and shame brought on by traditional moral doctrine ("the spirit of gravity"), and when it is liberated from the clouds of metaphysical deceit and illusion that obscure the symbol of truth itself (i.e., the sun, at the moment of noon, when there are no more vestigal shadows of the old God to be seen, when the sylvan Pan is said to be resting). This will be the fundamental opposition governing the character development of Zarathustra himself and his attempt to articulate the vision of the overman: the opposition between morality and truth—as it concerns the very conduct and significance of one's life.

ZARATHUSTRA'S TASK: THE ETERNAL RETURN

Thematically, we must start by examining Zarathustra's *task*; or, rather, by examining what our task is as interpreters of his teaching, and how we are to grasp the crucial notions of will, will to power, and ultimately, the eternal return. It should be noted at the outset that while these notions are closely interrelated or nested, and that our appreciation of them can help us to understand Zarathustra's task (and how that in turn can shed light on what Nietzsche ultimately means by the overman), we must be cautious in ascribing a system to Nietzsche's teaching. Literally, there *is* none. What can be said, however, is that these notions are essentially metaphorical, and as such, they are diffracted throughout his work. What must also be kept in mind is that the narrative complexity of *Zarathustra* makes conceptual clarification of these central notions extremely difficult. The text is at once poetic, overly rhetorical, and hortatory. By the same token it is a *dialogue* between an unnamed narrator, who sometimes engages Zarathustra himself, but principally, it is a dialogue between Zarathustra—a character who is himself constructed by Nietzsche to be both highly personal and historically allusive—and other figures, who often advance or represent positions that are more suggestive than precisely determined in any conventional conceptual sense.

The dialogue form is intended to engage the reader on a variety of levels as well, due to the richness of the stylistic elements it affords. Unlike a straightforward exposition, the dramatic dialogue personalizes the concerns of the author by lending to them a situational context, which is often highly emotionally charged, and this engages the reader in ways that alternately suggest and provoke the ordinary and extraordinary responses one takes in real life, concerning everything of *value*. It is precisely this value dimension of the individual's life—that which lends personal, social, ethical, moral, and aesthetic significance to human existence itself—that Nietzsche wishes to fully engage in *Zarathustra*. Finally, it is the dialogue form (modeled on the traditional narratives of Zoroaster, Jesus, Empedocles, Buddha, and Plato and borrowing from the rich rhetorical tradition of classical Greek tragedy, as well as from the German literary tradition, stemming from Luther's oratorical genius, through the dramatic prose of Goethe, Schiller, and Hölderlin) that would best express such a *practical philosophy* concerning the conduct of one's life. Life's values may well be engaged critically and theoretically in the course of the dialogue's narrative—and there is no shortage of such explicit discussion in *Zarathustra*—but their dramatic enactment or performance, by the figure of Zarathustra, has an immediacy and concreteness that draws upon our own deepest intellectual and affective resources as well. Things have to make sense, but happiness or joy alone lends individual existence its highest value. This simply cannot be taught, dictated, or universally legislated. It must be found personally, and from within, in consequence of a disciplined, well-disposed *will* that acts out of itself for its own pleasure and well-being.

In *Zarathustra*, the will is most often conceived of in extremely vital and dynamic terms: as a general strength of character, as the force of one's intellect and instinct, the courage to confront adversity and to overcome resistance and obstacles to one's considered objectives. Psychologically considered, then, the dynamic personalization of will is more broadly founded on what Nietzsche considers the dynamics of the natural world to be, namely, the ever-changing confrontation and exchange of energy and force—what he termed the "will to power." Perhaps Nietzsche's most concise account of the will to power is his remark in *Beyond Good and Evil*:

 Suppose . . . we succeeded in explaining our entire instinctive life as the development and ramification of *one* basic form of the will—namely, of the will to power, as *my* proposition has it; suppose all organic functions could be traced back to this will to power and one could also find in it the solution of the problem of procreation and nourishment—it is *one* problem—then one would have gained the right to determine all efficient force univocally as—*will to power*. The world viewed from inside, the world defined and determined according to its "intelligible character"—it would be "will to power" and nothing else.[28]

By conceiving the totality of natural existence as an enormous interplay of dynamic and differential forces—understood as a generalized physical doctrine—Nietzsche can advance an account of material reality as an ever-changing aggregation and reaggregation of force or energy. Thus, as a physical doctrine, one can say that "everything" is will to power, at every scale of natural and human existence: the scale and, indeed, the form of things, here being defined by the relative differences between aggregations or "congeries" of force—from the subatomic to the geologic scale of existence. Viewed at a distance, and from a *temporal* perspective, Nietzsche speaks of the *sum* of natural forces as the "eternal return." That is, given the finite sum of forces—constantly differentiating themselves into greater or lesser particular groupings of force—and an infinite time, the constituent forces will recur, or return, constantly, in subsequent aggregations. Thus, and this is one of the difficulties of interpreting what Nietzsche ultimately means by the "eternal return," "everything" returns, again and again. Hence the eternal return is an infinite repetition of "the same."

Oddly, what one understands by "the same" will govern one's interpretation of the "eternal return." On the one hand, the eternal return can be viewed—and has most often been viewed—as a historical or, even cosmological, *cycle* of repetition of the same events. At its most literal level, this means that every event, every individual subject, every historical age and geological epoch will be repeated, endlessly—granted the assumption of a finite quantum of force or matter, and predicated on the further assumptions of (1) the conservation of energy, and (2) an infinite time. On the other hand, and at an opposite extreme, one could also view the eternal return *not* as a *repetition* of the identical events, or of individual subjects, but rather as an eternal flux or interaction of the same dynamic forces—all being constantly reaggregated in an infinity of possible permutations of nature, and all being governed by the laws of nature, generally speaking. In the latter case, everything would indeed return or recur, but not as the same "thing"—rather, as the same constitutive field of forces, through which the multiplicities of forces would indeed form new "things," but not the "same" things. In this view, the same totality of force, through its

constantly differential interactions, remains, but not in the same particular series or sequence of identities (i.e., not as an identical cycle of the same events,
the same individuals, the same histories, and so forth).

These two principal views of the eternal return thus differ considerably: the
literal return of everything—in the same series and sequence—seems to suggest a kind of metempsychosis, a transmigration of the soul, or rather, the
rebirth of the individual through the process of an enormous cyclical recurrence.[29] In this respect, the account would appear to borrow traditional elements from Zoroastrian doctrine (e.g., the restoration of souls at the final
millennium, as advanced in the *Zend Avesta*),[30] thus strengthening the parallel
with the historical Zoroaster. But such a view also invokes the teaching of the
historical Empedocles and would ironically refer to Christian eschatology as
well, where all virtuous believers would be resurrected after death, following
the return of Jesus and the apocalyptic triumph over evil and the antichrist.

The second principal view of the eternal return, which, properly speaking,
seems to be Nietzsche's most considered view, postulates an endless flux and
metamorphosis of energy or matter, constantly transfiguring itself well into an
endless future. In which case, *every moment* is at once birth and death, a ceaselessly creative apocalypse. Such a worldview would be reminiscent of Heraclitus's understanding that all is in flux, or becoming, and that absolute
being—understood as permanence or fixity of being, whether of body or
soul—is illusory. Change is the only reality, whether by chance or necessity.

Both views differ as to plausibility and import. The first view has as its
strength the psychological injunction that one should act in such a way that
one would become well-disposed toward oneself and to life, to such a degree
of impassioned affirmation that one's highest wish would be to live life again,
in exactly the same way one has lived it, even despite the adversity one has
encountered—and, indeed, has suffered through—in life. This kind of injunction would be dramatically effective, however, only on the condition that such
a view of the eternal return were plausible, indeed, literally true.[31] Not only
would one have to demonstrate the perfect conservation of energy—with no
possibility, for example, of entropy (a much-debated issue in late nineteenth-
century philosophy of science and in popular culture as well)—to consider such
a view plausible, but one would have to qualify the very identity of the person
who maintained it. That is, one would have to *forget* that one has already lived
a previous number of identical lives, in order for it to serve as a plausible
psychological injunction—and such forgetting of one's own life would paradoxically demand a different subject.[32]

The second view of the eternal return seems far more plausible, in that the whole of nature seems to be constantly transfiguring itself in a series of atomic and chemical metamorphoses, even unto the scale of cosmic rebirth. But with the admitted nonrecurrence of one's individual identity, the psychological imperative behind the injunction to live as if one would repeat one's own life again and again to infinity—because it is said that one shall—clearly loses its force, indeed all motivational plausibility whatsoever (because it is extremely improbable that one will).

When Nietzsche first explicitly discusses the eternal return, however, in his earlier work, *The Gay Science*, (paragraph 341), he seems to advance the first account, which stresses the "strong" claim of a recurrent personal identity. The passage is a celebrated one: it is richly suggestive and rhetorically powerful— aided in part by the metaphorical comparison of reality (the finite sum of will to power) to the model of an hourglass, with its finite number of grains of sand, which, when turned over and over, will quite plausibly yield an identical positional aggregation among the particular grains themselves:

> *The greatest weight.*—What, if some day or night a demon were to steal after you *[eternal]* into your loneliest loneliness and say to you: "This life as you now live it and have *[recurrence]* lived it, you will have to live once more and innumerable times more; and there will be nothing new in it, but every pain and every joy and every thought and sigh and everything unutterably small or great in your life will have to return to you, all in the same succession and sequence—even this spider and this moonlight between the trees, and even this moment and I myself. The eternal hourglass of existence is turned upside down again and again, and you with it; speck of dust!"
>
> Would you not throw yourself down and gnash your teeth and curse the demon who spoke thus? Or have you once experienced a tremendous moment when you would have answered him: "You are a god and never have I heard anything more divine." If this thought gained possession of you, it would change you as you are or perhaps crush you. The question in each and every thing, "Do you desire this once more and innumerable times more?" would lie upon your actions as the greatest weight. Or, how well disposed would you have to become to yourself and to life to crave nothing more fervently than this ultimate eternal confirmation and seal?[33]

While this "strong" view of the eternal return is dramatically stated in *The Gay Science*, it is not really advanced as a straightforward, literal proposition (i.e., one that is capable of being verified or falsified). Rather, the viewpoint is figuratively expressed: it is advanced as a question and is stated—by a hypothetical demon, no less—in the conditional: "What if?" Its psychological force is strengthened by the circumstance of its utterance, namely, that one is enjoined to reflect upon such a personal destiny at the very weakest moment of personal depression or resignation, when one would desperately wish to relive one's own past moments of joy and happiness. It is this feeling of abjection followed by the complementary feeling of the possible restoration of happiness—of joy regained—that enters into the heart of the loneliest, the most forsaken individual, extending the prospect of real fulfillment, recuperation, and self-possession that is at issue here. This is meant to provoke our resolution, to discipline our own will and character, such that we might in turn act upon these feelings and attain happiness in consequence of our actions.

If the eternal return is only advanced as a metaphorical hypothesis, indeed, as a question cast in the conditional in *The Gay Science*, it is hardly more than evoked in *Zarathustra*, although quite frequently and quite intensely. It is claimed to be dramatically important—it is Zarathustra's ownmost "secret"—but it is not explicitly or literally discussed by Zarathustra at all: rather it is invoked by his animals, it is briefly mentioned as a "circle" by the dwarf, but Zarathustra can only seemingly refer to it while in a dream, or in a swoon—as if he were fully overpowered by the notion. Remarkably, in Nietzsche's unpublished notes from the period in which he composed book 5 of *The Gay Science* and *Zarathustra*, he writes extensively about it, advancing the "strong" as well as the "weaker" position, as well as many intermediate positions. Many of the unpublished statements about the eternal return are presented as quite literal claims that have to do with the possible scientific truth about eternal return,[34] about the psychological effects such a teaching would have on the individual, about how compelling its effects would be upon society at large, especially, with regard to human conduct in general. At one point Nietzsche says "there are a thousand formulas" for us to understand the eternal return.[35]

With a thousand ways of understanding the eternal return, and with Nietzsche's failure to publish one single explicitly literal account, the twofold question inevitably arises: why doesn't he explain the eternal return, and why does he belabor it so much in *Zarathustra*? The response to the first part of the question should be clear: he simply does not advance the eternal return as a verifiable truth at all, because it would be theoretically and observationally impossible to verify in either of the two extreme versions. The response to the second part of the question is that "the eternal return" is not an account of reincarnation, transmigration, or metempsychosis at all. Rather, the eternal return is precisely Nietzsche's antidote to the traditional metaphysical position that the soul is immortal. Understandably, then, the philosophical complexity of this antidote demands that it be engaged repeatedly, artfully, and at length. It is meant to eliminate every possible account of the soul's immortality once and for all. As Nietzsche remarked in a note from the fall of 1883, "Its immediate effect will be to take the place of the belief in immortality."[36]

Whether one advances the "strong" or the "weak" view of the eternal return, what is fundamentally excluded in both accounts is the order of transcendence—of eternal redemption, restoration, reward, or punishment of "the soul" in any "beyond" whatsoever: heaven or hell, Eastern or Western. It is the belief in the existential identity of the soul that inhabits the "strong" view and lends traditional "cyclical" accounts of recurrence, whether philosophical or religious, some modicum of plausibility.[37] But this is not Nietzsche's position. Identity in space and time, beyond space and time, or in a vast, millennial account of recurrence is simply impossible, given the fact of our empirical finitude in space and time, and hence the importance of truth, intelligibility, and a scientific account of human existence that would *exclude* the transcendent as any basis at all for determining empirical reality. Such a world would have no divine law, no moral purposiveness, and quite simply, no sin.[38] With the advent of God's death as elaborated in *The Gay Science*, belief in the immortality of the soul and the metaphysics of divine redemption are simply foreclosed. The eternal return, however conceived (most simply stated, the "second" or "weaker" account), becomes the remains, the leftovers, of traditional metaphysics and religion. In short, the eternal return is nothing other than the natural order itself: bereft of God, wholly immanent, radically finite.

At once, for Nietzsche, this need not be argued, since its "truth" is evident (its "truth" is simply that of "nature" or "life"), yet at the same time, since we are so deeply indebted to the traditional ways of conceiving ourselves, our world, and our culture, it is difficult to think through the full implications of a world without absolute, transcendent, and universal foundations: precisely those religious and metaphysical "truths" that have heretofore guided human conduct for millennia, lending "meaning" and "value" to human existence itself. This is why the eternal return is claimed to be so "enigmatic" and "burdensome" for Nietzsche. Because there are no transcendent foundations, no divine truths or universal absolutes to address these most difficult and most painfully human of issues—the age-old questions of life's meaning, purpose, destiny, and value—they can no longer be responded to in accordance with the suprasensible vocabulary that was traditionally used to raise them *as* issues in the first place.[39] Nietzsche's account quite simply devalorizes the traditional explanations as to the meaningfulness and purposiveness of human existence, and hence, it *cannot* respond to the issues as traditionally posed.[40]

Thus, what Nietzsche advances in *Zarathustra* is necessarily enigmatic, since his views cannot *resolve* the metaphysical and moral questions we have unwittingly inherited (i.e., positively or negatively, yes or no, black or white) *within* the intellectual purchase, the conceptual space of those questions. The entire conceptual framework for articulating the meaning of human existence, value, and purpose has been radically displaced by Nietzsche's nonfoundational, antimetaphysical, amorally conceived universe, a world of childlike innocence, before the fall. It is precisely this that makes the eternal return burdensome in turn, since its task is ultimately to show not only that the traditional teachings were themselves misplaced, indeed delusional, but that their very presuppositions were rooted in the incapacity to come to terms with the realities of human existence itself. In the end, the burdensome task of the eternal return—understood as the immanent unfolding of a dynamic and finite will to power—will be to render a truthful account of that reality, to articulate the intelligibility, the "thinkability" of this existence, such that it can be humanly comprehended and joyfully embraced, despite the quantum of pain and suffering that is necessarily ingredient to life.

We have already seen—in examining *The Gay Science*—that the place to *introduce* the notion of *will* (i.e., of a renewed and restored sense of human agency and autonomy) came after Nietzsche's explanation of the "death of God."[41] To willfully embrace the natural order was, for Nietzsche, both to *deny* the reality of a supernatural or extranatural existence, as well as to *affirm* the concreteness of empirical life. The highest affirmation of life was the joyful acceptance of the eternal return, whereby we *enjoin ourselves* to *become* naturalized in a world from which the gods have vanished. Indeed, this theme—the naturalization of humanity, with its correlate, the de-deification of nature—pervades the four books of *Zarathustra* and is advanced from the very outset in "Zarathustra's Prologue." In response to the very first character he encounters—and quickly takes leave of—Zarathustra remarks, "Could it be possible? This old saint in the forest has not yet heard anything of this, that *God is dead!*"[42]

In paragraph 3 of "Zarathustra's Prologue," Nietzsche reasserts the injunctions he set forth in *The Gay Science*, this time using them—in a highly oracular fashion—to raise the question of the overman:

> Behold, I teach you the overman. The overman is *the meaning of the earth*. Let your will say: the overman *shall be* the meaning of the earth! I beseech you, my

brothers, *remain faithful to the earth*, and do not believe those who speak to you of otherworldly hopes! Poison-mixers are they, whether they know it or not. Despisers of life are they, decaying and poisoned themselves, of whom the earth is weary: so let them go. Once the sin against God was the greatest sin; but God died, and these sinners died with him. To sin against the earth is now the most dreadful thing, and to esteem the entrails of the unknowable higher than the meaning of the earth.[43]

The death of God thus amounts to the removal of transcendent metaphysical principles that had formerly governed the traditional notion of nature as theologically meaningful and purposive (i.e., as tending toward fulfillment of the divinely ordained good) or as intrinsically rational (i.e., as guided by divine reason) or as a divinely created essence or substance. Thus *nature* is said to become *de-deified* upon the death of God.[44] Likewise, with no transcendent foundation of value, no divinely ordained vocation to human action and behavior, morality is no longer credibly held to be predicated upon the divine law or will. With no divine authority or governance, with no heaven to be attained or hell to be suffered, the most deeply held moral doctrines—the teachings of "sin," the "redemption" from sin, the "absolution" of "guilt," and the "salvation" of the "soul"—suddenly become weightless, meaningless. What had been implanted in human nature for millennia upon end—namely, the belief in a metaphysically conceived morality, operating as "the very wheel in the machinery of things"[45]—is henceforth withdrawn upon the announcement of God's death, in the prologue to the first part of *Zarathustra*, by the figure of Zarathustra himself. With this announcement, humanity, for once, shall find its meaning, authority, and purpose solely in terms of the intelligibility of the natural order itself: mankind thereby will become *naturalized*. The "returned" Zarathustra[46] will find this intelligibility of nature and of human nature in the dynamic understanding of will to power and, ultimately, in the teaching of the eternal return: this will be a "critical" teaching in that it sets limits to the "thinkability" of existence as such and by strictly *excluding* "otherworldly hopes" and any "esteem," much less any *truth* for the "unknowable." Nietzsche explicitly formulates this in the section entitled "On Self-Overcoming," in part 2 of *Zarathustra*:

> "Will to truth," you who are wisest call that which impels you and fills you with lust?
> A will to the thinkability of all beings; this I call your will. You want to *make* all being thinkable, for you doubt with well-founded suspicion that it is already thinkable. But it shall yield and bend for you. Thus your will wants it. It shall

become smooth and serve the spirit as its mirror and reflection. That is your whole will, you who are wisest: a will to power—when you speak of good and evil too, and of valuations. You still want to create the world before which you can kneel: that is your ultimate hope and intoxication.[47]

MORALITY OF THE MOTLEY COW

At the very outset of "Zarathustra's Prologue," Zarathustra starts out on his long journey by descending from the heights of his mountain retreat (where he lived for ten years) to wander far and wide and to spread his teaching, which he figuratively calls his "gift" of "honey." The itinerary of his extended journey, the places he visits, the individuals he encounters thus serve to structure the entire narrative development of the book, ultimately ending back at Zarathustra's cave on the mountain, at the close of part 4. Zarathustra's journey ironically recalls Jesus' travels throughout the period of his mission. Like Jesus, Zarathustra begins his quest at the age of thirty in search of disciples to whom he can impart his long-accumulated wisdom.[48] With Zarathustra's initial descent from the mountain, he exchanges his own lofty place of illumination and inspiration (i.e., the upper regions of spiritual light, of quickened breath, of elevated soul, etc.) for the shade-darkened lowlands, for the damp forests and sedentary villages.

Now, the first and only village to be named in the entire work is called "the village of the Motley Cow." This is a name that is rich in allusions and suggestions, one meant to stand in sharp contrast with Zarathustra's elevated mountain home and enlightened teaching. As an historical allegory, the village of the Motley Cow seems to refer to the ill-fated Greek city of Thebes. Under the counsel of the oracle at Delphi, King Cadmus was said to have founded the city of Thebes, in Boetia (the name for this region of Greece is literally "cow country"), by following a motley cow to the place it finally laid down to rest. The city is central to the tradition of Greek tragedy, since Cadmus's descendents constitute a veritable roll call of suffering, tragic figures, including Agave, Ino, Autonoe, Pentheus, Laius, Jocasta, Oedipus, and Antigone.[49] In Euripides' tragedy *The Bacchae*, this is the city where Dionysus wreaked deadly revenge on the would-be king Pentheus for challenging his divine status and for attempting to suppress the Dionysian cult worship and ecstatic ritual practices.[50] Thus, for the author of *The Birth of Tragedy*, a village so named would initially represent a repressive, austere, and foreboding place, one destined to yield to

the liberating sensuality of a Dionysus—whom Nietzsche frequently equated
with his figure of Zarathustra. By the same token, Zarathustra's mountain
would be associated with Mt. Cithaeron, the mountain outside Thebes to which
the followers of Dionysus (the Maenads, Bacchantes, etc.) would withdraw for
their sylvan celebrations.[51]

To maintain the parallel between Zarathustra and Jesus, however, the village
of the Motley Cow would suggest the biblical town of Galilee. According to the
Gospels, Jesus left the mountains of the wilderness to come down to Galilee,
where the disciple John the Baptist was placed under arrest. Jesus' coming
out of the wilderness thus signaled the beginning of his ministry, and his first
proclamation at Galilee was the announcement: "This is the time of fulfillment.
The kingdom of God is at hand. Repent, and believe in the gospel."[52] To those
who did not repent or who did not believe, Jesus' subsequent injunction was
that they shall be given over to the fiery underworld, to Gehenna.[53] Of course,
Zarathustra's first proclamation, upon descending from his wilderness (addressed to the old saint in the forest) was that God is dead and that there are no
afterworlds at all. The sarcastic contrast of the respective teachings is reflected,
finally, in the very name of the village itself, Motley Cow. A motley cow is a
variegated cow with splotches of two colors, usually black and white. Not only
would such a name designate the abode of a herdlike population, a group of
ruminant animals, cattle, sheep, and so forth, but their values would be what
Nietzsche consistently terms "herd values," which "trains the individual to be
a function of the herd and to ascribe value to himself only as a function,"[54] or
what he would later, in the *On the Genealogy of Morals*, call "slave values,"
that reflect the bitterness and resentment of the weak and suffering.[55] Both
"herd" and "slavish" values effectively devalue the worth of the individual and
invert the noble, active life of enjoyment and self-fulfillment into a regime of
passive, reactive, and unegoistic values, designating the latter as "good" and
the former as "evil." It would be due to the categorically rigid and simplistic
opposition of good and evil, black and white, divinely codified by the shepherd
of the herd and reinforced by the threat of a metaphysical afterworld—
ultimately, a set of unconditional values and imperatives that had become virtually instinctual to the herd, such that it could not tolerate creative change at
all, thereby putting the human community as a whole at risk of decline, degen-
eration, and nihilism—that the village of the Motley Cow would receive its
broadest and most poignant signification from Nietzsche: Village of Fools[56]
Europe. By the same token, however, this would be precisely the place from
which a higher form of humanity would eventually have to arise.

ZARATHUSTRA'S DESCENT

What is Zarathustra's initial descent or "down-going"? He first speaks of it to the sun; and in doing so, he identifies himself *with* the sun.[57] "I must descend to the depths, *as you do* in the evening, when you go behind the sea and still bring light to the underworld, you overrich star. *Like you* I must go *under*—go down, as is said by man, to whom I want to descend."[58]

Zarathustra, therefore, stands as a god, as an Apollonian source of divine illumination, to man; and like the Greek, he bears gifts. Now, in addition to the ironic parallel with Jesus[59]—a parallel that will be maintained throughout the four books of *Zarathustra*—there are two specific models for this descent, both of which come from Plato. Like *Zarathustra*, the *Republic* begins with Socrates' speech: "I went *down* to Piraeus," down to the filth and clamor of a port and market village—where, incidentally, a Bacchanalian religious festival for the Thracian goddess Bendis was taking place.[60] The second reference, of course, is to the cave image in book 6 of the *Republic* (514ff.). Also, as in the *Republic*, the image of descent follows the earlier account of the sun—the divinely metaphysical source of Goodness, Truth, and Beauty, which the Platonic philosopher alone is ostensibly capable of grasping (*Republic*, 506Eff.).

Nietzsche *as* Zarathustra, Nietzsche in the figure *of* Zarathustra, likewise shares an element of the divine with Socrates: both have a kind of *mania* or madness that is *demonic*—they both are spoken of as demons, halfway between man and God, and they both are demonic in the sense of being provocative, insistent, and frenzied. Yet Nietzsche's Zarathustra is *different* in one great respect from Socrates: in both cases of *descent* in the *Republic*, the philosopher is *forced* down, against his inclinations and better judgment. The unbridled herd *kills*! Socrates knows this, and Zarathustra is threatened more than once.

For Zarathustra's descent, however, there is no *apology*. He says, not only "must I go under" but "I *want* to descend." The Platonic Socrates seemed reactive, frightened, fearful for his own life. Not so Zarathustra. His descent is self-willed, that is, he affects himself, he possesses the auto-affective character of will, a self-legislative and animate will. Thus Zarathustra descends out of surfeit and superabundance. He descends to *give* the teaching of the overman. The teaching, just as the *Republic* speaks of the sun, will be "the greatest expenditure of the creator,"[61] a resplendent vision that will enable humanity to see as with divine eyes.

Zarathustra thus goes *down* to mankind, he goes down to man as he *is*. Far from idealizing humanity, however, Zarathustra knows full well that mankind is precisely a "laughing-stock and painful embarrassment," a breed of goat-herds, a giant accident: "Naked I saw both the greatest and the smallest man: they are still all-too-similar to each other. Verily, even the greatest I found all-too-human."[62]

Zarathustra's descent—or "down-going"—is motivated by his intent to *transform* the individual from the aberration he presently is into the overman: existent humanity is merely the opening, or overture, to the overman, a rude anticipation of what greatness humanity may yet attain. For the overman to come, however, humanity must first *undergo* a profound transformation, a dramatic change in its very being. Effectively, humanity must be redeemed *from* its redeemer, from two millennia of Christian moral and metaphysical formation.[63] Zarathustra will say, "What is great in man is that he is a *bridge* and *not* an end: what can be loved in man is that he is an *overture and a going-under*."[64] Thus, man's *undergoing* will be his *overcoming* of what he presently is, namely, all-too-human. Moreover, Nietzsche himself saw the whole of his work *Zarathustra* precisely as his own personal instrument in the service of this overcoming. In a letter to Erwin Rohde, he described his work as an "abyss" that will give rise to a transformed humanity:

> The three acts of my Zarathustra are finished. . . . It is a kind of abyss of the future—horrible, above all in its rapture. Everything in it is me alone, without prototype, parallel, or precedent; anyone who ever lived in it would come back to the world a different man.[65]

Four months later, in a note to Malwida von Meysenbug, he would say:

> My task is enormous, my determination no less so. What I want, my son Zarathustra won't tell you. But he'll challenge you to figure it out, and perhaps you can. This much is certain: I wish to force mankind to decisions which will determine its entire future—and it may yet happen that one day whole millennia will make their most solemn vows in my name.[66]

The task Nietzsche invokes here—motivated by his desire "to *take away* from human existence some of its heartbreaking and cruel character"[67]—would be explicitly framed in a later letter to Paul Deussen, wherein he describes it as "an immeasurably difficult and decisive task which, *when it is understood*, will split humanity into two halves. Its aim and meaning is, in four words, the *Transvaluation of all values*."[68] What is at stake, then, is an enormity: as Nietzsche would go on to remark about the profound social-historical consequences of God's death—especially, the undermining of the traditional system of values and morality—in book 5 of *The Gay Science*,

The event itself is far too great, too distant, too remote from the multitude's capacity for comprehension even for the tidings of it to be thought of as having arrived as yet. Much less may one suppose that many people know as yet what this event really means—and how much must collapse now that this faith has been undermined because it was built upon this faith, propped up by it, grown into it; for example, the whole of our European morality.[69]

It was Nietzsche's claim to have discerned the broad significance of this moral formation, its motivations conditioned by human bitterness and *ressentiment* about its own weakness, and the institutional reinforcement of this weakness through organized religion and the political-economic order itself. With the generally noted decline of conventional religious faith in the latter part of the nineteenth century in Europe, accompanied by the growing faith in science to help diminish human suffering, Nietzsche argued that value systems predicated upon the inherited morality nonetheless remained, but were sublimated and directed into other vehicles of valuation and activity—particularly the ideologies of emerging nationalisms and political extremisms, which offered a variety of utopian ideals of collective redemption and personal significance to the individual through national, party, class, or even racial identifications.

Historically, Nietzsche foresaw the extraordinary danger in replacing the traditional religious proclamations of salvation and redemption with the nascent ideologies of extremist nationalism and with the various political "egalitarian" movements following the French Revolution. Those not affiliated with the particular national state or with the specific social-economic class who stood to gain psychologically through identification with the larger collective spirit—or economically, from the growing prosperity brought about by rapid urbanization and the industrial revolution—could only come to be seen as enemies to be vilified. They would constitute the inassimilable "other," or, as he would express this in *On the Genealogy of Morals*, "you . . . the evil, the cruel, the lustful, the insatiable, the godless to all eternity": at once a threat and a danger to be eliminated.[70] It was with this historical prescience that Nietzsche foretold the disaster of the twentieth century in the final chapter of *Ecce Homo,* which in retrospect seems appropriately entitled "Why I Am a Destiny":

> For when truth enters into a fight with the lies of millennia, we shall have upheavals, a convulsion of earthquakes, a moving of mountains and valleys, the like of which has never been dreamed of. The concept of politics will have merged entirely with a war of spirits; all power structures of the old society will have been exploded—all of them are based on lies: there will be wars the like of which have never yet been seen on earth.[71]

The "truth" Zarathustra attempts to teach is not easily understandable, as we have been forewarned. Indeed, as we have already seen, it may not even be articulable, communicable—much less, generalizable—despite Nietzsche's repeated claim that his task is literally millennial in import. Alternatively, a teaching may be relatively straightforward, but for that very reason, it may be viewed as simplistic and of little apparent value. As Nietzsche remarked in his previous work, *Daybreak*, "It is not enough to prove something, one also has to seduce or elevate people to it."[72] It is perhaps in view of this rhetorical principle, as well as with regard to the deeply personal character of *Zarathustra*, that part 1—"Zarathustra's Speeches," following the prologue—has the curious, inverted structure it does. Rather than directly engage in a political or ideological program to arrest the coming conflagration of the centuries, Zarathustra proposes his own self-overcoming, his personal metamorphosis, as a model, in the first chapter, "On the Three Metamorphoses." Thus, it seems as if Zarathustra is determined to change his own nature prior to giving a thorough diagnosis of the general disorder to which humanity has been subjected, thence to ascertain the causes of it and to propose its remediation in turn, through his teaching and ultimately, by his own personal example, his *response* in the form of a "metamorphosis."

With this seeming inversion in mind, nonetheless, the ten sections of the prologue do introduce the many topics that will be developed in the course of *Zarathustra*, and they make it dramatically clear that Zarathustra will serve as an antidote, an opposite, to the prevailing moral order.[73] Quite simply, for Zarathustra, it is the existing moral order itself that has demeaned humanity, rendering it so ashamed of itself and its natural potential for growth and creativity that its citizens are literally equated with "trained dogs" and "corpses." There can no longer be any question of predicating the formation of a future humanity upon the continuing delusion of a supernatural afterworld or upon what for Nietzsche is the simply unintelligible metaphysical otherworld— whether of a Christian or Platonic variety. Following the death of God and the suspension of a religiometaphysically constituted immortal soul, a heavenly or hellish eternity of bliss or punishment, and the entire armature of moral values the West has erected upon these transcendent claims—even unto their specifically modern surrogates—there remains *only* the world of natural and human existence. But for failure to embrace this world, to honestly accommodate ourselves to the reality and truth of this vital natural existence—the "meaning of the earth"—is to do so at the very risk of our own survival. In failing to recognize the resources this meaning extends to us, it is as if (at least, for Zarathustra, in the prologue, mankind has squandered the potential for an enormous growth in its capacity for knowledge (which has seemingly become mere entertainment) and in its capacity to discover new values that would lend dignity and joy to the human condition: just as the tightrope walker is tricked, deceived into his fall.[74] The fall, of course, signifies the lack of a goal, a purpose, to humankind. With no purpose or direction to one's life, precisely because the goals humanity once had are now seen to be lies, the culture at large seems simply meaningless, without direction: we have arrived at the point of stasis, the dominion of what Zarathustra calls "the last man," where the only values seem to be a vestigial moral piety and an unthinking contentment with passivity and social conformity.

What is striking in the prologue is the patent rejection of Zarathustra's public teaching. He approaches the town "on the edge of the forest" with immense good will and generosity, seeking a public audience, and is met with incomprehension and derision. Mimicking Jesus' Parable of the Sower,[75] Zarathustra wishes to implant "the seed of his highest hope,"[76] his teaching that the goal of humanity is its self-overcoming in the overman, and that this would be the meaning of the earth, but he says, "They do not understand me; I am not the mouth for these ears. Must one smash their ears before they learn to listen with their eyes? Must one clatter like kettledrums and preachers of repentance? Or do they believe only the stammerer?"[77] Seemingly, Jesus' seed had taken root—even though he spoke in parables, since "the mysteries of the kingdom of heaven" have been granted only to his disciples—and this simply precluded Zarathustra's audience from "hearing" his own teaching. Admonishing the model of Jesus—as a shepherd and gravedigger (Jesus will send his angels to dispatch the unbelievers "into the fiery furnace" of hell "where there will be wailing and grinding of teeth")[78]—Zarathustra leaves the town (as did Jesus in the parable), realizing that he can speak only to the few, to the "hermits," to his future "living companions." Nonetheless, "the time is ripe," he says "to lure many away from the herd, for that I have come."[79] Effectively, Zarathustra pronounces himself the antichrist.

Sobered by the poor reception of his teaching, it becomes clear to Zarathustra that the project of human undergoing and overcoming will be far more complex than initially suspected. What must be dealt with at the outset is to analyze clinically the moral character of existent humanity as it is presently configured and as it serves as the practical basis for evaluating human action.[80] It then remains to present a critique of it, namely, to ascertain precisely how the present morality came to have the formation it has.[81] Once these two steps are made, the subsequent procedure will be to provide a counter-formation that would neutralize the power of the traditional morality—effectively, a negative undertaking—and finally, to present a positive, constructive account of the human situation so as to permit the creation of new values and new perspective estimations concerning everything of significance to one's life and conduct.

Zarathustra addresses these general concerns in sections 2–5 of part 1. In the second section, "On the Teachers of Virtue," he explicitly criticizes the palliative and unegoistic nature of the Ten Commandments[82] and the Beatitudes,[83] perhaps the most concise statements of our inherited moral imperatives. For Zarathustra, the signal virtue of these traditional moral teachings is that they promoted a sense of social ease and herdlike conformity, which enabled the individual to attain a good conscience about himself and in his relations with his neighbors, thus eliminating strife, enmity, and self-doubt. But Zarathustra sees that such a form of life is the very precondition of inaction and personal immobility, the cultivation of which serves to eliminate every form of individual doubt, self-questioning, experimenting, or personal "overcoming," anything that would even mildly disturb one's personal tranquility.[84] Drawing upon Christian Scripture itself, Zarathustra equates these moral teachings with the simple desire to attain an untroubled night's sleep: "Good sleep was sought, and opiate virtues for it."[85] Thus, a dreamless sleep is what the traditional morality basically aims for, and the recognition of this prompts Zarathustra to remark that if life itself were meaningless, sleep would indeed be a plausible goal. Zarathustra then points to the underlying justification of these inherited values, the divinely inspired traditional belief in an afterworld, an "other" world, behind the real world of lived, bodily experience—with the involved metaphysical claim that a spirit or soul likewise resides behind the body and that it is destined for immortality. But, for Zarathustra, such teachings are simply delusional forms of madness, invented by an earlier, primitive humanity to serve as a phantasmic compensation for the real suffering one undergoes in this world: "It was suffering and incapacity that created all afterworlds[86]—this and that brief madness of bliss which is experienced by those who suffer most deeply."[87]

Zarathustra announces that he, too, had once been given over to similar afterworldly delusions—whether (in the person of Nietzsche himself) by having fallen into pessimistic resignation in the face of an implacable, Schopenhauerian World-Will ("The work of a suffering and tortured god, the world then seemed to me") or by being transported by the emotional delirium of Wagnerian romanticism ("Drunken joy it is for the sufferer to look away from his suffering and to lose himself") or even by the Christian faith of his youth ("I too once cast my delusion beyond man, like all the afterworldly").[88] But he quickly realizes that this god was hardly "beyond man." Rather, "This god whom I created was man-made and madness, like all gods," that is, a fully human psychological construction and projection: "man he was and only a poor specimen of man and ego."[89] Such gods are merely "ghosts," imagined into existence so as to alleviate the pain of human suffering. Once one deals with the real causes of suffering and poses a purpose to, and meaning for, one's own existence—as the "awakened" Zarathustra had carried his ashes, phoenix-like, to his mountain—then the plausibility of these ghosts evaporates in the clear light of reason. It is human suffering, the incapacity to deal with that suffering, and the weariness—"a poor ignorant weariness"—bred from a lifetime of suffering, that inclines the sufferer to abandon the reality of this world for the delusion of redemption in another, higher world—in short, to "all gods and afterworlds."[90] Ultimately, for Zarathustra, the reality principle that serves as a countermeasure for such delusion is simply the *body* and the world it inhabits. Human suffering must not be deluded into thinking that one possesses an immaterial and immortal soul, which could propel oneself beyond the realm of the mortal and material, thereby to grasp or intuit a different, transcendent realm, some "dehumanized inhuman world which is a heavenly nothing."[91] Rather, the self is fully bodily, and the sense of self, or ego, is itself brought about by the body's own complex experience, that is, in its immediate life of pain and pleasure:

> The self says to the ego, "Feel pain here!" Then the ego suffers and thinks how it might suffer no more—and that is why it is *made* to think.
> The self says to the ego, "Feel pleasure here!" Then the ego is pleased and thinks how it might often be pleased again—and that is why it is *made* to think.[92]

Two major considerations should be added here concerning Nietzsche's account of the broader sense of the self or ego that arises from concrete, bodily experience: first, there is his discussion of the social-historical production of a refined sense of "self" and its "conscience," by which the self can claim any moral or practical responsibility, and second, there is account of "self-consciousness," which we use to clarify our sense of self and the world of our concerns. In *On the Genealogy of Morals*, Nietzsche would go on to give an account of the developed sense of self as having arisen out of the dynamics of social life, out of a primitive social existence where the tyrannical rule of authority obliged the individual to repress and sublimate his more aggressive, natural instincts. The fear of transgressing the rules set forth by that primitive punitive authority forced one to develop a memory, so as to be able to reckon or calculate the consequences of one's actions upon the community as a whole and to act accordingly and in conformity with the imposed rules.[93]

As for our own developed capacity of consciousness and reason, Nietzsche would explain this at length in book 5 of *The Gay Science*, particularly in section 354, "On the 'Genius of the Species,'" where he would claim that the strength and development of consciousness itself is proportionate to our "capacity for communication" and the "need for communication"—if we are to identify things, exchange goods and services, or to obtain help and protection—again, as postulated to have taken place in primitive society.[94] It will thus be the body, now understood to comprise our sensibility, self, ego, consciousness, and self-consciousness, as well as the instincts and passions, that Zarathustra will champion in part 1. The body is advanced as our intimate, continuous belonging to nature, to the natural world of human existence, thereby opposing and reversing the "antinatural" foundations of traditional moral doctrine: the divine, the soul, the otherworldly.[95] In its complexity, Zarathustra says that the body is at once a "plurality" and "a great reason"[96] that gives us exclusive and exhaustive access to the truth and meaning of the human condition for understanding the realistic causes of our personal distress in times of suffering and discontent, as well as the source for all human value, joy, and significance. To be true to his own teaching Zarathustra will have to privilege the body in his own person, for it is precisely through the body of the individual that he is an individual at all—that one's feelings, judgments, anxieties, moods, and overcomings are experienced and understood as such, even though they may not be fully expressible or articulable to an audience. Since the articulation of anything personally experienced can only be expressed verbally (i.e., in the general terms of the socially symbolic order of language), Nietzsche would remark,

> given the best will in the world to understand ourselves as individually as possible, "to know ourselves," each of us will always succeed in becoming [linguistically] conscious only of what is not individual but "average." . . . Fundamentally, all our actions are altogether incomparably personal, unique, and infinitely individual; there is no doubt of that. But as soon as we translate them into [linguistic] consciousness they *no longer seem to be*.[97]

Such is the very core of Nietzsche's "perspectivism" and "perspective evaluation" of things. The difficulty is not simply the epistemological concern of the subject-object divergence, or split, but the radically individuating lived experience afforded by the body when attempting to articulate a "teaching" to a public audience. Hence the necessity of Zarathustra's having to make himself into a "model" for the broader human "overcoming," in the form of his proposed "metamorphosis" in the first section of Zarathustra's speeches, rather than immediately confronting his moral and intellectual opponents. In such a confrontation or debate, it would be the opponents who would dictate the conceptual vocabulary of the discourse. Such a discourse would necessarily have to be generally accommodated to the existing symbolic order (the *only* generally articulable order of intelligibility), precisely the metaphysical discourse that has sustained, indeed permitted, the traditional account of "sin," "guilt," "shame," "transcendence," precisely what had led generation upon generation of thinkers to posit a "purpose" to human existence and a supervenient, "transcendent" meaning and value to life.

Much as René Descartes attempted to "search for truth" and to "acquire a clear and evident knowledge of all that is useful in life,"[98] by making a model of himself in his *Discourse on Method of Rightly Conducting One's Reason and Seeking Truth in the Sciences,* so Nietzsche has Zarathustra make a model of himself in his "On the Three Metamorphoses." Descartes's announcement of his project is strikingly similar to Zarathustra's approach: at once, disarmingly personal, written in a most unusual style, and most determined to avoid the conventional, scholastic vocabulary of his day.[99]

> I shall be glad . . . to reveal in this discourse what paths I have followed, and to represent my life in it as if in a picture, so that everyone may judge it for himself. . . . My present aim, then, is not to teach the method which everyone must follow to direct his reason correctly, but only to reveal how I have tried to direct my own. One who presumes to give precepts must think himself more skillful than those to whom he gives them; and if he makes the slightest mistake, he may be blamed. But I am presenting this work only as a history or, if you prefer, a fable in which, among certain examples worthy of imitation, you will perhaps also find many others that it would be right not to follow; and so I hope it will be useful for some without being harmful to any, and that everyone will be grateful to me for my frankness.[100]

It is in this sense that Zarathustra concludes section 9 of his prologue saying, "to my goal I will go—on my own way; over those who hesitate and lag behind I shall leap. Thus let my going be their going under."[101] And if Descartes claimed to present his discourse as a history or fable, this is because "the charm of fables awakens the mind, while the memorable deeds told in histories uplift it and help to form one's judgment if they are read with discretion."[102] Nietzsche's stylistic experiment with *Zarathustra* is similarly unusual. As he described it to Peter Gast, "Zarathustra has for the present the personal significance of being my book of 'edifying and encouraging discourses'—beyond that, it is dark and hidden and ridiculous to everyone."[103] Likewise, he styled it "a legendary air" to Carl von Gersdorff, filled with "plain and strange words."[104] Granted the stylistic powers of the fable or history—the edifying discourse or legendary air—the path is indeed personal: "The first time I came to men I committed the folly of hermits, the great folly: I stood in the market place. And as I spoke to all, I spoke to none."[105]

ZARATHUSTRA'S METAMORPHOSIS

Drawing upon the dramatic voice of his Zarathustra, Nietzsche employs a narrative technique that attempts to express his ownmost personal experiences, both emotional and intellectual. Deriving its intensity from the uniqueness of his own lived perspective, such a narrative would necessarily be, at least in part, figurative, metaphorical, poetic. The fact of Nietzsche's repeated insistence about the "personal" tone of *Zarathustra*, that only he could understand what was expressed therein, because only he had lived through it, combined with the fact that he reflected on the composition of part 1 for a period of eighteen months, results in a remarkably perplexing model for a more general, "human" self-overcoming. The specific model he offers is a set of personal "metamorphoses of the spirit," cast in terms of three *metaphors* given in Zarathustra's very first speech, "On the Three Metamorphoses." The terms of this metamorphosis[106]—what the metaphors enigmatically suggest—will be consistently maintained to help structure the narrative throughout the four parts of the work, and are advanced, as is the work as a whole, for "all and none." To further complicate matters, what Zarathustra *himself*—Zarathustra the "godless"—is to overcome, what his problem is, *as* the figure of Zarathustra, seems initially enigmatic as well.[107]

Zarathustra anticipates his metamorphosis to occur in three stages, and it is described according to three animal metaphors: "Of three metamorphoses of the spirit I tell you: how the spirit becomes a camel; and the camel a lion; and the lion, finally a child."[108] With regard to the first of the three metamorphoses, Zarathustra goes on to remark, "What is difficult? asks the spirit that would bear much, and kneels down like a camel wanting to be well loaded. What is most difficult, O heroes, asks the spirit that would bear much, that I may take it upon myself and exult in my strength?"[109]

When Nietzsche wrote the first draft of this section, he responded as follows: "(Chap[ter]) What would be *the most difficult* for Zarathustra? To *undo the old morality*."[110] By the time he completed the copy of the first part in late January 1883, he answered the same question, "What is most difficult?"—what would demand the greatest "strength" to deal with?—with a series of examples that suggest a sense of self-abasement bordering on self-destruction. The examples are clearly very personal in nature and indicate that his energies had indeed been directed at trying to stabilize himself after a host of personal disasters. What is most striking about the examples, perhaps, is the sense that Zarathustra seemed to "will" these disasters upon himself, that he ostensibly "wished" these events to happen to him, as a so-called "test" of his own strength. The responses, advanced as signs of this personal strength and endurance verge on the pathetic. What is most difficult?

> humbling oneself to wound one's pride . . .
> Climbing high mountains to tempt the tempter . . .
> for the sake of the truth, suffering hunger in one's soul . . .
> being sick and sending home the comforters . . .
> making friends with the deaf, who never hear what you want . . .
> stepping into filthy waters when they are the waters of truth . . .
> loving those who despise us and offering a hand to the ghost that would
>   frighten us.[111]

Wishing oneself to be humiliated, starving, disavowing friendship, being unheard and unloved, all this on the mountain in the wilderness, tempting the devil himself, and besmirching himself with the "truth" of it all is surely the desert of the hair-shirted ascetic, not an enviable travel destination for a forthcoming generation of "heroes." Hardly the Zoroaster of the *Zend Avesta*, this is the very embittered voice of Nietzsche himself emerging brokenhearted in his failed relation with the single real love of his life, Lou Salomé, compounded in this loss by what he felt to be Paul Rée's betrayal in having taken Lou from him, humiliated by the "tempter" Richard Wagner, the scandal at Bayreuth and the resulting dissociation of all family ties, the cold silence from his former friends, no job, no home, stateless, no readers to speak of, living on the constant edge of penury, exacerbated by a period of almost depraved illness and pain; indeed a winter of discontent in one's loneliest desert. Would one really wish this upon oneself? Would one ask the demon to repeat the whole, sorry affair yet once again? Would one say, "You are a god and never have I heard anything more divine"?[112] Rather, it would seem that Zarathustra is fairly well wrestling with demons in this desert, a place that is surely not of his own choice. Nonetheless, for the philosopher, as Nietzsche would later remark in *On the Genealogy of Morals*, there is something to be said for the desert, and there are many kinds of desert.

In the third essay of the *Genealogy*, Nietzsche discusses the philosopher's peculiarly positive inclination toward asceticism (usually viewed negatively, as the practice of an extreme austerity and self-denial)—"the meaning of the ascetic ideal" for them—namely, a not-infrequent "irritation" with regard to "sensuality" and bearing something of a penchant toward "poverty, humility, and chastity." But, rather than seeing these qualities in a negative or pessimistic way, thus leading to a kind of Schopenhauerian "resignation" to life, or as an abdication to suffering and the hope of some reprieve from life, Nietzsche makes a far more studied and positive evaluation of these ascetic qualities:

> The philosopher sees in [asceticism] an optimum condition for the highest and boldest spirituality, and smiles—he does *not* deny "existence," he rather affirms *his* existence and *only* his existence. . . . As you see, they are not unbiased witnesses and judges of the *value* of the ascetic ideal, these philosophers! They think of *themselves*—what is "the saint" to them! They think of what *they* can least do without: freedom from compulsion, disturbance, noise, from tasks, duties, worries; . . .
>
> . . . all dogs nicely chained up; no barking of hostility and shaggy-haired rancor; no gnawing worm of injured ambition; undemanding and obedient intestines, busy as windmills but distant; the heart remote, beyond, heavy with future, posthumous—all in all, they think of the ascetic ideal as the cheerful asceticism of an animal become fledged and divine, floating above life rather than in repose.[113]

For Nietzsche, it is with these protections, this distance, this sense of reserve and emotional self-control, that the philosopher can fully attain to his creative power and focus all his energies to the serious task to which he had all along devoted himself (i.e., "for the benefit of the evolving work").[114] To master one's task one must first master oneself, and to do this, favorable conditions must be sought (and met!) so as to maximize one's energy and will, to avoid distraction, and thence to find that real state of independence—a real freedom from dependency of all kinds—demanded for the successful fulfillment of that higher goal, the positive accomplishment of the creative task:

> Every animal—therefore *la bête philosophe*, too—instinctively strives for an optimum of favorable conditions under which it can expend all its strength and

achieve its maximal feeling of power; every animal abhors, just as instinctively and with a subtlety of discernment that is "higher than all reason," every kind of intrusion or hindrance that obstructs or could obstruct this path to the optimum. . . . Ascetic ideals reveal so many bridges to *independence* that a philosopher is bound to rejoice and clap his hands when he hears the story of all those resolute men who one day said No to all servitude and went into some *desert*.[115]

The loneliest desert, in which the camel would assume his great burden and most difficult problems, proves to be modest enough, however. "The desert, incidentally, that I just mentioned, where the strong, independent spirits withdraw," is contrasted with "the way educated people imagine a desert."[116] For these people, the desert would be "a stage desert"—perhaps, on the order of grand opera, like a production of Verdi's *Aida*—inhabited by actors "of the spirit," who could not possibly "endure life" in Nietzsche's desert. One is tempted to think of Wagner again, with the theatricality of Bayreuth, but Nietzsche does not pursue it further except to say that his own desert "is not nearly romantic or Syrian enough." "To be sure," he says, "there is no lack of camels" in their desert—camels in the sense of ridiculous and grotesque figures—"but that is where the similarity ends." Nietzsche then goes on to describe his own desert:

A voluntary obscurity perhaps; an avoidance of oneself; a dislike of noise, honor, newspapers, influence; a modest job, an everyday job, something that conceals rather than exposes one; an occasional association with harmless, cheerful beasts and birds whose sight is refreshing; mountains for company, but not dead ones, mountains with eyes (that is, with lakes); perhaps even a room in a full, utterly commonplace hotel, where one is certain to go unrecognized and can talk to anyone with impunity—that is what "desert" means here: oh, it is lonely enough, believe me![117]

If the model for the transformation of future humanity begins modestly enough with the wounded pride of "the hermit of Sils Maria"—as Nietzsche often signed his correspondence from his rented room in the summer in Sils, on the shore of Lake Silvaplana—nonetheless, the first metaphor is instructive enough in that the attempt to gain some form of self-mastery will inevitably involve some painful self-reflection and self-criticism. How "cheerful" the "vivisection" of the soul will be, however, remains to be seen.

If the first metamorphosis resulted in freedom from encumbrance, a reverence for one's self and one's pride, and a deeper self-understanding, Zarathustra goes on to say that the second metamorphosis, the next precondition for self-overcoming, is that one actually takes control of oneself. One must literally take control of—and responsibility for—one's own agency. One must "capture" or "create" one's own freedom, by liberating oneself from what Nietzsche had earlier termed "the old morality," what he here calls "the great dragon":

> In the loneliest desert, however, the second metamorphosis occurs: here the spirit becomes a lion who would capture his freedom and be master in his own desert. Here he seeks out his last master: he wants to fight him and his last god; for the ultimate victory he wants to fight with the great dragon.
>
> Who is the great dragon whom the spirit will no longer call lord and god? "Thou shalt" is the name of the great dragon.[118]

To become great, the spirit would have to divest itself of its tradition-bound moral laws and codes.[119] It must fight the seductive charms of the comforting moral order and its traditional imperatives, together with its "golden rules" of egalitarian "pity." To be capable of doing this, the spirit must become as a *lion*—the individual must *will* the end of the traditional moral era, the era of the "thou shalt," and convert it into an "I will." Such a will requires an unaccustomed strength of character and courage, precisely because, until now, the traditional values have constituted what was taught to be, what was learned to be, and what was felt to be value itself, value "in itself." Nietzsche states: "Values, thousands of years old, shine on these scales; and thus speaks the mightiest of all dragons: 'All value of all things shines on me. All value has already been created, and I am all created value.'"[120]

Of course, for Nietzsche, morality derives from the herdlike obedience to the customs and habits of the culture—the mores of a culture—and this obedience serves to strengthen and reinforce the authority of the tradition in turn: moral duty and obligation are thus created by the earlier culture and passed down, with all due respect, to subsequent generations. As Nietzsche expressed this in his earlier work, *Daybreak*,

> Morality is nothing other (therefore *no more!*) than obedience to customs, of whatever kind they may be; customs, however, are the *traditional* way of behaving and evaluating. In things in which no tradition commands there is no morality. . . . What is tradition? A higher authority which one obeys, not because it commands what is *useful* to us, but because it commands.[121]

Nietzsche thus points out not only that moral obedience is largely a question of habit but that, in many ways, it can be counterproductive to the individual's well-being, which is always concerned with one's own good and interests. While there is generally an element of "superstition" to the morality of custom, which induces obedience and compliance out of "fear in the presence of a higher intellect which here commands, of an incomprehensible, indefinite power, of something more than personal,"[122] Nietzsche goes on to argue that what really perpetuates the traditional morality is the very "hegemony" of customs and culture itself. In this sense, one is held to be "immoral" to the extent that one simply stands outside or resists that hegemony, whatever the motive. What is certain is that one is moral to the extent that one sacrifices one's own interests to the commands of custom: the greater the self-sacrifice, the greater the moral virtue and goodness.

While the traditional moral imperatives may have initially been framed with regard to some general motive of utility in an earlier age, times change but the imperative to act in a particular way remains in force and is still felt as a duty— not as a bearer or as an incarnation of its initial motives (which are often enough simply forgotten over the course of time)—but out of respect for the venerated tradition itself. The traditional morality of the "thou shalt"—or "thou shalt not"—is thus not only irrational but also militates against reasonable, thoughtful self-examination of its own nature, legitimacy, and underlying motivations.

> [Moral] duty is a compulsive feeling which impels us to some action and which we call good and regard as undiscussable (—we refuse to speak of its origin, limitation and justification or to hear them spoken of). The thinker, however, regards everything as having evolved and everything that has evolved as discussable, and is thus a man without a sense of duty—as long, that is, as he is functioning as a thinker.[123]

The resulting situation, for Nietzsche, is that the traditional morality aggravates one's discomfiture and makes one less able to deal with changing circumstances, thereby blunting one's ability to fare well in the complex circumstances of everyday life:

> Custom represents the experiences of men of earlier times as to what they supposed useful and harmful—but the *sense for custom* (morality) applies, not to these experiences as such, but to the age, the sanctity, the indiscussability of the custom. And so this feeling is a hindrance to the acquisition of new experiences and the correction of customs: that is to say, morality is a hindrance to the creation of new and better customs: it makes stupid.[124]

Ultimately, our sense of moral duty and virtue must be felt to be positive, purposive, and useful—beneficial—to the individual such that it would positively yield us pleasure:

A virtue must be *our own* invention, *our* most necessary self-expression and self-defense: any other kind of virtue is merely a danger. Whatever is not a condition of our life *harms* it: a virtue that is prompted solely by a feeling of respect for the concept of "virtue" . . . is harmful. "Virtue," "duty," the "good in itself," the good which is impersonal and universally valid . . . [are] chimeras and expressions of decline . . . the final exhaustion of life. . . . The fundamental laws of self-preservation and growth demand the opposite—that everyone invent *his own* virtue, *his own* categorical imperative. A people perishes when it confuses its duty with duty in general. Nothing ruins more profoundly, more intimately, than every "impersonal" duty, every sacrifice to the Moloch of abstraction.

An action demanded by the instinct of life is proved to be *right* by the pleasure that accompanies it. Yet . . . [the] Christian dogmatic . . . considers pleasure an *objection*. What could destroy us more quickly than working, thinking, and feeling without any inner necessity, without any deeply personal choice, without *pleasure*—as an automaton of "duty"? This is the very recipe for decadence, even for idiocy . . . [in the end,] one need not bother about reason—that is, when morality, when the sublime command "thou shalt," raises its voice.[125]

Of course, this is the problem, the inner emotional resistance to critique and of changing the very norms of moral evaluation. The sentiments of duty and obligation are so intimate and so thoroughly ingrained that they constitute our very identity as members of the broader culture at large. The "thou shalt" is understandably experienced as a deeply personal instinct, as a compulsion, a sentiment that has preserved the tradition we enjoy—and we with it. Hence the "undiscussable" character of the moral imperative. Through the effectiveness of our own moral formation, the "thou shalt" is immune to criticism and serves as a false consciousness, thus preventing the possibility of its own questioning. The difficulty in critiquing the tradition—precisely what requires the courage of a lion—is twofold: On the one hand, to do so is self-alienating, it drives the individual from the comfort of his shared heritage and communal belonging into the "desert," and only there can one begin to take a critical perspective upon the effects, the sentiments, one finds within oneself. On the other hand, such an isolation always tempts us to return to the traditional moral order, because it really is abundant, comforting, reassuring, welcoming:

> *The heritage of morality*:—In the domain of morality too there is a rich heritage: it is possessed by the gentle, the good-natured, the sympathizing and charitable, who have all inherited from their forefathers the good *mode of action* but not the reasons for it (its source). The pleasant thing about this wealth is that it has to be continually expended and spread abroad if it is to be felt to exist at all, and that

it thus involuntarily works to reduce the distance between the morally rich and
the morally poor: and, what is best and most remarkable, it does so not for the
sake of producing some future mean and average between poor and rich, but for
the sake of a *universal* enrichment and over-enrichment.[126]

But once one sees that the traditional morality can be inimical to the interests of the individual and of the well-being and adaptability of the community
at large, and that morality's foundations rest on a scientifically unjustified basis
in the old religiometaphysical order, then one realizes that morality's "hegemony" serves little more purpose than does inertia: "The dominant view of what
constitutes the moral heritage . . . it seems to me . . . is maintained more 'to
the greater glory' of morality than out of respect for truth."[127] What this means
for Zarathustra is that he has to thoughtfully and rationally examine his own
inner sentiments and compulsions and prepare to judge them truthfully. When
one does this to such deeply implanted moral sentiments as one possesses—
sentiments that compose our very identity—one may find them to be false
and without real purpose or justification. One finds, within oneself, that these
traditional beliefs and imperatives are themselves consequences of false and
erroneous judgments from a more primitive stage of civilization. As Nietzsche
would remark in book 1 of *Daybreak*,

> "Trust your feelings!"—But feelings are nothing final or original; behind feelings
> there stand judgments and evaluations which we inherit in the form of feelings
> (inclinations, aversions). The inspiration born of a feeling is the grandchild of a
> judgment—and often of a false judgment!—and in any event not a child of your
> own! To trust one's feelings—means to give more obedience to one's grandfather
> and grandmother and their grandparents than to the gods which are in *us*: our
> reason and our experience.[128]

More than just errors or mistakes that have become internalized and made
part and parcel of our moral being, these original judgments are now seen to
have been made in virtual contempt of reason and truth, in the disregard of
even a modicum of scientific understanding of causality and the natural
order.[129] With a historical understanding of morality's provenance, however,
one attains the recognition that its imperatives are, in many cases, simply the
consequences of *misinterpreting* nature and human experience itself. Who we
are and the moral sentiments we harbor are thus—due to no fault of our own—
consequences of a deep historical misinterpretation, and therefore, misunderstanding, of the real:

> The idea of a God is disturbing and humiliating as long as it is believed, but how
> it *originated* can at the present stage of comparative ethnology no longer admit

of doubt; and with the insight into this origination that belief falls away. The Christian who compares his nature with that of God is like Don Quixote, who under-estimated his own courage because his head was filled with the miraculous deeds of the heroes of chivalric romances: the standard of comparison applied in both cases belongs in the domain of fable. But if the idea of God falls away, so does the feeling of "sin" as a transgression against divine precepts, as a blemish on a creature consecrated to God. . . . Thus: a certain false psychology, a certain kind of fantasy in the interpretation of motives and experiences is the necessary presupposition for becoming a Christian and for feeling the need of redemption. With the insight into this aberration of reason and imagination one ceases to be a Christian.[130]

Recognizing the fictive and erroneous derivation of the religiomoral sentiments by conducting a historical and psychological criticism of them is what enables the individual to distance and liberate him- or herself from them, "a creation," Zarathustra says, "of freedom for oneself,"[131] so as to be able to will, and to evaluate, precisely *as an individual*, feeling responsible for the objectives and values entailed by the newfound autonomy. Nonetheless, and this will come to plague Zarathustra, there remains the residue, the residual moral after-effects of the old order that may imperceptibly reemerge from time to time, in a moment of weakness, perhaps, or in a period of despondency, loneliness, doubt, or despair; namely, the susceptibility of suffering from a variety of morally informed sentiments and feelings, something to which no one is entirely immune. It will demand a great deal of personal courage and fortitude to confront such a vestigial sense of moral sentiment (e.g., of conscience, guilt, and sin) precisely because they had been so deeply enracinated for so long in the human condition we inherit. Even though one consciously rejects the traditional moral imperatives, together with the entire religious and metaphysical apparatus that sustains them (this in the name of one's very autonomy), they nevertheless return unsuspected, in the very way neurotic behavior can arise out of an earlier, repressed trauma. Thus, even though one willfully and consciously distances oneself from "the idea of God," and the notion of "'sin' as a transgression of divine precepts," Nietzsche would remark,

> There probably still remains over that feeling of depression which is very much entwined with and related to fear of punishment by secular justice or the disapprobation of other men . . . [likewise,] the depression caused by the pain of conscience, the sharpest sting in the feeling of guilt.[132]

If such feelings do remain, albeit mostly on an unconscious level, Nietzsche argues that, since they resulted from *misinterpretations* of reality and human

experience in the first place, they can be *reinterpreted* in turn, and done so
effectively. He gives a rehearsal of his doctrine of eternal return as a means for
reinterpreting the vestigial moral sentiments one still unwittingly bears, which
prevent our full *enactment* of our new, freely willed values, in his work of 1878,
Human, All Too Human. This reinterpretation will give the individual a new
attitude that would desacrilize our worldview, and thus remove the very conditions of sin and guilt, with their attendant vestigial moral sentiments. But, remarkably, he will illustrate this reinterpretation, or reversal of interpretation,
with an example drawn from within the moral sentiments and religious attitude
of the Christian experience itself. The example again concerns the Christian's
felt need for redemption, a sentiment that weighs so heavily on the religious
conscience:

> Now if, as has been said, the Christian has got into the feeling of self-contempt
> through certain errors, that is to say through a false, unscientific interpretation of
> his actions and sensations, he also notices with the highest astonishment that this
> condition of contempt, the pang of conscience, displeasure in general, does not
> persist, but that occasionally there are hours when all this is wafted away from his
> soul and he again feels free and valiant. What has happened is that his pleasure in
> himself, his contentment at his own strength, has, in concert with the weakening
> which every profound excitation must necessarily undergo, carried off the victory:
> he loves himself again, he feels it—but precisely this love, this new self-valuation
> seems to him incredible, he can see in it only the wholly undeserved flowing
> down of a radiance of mercy from on high. If he earlier believed he saw in every
> event warnings, menaces, punishments and every sort of sign of divine wrath, he
> now *interprets* divine goodness *into* his experiences: this event appears to him to
> exhibit kindness, that is like a helpful signpost, a third and especially the whole
> joyful mood he is in seems to him proof that God is merciful. If he earlier in a
> condition of depression interpreted his actions falsely, now he does the same with
> his experiences; he conceives his mood of consolation as the effect upon him of
> an external power, the love with which fundamentally he loves himself appears
> as divine love.[133]

By thus reversing the earlier interpretation of divine agency and purpose,
an entirely different emotion rushes in to dispose the Christian to a world of
beatitude and grace. The new interpretation has transformed the Christian
experience of conscientious contempt into the joyous affirmation of plentitude
and abundance. The new attitude toward divine agency is no longer one of a
needful fear that breeds inadequacy and self-contempt, but rather one of a
divine love, effulgent in mercy and "the prelude to redemption," or, as Nietz-

sche often quoted Stendahl's concept of beauty, "the promise of happiness." But what Nietzsche pointedly asserts about this reversal of interpretation is that both views are equally erroneous, and both are predicated on the illusion of divine, purposive agency.[134] Rather, what has happened in practice is that the individual simply failed to see his own agency as the real, nonimaginary (if unrecognized) cause of his newfound and equally real happiness. Thus, Nietzsche concludes, "that which he calls mercy and the prelude to redemption is in truth self-pardon, self-redemption."[135]

If such a transformation of attitude derives from a new, albeit imaginary, *interpretation*, Nietzsche proposes that one make a *truthful* reinterpretation of divine agency and recognize it for what it is: nothing. Cosmic indifference. If one could come to *interpret* the real as being without purpose, without a goal, without any external demand (or reward) at all placed upon anyone or anything, then one would attain a human condition for practical action, for the real creation of value, without any felt constraint or limitation whatsoever. One would have achieved a human freedom of action, precisely due to the *indifference*—the benign indifference—of the universe.

> The pang of conscience, the sharpest sting in the feeling of guilt, is nonetheless abolished when one sees that, although one may by one's actions have offended against human tradition, human laws and ordinances, one has not therewith endangered the "eternal salvation of the soul" and its relationship to the divinity. If a man is, finally, able to attain to the philosophical conviction of the unconditional necessity of all actions and their complete unaccountability and to make it part of his flesh and blood, then that remainder of the pang of conscience also disappears.[136]

The teaching of real human freedom, in the face of an entirely indifferent cosmos—one of the principal formulations of the eternal return—is, of course, a preeminent Enlightenment teaching. It had its origins in ancient thought—especially in Epicurus and Lucretius—and its first modern proponent was Descartes, when he equated God with nature in his *Meditations*.[137] He did this precisely to rid our understanding of nature as *purposive*. Spinoza would in turn formulate nature, according to a pantheistic physical doctrine, as self-creating and as self-created. The absence of an *external* source of creation and purpose, however, led Leibniz to criticize such unchristian freedom as "the liberty of indifference." With no divine constraints or prerogatives whatsoever, with a freedom to apply this interpretation to one's life and to create new values that would finally result in humanity's self-overcoming, Zarathustra proposes the third and final metamorphosis, that of the child.

But say, my brothers, what can the child do that even the lion could not do? Why must the preying lion still become a child? The child is innocence and forgetting, a new beginning, a game, a self-propelled wheel, a first movement, a sacred "Yes." For the game of creation, my brothers, a sacred "Yes" is needed: the spirit now wills his own will, and he who had been lost to the world now conquers his own world.[138]

The third stage of the spirit's metamorphosis, or overcoming, would then be its rebirth as a new and higher individual: the age of the *child* who can affirm a sacred "yes." And, in doing this, the spirit becomes capable of *creating new* values. Yet, why a child, why the value of innocence? Perhaps we can here begin to see that the three metamorphoses really express much the same thing. Camel, lion, and child are different ways of saying that the *old* tablets of morality and metaphysics must be broken, that the old phantoms and shrouds of the dead God must be disgorged. In short, it is to say that the old *will* must be overcome, straightened out, and best of all, *forgotten*: "The child is innocence and forgetting."

The child: youth, innocence, and forgetting. Tradition has it otherwise. Plato and Aristotle both tell us that the philosopher, the great-souled man of intellect and virtue, must above all else have a *good memory*. This is the first requirement to be met if one wishes to pursue the life of philosophy. We have only to examine practically any classical text at random to find this: for example, the *Meno, Theaetetus, Republic*, or *Ethics*. Second, the philosopher—as traditionally understood—must be *old*: the medieval philosopher Moses Maimonides even went so far as to say that one's testicles must first desiccate before he can become a philosopher. Nietzsche, however, has the temerity to say not only that the higher man should be young, but that he should be a child, precisely because he would *not* have a memory, precisely because he naturally *forgets* and has little if anything to remember anyway. The important consideration, for Nietzsche, in any case, is the value of the *future* and the infinitizing possibilities that it extends to the child—and *not the past*, which is the source of our present discomfiture and restriction.

MEMORIES

We might be tempted to argue that Nietzsche simply urges us to forget the whole tradition of ontotheology.[139] Clearly, this is indeed true to some extent. The difficulty of attaining a singular individuality and a rigorous sense of personal autonomy and the ability to form one's own values—to be able to evaluate on one's own—often in contradiction to the prevailing common morality and social mores, are themes Nietzsche explores from his earliest through his latest works.[140] But just as important as the ability to distance oneself from the received tradition—to actively forget certain general beliefs and teachings encoded in it—is the attitude one takes toward the memory of one's own personally experienced past. It is imperative, Nietzsche argues, that the individual *needs to forget certain* aspects of his *own past*, for the sake of his very *future*, for his future comportment and growth. What must be transformed, for Nietzsche, is our fearful and enervating dependency on the past, on what he calls the "it was." The *past itself* stands to thwart the individual's future, since the past and its continuous reverberations *operate* as the origin of our own present weaknesses, our own distorted and inverted wills. Strictly speaking, of course, the past is not. Nonetheless, as Nietzsche would later observe at great length in *On the Genealogy of Morals*, the persistence of the past in memory, constantly repeated and invoked, lies at the very heart of bad conscience, of sin and guilt, of slave morality itself. Indeed, slave morality was a compensatory formation to relieve suffering, conflict, and strife. It is for precisely this reason that any critique of the broader tradition of morality and metaphysics must be initially internalized into an autocritique—of the person who was formed by it. In any case, for Zarathustra, present humanity stands as deficient to the higher man precisely because we are unwittingly chained to the past, because, for example, we *cannot forget* the personal wrongs done against us—or, equally, because we *cannot forget* the pleasures we *once had* and *no longer* have. Our *past* and our *memories* concerning the past thus stand as an abiding interpretive grid, as an intellectual and emotional block, a psychological force that exercises its resistance *against* the present, against our concern with the future. In short, the emotional and oftentimes obsessional relations we hold toward our personally experienced past stand against the free exercise of life itself.

Because of a wrong committed against us in the past, for which we suffered, we cannot humanly forget it (i.e., given our present psychological formation). We turn bitter, resentful, full of spite and rancor and loathing. We crave revenge or harbor pettiness, and we become nasty, brutish. We cannot affirm the present for we have already become powerless to act naively, openly, in the face of it, in the face of our preoccupations in the present about the past. Our minds seethe with the prospect of revenging the past, of literally rectifying it. In such a condition, the will turns sick, weak, and festering. All energies turn toward retribution, perhaps under the euphemistic title of "justice." The individual cries out: "We want justice!" Nietzsche points out, however, that what is being said in such cases is really quite different: what is really called for is retribution—perhaps in the person of an avenging judge, or hangman—some form of retribution—to serve as a soothing antidote for our wounded pride and arrogance.[141] Or perhaps we might take a less direct course of action and repress the festering pallor of our resentment even further—in our own self-denial—in which case we become pious, ascetic, self-righteous, and morally unctuous:

> Once a man has been brought to a state of extraordinary tension, he can resolve equally well to take a fearful revenge or to break himself of his thirst for revenge. Under the influence of violent emotion, he desires in any event the great, tremendous, prodigious [release], and if he happens to notice that the sacrifice of himself satisfies him as much as, or even more than the sacrifice of another, he chooses it. All he is really concerned with, therefore, is the discharge of his emotion; to relieve his state of tension he seizes the spears of his enemies and buries them in his own breast . . . there is something great in self-denial, and not only in revenge. . . . As the overcoming of the foe hardest to conquer, the sudden mastering of an affect—that is how this denial *appeared*; and to this extent it counted as the summit of the moral.[142]

The obsessive preoccupation with a past hurt or wrong can easily condition all subsequent human relationships for the individual. Each personal encounter then becomes a renewed vendetta, and the human world of social intercourse becomes a place of opprobrium, of enmity. The *world* becomes *evil*, and trust, much less affection, is nowhere to be found, save perhaps in the compensatory religious metaphysics of an afterworld or otherworld.

On the other hand, perhaps we *once* had a love, a love *so* grand, so profound, that our waking universe paled in comparison. What if fortune took away that love? We would torture our souls in anguish over that memory—we would see every other love as a dim reflection of that *one* truly ideal and once real love. We would wander the earth like Homer's wraiths or like Aristophanes' split lovers, looking for our departed complements.[143] Our lives would become completely debilitated by this loss of someone who once was and who meant so much to us, so long ago. Perhaps we might, for an instant, catch a glance of a face in the crowd—by the Café Wagner, on the Place de l'Opéra, perhaps down the Avenue Wagram by the Place des Ternes: we would run and hail to it, only to be bitterly disappointed, time and again. We would want to return, to go back, to flee—to find our lover somewhere on a warm evening hillside in Umbria, on a midnight seacoast in the Yucatán, in a small village set close to the Loire, or perhaps, dead. Only a letter, an old photo, is left. What unspeakable torments of misery these little shards of the past might trigger. "It was"—and nevermore shall be.

Can anything be more life-denying than this kind of personal debilitation, this completely unproductive and anguishing self-indulgence? In all these cases, the will—our entire personality and character—becomes inverted, turned back upon itself, and languors in impotence, helplessly. We know full well *where* its bitterness will be directed. As Nietzsche already remarked in *The Gay Science,* "One thing is needful: that a human being should *attain* satisfaction with himself. . . . Whoever is dissatisfied with himself is continually ready for revenge, and we others will be his victims, if only in having to endure his ugly aspect. For [even] the sight of what is ugly makes one bad and gloomy."[144]

WORKING THROUGH

In the second part of *Zarathustra,* in the section titled "On Redemption," Nietzsche gives his proper account of the *ill will* that is borne by the "it was."

> "It was"—that is the name of the will's gnashing of teeth and most secret melancholy. Powerless against what has been done, he is an angry spectator of all that is past. The will cannot will backwards; and that he cannot break time and time's covetousness—that is the will's loneliest melancholy. "It was" is the name of the stone he cannot move. Thus the will took to hurting; and on all who can suffer he wreaks revenge for his inability to go backwards. This, indeed, this alone, is what revenge is: the will's ill will against time and its "it was."[145]

The spirit of revenge is found at the heart of all rancor, bitterness, loathing, and resentment. We crave revenge against the past, against the "it was." If we could only recapture that one moment of joy, of happiness, that we once experienced in the past. If we could only extirpate that moment of pain, of pique—once committed against us so long ago. But we are powerless to do so. We are bound by our own impotence—we cannot move that stone of the past. Consequently, we cannot naively enjoy the present or joyfully anticipate the future. We are quite simply bound by our own, extremely personal, psychological obsession with the past—with the joy *or* sorrow we *once* experienced *in* the past. In short, the "it was" can easily assume the weight of a debilitating trauma, and this was in fact Nietzsche's personal condition at the time.

Prior to the disastrous breakup with Lou Salomé, Nietzsche seemed to have regarded his health and goodwill with such a high degree of satisfaction that he desired to embrace the totality of existence itself:

> No revenge, my sweetest thought: I want to learn more and more to see as beautiful what is necessary in things; then I shall be one of those who make things beautiful. *Amor fati*: let that be my love henceforth! . . . Now we see how everything turns out for the best. Every day and every hour, life seems to have no other wish to prove this proposition again and again.[146]

Following the Lou affair and the collapse of his health, however, Nietzsche found himself in total despair, verging on a complete spiritual breakdown. His despair is clearly evoked in "The Night Song" of part 2, which he wrote in his "melancholy spring [1883] in Rome, where I put up with life."[147] In a room overlooking the fountain in the Piazza Barberina, "the loneliest song was written that has ever been written, the 'Night Song.' Around that time a melody of indescribable melancholy was always about me, and I found its refrain in the words, 'dead from immortality.'"[148] The poem compares Nietzsche himself to a "fountain," because, as he later described his condition at the time, in *Ecce Homo*,

> I drink back into myself the flames that break out in me. I do not know the happiness of those who receive; and I have often dreamed that even stealing must be more blessed than receiving. This is my poverty, that my hand never rests from giving . . . Oh, ravenous hunger in satiation! They receive from me but do I touch their souls? . . . I should like to rob those to whom I give; thus do I hunger for malice. To withdraw my hand when the other hand already reaches out to it . . . thus do I hunger for malice. Such revenge my fullness plots: such spite wells up out of my loneliness. My happiness in giving died in giving.[149]

If "The Night Song" is "the immortal lament at being condemned . . . not to love,"[150] Nietzsche at first responds to this lack of love, this lack of any emotional reciprocation whatsoever, with a sense of irony, indeed sarcasm—by writing about it and working through it—in the section titled "On Little Old and Young Women," in part 1, especially in the famous passage that closes the section:

> "It is strange: Zarathustra knows women little, and yet he is right about them. Is this because nothing is impossible with woman? And now, as a token of gratitude,

accept a little truth. After all, I am old enough for it. Wrap it up and hold your hand over its mouth: else it will cry overloudly, this little truth."

Then I said: "Woman, give me your little truth." And thus spoke the little old woman:

"You are going to women? Do not forget the whip!"[151]

In the preceding section, "On the Way to the Creator," and in the following section, "The Adder's Bite," many of Zarathustra's remarks point to the failed affair with Lou, and the mention of the "whip" in the above passage clearly bears reference to the group portrait photograph Nietzsche staged with Lou and Rée in the spring of the previous year. The well-known photograph depicts Nietzsche and Rée each pulling a handle of a wooden-wheeled farm cart, a small wagon, with Lou inside rather sheepishly brandishing a whip in her hand, which Nietzsche had carefully entwined with flower blossoms.[152] A close examination of the picture reveals a look of intensity on Nietzsche's face, a knowing smile, with more than a bit of irony to it. Rée looks confused, befuddled, and Lou a bit uncertain and perplexed about the whole scene. Given the variety of props available to the still photographer in his studio, the "malice" of this staged pose is pointed (in Nietzsche's selection of the props) and is as much directed in "revenge" against Rée as Lou, Nietzsche having been outmaneuvered by Rée for Lou's affections. The deception Nietzsche employs is to humiliate Rée without the latter's realizing it (no point in burning all the bridges, yet!), thus asserting some form of his own superiority over Rée—at least to his own mind—whether psychological, intellectual, or even in the capacity for a kind of jailhouse humor.

The scene derives from an apocryphal medieval story about Alexander the Great and his lover, the beautiful young Phyllis, and it involves a staged humiliation of the great Aristotle himself. The story was often retold in popular literature, poetry, song, and sermon, when addressing such entertaining moral topics as sexual "deception," "feminine tricks and wiles," "foolish loves," and so forth, and its origins go back at least to the thirteenth century.[153] The legend, or fable, has it that when Philip of Macedon summoned Aristotle to his court to give young Alexander instruction in the sciences and rhetoric, Aristotle was so demanding of Alexander's time—begrudgingly devoted to his studies at his father's insistence—that Phyllis and Alexander despaired over their now loveless separation. The two plotted a trick that, hopefully, would send Aristotle away, thereby allowing the resumption of their impassioned affair. The trick was to seduce Aristotle into thinking he had gained Phyllis's affection and then to expose his purported "lechery." One warm spring day, when Alexander feigned illness, so as to avoid his regular lessons, Phyllis approached the window of Aristotle's study (see below left) and paused there to pick blossoms from the branch of a fruit tree. Standing next to the window, Aristotle looked out, and seeing Phyllis dressed in a most décolleté gown, he was simply stunned, transfixed, by her beauty and quickly invited her into his study. When Phyllis told Aristotle of her shock that he was so handsome and far younger than she had expected—and not just that he was the world's most brilliant philosopher!—Aristotle fell all over himself in praising her beauty. Phyllis responded by readily offering her affections to Aristotle, if he might—just possibly, maybe, please—serve one of her girlish whims, first. If he could just indulge one small, prankish wish—namely, to play "pony," "horsy," with Phyllis on his back. Beside himself with the prospects of Phyllis's attentions, Aristotle agreed, and Phyllis mounted his back, carrying the flowering branch as a "whip" (see below right). Crawling on hands and knees from his study, out into the courtyard, where the entire court nobility was hiding behind curtains, hav-

Detail from Freiburg Tapestry (ca. 1320) depicting Aristotle (*left*) (in his study) and Phyllis (*right*) (courtesy of Saskia Durian-Ress, Augustinermuseum, Freiburg im Bresgau).

Detail from Freiburg Tapestry (ca. 1320) depicting Phyllis riding Aristotle (Aristotle's head is on the left) (courtesy of Saskia Durian-Ress, Augustinermuseum, Freiburg im Bresgau).

ing been set up for the joke by Alexander, everyone leapt out, shouting in peals of laughter. Completely humiliated, Aristotle fled Philip's court the next day, and the lovers were reunited.

Clearly, Nietzsche had this story in mind when he staged the studio portrait, having Lou hold a short whip, entwined with flowers. The joke is particularly directed at Rée, however, since he—as well as anyone—should have known better: What ignorance! Rée had studied Aristotle at the University of Basel, where the great Aristotelian Sebastian Brant had taught and written his doctoral dissertation in philosophy on the history of ethics and moral theory! Let Rée play Aristotle himself and heap even more shame on him for having violated their friendship in the first place, friendship being so central to Aristotle's model of developed, human character. By successfully staging the trick, Nietzsche smiles knowingly right at the camera, as Alexander—all the while, realizing that precisely the kind of pony cart they posed with was known in medieval times as "the ship of fools."[154]

If Nietzsche did get some small psychological satisfaction by invoking his own pleasure at Rée's inability to understand the "whip" staging—and recasting this as the "Little Old and Young Women," inducing Rée to unwittingly make a fool of himself—such satisfaction, at this point, could be little more than anecdotal. The real problem and the source of Nietzsche's inability to deal with his rage and depression following the final breakup in the fall of 1882 was that his feeling for revenge would have to be directed in some fashion against Lou.[155] He would have to stamp the mark of his own suffering on her: *in re* or *in intellectus*, and this would at least restore some semblance of balance to his painfully wounded pride. Rather than strike back at someone's person, or retreat to the delusion of a redemptive faith or "idealism," Nietzsche would really have to deal with his own suffering and pain—which inhabited him like a "ghost"—by confronting them, by creatively employing them in his own service of self-overcoming. Effectively, he has to exorcise the ghost of a ghastly *memory* of the Lou affair, and he does this in his unpublished drafts written during this period by making a symbolic sacrifice; namely, the alter ego of the "suffering" Zarathustra has to be *killed* in order to somehow reclaim the naiveté of an "awakened" and "transformed" Zarathustra, in the end, to undergo the third metamorphosis, that of the child.[156] Given the intensity of his embittered feelings and hostile aggressions toward Paul Rée and, ultimately, toward Lou herself, such emotions would have to be either internalized or externalized. But even if it were possible to internalize them, it would be at the cost of their further intensification and his own suffering—perhaps in the form of an extreme self-laceration or what he thought might prove to be a final servility.[157] Rather, he would externalize them by projecting them in his writing—his very drafts of *Zarathustra*—onto a *symbolic Lou*, who would in turn kill off what she herself had created; namely, a fractured, brokenhearted Nietzsche. Realistically, this scenario takes the form of a most determined sublimation, the sublimation of painful affect through *work*, through his own art, his writing.

In the early drafts of *Zarathustra*, Nietzsche had figured a feminine character to play a prominent role in the work, and the name he bestowed to this protagonist was Pana. The name Pana at first appears to be a feminization of the mythical Greek god Pan—friend of Dionysus, god of the mountains and pasture, of the goats and shepherds, who would frolic with the nymphs, seducing them with his flute: playful, capricious, petulant, and lustful. But "Pana" also suggests "Pantheia," the woman who Empedocles was said to have brought back to life in the Sicilian city of Acragas.[158] Nietzsche had started several drafts of a projected tragedy concerning the life of Empedocles, whose philosophy, Nietzsche thought, prefigured his own notion of the eternal return, and whose public teachings were held blasphemous and were met with such disfavor that he was exiled—seemingly, a portentous omen of Nietzsche's own situation at the time. Nonetheless, he was reputed to be highly skilled in rhetoric, medicine, anatomy, and engineering. Nietzsche's drafts for "Empedocles" date back to the time preceding *The Birth of Tragedy* (1870–71) and continue through the mid-1870s.[159] By 1882–83, the dramatic character of the earlier Empedocles merges into, and is fully eclipsed by, Zarathustra himself. The historical figure of Pantheia is also to be found in Hölderlin's drafts for a similar tragedy, "The Death of Empedocles," written in 1799–1800. But the name Pana that Nietzsche uses in his later *Zarathustra* drafts is also suggestive of Pandora, the first woman created by Zeus to torment mankind for having accepted Prometheus's gift of fire. The traditional (if erroneous) etymology of Pandora is "she who receives all gifts," and this certainly is in keeping with Nietzsche's own accounts of *his* giving, and receiving nothing but heartbreak: "I drink back into myself the flames that break out in me. I do not know the happiness of those who receive."[160] Finally, "Pana" also suggests the familiar Polish term for a young maiden, Panna (as did the image of the Jungfrau— literally, "young woman," or more typically, "virgin").[161] All these allusive figures seem to fuse into the role of Pana, the person who will kill Zarathustra more than once in the course of Nietzsche's *Zarathustra* drafts: "Pan[thei]a," for Empedocles and Hölderlin, and "Pana" for Zarathustra, the "godless."

In the unpublished notes from *The Birth of Tragedy* period, the figure of Pantheia[162] is cast as Empedocles' lover, completely enraptured by him—to the point of committing suicide for him—and she is described as "the most beautiful woman" in Agrigento.[163] By the time the Empedocles project is transformed into *Zarathustra*, Nietzsche reestablishes the "love" of the Pantheia/Corrina figure into Pana's love for Zarathustra, again, to the point of death: "'I want to die like this! And to die again! And to live to die like this!' And in dying she smiles: because she loved Zarathustra."[164]

After mentioning two of the central dramatic scenes that were carried over from the various earlier Empedocles drafts, for example, a general public panic in anticipation of the plague and the arrival of the plague, Pana draws Zarathustra into an affectionate embrace: "She drew Zarathustra's arm over her breast. / And once again the abyss breathed: he groaned and his flames roared upwards."[165]

Again, Nietzsche goes on to incorporate several scenes drawn from the earlier Empedocles: now, it is Zarathustra's "cure of the woman," the "outbreak of the plague," "cadavers," and then Zarathustra addresses Pana, fully acknowledging his love of her, but he is perplexed as to the motivation behind her love:

OMENS . . .

"But you well know, Pana, my child, my little star, my golden ear—you certainly
    know that I, too, love you?"
The love you have for me convinced you, I see: but I still don't understand the
    will of your love, Pana![166]

Upon reflection, however, Zarathustra realizes that hers is not a noble and joyous love, but one bred from pity and need. Upon disclosure of her concealed truth, she—like the statue in Schiller's poem, "The Veiled Image at Sais"—wishes death upon him:

But when he saw his serpent dart his tongue at him, his face, slowly, slowly,
slowly, became transformed: the door of understanding opened up for him, unwittingly: it was like a bolt of lightning plunging from the deepest depths of his
eyes, then again, like lightning: it took him a moment to grasp. . . When the woman
saw this change, she shout out a cry of extreme distress. "Die, Zarathustra." . . .
    "And what should I do with this knife, Pana? Should I cut off the yellow
grapes at the foot of the vine?"[167]

Rewriting the death scene in the fall of 1883, some months later, Nietzsche again has Pana kill Zarathustra—not by his own hand, but out of pity for her!

"When he unveils Pana, Zarathustra dies of pity for her pity. Before, the moment of the great contempt (supreme beatitude!)."[168]

Nietzsche restages the death scene in the very next notebook entry, and the knife is now wielded by Pana:

> First of all, everyone turns away from Zarathustra (do *a progressive elaboration* of this!). A delighted Zarathustra senses nothing. Pana wants to kill him. *At the very moment when she thrusts the knife Zarathustra understands everything and dies of pain in seeing this pity. This is what has to be made clear!*[169]

Finally, realizing that everything depends on his own happiness, and that Pana is incapable of grasping the secret of the eternal return, which is predicated on that happiness, Pana is again driven to kill Zarathustra out of bitterness and revenge. She is unwilling to accept things as they are and to simply acknowledge the blessings they bring. She dies, broken on the ground by this truth—exacting a final revenge on Zarathustra: her suffering causes Zarathustra to die laughing!

> Redemption of accident: what I *let* happen, I know afterwards, makes it good for me: and by this fact, *to will* afterwards what I did not will beforehand.
>
> A goal complete in itself.
>
> On this, Zarathustra recounts, *on the basis of the happiness of the overman*, the secret of the return of all things.
>
> Effect. Pana wants to kill him.
>
> He finally understands, passes through all the metamorphoses right up to the most victorious, but when he sees her lying broken on the ground—he *laughs*. Laughing, he climbs up the rock: attaining the summit he dies happy.[170]

Seemingly pausing here, at the very threshold of the last metamorphosis, the "brokenhearted" Zarathustra dies happy—with the *knowledge* of what must be done and knowing full well that "redemption" will not come from without, and certainly not from Lou. With Pana dead, it remains for a "transformed" Zarathustra to act upon his new knowledge and create his own happiness—absent Pana. Revenge, Nietzsche well knew, must finally be laid to rest.

In the section entitled "On Redemption" in part 2 of *Zarathustra*, Nietzsche says: "*The spirit of revenge*, my friends, has so far been the subject of man's best reflection."[171] Perhaps more pointedly, man's best reflections have been conceived *in* this spirit of revenge, in the desire either to *recapture* or to *obliterate* the past; that is, to deal with and to rectify what *has been*, the "it was."

In both cases—that of the past joy or hurt—the consequences reverberate into the present. We are haunted by the past in the form of an enduring *pain* that we are oftentimes incapable of dealing with. But also, this pain is often accompanied by a *fear* that stems from the awareness of our evident frustration or powerlessness to act in the face of the past. Consequently, we are haunted by our *finitude* with regard to time and eternity. We are hurt, we suffer, and we are powerless to do anything about it. This is our all-too-human condition.[172]

Because of these four considerations—this pain, our powerlessness, the fear it induces, and our finitude—we not only see that the "it was" is not only a source of psychological debilitation, but that its trace, its effect, is also to be found at the very source of traditional metaphysics and Judeo-Christian morality: the "it was" gives rise to the ontotheologically conceived world order in general as a compensation for our felt helplessness in the face of our personal suffering. Accordingly, Nietzsche remarked in *The Gay Science*, that

> the greatest *sufferer*, the man poorest in vitality, would have most need of mildness, peace, and kindliness in thought and action: he would need, if possible, a God who is specially the God of the sick, a "Savior"; similarly, he would have need of logic, the abstract intelligibility of existence—for logic soothes and gives confidence;—in short, he would need a certain warm, fear-dispelling narrowness and imprisonment within optimistic horizons. . . . My vision has always become keener in tracing that most difficult and insidious of all forms of retrospective inference . . . [such as] the tyrannical will of a sorely suffering, struggling or tortured being, who would like to stamp his most personal, individual, and narrow characteristics, the very idiosyncrasy of his suffering, as an obligatory law and constraint on others; who, as it were, takes revenge on all things, in that he imprints, enforces and brands his image, the image of his torture, upon them.[173]

But what is Zarathustra's teaching? Zarathustra teaches the eternal return, the most "abysmal thought," the most "riddle-laden" and problematic thought. Only the teaching of the eternal return can deliver us from the spite and peevishness of a debilitating revenge. But what is needed for this most abysmal thought? Zarathustra tells us that we need, above all, courage, for courage alone can slay pity and self-pity. True, sincere pity is the danger of seeing too deeply into life and into the *necessary suffering in and of life*.[174] Nietzsche had earlier claimed, in *The Birth of Tragedy*, that classical, pre-Platonic Greece could deal with this, by purposefully cultivating an agonistic dimension of culture and, ultimately, by its balanced appreciation of the tragic condition through the conjunction of the Apollonian and Dionysian attitudes. Nonetheless—and we ignore this at our peril—it remains that suffering, destruction, loss, pain, and so forth are *necessary for life*, since they are ingredients to the economy of natural existence as such. They can neither be wished nor imagined away, nor can they be concealed or gotten around by a moral metaphysics of the unnatural or supernatural. This recourse, the belief that one can fully evade suffering, is only a moral and ideological delusion. Rather, one must be vigilant in ascertaining the unnecessary sources of pain and suffering through a critique of those practices and agencies that needlessly augment our suffering. Hence Zarathustra's accusation of the "dishonesty" of the traditional faith: in promising redemption, it perpetuates the illness that calls for redemption and cure.

ENDGAME . . . "HONEY"

Abandoning the notion of redemption (i.e., through another's agency, human *or* divine), yet fully cognizant of the reality of human pain and suffering that may well mark and disfigure one's life, Zarathustra claims that a new attitude toward life is fully possible to attain—an attitude that will overcome our bitterness toward life in general, our pitying resignation to suffering, and our fully futile revenge against the past, the "it was." Of course, it is Zarathustra's "task" to convey this attitude as a "gift," in his teaching of the eternal return. Nonetheless, there is an ambivalence about the teaching that provokes resistance to its ready acceptance. If the world, as viewed through this teaching, is merely a vicious circle of meaningless change, bereft of purpose and any higher significance—the pointless rambling-on of a "hurdy-gurdy song"[175]—then such a view might well be tantamount to nihilism and a recipe for ruin. Alternatively, if such a view extended the prospect of creating new values and the celebration of a new meaning for the very earth itself, freeing us at the same time from our enervating dependency on the past, then such a prospect would positively transfigure human existence and one would do well to embrace it with enthusiasm. Confronted with such an ambivalent teaching as the eternal return, one whose "truth" is uncertain and the risks high, one would understandably be tempted to forgo novelty for the familiarity and assurance afforded by the traditional order, whose wisdom and value have, for millennia, become habit: flesh and bone.

It could equally be said, however, that the ambivalence in question is to be found less in the teaching itself than in the mind of the beholder, and that this is what provokes resistance to the teaching. Stated somewhat differently, perhaps, does an embrace of the teaching result in a transformation of attitude, or is a new attitude called for that will permit the embrace—and consequently, the interpretation—of the teaching? The latter seems to be the case in part 3, as presented in the important section, "On the Vision and the Riddle," where Zarathustra excitedly enjoins the young shepherd to have the "courage" to accept the teaching of the eternal return. In this very dramatic and complex scene, Zarathustra realizes that it will require a great deal of courage to humanly incorporate the teaching—literally, to "swallow" its "truth"—that the individual must embrace the whole of natural existence, together with its all-too-pressing deficiencies, its necessary component of pain, suffering, and pity. The courage called for demands the strength and determination to deal frankly with personal hardships, indeed, personal disaster, and Zarathustra realizes that such courage itself has to be—at least, provisionally—emotionally roused, enjoined, incited. It will require courage to bite off the head of the snake depicted in the encounter with the shepherd and to swallow *its truth*, which is also the truth of this suffering and pity. Among other meanings, the snake with the tail in its mouth has always been the symbol of *cyclical eternity*. Thus, to burst out in the laughter that Zarathustra requires, the laughter of the awakened shepherd, one must have the courage to bite off the head of this serpent which is both poisonous and wise as well as seductive. Zarathustra describes his encounter with the shepherd and the serpent:

> A young shepherd I saw, writhing, gagging in spasms, his face distorted, and a heavy black snake hung out of his mouth. Had I ever seen so much nausea and pale dread on one face? He seemed to have been asleep when the snake crawled into the throat, and there bit itself fast. My hand tore at the snake and tore in vain; it did not tear the snake out of his throat. Then it cried out of me: "Bite! Bite its head off! Bite!" Thus it cried out of me—my dread, my hatred, my nausea, my pity, all that is good and wicked in me cried out with a single cry.[176]

The richness of symbolism and allusion renders this passage particularly complex, both with regard to a variety of biblical references and with regard to Nietzsche's personal circumstances. When "On the Vision and the Riddle" is presented in part 3, it follows the first relatively clear articulation of the eternal return, which Zarathustra terms his "most abysmal thought." This *abyss*—whether it be ironically contrasted with the Zoroastrian "lake of fire," the New Testament Gehenna, or its Old Testament equivalent for the underworld, Sheol—is Nietzsche's own deepest or most profound thought, precisely the teaching that there are no netherworlds or afterworlds at all, that natural existence is fundamentally amoral or innocent—or, as he would later term it, "the innocence of becoming."[177] The world and human existence are fully natural, and as such, the metaphysical and moral dogmas of tradition are simply ideological constructions designed to compensate for human fear and suffering. Of course, it is Nietzsche's further claim that the entire religious apparatus of salvation and redemption has only added to the increase in human suffering, in that it casts the whole of natural existence in "moral" terms. To the extent that human existence is "natural," the religious teaching places it under the burden of sin and guilt, for which it is said one suffers in the first place.[178] Only through the ritual atonements of further suffering and self-denial, prescribed by the orthodox practices of religious asceticism, can redemption and salvation from this world be hoped for. Hence, it is this abyss of suffering, brought on by the moral metaphysics of traditional religious thought, that Nietzsche wishes to overcome: precisely by Zarathustra's "abysmal thought" that there are no metaphysical abysses at all. The "shepherd"[179] into whose mouth the snake crawls is thus to be initially identified with Jesus, as the originator of the Christian dogma, who will be forced by Zarathustra's cries to abjure his former teaching. By a narrative shift in the section "The Convalescent," however, Zarathustra will later recall that the serpent in fact crawled into *his*, Zarathustra's, own throat.[180] Thus Nietzsche's remarks in *Ecce Homo* as to why he entitled the work *Zarathustra* in the first place are here dramatically illustrated:

> I have not been asked . . . what the name of Zarathustra means in my mouth, the mouth of the first immoralist. . . . Zarathustra was the first to consider the fight between good and evil as the very wheel in the machinery of things: the transposition of morality into the metaphysical realm. . . . Zarathustra created the most calamitous error, morality; consequently, he must also be the first to recognize it[181]

—and to exorcise, to expel or reject, his earlier teaching.

This highly dramatic incident is constructed in reference to two passages from the New Testament, the miraculous exorcism of the demon,[182] and Revelation's account of the gift of the scroll to St. John the Divine.[183] Once the demon—or unclean spirit—is exorcised from the madman, in Mark 1:27, it is said that "all were amazed and asked one another: 'What is this? A new teaching with authority. He commands even the unclean spirits and they obey him.'" In Revelation 10, an angel visits St. John and, at the behest of God, gives him a scroll announcing the end of the world. The divine voice enjoins St. John to "swallow" the scroll: "He said to me, 'Take and swallow it. It will turn your stomach sour, but in your mouth it will taste as sweet as honey.'" The passage is traditionally understood to mean that the scroll would taste sweet, because it ultimately foretold the victory of God's people, but that it was sour because of the suffering they would have to endure until the end.

What is to be done, then, even in the face of personal adversity, is clear: to have the courage to *accept* the teaching of the eternal return. But does even Zarathustra have this courage? By part 4, in the "Honey Sacrifice," he shouts out, "I am still waiting for the sign that the time has come for my descent, I still do not myself go under, as I must do. . . . That is why I wait here, cunning and mocking on high mountains."[184] Of course, in biblical literature, it is precisely the unbelievers who are in need of such signs.

Effectively, Zarathustra himself has *not yet affirmed* his *own* teaching! He teaches *of* the overman, he talks *about* the overman. He says that he "longs for" the overman, he longs for that resolution of courage by which he can accept the eternal return—this enigma of the eternal present—the enduring transience, the always and forever becoming.[185] Zarathustra's shout for the shepherd, after all, was in a *dream* whose meaning *he asks to be explained.* He still *asks*, or *implores*, for this courage to bite it off, to accept the eternal return. In the "Honey Sacrifice," he exclaims, "Out my fishing rod! Down, down, bait of my happiness! Drip your sweetest dew, honey of my heart! Bite into the belly of all black melancholy."[186]

What is this chunk of black melancholy—the belly of the great fish that carried Jonah, crying out in distress for deliverance, to the netherworld?[187] It is precisely the spirit of revenge and resentment that refuses the eternal return. The spirit of revenge is the time-honored and time-bound ill will that must be, but has not yet been overcome. Above all, this is the perverted will that dwells on in enduring pity and self-pity. But what is it that prepares one for such courage to overcome the ill will of pity and revenge, if not a kind of strong-willed discipline? In a very curious entry from one of Nietzsche's notebooks dating from 1880, there is the suggestion of an explanation that draws out a bit the complex imagery of the "snake," the "honey," of "joy," and of "significance" or "meaning." The note focuses on the term "semen":

> The reabsorption of semen by the blood is the strongest nourishment, and perhaps more than any other factor, it prompts the stimulus of power, the unrest of all forces towards the overcoming of resistances, the thirst for contradiction and resistance. The feeling of power has so far mounted highest in abstinent priests and hermits.[188]

It is this *semen* that Zarathustra will term the "honey-drippings" of his "fishing rod" here in the "Honey Sacrifice" section. Or, as he says, "it is the honey in my veins that makes my blood thicker and my soul calmer. . . . [and] when I desired honey, I merely desired bait and sweet mucus and mucilage."[189] The equation of honey and semen is traditional, as when in *The Bacchae*, for example, Euripides writes about the gentle revelry of the languorous Bacchantes. In his report to King Pentheus, the cowherd described the Dionysian phallic staff carried by the revelers on Mt. Cithaeron: "From their ivy-twined thrysi came honey, dripping in delicious streams. Had you been there to see this you'd pursue with prayers the very God that now you rate with contumely."[190] Semen: seed of the joyful phallus, which is also the seed of life itself, the natural life of body and nature whose highest expression is ultimately the eternal return, the Dionysian will to embrace the whole of existence—repeatedly, ecstatically, eternally.[191] This *seed* of life is also the *meaning* of life—or, as he suggested, in *The Birth of Tragedy*, that which prompted the highest veneration for life. Thus, from the German (*Samen*), back through the Latin (*semen*), back to the Greek (Σεμελε: *semele*), it would almost seem that "semele" (seed, semen, and also the name of Dionysus's mother, Semele) shares a common etymological root with "semea" (Σεμεα: *semea*): "sign," or "significance," that is, "meaning." Seed or germ, but also sign or meaning; thus, at the origin, the same root for "seminal," "semiotics," and "semantics." Indeed, in *Twilight of the Idols*, Nietzsche describes the Christian teaching as "castratism," imposed precisely as the institution of universal law—divine, human, natural, and moral law—in short, the law of the repressive Father. The whole doctrine of a "joyful wisdom" or "gay science"—which unites a truthful account of existence with an intense human delight and joy with that same human existence—will consist in unblocking or foreclosing this constraint imposed by the Father-Divine. Hence, for Nietzsche, the traditional account of Being as metaphysically and morally purposive would be replaced with the nonmetaphysical account of "will to power." Traditional "rationality" would be supplanted by a broader notion of "semiotics," that is, by the functional sign-system of language itself[192] and its perspective interpretation, and the traditional Christian moral teachings would be unbound, freed from the constraints of *ressentiment* directed against the "it was." More than a reversal or inversion of metaphysics, Nietzsche more precisely considers this to be an "overcoming" of the tradition.

That Nietzsche wishes to stress an extremely sensualistic vocabulary and symbolism—so as to celebrate the vitality of human existence, with a liberating respect for its richly sensual and often ecstatic emotional capacity for pleasure, joy[193]—seems particularly apparent in the "Honey Sacrifice" section. The teaching of Zarathustra is offered as "honey," precisely in parallel to the angelic scroll of the millennium in the apocalyptic vision of St. John the Divine in the book of Revelation. In the "Honey Sacrifice," just prior to dripping his honey from his fishing rod, Zarathustra says—again, in an apocalyptic tone—"What must come one day and may not pass? Our great *Hazar*: that is, our great distant human kingdom, the Zarathustra kingdom of a thousand years."[194] The word *Hazar* is the Persian term for the millennium. A related Arabic term, *az zahr* is the name of the traditional dice game "hazard," as well as the etymological origin of "hazard," as "chance," "accident," "without purpose," "unintentional," "fortuitous," "fortune," and so forth. Hence, Zarathustra's teaching is to completely reverse and overcome the purposive, lawful, and rational determination of the Father's creation. The creative and symbolic agency of the father is indeed repudiated.[195] Effectively, Zarathustra's gift is the teaching of the antichrist.[196] Instead of the heavenly scroll, which sits sourly, bitterly, in the stomach, Zarathustra gives us unabated honey—"sweetest dew, honey of my heart"—a honey that is fully natural, organic, indeed, delightfully orgasmic. This "joyful wisdom" is the "glitter bait" that our new fisherman extends to "the most beautiful human fish"; not the webs and nets cast by the old "fisher of men," namely, Christ, but precisely the joyful gift of the "antichrist." Here, then, is what Zarathustra would term *his* millennium: "the heaven accident and chance"—following upon Heraclitus's gods, childlike, and throwing dice in a perpetual game of innocent creation.[197] Zarathustra's remark, after the announcement of "our great Hazar"? "Laugh, laugh, my bright wholesome sarcasm!"

Where does this somewhat agitated rhetoric—a sort of inverted phallocentrism—lead us? Zarathustra cannot yet affirm his seed or his meaning and is still *afraid* of it and its *power*. To embrace this meaningful seed of life would be to ensure his own *overcoming*. But, perhaps, then, he would know too much about life. In the section titled "On the Three Evils," he tells us that this attitude could well lead to the monastery—is this what the asceticism of Pascal produces? Or of Maimonides? Or Kant and Spinoza? Or is it the excessive wisdom of Silenus, the tragic and lacerating knowledge that all is excess, pain, and death?

But Zarathustra has not embraced this seed, this meaning, yet. He was not strong enough. He has to give the semen—he has to inseminate and propagate, but as yet, he can only dream and implore. His gift appears to be little more than onanism—he spills his seed—even in his sleep![198] Thus it would seem that Zarathustra does not have the discipline to prepare himself for the necessary courage to understand and to accept his own teaching.

Perhaps it is the other way around. Perhaps Zarathustra is already too much the ascetic. Every attempt at insemination, that is, of articulating and present-ing his teaching, simply drives him back up the mountain in a state of nausea! He must let his honey drip, he must allow his seed to fall, but perhaps he does not have enough joy to accept his followers, where, after all, the seed has to be implanted. This would appear to be the case from one of the poems that form a kind of preface to *The Gay Science*, called "The Scorner."

> There is much I drop and spill:
> I am full of scorn, you think.
> If your beaker is too full,
> There is much you drop and spill
> Without scorning what you drink.[199]

When Zarathustra's followers do come up to the mountain cave to learn his teaching in part 4, when they arrive in numbers, he regards them as fools, madmen, or god-intoxicated parasites and hangers-on. They themselves realize this, they praise and worship Zarathustra as a god, yet they fail to understand him. Incidentally, two months after Nietzsche told Peter Gast that his friend Heinrich von Stein could not understand any more than twelve sentences from the whole of *Zarathustra*, he dedicated a poem to von Stein and sent it off to him, titling it "From High Mountains." Part of the poem read, "Where are you, friends? Come! It's time! It's late! And my sweet honey—who has tasted it? . . . Am I another? Self-estranged? . . . Wounded and stopped by his own victory?"[200] If Zarathustra's followers do not understand him, does this mean that Zarathustra himself is too weak or too slow-footed to make himself clear? Does Zarathustra himself wobble or limp, and *not* fly? Is he the weak-footed Oedipus, abandoned as a child on Mt. Cithaeron, who has merely replaced the Father by virtue of the fast knife blade? As the Wanderer said, "in the case of the Gods, death is a mere prejudice."[201]

The problem is that Zarathustra is not the overman. He, too, is subject to the distance between himself and the world, to the duality of life, woe and sorrow, joy and happiness, yea and nay, pity and overcoming. In this respect, Zarathustra has not attained the joyfulness of naiveté like that of the child, one of the signal virtues Nietzsche most admired in the person of Christ. As the apostle Paul remarked in 2 Corinthians 1:19, "There was not in Christ yea and nay, but in him was yea." Consequently, where the eternal return *is* discussed, and not merely chanted or ritually invoked, Zarathustra is himself *asleep* in "The Stillest Hour," "On the Vision and the Riddle," and the section "At Noon." Elsewhere, when he is not asleep, he is nonetheless in a swoon, comatose, as in "The Convalescent." In the latter case, it is Zarathustra's *animals* who talk about the eternal return. In the "Great Longing," he dreams of deliverance and comfort. But is this not too soft? Too weak-willed? All-too-human?

It seems that the final metaphor, the third metamorphosis in Zarathustra's own transformation, is in question: to become a child, to embrace the innocence of becoming and to forget that he remains a man, that he is all-too-human.[202] The camel, yes. The lion, perhaps—in fact, part 4 ends with Zarathustra and his lion wandering off into the sunset, in search of ever more adventures.

But why the problem with the child, the loss of memory? Is amnesia—true forgetting—only possible for Zarathustra as a dream state? Can he forget only in his sleep? Moreover, didn't Zarathustra tell us that sleep was the preparation, the very "house" of metaphysics?[203] Where one dreams of the past, of the long-dead? Isn't this the dream of sleepy thinkers and theologians of all ages? Yet, in "The Old and New Tablets," he tells us: "Whoever wanted to sleep well talked of good and evil before going to sleep. I disturbed this sleepiness when I taught; what is good and evil, no one knows yet, unless it be he who creates."[204]

But who is it in the end that finally overturns the tablets? Who is it that finally creates new values and not the reverberations of the old God and conventional metaphysics? Who creates? Only the overman. But Zarathustra is not the overman; he teaches about the overman and the eternal return only in the conditional, in the subjunctive. In short, it would seem that Zarathustra sleeps all too much.[205]

Why does Zarathustra continue to resist assuming an attitude of being well-disposed toward his own teaching of the eternal return? The fact is that he must willfully embrace everything, however petty or distasteful, that has encumbered him—and that continues to do so.[206] Whether in suffering or in delight, it remains that the duality of life, of will to power, consists in the flux of woe *and* joy, sorrow *and* happiness. The two strophes or movements of life itself can only be affirmed *together* in the abysmal thought of the eternal return. But the deepest *woe* of life, within that duality, must *first* be overcome. Zarathustra says that courage alone can kill the abyss of woe, of *pity*. This courage stems from *joy itself*, from *happiness*. Joy is even deeper than woe, happiness extends deepest and farthest into all that is: "All joy wants eternity, wants deep, deep eternity."[207] Here, we should look at his teaching in the section titled "At Noon."

> Oh happiness [says Zarathustra], how little is sufficient for happiness! . . . it is *little* that makes the *best* happiness. . . . What happened to me? Listen! Did time

perhaps fly away? Do I not fall? Did I not fall—listen!—into the well of eternity? What is happening to me? . . . I have been stung, alas—in the heart? . . . How? Did not the world become perfect just now? Round and ripe? Oh, the golden round ring—where may it fly? . . . (And here Zarathustra stretched and felt that he was asleep.) "Up" he said to himself! Up you sleeper! you noon-napper.[208]

But, perhaps Zarathustra is too inclined to sleep, to dream. To dream the noon-teaching of the eternal return. As the Soothsayer said,

Anyone coming to this height, looking for that man, would come in vain; caves he would find, and caves behind caves, hiding-places for those addicted to hiding, but no mines of happiness or treasure rooms or new gold veins of happiness. How should one find happiness among hermits and those buried like this?[209]

There is not enough happiness in Zarathustra, and thus he cannot overcome his woe. To make even the briefest happiness endure, to recall it, to say "abide moment," is to want *all* of it, to want it all to endure, for woe and happiness to recur eternally, for they are ensnared, entangled, and enamored with one another.[210] What is the final moment in *Zarathustra*?—the last section to be written in part 4, after a period of more than a year's reflection by Nietzsche? The book closes with Zarathustra's final *sin*—"sin," a term that seems to be squarely within the sense of traditional ontotheology—namely, his *pity* for the higher man.

As the old pope had recounted, it was pity that killed God. Here, it is pity for the higher man that kills him, too. To overcome pity, the sorrow and woe upon oneself that one suffers for a lifetime—and for no end or greater purpose—*one must become joyous* and happy. But, Zarathustra says, at the conclusion of part 4, "My suffering and my pity for suffering—what does it matter? Am I concerned with *happiness*? I am concerned with my *work*!"[211] Now the lion comes, roaring with laughter, now one can meet the Great Noon. But what can this be but even more sleep? Yet shouldn't he precisely will happiness? This poses the most difficult question: one cannot simply will happiness, one must first possess it!

FINAL PARADOXES

The paradox that Zarathustra confronts—the meager company attending him in his "cave," who are unable to understand his not quite fully articulable teaching and the deeply felt importance of his "work," that is, of his continuing life's task to develop and articulate his critical, philosophical insights—renders him silent at the end and forces him once more back into solitude. This paradox is clearly Nietzsche's own: his solitude drives him into periods of intense loneliness and depression, and his repeated attempts to overcome this and to find happiness in the intellectual and affective companionship of others constitute a veritable roster of personal failures. The plaintive tone of the "Honey Sacrifice," with all its suggestive and painful allusions, resonates throughout the whole of *Zarathustra* and it clearly reflects the series of expectations, frustrations, and disappointments Nietzsche himself underwent throughout the period of its composition, indeed, for a very long time.[212]

Ever the psychological vivisectionist, Nietzsche begins to carefully analyze the dynamics of his situation—again, in striking parallel to the dramatic situation of Zarathustra at the end of part 4—seeking to establish its etiology and thereby, its remediation, its cure. He gives a pointed analysis of what he calls the "pity" of the "higher men" in section 269 of his very next work, *Beyond Good and Evil*, and he once again locates the source of suffering, pity, and self-pity in the individual's disposition toward the "it was," that is, in the memories of the past and the pain caused by those memories. What triggers this awareness and renders it manifest is the higher individual's desire to be accommodated by the "normalcy" of others' relations toward him.

> The more a psychologist—a born and inevitable psychologist and unriddler of souls—applies himself to the more exquisite cases and human beings, the greater becomes the danger that he might suffocate from pity. He *needs* hardness and cheerfulness more than anyone else. For the corruption, the ruination of the higher men, of the souls of a stranger type, is the rule. . . . The manifold torture of the psychologist who has discovered this ruination, who discovers this whole inner hopelessness of the higher man, this eternal "too late" . . . may perhaps lead him one day to turn against his own lot, embittered, and to make an attempt at self-destruction. . . .
>
> In almost every psychologist one will perceive a telltale preference for and delight in association with everyday, well-ordered people: this reveals that he always requires a cure, that he needs a kind of escape and forgetting, away from all that with which his insights, his incisions, his "craft" have burdened his conscience. He is characterized by the fear of his memory. He is easily silenced by the judgments of others; he listens with an immobile face as they venerate, admire, love and transfigure where he has *seen*.[213]

It is clear that this analysis is self-referential, for Nietzsche explicitly says so; he addresses precisely this understanding of himself in a letter to Gast, written at the very same time, in the summer of 1885: "In all my states of sickness I feel, with horror, a sort of downward pull toward the weakness of the rabble, the gentlenesses of the rabble, even the virtues of the rabble—do you understand this? You picture of health!"[214] But such relations are deceptive and paradoxical because what these "souls of a stranger type" have attained in their reflection is generally misunderstood by a broader, more normal, public, supposing the air to be somewhat less rarefied at their level. The initial misunderstanding is compounded by the public's equation of the accomplished "work" with the person who created it, thus, effectively "doubling" the subject. As a figure of public recognition and reputation, the subject becomes fractured and increasingly dependent on others' approbation to maintain a sense of self-esteem. The original motivation behind the work, "whether of the artist or the philosopher," may well have been simply "enthusiastic, sensual, childish, frivolous," and, Nietzsche continues, such figures

> usually try to conceal some fracture; often taking revenge with their works for some inner contamination, often seeking with their high flights to escape into forgetfulness from an all-too-faithful memory; often lost in the mud and almost in love with it.[215]

But the lack of communication, the disparity between the person and the public persona, and the increasing dependency upon others for a confirmation of self-worth ultimately break such creative individuals, forcing them to become ever more despondent and to lose "all belief in themselves." It is at this moment when the "higher" individual is most vulnerable to love, pity, and compassion:

> It is easy to understand that *these* men should so readily receive from woman . . . those eruptions of boundless and most devoted *pity* which the multitude . . . does not understand and on which it lavishes inquisitive and self-satisfied interpretations. This pity deceives itself . . . to believe that love can achieve *anything*.[216]

Bred in despondency and dependency, such love cannot be the cure for the embittered individual who still desperately seeks a modicum of happiness. On the contrary, "whoever knows the heart will guess how poor, stupid, helpless, arrogant, blundering, more apt to destroy than to save is even the best and profoundest love."[217]

Ultimately, such a cure is recognized as worse than the illness itself, an unfulfilled, unrequited love, driven by a pathological despondency of need. Nietzsche clearly associates himself with this terminal state of self-destruction:

the deeply enrooted religious demand for redemption, carried by the vestigial sense of "sin," what he so wickedly exposed in the dynamics of Romanticism and in the Wagnerian opera. The paradigm example he offers of this love as a demand for redemption, salvation, and final approbation is not Amfortas, but Jesus himself:

> The martyrdom of the most innocent and desirous heart, never sated by any human love; *demanding* love, to be loved and nothing else, with hardness, with insanity, with terrible eruptions against those who denied him love; the story of a poor fellow, unsated and insatiable in love, who had to invent hell in order to send to it those who did not *want* to love him—and who finally, having gained knowledge about human love, had to invent a god who is all love, all *ability* to love—who has mercy on human love because it is so utterly wretched and unknowing. Any one who feels that way, who knows this about love—*seeks* death.
> But why pursue such painful matters? Assuming one does not have to.[218]

The desperate need for a reciprocated love, a needful dependency, some redemptive sense of affection and approbation, are all in some way or another compensations for the past sufferings and joys—the painful memory of the "it was." It is precisely this that must be "cured" to achieve the state of "innocence," the metamorphosis of a youthful "affirmation," to fully attain one's own self-overcoming. How this is attained, how Nietzsche himself finally came to terms with his own situation of despondency and alienation, is related in detail in the new prefaces he wrote, in the following summer of 1886, to parts 1 and 2 of *Human, All Too Human*. The prefaces are autobiographical in nature and spirited in tone, and they convey a detailed application of the many injunctions he had set forth earlier in the section "On Old and New Tablets," in part 3 of *Zarathustra*.

The central teaching of "On Old and New Tablets" was that all "values" are the result of human estimation, human valuing, the ability to take new perspectives upon things, to affirm and deny, to lend purpose and direction to the objectives of one's actions, and this effectively amounts to one's own "creation" of values. By the same token, this would be precisely the capacity to liberate *oneself* from the spirit of gravity, the constrictive value system one unwittingly inherits: "I also found again my old devil and arch-enemy, the spirit of gravity, and all that he created: constraint, statute, necessity and consequence and purpose and will and good and evil."[219]

For Zarathustra, the enactment of the will is as basic to the individual as the simple performance of every choice, every inclination, every act of interpretation—each lends a sense of purpose and perspective estimation to things, each act is thus creative of worth, orientation, significance. But, if "To will liberates, for to will is to create,"[220] then how is this actually performed in the face of the spirit of gravity, the morality of mores that finds expression as, for example, conventional morality, ideology, traditional religion, and nationalism,[221] all of which are precisely all-too-human constraints, bonds? The difficulty in resolving this issue of self-liberation is repeatedly addressed in *Zarathustra*, and it seems to cloud the formal structure of the work as a whole—especially the concluding scene at the finale of part 4—and it also seems to have plagued Nietzsche in person. How can both Zarathustra and Nietzsche attain the attitude that will permit a joyous acceptance of their own person and, most importantly, of the eternal return itself, the very sum of existence? What serves to occlude or forestall the resolution in *Zarathustra* is that, due to Nietzsche's highly dramatic portrayal of the figure of Zarathustra, he appears to be overly grandiose in stature, often imperious, overbearing, dismissingly authoritative, if not authoritarian, and far too directive. His pronouncements themselves appear to be statutory rules, lawlike injunctions; in short, "tablets" of constraint upon a diverse audience, each statute or tablet seemingly imperative and univocal—this despite his repeated assertions to "Go your *own* ways,"[222] that "there are many ways of overcoming," that you must "overcome yourself."[223] The problem, then, is that Zarathustra's teaching of self-overcoming either appears as yet another set of formal maxims and rules, and thus remains bound to the traditional morality of the "thou shalt," or it seems to be hollow, without content for the particular individual, with his or her remarkably complex individuality of character and sensibility.

To make matters even more difficult, had Zarathustra explicitly succeeded in his own self-overcoming, by attaining a specifically delineated metamorphosis into the "child," this would have paradoxically lessened the value of his teaching, since it would have been projected as a model, a template, for all. The "I will" would be replaced, once again, with the pathology of the "thou shalt," meaning, do as I do! Again, such a perspective would tend to diminish the agency of the individual, rather than enhance it, and this in turn would weaken the "liberating" or "emancipatory" quality of individual value creation. At the end of part 4, and ever confident, Zarathustra yet again leaves his cave and descends. But to where? To his solitude? To slay more dragons? To finally enact his self-overcoming? Unclear, indeed, and almost impossibly so.

Nonetheless, Nietzsche does provide a resolution to *Zarathustra*'s paradox, at the same time that he clarifies his own self-overcoming, what he calls his

"Great Liberation," in the new prefaces to *Human, All Too Human*.[224] The clarification is given in the first person singular—wary of rendering universal judgment from the individual experience—and it thus avoids the presumption of the imperative maxim, law, or statute. By the same token, his account of his own "cure" or self-overcoming avoids the danger of mere formalism, of injunctions that are empty of content, precisely because he describes his own personal experiences and the strategies he employs in the service of the cure. He succinctly restates the *problem*—and the difficulty of the problem—in another of his works at the time, book 5 of *The Gay Science*, written in the same year (1886):

> "The Wanderer" speaks.—If one would like to see our European morality for once as it looks from a distance, and if one would like to measure it against other moralities, past and future, then one has to proceed like a wanderer who wants to know how high the towers in a town are: he *leaves* the town. "Thoughts about moral prejudices," if they are not meant to be prejudices about prejudices, presuppose a position outside morality, some point beyond good and evil to which one has to rise, climb, or fly—and in the present case at least a point beyond *our* good and evil, a freedom from everything "European," by which I mean the sum of the imperious value judgments that have become part of our flesh and blood. That one *wants* to go precisely out there, up there, may be a minor madness, a peculiar and unreasonable "you must"—for we seekers of knowledge . . . the question is whether one really *can* get up there. . . . [To do this] one must have liberated oneself from many things that oppress, inhibit, hold down, and make heavy precisely us Europeans today.[225]

The cure for his despondency and alienation begins with a *ruse*, a deception, namely, the creation of an imaginary interlocutor. Much as Descartes devised his "evil demon" to test the limits of his resolute reflection,[226] so too does Nietzsche say that he "invented" a series of companions—sometimes called "free spirits," or "shadows," or even "good Europeans"—with whom he could engage in a spirited dialogue. What motivated this—he says in the preface to part 1 of *Human, All Too Human*—was precisely his profound sense of isolation and loneliness and his need to be, at least at the outset, *diverted away* from his almost obsessive preoccupation with it:

> I had need of them at that time if I was to keep in good spirits while surrounded by ills (sickness, solitude, unfamiliar places, torpor, inactivity): as brave companions and familiars with whom one can laugh and chatter when one feels like laughing and chattering, and whom one can send to the Devil when they become tedious—as compensation for the friends I lacked.[227]

The products or results of these dialogues are, of course, his works, his books, his notes of the period. Their content derived from his recognition of the causes and origins of his own restrictions, inhibitions, and suffering, precisely what he had been debating with his feigned interlocutor. The alterity—or otherness—of the imaginary companion makes concrete the range of his or her own imagination by continually varying a perspective, contradicting an initial judgment, or insistently prodding him- or herself into recognizing a secondary or tertiary consequence of a position. This imaginary exchange may take the form of a jest or a question, as well: "Is that what you *really* believe?" "Is there a *deeper* motivation for you saying that?" "Is that what *you* think, or is it what most people maintain?" Effectively, such a seriously maintained self-conscious dialogue serves as a metacritique of beliefs, values, positions, explanations— and it raises underlying questions of conditionality, legitimacy, verifiability, truth-functionality, agency, and efficacy, all of which are discussed repeatedly in Nietzsche's published and unpublished "work" of the period.

What initially results from this discursive questioning in Nietzsche's pursuit of a "cure," or a "self-overcoming," is his discovery of the particular elements that bind or restrict him, and he finds these elements to be the causal agents, the cohesive factors, that structure the morality of mores and define the individual as such within the traditional system of morality. He terms these defining and determining elements "fetters," and he claims that they serve to constitute normalcy itself, one's "home," or one's "being at home," the regularity and normalcy of convention, of all that is usual, familiar, and "day-to-day" in social life. He enumerates those "fetters" that most palpably bond the individual not only to the traditional order but also to his own personally experienced past, thereby preventing his liberation:

> What fetters the fastest? What bonds are all but unbreakable? In the case of men of a high and select kind they will be their duties: that reverence proper to youth, that reserve before all that is honored and revered from of old, that gratitude for the soil out of which they have grown, for the hand which led them, for the holy place where they learned to worship—their supreme moments themselves will fetter them the fastest, lay upon them the most enduring obligation.[228]

It is upon conducting this intense and highly-focused experience of analyzing the nature of his fetters and of being able to critically articulate them— their number, type, and range; their purchase upon himself and upon the culture at large—that something personally dramatic occurs to Nietzsche. He is struck by the *feeling* (literally, an emotional *shock*) that many of these formerly revered duties, values, obligations, and past memories are simply mean-ingless, nonsensical, absurd, and that they merit little more than his honest contempt for their obtrusive pettiness and small-mindedness. Once this emo-tionally charged thought befalls him, he realizes that he has himself changed, and this is the first step in his self-liberation. *He* can no longer hold these "fetters" in respect and esteem, and by this very fact, *they* no longer bind him. What it was, formerly, to be "at home" is now revealed to him under an entirely new sensibility—and this is felt as a new "drive" or "impulse"—as unworthy of residence; indeed, they are felt to be contemptible: "'Better to die than to go on living *here*'—thus responds the imperious voice and temptation: and this 'here,' this 'at home' is everything it had hitherto loved."[229]

Nietzsche described the immediate effects of his new revelation as being twofold: he experienced a practically intolerable feeling of *shame* for the loss brought about by his obsessive inquisitiveness, his going to the utmost limits of his imagination to *understand* his distress, and by doing so, having lost the veneration and respect for everything that until then constituted belonging, identity, value, and honor, everything worthy of love and worship. But this feeling of loss was tempered, then overwhelmed, by a new feeling for the enor-mity of what he had accomplished, a feeling of immense *pride* and personal *exultation* that it was *possible at all* and that his contempt could overturn the very norms by whose agency he had previously suffered. Then he was tempted, even dangerously, to test other norms, limits, prescriptions, and proscriptions, to question what was formerly forbidden and find it delightful, joyous, the sweetest fruit. From this feeling of exultation and delight there follows a deter-mination to will and esteem, to evaluate, on one's *own* account, in one's *own* name—and one leaves "home," the "at home," seeking to relish and to develop the further capacity of self-determination through new, multiply transforming and overturning, valuations and estimations. Literally and figuratively, for Nietzsche, this involves the determination to *travel*, to get *beside* himself,[230] to self-consciously seek other, *strange* abodes and customs, other entire systems of valuation, other realms of the human spirit itself: to be an "Argonaut of the ideal."[231] Thus, *one uses oneself as an experiment*, as an open-ended source of experiences for experiment[232] in the construction of one's developing hierarchy of values—one's own considered construal of what really *is* important, what *is* significant, of worth and merit—what is worthy of admiration, affection, and esteem: again, in one's own name and in one's own service.

At the same time, one progressively uncovers the truth of things, of people, and of events. By withholding the conventional value-positing perspective, the prevailing mode of esteem or belief that enshrouds something, by "turning it around," one can uncover the distorting biases that contextualize and determine the very significance, the symbolic "truth," of things. Gradually they begin to appear to a less biased eye as things yet unseen, marvelous in their complexity of texture, their simplicity of intent, ever adaptable to the disposition of the observer—mutable in their very disclosure:

> With a wicked laugh he turns round whatever he finds veiled and through some sense of shame or other spared and pampered: he puts to the test what these things look like *when* they are reversed. It is an act of willfulness and pleasure in willfulness, if now he perhaps bestows his favor on that which has hitherto had a bad reputation—if, full of inquisitiveness and the desire to tempt and experiment, he creeps around the things most forbidden.[233]

Spurred on by the possibility that "*all* values" may be turned around, Nietzsche says that he began to cultivate a curious sort of cynicism, thinking that the very absolutes themselves may well have been little more than platitudes. This acquired cynicism and a certain irony attendant to it provoke even further "wandering" and testing of limits until he is quite far afield, in "the desert" of his tempting experiments. This "experimentalism" produces in him, Nietzsche says, a kind of "solitude," sometimes even a "morbid isolation," but one that has gathered into itself such a breadth of values and penetrating perspectives that he no longer feels constrained at all, least of all by the old "fetters": "One lives no longer in the fetters of love and hatred, without yes, without no, near or far as one wishes . . . also [without] the quantum of stupidity that resides in antitheses of values and the whole intellectual loss which every For, every Against costs us."[234]

Having broken these fetters, one has the feeling of a great elation, namely, "that *mature* freedom of spirit which is equally self-mastery and discipline of the heart, and permits access to many and contradictory modes of thought."[235] Freed from "the spirit of gravity" and free to will one's own "scale of values," one is no longer compelled by the old fetters or compelled to suffer from them. This sense of elation or "weightlessness" one has attained, together with the fact that one has welcomed *so much* in gratifying one's inner temptation to experiment with a plethora of experiences, means that one *returns* from one's desert transformed. One possesses a generosity of spirit, an "inner spaciousness and indulgence," such that everything appears benign and innocent, drained of ominous portent and freed from malice of intent. One gains the stability of one's own power over one's perspective, and this at once liberates the individual from bitterness and recrimination while it places one above—at a distance, with a feeling of distance from[236]—the pettiness and vindictiveness of others. Rather, with a spirit of exuberance and freedom, in which "curiosity is united with a tender contempt":

> It again grows warmer around him, yellower, as it were; feeling and feeling for others acquire depth, warm breezes of all kinds blow across him. It seems to him as if his eyes are only now open to what is *close at hand*. He is astonished and sits silent: where had he been? These close and closest things: how changed they seem! what bloom and magic have they acquired! He looks back gratefully— grateful to his wandering, to his hardness and self-alienation, to his viewing of far distances and bird-like flights in cold heights. What a good thing he had not always stayed "at home," stayed "under his own roof" like a delicate apathetic loafer! He had been beside himself: no doubt of that. Only now does he see himself—and what surprises he experiences as he does so![237]

Attaining such a state, such an attitude of mind, one is "cured," as of a past illness and a long convalescence, by the "Great Liberation." Everything is welcomed, without addition or loss, even "the *necessary* injustice . . . as insepa- rable from life, life itself as *conditioned* by the sense of perspective and its injustice."[238] Thus, finally having gained possession of his own self-mastery through controlling his sense of perspective, having freed himself from bond- age to the imperative of the "thou shalt"—and the personal discontent caused by it—Nietzsche would reflect, "You come to realize how you have given ear to the voice of nature, that nature which rules the whole world through joy."[239] Reviewing the joys that nature itself bestows upon someone so "cured" as him- self, Nietzsche ends the discussion of his own "liberation" with a series of light- hearted "injunctions"—the last of which affirms the resolution to Zarathustra's paradoxical departure: smiling, strong as bronze, accompanied by his laughing lion:

> You shall . . . You shall . . . You shall . . . You shall—enough: from now on the free spirit *knows* what "you shall" he has obeyed, and he also knows what he now *can*, what only now he—*may* do.[240]

4

ON THE GENEALOGY OF MORALS

THE GENESIS OF THE *GENEALOGY*

Following the appearance of *Beyond Good and Evil* in July 1886, Nietzsche began work on preparing for a second edition of all his major works, except for his recently published *Thus Spoke Zarathustra*. By mid-August he had completed a new preface for volume 1 of *Human, All Too Human*, and by the end of the month he completed his "Attempt at a Self-Criticism," which would serve as the second preface for his *Birth of Tragedy*. He sent out his preface for the second volume of *Human, All Too Human* on September 2, 1886, and by the end of October, all three volumes would be in print. Over the late fall and early winter, beginning in Ruta (near Genoa, on the Ligurian coast of Italy), and then continuing on in Nice, he would write prefaces to the new editions of *Daybreak* and *The Gay Science*—as well as adding an additional section to the latter work, book 5, and a set of poems he appended to it as a postface, "The Songs of Prince Vogelfrei." Both of these works would appear in June of the following spring. While Nietzsche's health vacillated from periods of relative calm to violent attacks of his recurring illness during this period, he engaged these projects with a renewed enthusiasm, since, for once, his work was beginning to draw serious public attention. He was encouraged both by the sales of *Beyond Good and Evil*—within two months, the printing was already half sold-out—and by the good fortune of finding a new publisher (E. W. Fritsch, of Leipzig), who would handle the second edition of his works, expecting to benefit from the interest aroused by the just-published *Beyond Good and Evil*. His earlier publisher, Schmeitzer, had withheld distribution of his previous books, causing Nietzsche great anguish and increasing his feeling that not only was he misunderstood, he was not even being read. Nietzsche expressed these concerns in a letter to Franz Overbeck (his old friend and former Basel colleague) in the summer of 1886:

> During ten years, no copies have been sent to booksellers, also no review copies; not even a distributor in Leipzig; no *reviews*—briefly, my writings since *Human, All Too Human* are "anecdota." The parts of *Zarathustra* have sold sixty or seventy copies each, and so on, and so on.[1]

Developing and intensifying his critique of morality in the new prefaces, and through his continuing study of traditional moral theory, Nietzsche became ever more preoccupied with the complex origins of morality and its close association with traditionally practiced religion. He had already sketched several draft studies on this relation, especially during the period in which he was working on the fourth of the *Unmodern Observations*, "Richard Wagner in Bayreuth," by the spring and summer of 1875.[2] On the bottom of the original title page of the *Genealogy*, Nietzsche pointed out that the present work is "A Sequel to My Last Book, *Beyond Good and Evil*, Which It Is Meant to Supplement and Clarify." He goes on, in the preface, to say that, in fact, the *Genealogy* is a continuation of several themes he had earlier articulated—indeed, going all the way back to his own childhood—but particularly an amplification of the "twofold prehistory of good and evil" that he had elaborated in *Human, All Too Human*, volume 1 (sec. 45), and of "the morality of mores" he treated in volume 2 (sec. 89) of the same work. He also draws attention to his earlier discussion of "justice" in *Daybreak* and to his account of "punishment" in "The Wander and His Shadow" (part 2 of vol. 2 of *Human, All Too Human*), and in section 7 of the "First Essay" of the *Genealogy*, he invokes his previous discussion of "slave morality" in *Beyond Good and Evil* (sec. 195). Effectively, then, the *Genealogy* continues his earlier concerns with morality and it anticipates his later writings as well: "Essay Three" anticipates *The Case of Wagner* and *Nietzsche contra Wagner*, and most importantly, perhaps, his reflections on "the revaluation of values" in "Essay One" of the *Genealogy* foreshadow his projected work on a "transvaluation of all values," of which *The Antichrist* was to have been the first chapter and for which *The Will to Power* notes would have presumably been employed. Such a project had already been clearly anticipated—and simply stated—in the very subtitles of two previous works, *Daybreak* and *Beyond Good and Evil* (i.e., "Thoughts on the Prejudices of Morality," and "Prelude to a Philosophy of the Future"). In fact, Nietzsche had come to see the development of these two themes as the very heart of his own philosophical "task." During the period just prior to, and continuous with, the publication of the *Genealogy*, Nietzsche writes of this "task" with an increasing frequency and with a growing personal intensity. In a letter to Franz Overbeck of August 5, 1886, he evinces this intensity of feeling concerning his task, and at the same time he realizes that one of the consequences of pursuing it—as he must!—is that such a project might well further alienate him from the general public, from those very readers to whom he had long sought to reach out:

> If only I could give you an idea of my sense of *solitude*! Among the living, as among the dead, I have nobody with whom I have any affinity. It gives me the shudders—indescribably; and only my practice in enduring this sense and my gradual development of it from earliest childhood enable me to understand why it has not yet been the death of me. As for the rest, I can see clearly before me the task for which I live—as a *factum* of indescribable sadness, but transfigured by my consciousness that there is *greatness* in it, if ever there was greatness in the task of a mortal man.[3]

[margin annotation: solitude]

He posed his task as a "problem" in a letter to his old friend and colleague from Basel, the historian Jakob Burckhardt, namely, his awareness of the "extremely dubious relation," or "the contradiction between every moral concept and every scientific concept of life," adding that "to express it is perhaps the most dangerous venture of all, not for the person who ventured it but for those to whom he speaks of it."[4] Indeed, Nietzsche would specifically advise his own mother *not* to read his work and would warn his sister as well that certain passages of the *Genealogy* simply were not for her ears.[5] Nonetheless, Nietzsche felt that the magnitude of his task was compelling enough to risk this alienation. In March 1887 he told Overbeck, "There is the hundredweight of this need pressing upon me—to create a coherent structure of thought during the next few years."[6] By May, as he recounted this to Malwida von Meysenbug, "I feel *condemned* to my solitude and fortress. There is no choice any more. The unusual and difficult task which commands me to go on living commands me to avoid people and to bind myself to no one any more."[7] Barely a week before he began the draft of the *Genealogy*, Nietzsche seemed to resolve this tension between the importance of his forthcoming work and the likelihood of his being sorely misunderstood, ignored, or maligned once again by his prospective audience. His resolution, as he first expresses this to von Meysenbug, would be to consciously write for a more narrowly circumscribed audience: "I have cast my book to the 'few,' and even then without impatience."[8] By the beginning of July, this perceived audience of the 'few' would prove be quite literal. In a letter to Hippolyte Taine, thanking him for his kind remarks about *Beyond Good and Evil*, Nietzsche's resolution was effectively one of resignation:

> I no longer trouble much about readers and being read; yet. . . . I have never lacked a few excellent and very devoted readers . . . among them, for instance, the old Hegelian Bruno Bauer, my esteemed colleague Jakob Burckhardt, and that Swiss poet whom I consider to be the only living *German* poet, Gottfried Keller. I would be very happy if my readers were to include the Frenchmen whom I hold in the highest esteem.[9]

Few indeed. Bauer had been dead for five years at this point, Keller never seemed to have read Nietzsche at all, and after *Beyond Good and Evil,* Burckhardt himself seems to have stopped reading Nietzsche altogether. In fact, in a letter Burckhardt sent to Nietzsche, in the fall of 1886, his remarks about *Beyond Good and Evil* were most equivocal: they were filled with praise for Nietzsche's historical insights and his "astonishing" command of the contemporary intellectual landscape, yet at the same time they expressed his real incomprehension of the book's philosophical value. Ultimately, Burckhardt confessed that he wasn't quite able to understand Nietzsche's ideas, given the fact that he "really didn't have a head for philosophy"; also, he admitted, his own engagement with classical philosophy was now something that belonged to the past. In conclusion, Burckhardt added, with a note of concern, "I would have been really pleased to find—in your respectful letter—some news about your health. As for me, due to my advanced age, I have given up teaching history, to keep up my interests in art history."[10]

Though Burckhardt was unable to grasp Nietzsche's profound concerns at the time, Nietzsche was nonetheless delighted to find one reader who apparently could, and this was enough, it seems, to provide real encouragement. The reader in question was Joseph Widmann, who wrote an extraordinary review of *Beyond Good and Evil* in the liberal Basel newspaper *Der Bund*.[11] Widmann was the book review editor, and for Nietzsche, almost the ideal reader: on the one hand, he had the philosophical background to understand Nietzsche's work (having studied theology, philology, and philosophy, first at the University of Basel, then at Heidelberg and Jena); on the other, he had a solid professional formation in music and was a close personal friend of Brahms, thereby being in a position to distance himself from those who might suspect him of Wagnerian sympathies. Widmann grasped the radicalness of Nietzsche's philosophical positions as expressed in *Beyond Good and Evil*, especially Nietzsche's critique of the traditional philosophical account of knowledge and his elevation of perspectivism—both of which would irrevocably alter the totalizing claims of reason's universal agency and philosophy's pretense of unbiased, intellectual autonomy. Widmann compared *Beyond Good and Evil* to the "stocks of dynamite" then being used to blast open the new Gotthard tunnel; like them, Nietzsche's book was equally "dangerous" and should be "marked by a black flag, indicating mortal danger." He went on to remark that "Intellectual explosives, like the material sort, can serve very useful purposes. . . . Only one does well to say clearly, where such explosive is stored, 'There is dynamite here!'" After proudly relating this review to Malwida von Meysenbug, Nietzsche closed his remarks by again quoting from it, in recognition that, finally, a serious reviewer had glimpsed the magnitude of what he felt to be his own task: "Nietzsche is the first man to find a way out, but it is such a terrifying way that one is really frightened to see him walking the lonely and till now untrodden path."[12]

Encouraged by Widmann's review and the prospect of its generating real philosophical interest in his work, Nietzsche began extensive research in preparation for the *Genealogy*. Despite his failing eyesight, a bitterly cold, wet, and thoroughly wretched winter season in Nice, topped off by a series of devastating earthquakes during the month of February, he was nonetheless able to read voraciously and to begin assembling his new reflections on morality. His discussions with Overbeck on the early Patristic period of church history, during their Basel years of the 1870s, had familiarized Nietzsche with much of the neo-Platonic tradition. Returning to that subject matter in January 1887, Nietzsche was struck by the work of Simplicius, especially his commentary on Epictetus.

Epictetus (ca. A.D. 50–135) was the author of a major Stoic tract, the *Enchiridion* (actually copied by his student Arrianus), that was a virtual handbook or catechism of conservative moral conduct. Himself a freed Roman slave, Epictetus founded his own school of philosophy, a rigorously traditional kind of Stoicism, at Nicopolis in northern Greece. He was celebrated for his teachings that we can control only those things within our own power (specifically, our judgments and our will), but not those things that lie outside our power, which are governed by God.[13] For Epictetus, then, we ought to control ourselves and to follow virtue, duty, prudence, and conscience: effectively, we must submit ourselves and act in accordance with divine prescription, precisely because God—according to Stoic physics—is subtly present everywhere and governs all things. Its teaching is an example of what Nietzsche would discuss at length in the first essay of the *Genealogy* (i.e., "slave morality"), and in fact, later neo-Platonists would come to see Epictetus as a precursor, if not a concealed practitioner, of Christian religious philosophy.

Simplicius (an early sixth century A.D. Greek neo-Platonist philosopher), while not himself a Christian philosopher, commented on Epictetus's *Enchiridion*, heavily stressing its teachings of ethical and moral virtue, but he tried to bring its broader philosophical doctrines much more in line with the Eleatic tradition (especially, that of Xenophanes and Parmenides), whose metaphysical teachings culminated in Plato's doctrine of "ideal" being—the transcendent "unity" of "the good," "the true," and "the beautiful." This would be precisely what Nietzsche inveighed against for so long as "moral metaphysics": the fictional translation of morality into the very machinery of nature. In his study of Simplicius, Nietzsche came to realize the immense influence this "pagan" philosopher had on the subsequent medieval and Renaissance tradition of Christian thought, which was deeply neo-Platonic and hence profoundly anti-materialistic—and thus, for Nietzsche, resolutely anti-scientific. Interestingly enough, Epictetus himself had been allied with the more materialistic schools of early Ionian, "atomistic" philosophy, which Nietzsche saw as his own intellectual forerunners, especially the teachings of Epicurus (ca. 341–270 B.C.), and to some extent, the Milesian philosopher Heraclitus (ca. 540–480 B.C.). These thinkers, in Nietzsche's estimation, had roughly anticipated certain aspects of his own formulation of the "will to power," which he would specifically characterize as his philosophy of "anti-Platonism." In a letter to Overbeck, who was still a professor of church history at the University of Basel, Nietzsche's summary of his views on Simplicius was both succinct and overdramatized, but it would effectively link his reflections on Christian moral teaching back to the period of late antiquity, with its sources in Plato and the earlier Eleatic school:

> It is a hard winter here too; instead of snow, we have had whole days of rain—the foothills have for some time been white (which looks like coquetry on nature's part, in a landscape so drenched in a variety of colors). This variety includes my *blue* fingers, as usual, likewise my *black* thoughts. I have just been reading, with thoughts of that kind, Simplicius' commentary on Epictetus; here one can see clearly before one the whole philosophical scheme in which Christianity became imbedded, so that this "pagan" philosopher's book makes the most Christian impression imaginable (except that the whole world of Christian emotion and pathology is missing—"love," as Paul speaks of it, "fear of God," and so on). The falsifying of everything actual by morality stands there in fullest array: wretched psychology, the "philosopher" reduced to the stature of "country parson." And it is all Plato's fault! He is still Europe's greatest misfortune.[14]

It should be said that at least two other incidents lent direction to Nietzsche's reflections on the relation between the origins of morality and early Christian religious practice, two of the principal themes to emerge in the *Genealogy*. In the first case, it was an extended period of discussion with Paul Rée, when they spent the winter and spring season of 1876–77 with Malwida von Meysenbug at the Villa Rubinacci in Sorrento, near Naples. Nietzsche had taken a year's leave of absence from the University of Basel, due to a particularly protracted and painful series of attacks on his health.[15] Malwida, a close friend of the Wagners, had invited Nietzsche to spend the winter season with her in Italy, so that he might recuperate from his illness and, hopefully, rejoin the Wagners during the course of their own travels in Italy, as well as repair the damaged personal relations Nietzsche had experienced with them the previous summer in Bayreuth.[16] Nietzsche brought Rée with him from Switzerland and was joined on the way, in Geneva, by one of his Basel students, Albert Brenner. Nietzsche had met Rée in the spring of 1873, when he was then completing his doctoral dissertation on Aristotle's *Ethics*. They had since become close friends—Rée was also a friend of Malwida and was a familiar figure in Bayreuth—and Nietzsche was most impressed by Rée's recent investigations into the area of psychological motivation theory, especially his epigrammatic work of 1875, *Psychological Observations*. Nietzsche had hoped that Rée's convergent work on ethics and psychology would prove to be intellectually stimulating, and that the group as a whole—Malwida, himself, Brenner, and Rée—would effectively constitute an intellectual community of "kindred spirits."[17]

The effects of Nietzsche's discussions with Rée were immediate and consequential. Rée himself was in the process of completing his next book, *On the Origin of the Moral Sensations*, which would appear in 1877, and Nietzsche was working on what would become the first volume of *Human, All Too Human*, to be published in 1878.[18] Two especially important chapters from the latter work would dramatically indicate the extent to which Nietzsche shared the same insights and concerns as those of Rée: chapter 2, "On the History of the Moral Sensations," and chapter 3, "The Religious Life." There Nietzsche focused on the remarkable agency of psychological insight to uncover the origins of morality and to ascertain the complex formation of religious beliefs. These two concerns, properly examined, would yield the understanding that the very world we inhabit—and claim to know—is a falsified construction, a metaphysical projection of religiomoral beliefs:

At its present state as a specific individual science the awakening of moral observation has become necessary, and mankind can no longer be spared the cruel
sight of the moral dissecting table and its knives and forceps. For here there rules
that science which asks after the origin and history of the so-called moral sensations and which as it progresses has to pose and solve the sociological problems
entangled with them. . . . It has been demonstrated in many instances how the
errors of the greatest philosophers usually have their point of departure in a
false explanation of certain human actions and sensations; how on the basis of an
erroneous analysis, for example that of the so-called unegoistic actions, a false
ethics is erected, religion and mythological monsters are then in turn called upon
to buttress it, and the shadow of these dismal spirits in the end falls across even
physics and the entire perception of the world.[19]

Having pointed out the extent of this construction—a trajectory from "moral
sentiments" to "physics and the entire perception of the world"—Nietzsche
went on to credit Rée with having had the psychological insight to dissociate
morality from any such metaphysical presumption of determining material reality:

Already it is becoming apparent that results of the most serious description are
emerging from the ground of psychological observation. For what is the principle
which one of the boldest and coldest of thinkers, the author of the book *On the
Origin of the Moral Sensations*, arrived at by virtue of his incisive and penetrating
analyses of human action? "Moral man," he says, "stands no closer to the intelligible (metaphysical) world than does physical man." This proposition, hardened
and sharpened beneath the hammer-blow of historical knowledge, may perhaps
at some future time serve as the axe which is laid at the root of the "metaphysical
need" of man—whether as *more* of a blessing than a curse to the general well-
being, who can say?[20]

In the previous paragraph of *Human, All Too Human* (sec. 36), Nietzsche
had praised Rée's earlier *Psychological Observations* and went on to equate
his insights with those of the "French master of psychical examination," La
Rochefoucauld, saying that they are "like skillful marksmen who again and
again hit the bullseye." His only qualification, and it seems minor at this
point—but one that would be extensively developed in the *Genealogy*—is the
caveat, "but it is the bullseye of human nature." Thus, while acknowledging his
debt to Rée, already by the time of their Sorrento discussions, Nietzsche seems
to have indicated that Rée's own psychological approach stops with "human
nature" as the fixed origin of moral sentiments, and in consequence, he is
insufficiently aware of their profound prehistory. Such philosophers, he had

remarked in section 2 of the first chapter of *Human, All Too Human*, have a "lack of historical sense." They "even take the most recent manifestation of man, such as has arisen under the impress of certain religions, even certain political events . . . as the fixed form from which one has to start out."[21]

Some five years later, in 1882, Rée would introduce Nietzsche to Lou Salomé at Malwida von Meysenbug's salon in Rome.[22] Lou was a university student at the time, in Zurich, and had come to Switzerland with her mother from St. Petersburg, where she had recently fled from a poignant and heart-breaking relationship with a married protestant pastor, Hendrick Gillot. Nietzsche had proposed marriage to Lou within hours of meeting her, only to be rebuffed. Lou's sensibilities were fragile in consequence of the earlier relationship, and while she enjoyed the company of Rée and Nietzsche, her concerns were principally intellectual and spiritual in nature. In fact, she had been struggling with her own loss of faith and had sought help first from Gillot, and then from Nietzsche, to understand the historical evolution of Christian thought and moral doctrine—in straightforwardly realistic terms—so as to help her deal with the magnitude of this personal loss and, thereby, to regain a sense of her own emotional stability. Nietzsche willingly helped her in discussing these matters, and in the summer of 1882, they spent a considerable period of time analyzing the historical impact of the early Christian Patristic philosophers upon subsequent church doctrine. These discussions renewed Nietzsche's earlier interests in the Patristic period, which he had developed in conversations with his old friend and colleague, Franz Overbeck, a theologian who specialized in New Testament interpretation and early church history at the University of Basel.[23]

For Lou, this period of common reflection resulted in a work she began in 1883, *Struggling for God*, a novelistic account of a protagonist confronting the loss of his religious faith—a loss scarred by his accompanying feelings of profound guilt and shame—but who is ultimately buoyed by the strength of new-found ideals and an impassioned love of life.[24] From these same reflections, Nietzsche seems to have gained a focus on the compelling nature of religious guilt itself—a theme he would draw out in detail in the second essay of the *Genealogy*—as well as on the psychological element of *ressentiment*, with its attendant mechanism of a fantasized "compensation" for the unpleasant, but ubiquitous, fact of human suffering. He would expand on the latter themes at length throughout the *Genealogy*, but he would draw forth a particularly dramatic characterization of *ressentiment*-charged fantasy in the figure of the early church father Tertullian (ca. A.D. 155–225), in section 15 of the first essay, a characterization that would date back precisely to his discussions with Lou from the summer of 1882.

While Lou is not mentioned in the *Genealogy*, Rée is, and Nietzsche practically vilifies him in sections 4 and 7 of the preface. He there describes Rée's *On the Origin of the Moral Sensations* as a "precocious little book," one of an "upside-down and perverse" nature, and goes on to say, "Perhaps I have never read anything to which I would have said to myself No, proposition by proposition, conclusion by conclusion, to the extent that I did to this book."[25]

Nietzsche then relegates Rée to the doubtlessly opprobrious realm of the "English moral genealogists" (i.e., to the "English psychologists" and "utilitarians"), neglecting to point out that Rée was in fact from Prussia, and of Jewish, not English, descent. In a final rebuke, he dismisses Rée as an "ultramodern unassuming moral milksop . . . wearing an expression of a certain good-natured and refined indulgence."[26]

This seemingly embittered tone toward Rée, in the preface to the *Genealogy*, clearly indicates that the old friendships were long since at an end.[27] Indeed, Nietzsche had last seen Lou and Rée in Leipzig in November 1882. They left Nietzsche and moved on to Berlin, where they lived together until Lou, in turn, left Rée to marry Carl Friedrich Andreas. Nietzsche received news of her engagement on his way to the Engadine, in the early summer of 1887, where he was to begin writing *On the Genealogy of Morals*. He had planned to stay that summer in the Celerina area, between Samedan and Saint-Moritz, but when he arrived there, he learned that the friend with whom he was to stay, an elderly retired military officer, General Simon, had just recently died, so he continued on to his usual haunt, Sils-Maria. Exhausted and in exceedingly poor health, he quickly received another shock, namely, that another of his good friends, Heinrich von Stein, had died on June 20. On June 24, Nietzsche sent off his musical transcription of Lou Salomé's poem, "Hymn to Life," for publication. It was to be the only piece of music he published in his lifetime, and he had been continually revising the composition, with the help of his friend, composer Peter Gast, ever since he received it as her parting gift—her final memento from their brief, but memorable, summer together in Tautenberg—on August 25, 1882.

Nietzsche started work on the *Genealogy* on July 10, 1887. He sent it to the printer on July 30.

PREFACE

Like most classical writers, Nietzsche writes prefaces and prologues, and he frequently enough informs us that he intends them to be taken seriously. The preface says or announces something beforehand (L: *praefatio*—"a saying beforehand"), it tells us, quite simply, *how to read* the text that follows. Although the text itself might welcome or even require our own interpretation, we can nonetheless anticipate some knowledge of what the writer wants to say by focusing upon his stated intentions, his given instructions to the reader in the preface. In the preface to *On the Genealogy of Morals*, for instance, Nietzsche demands that the reader practice "the art of exegesis," that is, of deciphering, of interpretation, and ultimately, he says, of "rumination." The reader should approach the text as if he were a "cow": a gentle, ruminant animal, one without guile, meanness, prejudice, or preconceived intent. But also, according to this "ruminant" metaphor, the reader should chew the cud over several times so as to taste what the text offers up; on subsequent reading, in further reflective reexaminations, always attentive to what one might have overlooked on first examination, for example, concerns of detail or context.[28]

We should thus pay serious attention to what Nietzsche says in the preface, with the same intent (at least, to the extent that this is announced to us) as the writer himself. The first words of the preface to the *Genealogy* are "We are unknown to ourselves." Nietzsche goes on to say several times again, in succession, "we are not 'men of knowledge' with respect to ourselves," "we are necessarily strangers to ourselves."[29] With this admission in mind—Nietzsche warns us six times in the first paragraph about this lack of real self-understanding—he then begins to discuss the proper subject matter of the book itself, namely, the various and complex *origins* of traditional moral evaluations. In anticipation of this theme, he refers us to several passages in his earlier work, and the last such text he mentions—even while he is telling us how to read the *present* work—is perhaps his most famous book, *Thus Spoke Zarathustra*. Specifically, Nietzsche refers the reader to the section in *Zarathustra* concerning values. The explicit discussion of good and bad, good and evil, is found in the chapter of *Zarathustra*, part 3, entitled "On Old and New Tablets." One of the most striking remarks of the chapter is found there:

> When I came to men I found them sitting on an old conceit: the conceit that *they* have long known *what* is good and evil for man. All talk of virtue seemed an old and weary matter to man, and whoever wanted to sleep well still talked of good and evil before going to sleep. I disturbed this sleepiness when I taught: what is good and evil *no one knows yet*, unless it be he who creates.[30]

Two elements in this passage from *Thus Spoke Zarathustra* should be stressed: (1) Nietzsche himself does *not* claim to know what good and evil *are*, despite the often strident accusations directed against him by his critics. This

reluctance to make a distinctly positive value claim is also confirmed by the
highly ambiguous character of Zarathustra himself. (2) *What* the values of good
and bad, good and evil are, what they have been, or might well be, is nonetheless said to be related to creation (i.e., to construction, to invention). From this,
we can at least conclude that new values are yet to be created, and that what
has so far *passed* for good and evil has indeed been a *human* creation. Thus,
we should look to the future, to what conditions the possible future creation of
value, as well as to the past and to its conditions. In short, we are enjoined to
turn to *history* and to examine the historical origins of morality, that is, to
review the variety of conditions that led to the creation of different types of
moralities and moral systems generally.

In strong opposition to the large part of traditional claims, then, Nietzsche
directs his attention neither beyond the world nor behind the world, to some
purported transcendent ground of value in Heaven, in the Stars, or from God's
divine legislation, but rather, he turns toward the world of historical immanence for the origin of what he terms "moral prejudices."[31] His question for
the *Genealogy* then becomes:

> Under what conditions did man devise these value judgments; good and evil?
> *And what value do they themselves possess?* Have they hindered or furthered
> human prosperity? Are they a sign of distress, of impoverishment, of the degener-
> ation of life? Or is there revealed in them, on the contrary, the plenitude, force,
> and the will of life, its courage, certainty, and future?[32]

Looking within world history for the answers to these questions, for the
origins of good and evil and for the origins of morality itself, Nietzsche realizes
he must first distinguish the several contributing elements called upon here,
that being the historical facts and conditions for moral systems generally. This
includes a review of various ages or historical epochs, an examination of different cultures and peoples, various orders, ranks and types of individuals, and so
forth. Also, and by means of a historical perspective, he looks for an order of
social stratification, one that might account for both the origins and the hierarchy of specific moral judgments found within any given society.[33]

All this is only preparation, however. What is really involved here is his
critique, his criticism of morality, the question as to the value of morality as
such: the value of value.[34] If our own code of traditional morality itself has little
or no value—as Nietzsche regrettably suspects—then perhaps he is correct to
call that *nihilism*: the belief that *nothing* is of intrinsic value, that there is no
universal or absolute foundation of value at all, that nothing truly matters, that

one position is equally good or just or reprehensible as any other.⑤ Thus, for Nietzsche, what has up until now passed for morality appears to be quite literally without value—worthless, unworthy of our critical estimation and moral adherence.

Nietzsche insistently directs his attacks against the _traditional_ morality, the morality that enjoins us to champion the weak and defenseless, the meek and humble, the less fortunate members of our society. Such an ethics is one of sympathy, of pity, an ethics of selflessness. But these—properly Judeo-Christian—_values_ are precisely the ones he calls nihilistic. Why should this be the case? First of all, because they claim to be self-evident values, a priori values, values that are supposedly self-evident; values that purport to be intuitively obvious to anyone, anywhere, any time, even _before_ one might have the occasion to experience them in a particular society at a given period in its development. But Nietzsche would deny the very possibility of this status. He would say that a priori values would simply amount to the claim that the values in question were utterly _indifferent_, that they would be simply detached, unrelated _to_ and unmotivated _by_ particular historical, social, or economic conditions. For Nietzsche, a priori values would be acceptable _if_ the particular human subject happened to live _outside_ of history, outside a particular society, nation, state, or community, or if such a person were entirely free from the practical demands of an economic order.

But second, and more importantly, he holds these traditional values of pity in a generally _negative_ attitude because they ultimately, if taken strictly, and in the long run, _deny_ life and the conditions for life. In this sense, they are inconsistent with the requirements for their own possibility. To be valuable, if not viable, it is supposed at the very least that the values one lives by are life-sustaining, indeed, life-enhancing.

> It was precisely here that I saw the _great_ danger to mankind, its sublimest enticement and seduction—but to what? To nothingness? It was precisely here that I saw the beginning of the end, the dead stop, a retrospective weariness, the will turning _against_ life, the tender and sorrowful signs of the ultimate illness: I understood the ever-spreading morality of pity that had seized even on philosophers and made them ill, as the most sinister symptom of a European culture that had itself become sinister, perhaps as its bypass to a new Buddhism? To a Buddhism for Europeans—to _nihilism_?[36]

For Nietzsche, this Judeo-Christian ethics of pity—or, what is much the same, in a _secular_, nonreligious sense, the _utilitarian_ morality, which teaches the desirability of the greatest happiness for the greatest number of people—is held to be *dangerous*. But why should this appear at all dangerous? Nietzsche sees the traditional moral code to be especially dangerous since it *indicates* a deeper state, both cultural and personal, of profound weariness or fatigue. All it seems to aim for is the finality of pleasure and an absence of pain: essentially, peace, bliss, sabbath. Narcotically, the traditional code of values induces an exhausted state of conformist tranquility where pleasure is maximized and pain minimized. Under such conditions, the human spirit weakens, atrophies. The exceptional person—one who introduces new ideas and calls for advancement, for active development and improvement—then appears as a threat: a threat of disruption, of social disequilibrium.As such, he must be rooted out and suppressed. The result, for Nietzsche, is that, under these circumstances, mediocrity is almost destined to prevail. Any question of struggle, achievement, or growth in what humanity can be or become is abandoned from the start. Such a traditional morality encourages little activity at all, save for pleasurable diversion or leisure. Ultimately, Nietzsche argues, it is the moral order itself that is instrumental in bringing about a culture of *nihilism*—"Buddhism," so called. In short, the value of *passivity* and resignation is elevated to the highest order and action is diminished to the lowest.[38] This gets elaborated in the first essay of *The Genealogy of Morals*, when Nietzsche discusses the emergence of slave and reactive values.

What this traditional morality of pity, pleasure, and passivity results in, for Nietzsche, is ultimately a morality of total *conformity*, where the democratic mass—or, more properly construed, the egalitarian mass, the "herd"—calls *good* that which is beneficial to *them*, at the least possible expense.[39] To paraphrase John Stuart Mill's formulation of this in his influential work of 1861, *Utilitarianism*, "The more who derive benefit from an action, the better it is." Nietzsche argues that to be effectively realized, however, such a morality must assume the viewpoint of the passive majority who receive and benefit from an action, and not that of the few individuals who are active agents, who willingly undertake to *do* something for themselves, to initiate their own growth and development. This pervasive morality of the West designates pity, selflessness, and altruism as virtues. Why is it dangerous then? Nietzsche's response to this question is generally twofold. In his *Gay Science*, section 21, Nietzsche explains that the utilitarian morality depreciates the individual in favor of the larger, social whole. Thus, the individual's value is merely *instrumental* to the benefit of others. "A man's virtues (like industriousness, obedience, chastity, filial piety, and justice) are usually harmful for those who possess them," and invariably,

through one's education in these virtues, one becomes their "victim." Remarkably, however, society at large (i.e., the domain of one's "neighbor") praises
these virtues in the individual for precisely the reason that possession of them
is beneficial to the greater whole. Thus, what is praised in *principle*—
selflessness—is contradicted by its *motives*, namely, a generalized selfishness:

> That is how education always proceeds: one tries to condition an individual by
> various attractions and advantages to adopt a way of thinking and behaving that,
> once it has become a habit, instinct, and passion, will dominate him *to his own
> ultimate disadvantage* but "for the general good." . . .If this education succeeds,
> then every virtue of an individual is a public utility and a private disadvantage.[40]

Furthermore, the self-sacrificial character of utilitarian morality ultimately
results in a real danger to the individual; it results in the individual's lack of
concern for his or her own best interests, health, wealth, honors, promotion,
and for the expansion of his or her own power. Collectively, then, and in the
long run, such a morality is debilitating, enervating; it clogs and deadens the
human spirit, it weakens us through atrophy, and especially, it deprives *life* of
all value. The active exercise of life loses all value for a morality that cultivates
passivity, rest, torpor, sleep, and narcotized diversion. In this sense, the culture
of nihilism shows itself as a kind of—what Herbert Marcuse, in his *One-Dimensional Man*, would later call "repressive desublimation." This is a situation
in which one is encouraged to find pleasure and happiness in the conformist
consumption of leisure, gadgets, and socially sanctioned forms of entertainment. All these pleasurable diversions are purchased at the cost of excessive
and painful labor, however, precisely to counteract the pain and tedium produced by that labor.[41]

In more general terms, then, for Nietzsche, what is the value of morality as
such—of any morality—and what are its motives and consequences? Why
should we entertain this, our present morality, rather than any other? What
follows if we abide by one rather than by another morality? In other words—
and this is really the point of the preface—Nietzsche argues that there is no
simple face value to morality. If this is the case, if there is no simple and evident
value to it on the surface, then Nietzsche will discern the very institution of
morality in terms of something *else*, in terms of something *other* than what it
claims to be.[42] Thus, for example, Nietzsche will come to view morality *as*, or
in terms of, for example, its motives, or in terms of its consequences; or, morality *as* a symptom of an age; or, *as* a mask; perhaps, *as* self-righteousness; or, *as*
an illness; or, *as* a misunderstanding; or, *as* the cause of something else; or, *as*

a remedy to a prior state of affairs; or, *as* a stimulant, *as* a restraint, or even *as* a poison. Thus, Nietzsche will assert in section 6 of the preface:

> One has taken the *value* of these "values" as given, as factual, as beyond all question; one has hitherto never doubted or hesitated in the slightest degree in supposing "the good man" to be of greater value than "the evil man," of greater value in the sense of furthering the advancement and prosperity of man in general (the future of man included). But what if the reverse were true? What if a symptom of regression were inherent in the "good," likewise a danger, a seduction, a poison, a narcotic, through which the present was possibly living *at the expense of the future*? Perhaps more comfortably, less dangerously, but at the same time in a meaner style, more basely?—so that precisely morality would be to blame if the *highest power and splendor* actually possible to the type man was never in fact attained?—So that precisely morality was the danger of dangers?[43]

Now we can understand why, in the very first sentence of the preface, Nietzsche stressed the importance of interpretation. Morality, quite simply, has to be interpreted, because there is no face value to it. Indeed, he compares morality with the study of signs, of *semiotics*: everything about morality has to be deciphered, related, and interpreted, precisely because, like a sign or a symptom, it *points to* something *other* than itself to secure a meaning *for* itself. It must turn elsewhere to ground its own sense or meaning. What constitutes morality is, as he suggests, a complex and deeply historical series, or chain, of signs: effectively, a "hieroglyphic record, so hard to decipher."[44] Its remote, indeed archaic, origins must literally be uncovered, exhumed.

If morality has to be interpreted to be understood, and to be evaluated in turn, this is precisely because—once again—there is no surface truth, no face value to morality itself. In other words, for Nietzsche, there are simply no "moral facts" in and of themselves. There are only moral "interpretations" or, as he says, "misinterpretations." He develops this thought at length in one of his later works, *Twilight of the Idols*, written in 1888:

> [Here is] an insight which I was the first to formulate: that *there are altogether no moral facts*. Moral judgments agree with religious ones in believing in realities which are no realities. Morality is merely an interpretation of certain phenomena—more precisely, a misinterpretation. Moral judgments, like religious ones, belong to a stage of ignorance at which the very concept of the real and the distinction between what is real and imaginary, are still lacking; thus "truth," at this stage, designates all sorts of things which we today call "imaginings." Moral judgments are therefore never to be taken literally; so understood, they always contain mere absurdity. Semiotically, however, they remain invaluable; they re-

veal, at least for those who know [how to decipher], the most valuable realities of cultures and inwardnesses which did not know enough to "understand" themselves. Morality is mere sign language, mere symptomatology; one must know what it is all about to be able to profit from it.[45]

A striking example of just how a particular moral system misinterprets the real to such an extent that reality becomes transformed into the imaginary—and again, this is Nietzsche's own interpretation—is given in his last work, *The Antichrist*, where he characterizes, if not caricatures, his view of the traditional Christian-moral system of values.

> In Christianity, neither morality nor religion has even a single point of contact with reality. Nothing but imaginary *causes* ("God," "soul," "ego," "spirit," "free will"—for that matter, "unfree will"), nothing but imaginary *effects* ("sin," "redemption," "grace," "punishment," "forgiveness of sins"). Intercourse between imaginary *beings* ("God," "spirits," "souls"); an imaginary *natural* science (anthropocentric; no trace of any concept of natural causes); an imaginary *psychology* (nothing but self-misunderstandings . . . with the aid of the sign language of the religio-moral idiosyncrasy: "repentance," "pangs of conscience," "temptations by the devil," "the presence of God"); an imaginary *teleology* [or doctrine of final ends] ("the kingdom of God," "the Last Judgment," "eternal life").
>
> This *world of pure fiction* is vastly inferior to the world of dreams, insofar as the latter [at least] *mirrors* reality, whereas the former falsifies, devalues, and negates reality. Once the concept of "nature" had been invented as the opposite of "God," "natural" had to become a synonym of "reprehensible."

Nietzsche now proceeds to dramatically state his interpretation of what the traditionally received moral system "points to." In this case, it indicates a deeper motivational substructure, namely a whole "world" of fantasy compensation and psychological projection, predicated upon human frailty and suffering:

> This whole world of fiction is rooted in *hatred* of the natural (of reality!); it is the expression of a profound vexation at the sight of reality.
>
> *But this explains everything.* Who alone has good reason to lie his way out of reality? He who suffers from it. But to suffer from reality is to be a piece of reality that has come to grief. The preponderance of feelings of displeasure over feelings of pleasure is the cause of this fictitious morality and religion; but such a preponderance provides the very formula for decadence.[46]

Should we say, then, that Nietzsche is simply *for* life, and that life-affirming values are good? That "vitalism" is the sole good? Should we say this despite his caution, his saying six times in the first paragraph of the preface that he does not know? Or, perhaps, we might say that he does not know life very well. Nietzsche tells us, after all, that "we are unknown to ourselves . . . we do not know ourselves." Yet, even in a real historical sense, we rarely do know what our own life or personality is—with any remarkable exactitude—or, what it ultimately means, especially in an age of cultural confusion and personal indecision, of pretense and dissimulation. How, then, are we to know what is good and evil? Or, even more so, what should be held as good and evil? In any event, the preface to *On the Genealogy of Morals* counsels caution, it speaks in the subjunctive. As a critique of values, it first raises the question as to where we should look for the answers concerning the very institution of morality, its effective practice, and its broad significance.

THE ORIGINS OF "GOOD AND EVIL," "GOOD AND BAD"

In the first essay of *On the Genealogy of Morals*—" 'Good and Evil,' 'Good and Bad,' "—Nietzsche points out that the "English psychologists," people such as such as Jeremy Bentham, James Mill, David Hume, John Stuart Mill, and Herbert Spencer, all predominantly utilitarian philosophers, were *interesting* because they directed their attention to what was not obvious, to what was not immediately evident about morality: namely, they sought to uncover the concealed provenance, the hidden origins, of moral sentiments, as they found expression in morally guided judgment and action. They looked to the unconscious, to the life of acquired habits, of internal and nonapparent sources of motivation, to explain human moral behavior, that is, to "the truly effective and directive agent, that which has been decisive in its evolution."[47] They focused on what seemed to be the most "inertial" and perhaps unnoticed aspects of experience. In this sense, they too, like Nietzsche, began to approach morality as a system of signs, of signifiers, that would point to another text, to a deeper and hidden inscription they would call "human nature."

Interesting, but still wrong. Not far enough. As Nietzsche rather coyly remarked, the English look into the "swamps," into the lowliest and most fetid part of man—from whence their moral "feelings" were thought to have emerged. What they failed to understand is that these habits and unconscious dispositions are not simply innate or permanently fixed, preestablished elements of human nature, but rather, that they are themselves *products* of a specifically historical evolution, that morality and its valuations are already the finished products, or consummation, of an age. As Nietzsche had already observed in his work of 1882, *The Gay Science*: *Conscience*

> Your judgment "this is right" has a pre-history in your instincts, likes, dislikes, experiences, and lack of experiences. "*How* did it originate there?" you must ask, and then also: "What is it that impels me to listen to it?" You can listen to its commands like a good soldier who hears his officer's command. Or like a woman who loves the man who commands. Or like a flatterer and coward who is afraid of the commander. Or like a dunderhead who obeys because no objection occurs to him. In short, there are a hundred ways in which you can listen to your conscience. But that you take this or that judgment for the voice of conscience—in other words, that you feel something to be right—may be due to the fact that you have never thought much about yourself and simply have accepted blindly that what you had been told ever since your childhood was right. . . . And, briefly, if you had thought more subtly, observed better, and learned more, . . . your understanding *of the manner in which moral judgments have originated* would spoil these grand words for you.[48]

Even the simple fact of a particularly conditioned moral feeling or judgment is therefore deeply historical, it represents but a mark on a vast surface. Nietzsche calls for a *genealogy*, therefore, and not merely a psychological self-scrutiny: "The *historical spirit* itself is lacking in them . . . the thinking of all of them is by *nature* unhistorical . . . these investigators and microscopists of the soul."[49] Prepared by the development of what he termed his own "historical sense," then, Nietzsche proposed a different approach: to trace down the historically obscured dynamics of the moral sentiments, to track down the effaced traces of all that underlies and conditions our contemporary moral sensibilities.[50] What the English school views as a straightforward moral feeling or moral sentiment is—for Nietzsche—really an atavism, a throw-back or vestige of a series of complex social conditionings that has transformed (and thereby, concealed) the earlier, more primitive codes and practices of moral conduct. What the English call an individual's personal "moral feeling," or "moral sentiment," Nietzsche interprets as the already evolved and internalized value system of the "herd," the many.

By 1879, Nietzsche had characterized this moral conditioning as the "morality of mores" (*Sittlichkeit*), that is, as simple obedience to traditional customs. One's own moral feelings would thus be a reflection of society's broader codes of moral values, indeed, would be a particular interiorization of these customary values:

So we continue on with custom and morality [*Sittlichkeit*]: which latter is nothing other than simply a feeling for the whole content of those customs [*Sitten*] under which we live and have been raised—and raised, indeed, not as an individual, but as a member of the whole, as a cipher in a majority.[51]

Nietzsche extends this analysis in part 2 of the second volume of *Human, All Too Human*, the section titled "The Wanderer and His Shadow" (1880), when he notes that the moral content of our conscience, which "excites that feeling of compulsion," is formed during our childhood years, and it demands our moral compliance, but it does this "without reason." Rather, we have been instructed by people we honor or fear, by parents and by those in authority. The feelings of our own moral conscience, which compel us to act in a certain way, are precisely those feelings for which we have no "reasons": "The belief in authorities is the source of the [moral] conscience: it is therefore not the voice of God in the heart of man but the voice of some men in man."[52] By the time of *Daybreak* (1881), Nietzsche would lend more precision to this analysis by distinguishing moral feelings from moral concepts, claiming that they had markedly different historical origins, but that they were nonetheless convergent in our own lived experience. In childhood, one imitates—"as born apes"—those moral inclinations and aversions that are exhibited by adults. Yet, in later life, when one is quite familiar with these acquired moral sentiments, one looks for a "reason" by which their moral correctness can be justified or accounted for. Simply by virtue of the demands of human rationality, one feels compelled to give reasons that would render these sentiments plausible and socially acceptable. The demand that these moral sentiments make sense and that they are reasonable thus overlies their already compelling moral agency, but only retrospectively yields rational or intellectual justification. Nietzsche would remark, "To this extent the history of moral feelings is quite different from the history of moral concepts. The former are powerful *before* the action, the latter especially after the action in face of the need to pronounce upon it."[53]

In this sense, the personal "urge" or the individual's "feeling" to act morally—the dispassionate, detached, or altruistic feeling in the case of the English utilitarians—is largely an expression of the moral values held by Englishmen generally, and by English philosophers specifically. What is felt to be truly good is to do things for others, to be charitable, to take pity on the humble unfortunates (one does not tend to pity the "unruly" unfortunates, unfortunately). When the Englishman does this, he enjoys a reassuring moral feeling in return. Of course, this reassuring moral feeling is one of personal pleasure, and it serves to positively reinforce the initial value of what was purportedly an "un-egoistic" act of "disinterested" virtue. In short, one does good for others: *there-fore*, one "feels" better and is all the more *moral* for having done so. For Nietzsche, however, such a claim is clearly disingenuous and conveniently mis-interpreted:

> "Originally"—so they decree—"one approved unegoistic actions and called them good from the point of view of those to whom they were done, that is to say, those to whom they were *useful*; later one *forgot* how this approval originated and, simply because unegoistic actions were always *habitually* praised as good, one also felt them to be good—as if they were something good in themselves." One sees straightaway that this primary derivation already contains all the typical traits of the idiosyncrasy of the English psychologists—we have "utility," "forget-ting," "habit," and finally "error," all as the basis of an evaluation.[54]

But Nietzsche claims that it is a relatively late historical development to interpret value simply in terms of an action's effects upon others. This is largely due, he says, to the inability to impose one's own will and to bring about what is desired for oneself. In broader terms, Nietzsche typically locates this inability or weakness at the very origin of Western morality itself. This is why Nietzsche charges that the Judeo-Christian tradition begins with a change or with a dis-ruption of values, with what he terms a "revaluation" of previously existing values.[55] The change consists in an inversion of value, such that an action is no longer judged according to the forceful imposition of one's personal gain or one's own positive end in view. Rather, it is henceforth to be judged by the effects these actions have on others. The movement of inversion is thereby twofold: from the positive imposition of value to the negative reception of value. From active agent to passive recipient. In the former case, something is good because I do it. In the latter, it is good because it helps them, the others. Because it helps others, I feel good in turn; I have a pleasurable moral feeling or sentiment.

We shall examine this issue of value inversion, of the "revaluation of values," in detail in a moment, but it should at least be noted here that Nietzsche deals with the same psychological "facts" as the English moral philosophers claim to advance. Due to what he calls his own "historical sense," however, Nietzsche *interprets* these facts quite differently. What they take as an internal psycholog-ical datum (i.e., the so-called "moral sentiment" or "the moral urge of con-science") is interpreted by Nietzsche as a historically constituted product or effect, in this case, an "atavism." All of which means that the individual subject who acts out of the "moral urge" is not even aware that he is invoking, that he is acting out of, the resentment-laden values of the previous age, the Judeo-Christian age. Thus, what the individual thinks is a *personal*, subjective urge to act morally is, for Nietzsche, the evolving historical product of past *social* conditioning.

Nietzsche claims to carry out a "genealogy" in a second sense, when he asks for the etymological origin of certain crucial moral terms, that is, of certain traditionally important words in our moral vocabulary. He views the use of these key words or terms as enduring traces carried on from the past, much in the same way as family names or *surnames* testify to an ancestral origin or a historical line of succession. What he finds in each case—for the Greeks, Romans, Goths, Saxons, and Indo-European cultures in general—is that *moral terms* tend to begin with the emergence of strict social and class distinctions. The distinctions originally occur between the ruling classes and the ruled or governed classes, and Nietzsche observes that moral terms themselves are coined from the perspective of each class, respectively. From the perspective of the ruling class, morally *positive* terms, terms of moral approval or approbation, are framed to reflect what are held to be the distinctive qualities belonging to the members of the higher established social order. Thus, terms designating "good," "noble," "virtuous," "strong," "happy," "pleasing," and so forth were originally meant to describe the *ruling class* itself. In the case of ancient Greece, *kalos* meant "noble," and *agathos* or *agathon* meant "good." What the ruling aristocratic class called itself in ancient Greece, then, was the *kaloi kagathoi*, "the noble and good." By *opposition*, and still from the perspective of the ruling class, the *subordinate* class, far greater in number and far weaker in virtue, were called the *hoi polloi*, "the undistinguished multitude," the many, the *demos*, the wonder-loving herd. Nietzsche, the classical philologist, is understandably first drawn to this second sense of genealogical analysis, which he then extends to the broader case:

> The signpost to the *right* road was for me the question: what was the real etymological significance of the designations for "good" coined in the various languages? I found they all led back to the *same conceptual transformation*—that everywhere "noble," "aristocratic" in the social sense, is the basic concept from which "good" in the sense of "with aristocratic soul," "noble," "with a soul of a high order," "with a privileged soul" necessarily developed: a development which always runs parallel with that other, in which "common," "plebeian," "low" are finally transformed into the concept "bad."[56]

With this notion of the "good" derived from the self-characterization of the aristocratic noble class—and the parallel derivation of the "bad" from the nobility's characterization of the lower class—we must nonetheless remember that the socially ascendant class, the upper class, first *imposes* the terms "good" and "bad" from *above*. Quite simply, they do this from their own position of power. But for them, this *power* also, and importantly, designates certain highly esteemed character traits, or strength of spirit.[57] These terms not only signify the strong but *also* the truthful, the faithful, the courageous in battle, the god-like. Thus, what came to be called *good* in Latin—the *bonus* or *bonum*—was first a term of warfare, *bellum*: "One sees what constitutes the 'goodness' of a man in ancient Rome." Likewise, Nietzsche continues, "Our German *gut* [good] even: does it not signify 'the godlike' [*den Göttlichen*], the man of 'god-like race' [*göttlichen Geschlechts*]? And is it not identical with the popular (originally noble) name of the Goths [*der Gothen*]?"[58]

Given the traditionally established aristocratic values in antiquity, Nietzsche argues that these moral traits of the ruling class and the terms used to signify them *first* became threatened from within the aristocratic class itself. This first stage in the "revaluation of values" takes place with the emergence of certain high-born people who were not themselves warriors, but rather, priests and administrators: what Nietzsche collectively calls the "priestly" caste.

> To this rule that a concept denoting political authority always resolves itself into a concept denoting superiority of soul it is not necessarily an exception . . . when the highest caste is at the same time the *priestly* caste and therefore emphasizes in its total description of itself a predicate that calls to mind its priestly function. It is then, for example, that "pure" and "impure" confront one another for the first time as designations of station; and here too there evolves a "good" and a "bad" in a sense no longer referring to station. . . . There is from the first something *unhealthy* in such priestly aristocracies and in the habits ruling in them which turn them away from action and alternate between brooding and emotional explosions . . . how easily the priestly mode of valuation can branch off from the knightly-aristocratic and then develop into its opposite . . . but why? Because they are the most impotent. It is because of their impotence that in them hatred grows to monstrous and uncanny proportions, to the most spiritual and poisonous kind of hatred.[59]

Thus the prevailing set of values became transformed by the addition of other aristocratic factions who could no longer sustain the culturally esteemed warrior values—"a powerful physicality, a flourishing, abundant, even over-flowing health, together with that which serves to preserve it: war, adventure"—but, instead, replaced them with values that were more in accord with their weakened ecclesiastical and civil functions. Cunning, ruse, and intelligence replace valor and courage, strength and power.[60]

THE "SLAVE REVOLT" IN MORALS: *RESSENTIMENT*

Briefly stated, the most significant historical *transformation* of values for Nietzsche is the moment of their complete reversal, their overturning. This great "inversion of values," which marks the transition from the classical Greek and Roman aristocratic morality to the modern Judeo-Christian (or utilitarian and egalitarian) morality, is what Nietzsche terms the "slave revolt" in morals. Effectively, the "slave revolt" in morals consists in the replacement of the aristocratic scale of values with those of the underclass, the slave values. The process is complicated, and Nietzsche dwells at length upon the social and psychological dynamics of this transformation. Nonetheless, the outline of this larger position can be briefly set forth: from the standpoint of slave morality, what the aristocratic morality had valued as "good" (e.g., aggressiveness, strength, bellicosity, etc.) becomes inverted and devalued—into "evil"—and what was formerly held to be "bad" for the aristocratic morality (e.g., weakness, passivity, timidity, etc.) is henceforth presented by the slave morality as "good."

The transition from the aristocratic "good" to the slavish "evil" is the key to the slave revolt. What Nietzsche sees at work in this inversion and devaluation (from "good"—not to "bad"—but to "evil") is the enormous upwelling of a long-repressed bitterness, bred from the slave's impotence and suffering, that finally finds expression and satisfaction in his revolt against the master. At first, the opposition and revolt would appear to call for a political, if not military, means of resolution, since the lower classes traditionally outnumber the aristocratic class. But Nietzsche argues that, since the lower classes are initially powerless, the revolt must, at least at the start, be one of a psychological-moral variety (i.e., a substitute for real action). The overthrow of the master morality by the slave is thus, quite simply, a "moral" victory. What induces the slave to positively embrace these negated, inverted values is the promise of a real, if not deferred, compensation—in the form of a divine "salvation" or "redemption" from earthly suffering altogether: precisely, the promise of heaven as a reward for the true believer who suffers at the hands of the evil overlord. The agent of this promise is precisely the "priest," the cunning and intelligent manipulator of human suffering. Under the religiometaphysical teaching of personal immortality through divine redemption, the priestly caste ultimately garners the moral adherence (and the enormous practical support) of the populous lower classes as well as the political self-subjugation of the ruling class itself.

In time, the classical world of Greece and Rome passes over to the medieval world of feudal, aristocratic regimes, which in turn—given the Christian doctrine of the equality of all souls before God—becomes transformed through the revolutions and liberation movements, beginning in the eighteenth century, into modern, democratic societies. Ultimately, the "slave revolt" succeeds, historically and politically. Yet the values we have inherited in the process of this two-thousand-year revolt remain strikingly problematic for Nietzsche.

If the "slave revolt" in morals is first incited and propagated among the lower classes by the priests and ecclesiastics, the specific motivation to "invert" the system of aristocratic moral values takes place as an act of resentment, or as Nietzsche regularly uses the French term, *ressentiment*. This latter use carries the sense of the ongoing bite or sting of an embittered feeling, the lingering or resonating sentiment of a "sickly" revenge, one that cannot be directly exercised and that, due to lack of power or will, must be repressed, deferred, and ultimately, *sublimated*. It connotes the persisting aftertaste of a sorely "unhappy" consciousness. *Ressentiment* bears witness to a subversion of the will, *a subversion of direct action*.[61] We could compare the two usages by saying that an act of revenge or resentment, pure and simple, would be a direct striking-back at the source of one's hurt, an attempt to deal with the oppressor, agent, or inflictor of one's pain, one's discomfiture, and to act upon it. In this sense, Nietzsche often speaks of simple revenge as the act of an ordinarily strong and well-adjusted nature—hardly uncommon, and perfectly understandable. In this sense, revenge is positive and cathartic, and the feeling for revenge disappears when vengeance—direct or deferred—has been taken. *Ressentiment*, however, in Max Scheler's celebrated discussion of the phenomenon,

> is a self-poisoning of the mind which has quite definite causes and consequences. It is a lasting mental attitude, caused by the systematic repression of certain emotions and affects which, as such, are normal components of human nature. Their repression leads to the constant tendency to indulge in certain kinds of value delusions and corresponding value judgments. The emotions and affects primarily concerned are revenge, hatred, malice, envy, the impulse to detract, and spite.[62]

It should be noted that this distinction between resentment and *ressentiment* parallels the broader distinction between noble and slave, that is, at the basis of the good–bad/good–evil distinction. When Nietzsche first formulates this distinction, in his work of 1878, *Human, All Too Human*, he initially distinguishes the origin of these moral values according to what characterizes the *power relations* between the two social classes. The noble or ruling class has the power to strike back in an *aggressive* sense. But, equally, it has the power *to give back*, to repay, in a *benevolent* sense. The master has this power, the slave simply does not. The conquering tribe or ruling caste, by virtue of its position of power, is able, Nietzsche claims, to *requite*: that is, to retaliate, to return, or to repay a bad *or* a good deed.[63] As masters, they are empowered, and thus, they are fully free to express, to exteriorize their inclinations, their aggressions or passions.

The slave, of course, is hardly free to do this, precisely due to his lack of power and his inability to express himself at will. Paying back, compensation, or, as Nietzsche terms it, "requital" can only be covert, unexpressed, or "spiritual." In this sense, the slave can compensate himself, for the suffering inflicted upon him by the master, only *indirectly*—through a kind of spiritual, or emotional, hatred of the master, by feeling anger or wrath toward the master, the overlord, and this serves as a psychological substitute for real action, requital. His own aggressions must be initially repressed and can only be expressed in a sublimated way, that is to say, redirected through indirect release, covertly, spiritually, in the form of a kind of rage or hatred that may also assume the form of an ideological or moral or religious denunciation of the oppressive ruling class.[64] The vengeful aggressions cannot be expressed directly, in the fashion of outright revenge, precisely because the slave has no power to do so. The slave, after all, is already powerless: defeated, incarcerated, humiliated, subjected by the overclass. As Nietzsche would express this in section 45 of *Human, All Too Human*—and recall that Nietzsche refers the reader to this passage in his preface to the *Genealogy*, along with many other references for clarification:

> The concept good and evil has a two-fold prehistory: firstly in the soul of the ruling tribes and castes. He who has the power to requite, good with good, evil with evil, and also actually practices requital—is, that is to say, grateful and revengeful—is called good; he who is powerless and cannot requite counts as bad. As a good man, one belongs to the "good," a community which has a sense of belonging together because all the individuals in it are combined with one another through the [shared] capacity for requital. As a bad man, one belongs to the "bad," to a swarm of subjected, powerless people who have no sense of belonging together. The good are a caste, the bad a mass, like grains of sand. Good and bad is for a long time the same thing as noble and base, master and slave. On the other hand, one does not regard the enemy as evil: he can requite.[65]

Nietzsche *then* goes on to show how the Greeks could be mortal enemies with one another, yet never fail to have respect for one another, because that respect was based on the other's real capacity for requital—which, in turn, ensured respect. He gives a historical example of this with the case of the Trojan War. Throughout the whole of Homer's epics the *Iliad* and the *Odyssey*, both the Greeks and the Trojans are counted as good; the warriors, the characters, even Homer himself, hold both parties in the highest respect, admiration, even veneration. Basically, respect is given among equals, and this constitutes the aristocratic morality. The slave class earns no respect from the aristocrats, since they are literally incapable of requiting evil or good. Hence Nietzsche's statement about the second element involved in the prehistory of good and evil, namely, the moral judgment from the standpoint of the oppressed class, the slave, again from section 45 of *Human, All Too Human*:

> Then in the soul of the subjected, the powerless [and from this point of view] . . . every *other* man, whether he be noble or base, counts as inimical, ruthless, cruel, cunning, ready to take advantage. [In this case,] Evil is the characterizing expression for man, indeed for every living being one supposes to exist, for a god, for example; human, divine mean the same thing as diabolical: evil. Signs of goodness, benevolence, sympathy are received fearfully as a trick, a prelude with a dreadful determination . . . in short, as refined wickedness. When this disposition exists in the individual a community can hardly arise, at best the most rudimentary form of community; so that wherever this conception of good and evil reigns the downfall of such individuals, of their tribes and races, is near.[66]

Hence, when Nietzsche discusses "the slave revolt in morals" in the *Genealogy*, he specifies social and class distinctions, and basically—fundamentally—this distinction is grounded on an unequal distribution of real *power*. It is the absence of power—effectively, impotence—that drives *ressentiment* beyond the state of revenge, envy, or the will to detract.

> *Ressentiment* can only arise if these emotions are particularly powerful and yet must be suppressed because they are coupled with the feeling that one is unable to act them out—either because of weakness, physical or mental, or because of fear. Through its very origin, *ressentiment* is therefore chiefly confined to those who serve and are *dominated* at the moment. . . . Accompanied by impotence . . . the oppressive sense of inferiority which always goes with the "common" attitude cannot lead to active behavior. Yet the painful tension demands relief. This is afforded by the specific value delusion of *ressentiment*. To relieve the tension, the common man seeks a feeling of superiority or equality, and he attains his purpose by an illusory devaluation of the other man's qualities or by a specific

"blindness" to these qualities. But secondly—and here lies the main achievement of *ressentiment*—he falsifies the values themselves which could bestow excellence on any possible objects of comparison.[67] *Scheler*

That Nietzsche specifies the Jews as a historical case of slave morality is thus a prime instance—not of racial difference, or of race as such—but rather, of the situation of a subjected people. The history of this subjection and persecution began under Ramses II and continued periodically under the Philistines, Assyrians, Egyptians, Babylonians, Greeks, and Romans, with the Jews finally being driven from Jerusalem with the fall of the Second Temple in the year 70. Understandably, many classical historians—the Roman historian Tacitus, especially—would term the Jews "subject" peoples, and their historical identity, while initially derived from the political identity of the Kingdom of Judah, would progressively be determined in religious terms as the followers of "Judaism." It is in this sense that Nietzsche describes the Jews both in political or class terms—as "subjects" or "slaves"—as well as in religious and aristocratic terms (i.e., precisely, as "priestly").

Far from being eliminated, or suffering a complete collapse of "community" as Nietzsche suggested was the case with most "subject" peoples, the Jews, to Nietzsche's great admiration, suffered through their historical adversity to become one of the great peoples of the West. That the Jews mark the beginning of "the slave rebellion" in morals, and that they were successful in bringing this about, testifies to what Nietzsche himself calls "a miraculous feat," one that ultimately subverted all their ancient rivals, their supposed "masters." It was precisely their suffering, Nietzsche argues, that enabled the Jewish people to formulate an unimaginable spiritual strength, a strength that grew from the wrath of the ancient prophets to the heights of spiritual sublimity and moral authority.[68]

Some references to Nietzsche's other writings will be helpful in addressing his views on this matter, especially because they seem so abruptly stated in section 7 of essay 1 of the *Genealogy*, and because they have so often been painfully distorted by his contemporaries and by subsequent interpreters (both willfully and unwittingly). First of all, Nietzsche often remarks on how the conditions of adversity—subjection, slavery, and the suffering it entailed—historically served to strengthen the spirit of a people:

> The discipline of suffering, of *great* suffering—do you not know that only *this* discipline has created all enhancements of man so far? That tension of the soul in unhappiness which cultivates its strength . . . and whatever has been granted to it of profundity . . . spirit . . . greatness: was it not granted to it . . . through the discipline of great suffering?[69]

As for the specifically Jewish response to this ordeal, Nietzsche remarks in *Daybreak* (1878):

> The Jews have experienced anger [and wrath] differently from us and they pro-
> nounced it holy. Thus they saw the gloomy majesty of the man with whom it
> showed itself associated at an elevation which a European is incapable of imagin-
> ing; they modelled their angry holy Jehovah on their angry holy prophets. Mea-
> sured against these, the great men of wrath among Europeans, are as it were,
> creations at second hand.[70]

It was such a spiritual formation through adversity that gave rise to perhaps the greatest moral document of the West, at least in Nietzsche's view. In 1886, he would claim in *Beyond Good and Evil*:

> In the Jewish "Old Testament," the book of divine justice, there are human be-
> ings, things, and speeches in so grand a style that Greek and Indian literature
> have nothing to compare with it. With terror and reverence one stands before
> these tremendous remnants of what man once was. . . . To have glued this [Chris-
> tian] New Testament . . . to the Old Testament to make one book, as "the Bible"
> . . . this is perhaps the greatest audacity and "sin against the spirit" that literary
> Europe has on its conscience.[71]

In one of his most extended reflections on the Jews, and on the adversity they overcame and transformed into greatness, Nietzsche would come to welcome their spiritual contributions as one of the highest possible blessings for modern Europe. The following is from section 205, "Of the People of Israel," from *Daybreak*:

> In Europe [the Jews] have gone through an eighteen-century schooling such as
> no other nation of this continent can boast of—and what they have experienced
> in this terrible time of schooling has benefited the individual to a greater degree
> than it has the community as a whole. As a consequence of this, the psychological
> and spiritual resources of the Jews today are extraordinary. . . . Every Jew pos-
> sesses in the history of his fathers and grandfathers a great fund of examples of
> the coldest self-possession and endurance in fearful situations, of the subtlest
> outwitting and exploitation of chance and misfortune; their courage beneath the
> cloak of miserable submission, their heroism in "scorning being scorned" sur-
> passes the virtues of all the saints. For two millennia an attempt was made to
> render them contemptible by treating them with contempt, and by barring to
> them the way to all honours and all that was honourable, and in exchange thrust-
> ing them all the deeper into the undesirable trades. . . . But . . . they themselves
> never ceased to believe themselves called to the highest things . . . they possess

by far the greatest experience of human society, and even in their passions they
practice the caution taught by this experience. . . . And whither shall this assembled abundance of grand impressions, which for every Jewish family constitutes
Jewish history, this abundance of passions, virtues, decisions, renunciations,
struggles, victories of every kind—whither shall it stream out if not at last into
great men and great works? Then, when the Jews can exhibit as their work such
jewels and golden vessels as the European nations of a briefer and less profound
experience could not and cannot produce, when Israel will have transformed its
eternal vengeance into an eternal blessing for Europe: then there will again arrive
that seventh day on which the ancient Jewish God may rejoice in himself, his
creation and his chosen people—and let us all, all of us, rejoice with him![72]

While Nietzsche's judgment of the Jewish struggle, which results, as we
have seen, in his own broader perspective, with the triumphant self-affirmation
of a world-historical people, seems more in accord with Hegel's account of
"lordship and bondage" in his *Phenomenology*, Nietzsche nonetheless relies
upon the example of the Jews for his account of slave morality.[73] He does this
for a number of reasons. Historically, he follows the traditional view that the
Jews were a politically subjected people: from the Exodus to the Babylonian
Captivity to the Diaspora, following Titus's destruction of the Second Temple.
As a subject people, they could hardly exact collective military revenge against,
for example, the Romans and hope to prevail. Such revenge had to be sublimated, then, which is generally characteristic of *ressentiment,* rather than revenge. But, as Nietzsche himself had already pointed out, developing under
the "discipline of suffering," this subjection and vengefulness ultimately transformed itself into a body of great literature, an entire mythology and religion,
an unprecedented strength of spirit, intellect, and moral majesty—in the Jews'
own historical development.

More important, however, Nietzsche uses the example of the Jews' subjection as a transition to his larger concern, namely, the immense fund of *ressentiment* he found so strongly characteristic of early Christianity, especially, that of
the Pauline tradition. That the Jews were a "chosen people" testified to their
"priestly" morality, and their subsequent creation of a great religious morality
was demonstrative of their chosen "role": namely, to be spiritual leaders. All
this is consistent with Nietzsche's account of "the slave revolt in morals." But
Nietzsche goes on to stress that Christianity's *ressentiment*, developing within
the Roman civilization (and not just as a trait belonging to a distinct, subject
people), finds its compensation not merely in the active exercise of spiritual
authority but in the reactive creation of a metaphysical worldview that would

have the overlords, the masters, literally burned in hell as compensation for Christian suffering: hence, Nietzsche's acerbic remarks about the apostles and St. Thomas, and especially his scathing invocation of Tertullian, in section 15 of the first essay.

Nietzsche's use of the Jews as an example of slave morality is thus intended to open wider the discussion of *ressentiment* and its principal inheritor, the Christian religiomoral teaching. In fact, Nietzsche ends section 7 of the first essay by saying "one knows *who* inherited this Jewish revaluation." In this sense, the slave revolt in morals "has a history of two thousand years behind it and which we no longer see because it—has been victorious."[74] The slave revolt thus grows into "something equally incomparable"—a "new love," that of Christianity. Section 8 of the first essay indicates the transition Nietzsche wants to make between the brief historical account of Jewish subjection, or slavery, and the sublime psychological and metaphysical construction of *ressentiment* that he will develop in section 10. As for the transition from a "vengefulness and hatred" that characterized the slave revolt, which was basically rooted in a suppressed "revenge," the Christian gospel of love is *not a denial of revenge,* as might be expected, but rather, its bitterest, most poisonous transfiguration (out of revenge) into *ressentiment,* where all pretext of honor and requital and any sense of an aristocratic value standard are abandoned.[75]

According to Nietzsche's formulation, *ressentiment* is a far more subtle and ingenious way of retribution than simple resentment or revenge. Rather than attacking the offending object or perpetrator and engaging it straightforwardly as an enemy, as a restriction, or limitation, and as something to be quickly repulsed, the act of *ressentiment* instead subverts the value of the object in question, in this case, the source of one's distress. Rather than striking back at an aggressor, as in the case of revenge, one merely *denigrates* him and *pronounces* that he is worthless, beneath contempt, *evil.* Here, the very agency of value-formation has changed. No longer is value a function of the subject's action, his forceful self-affirmation; it is now a matter of creating value by weak and impotent *reaction.* Here the subject *cannot* strike back, for he is terrified, overpowered, and sorely embittered by his own impotence and lack of self-confidence, so he does the next best thing: he changes the rules of the game. If he cannot attain his *real* goal of successful retribution (of recompense or of restoration of his honor), *he lessens its value,* and consequently the likelihood of obtaining it. In the simple words of Aesop's fable, one assumes an attitude of "sour grapes"! In morally evaluative terms, if I cannot deal with strength and self-affirmation, I must *invert* these values and call weakness and self-denial *good.* Nietzsche says that "this act of *spiritual* revenge is carried out with awe-inspiring consistency." The *ressentiment*-laden *individual*, or *class*, or *culture*, or *people*

> inverts the aristocratic value equation (good = noble = powerful = beautiful = happy = beloved of the gods) and hangs onto this inversion with his teeth, saying that the wretched alone are the good; the poor, the impotent, and lowly are the good; the suffering, deprived, sick, and ugly alone are pious, alone are blessed by God—blessedness is for them alone—and *you*—the powerful and noble, are on the contrary the *evil*, the cruel, the lustful, the insatiable, the God-less to all eternity.[76]

What slave morality calls "evil," then, had formerly been characterized as the "good" by the aristocratic value equation. Slave morality is essentially a negative creation of value, and it drips with the poison of psychological rancor, the seething powerlessness of *ressentiment*. Nietzsche clarifies the negative and reactive role played by *ressentiment* in the formation of slave morality:

> The slave revolt in morality begins when *ressentiment* itself becomes creative and gives birth to values; the *ressentiment* of natures that are denied the true reaction, that of deeds, and compensate themselves with an imaginary revenge. While every noble morality develops from a triumphant affirmation of itself, slave morality from the outset says No to what is "outside," what is "different," what is "not itself"; and *this* No is its creative deed. This inversion of the value-positing eye—this *need* to direct one's view outward instead of back to oneself—is of the essence of *ressentiment*; in order to exist, slave morality always first needs a hostile external world; it needs, physiologically speaking, external stimuli in order to act at all—its action is fundamentally reaction.
>
> The reverse is the case with the noble mode of valuation; it acts and grows spontaneously, it seeks its opposite only so as to affirm itself more gratefully and triumphantly—its negative concept "low," "common," "bad," is only a subsequently-invented pale, contrasting image in relation to its positive basic concept—filled with life and passion through and through—"we noble ones, we good, beautiful, happy ones."[77]

Once again, this "revaluation of values" is not a simple mechanical inversion or reversal: it is complicated by the addition of this embittered feeling of *ressentiment*, by the psychological or personal inability to see one's enemy as an equal, the inability to respect and to have reverence for one's opponent (see figure 4.1). Only by regarding the enemy, the adversary, as absolutely despicable, as reprehensible filth, as unclean and unchaste, as *evil* and *sinful*, does one give *oneself* any moral (and, indeed, psychological) status at all. By denigrating

Figure 4.1   Schema of the slave's "inversion" of aristocratic values.

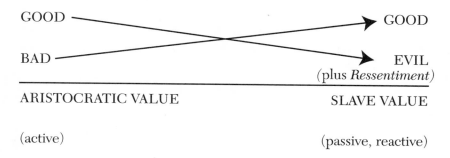

ARISTOCRATIC VALUE   SLAVE VALUE

(active)   (passive, reactive)

or by positively devaluing the "other," one thereby—and only indirectly—elevates oneself. Of course, from the viewpoint of aristocratic value, one would maintain that it is unworthy of a noble to have such a *lowly* opponent: one would have to stoop far too low even to engage an enemy who was so vilified. As Nietzsche had already recalled in *The Gay Science*:

> An easy prey [an easy victim] is something contemptible for proud natures. They feel good only at the sight of unbroken men who might become their enemies and at the sight of all possessions that are hard to come by. Against one who is suffering they are often hard because he is not worthy of their aspirations and pride; but they are doubly obliging toward their *peers* whom it would be honorable to fight if the occasion should ever arise. Spurred by the good feeling of *this* perspective, the members of the knightly caste became accustomed to treating each other with exquisite courtesy.[78]

Hence, for the aristocratic morality—where *ressentiment* is not a contributing factor of judgment—"bad" is not a term of vilification (as "evil" *is* from the viewpoint of slave morality).[79]

As a reversal and devaluation of noble values, the *ressentiment*-laden slave values are typified by their reactive and passive nature, both of which characterizations stand in fundamental opposition to the emphasis placed on the *active* character of noble values. At one rhetorical extreme of his extended account, Nietzsche tends to emphasize the active quality of these values to such a degree that they would seemingly embrace the violence of primitive, barbaric behavior. In section 11, for example, he applies this rather overdramatized characterization to the early Germanic peoples, the Goths, as well as to the Vandals, the Scandinavian Vikings, the Arabian and Japanese nobility, and the Greeks and Romans, all viewed as typical bearers of a "master" morality (again, in rhetorically exaggerated contrast to the "slave" morality). So conceived, their warlike and violently aggressive instincts would find direct expression in the ruthless subjugation of their enemies in predation and battle and would stand as an affirmation of strength, valor, and courage, values necessary to establish a primitive political state by force; hence, Nietzsche's characterization of such primitive warrior peoples as "animals," "beasts of prey," and "blond beasts." Hardly averse to rhetorical hyperbole himself, Sigmund Freud would likewise describe these archaic, tribal founders of civil society as "the primal horde."[80] For both thinkers, civilization would consist in a process of "taming" the aggressive "barbarian" instincts, through their repression and sublimation, such that peaceful coexistence could eventually prevail among their constituent members.

In making the transition from the earlier barbarian model to the aristocratic model of Greco-Roman antiquity, Nietzsche quotes from Pericles' funeral oration, which testifies to these still-retained aggressive warrior instincts—an archaic delight in "boldness" and "wickedness"—that even in his civilized Athens of the classical period could once again find expression as bloody excess, in warfare, retribution, looting, pillaging, and so forth. But Nietzsche ultimately wishes to emphasize the active character of aristocratic, noble morality in the later classical period and to dissociate it from the simpler "barbaric" model of an uncaged beast (he largely reserves this characterization for his argument in the second essay of the *Genealogy*, on "guilt" and "bad conscience"). For his positive characterization of the classical "active" mode of aristocratic valuation, Nietzsche generally follows Aristotle's traditional injunction that *happiness* consists in *doing well*: "The 'well-born' . . . knew, as rounded men replete with energy and therefore *necessarily* active, that happiness should not be sundered from action—being active was with them necessarily a part of happiness (whence *eu pratein* [to do well, to fare well, to be successful] takes its origin)."[81]

In this sense, happiness stems from human *action*, from the active exercise of those human faculties—of the spirit and body—which, in themselves, yield happiness, virtue, prosperity, and pleasure. Such an actively determined happiness testifies to one's independent agency, one's own sovereign capacity to find value and happiness in oneself, through one's own deeds, and in function of one's own pride and self-esteem.[82] Such an individual is well-disposed toward himself and his peers, and as a class, the traditional aristocracy holds itself forth precisely as a model and source of what it values as the good. As such, the aristocratic morality is neither dependent on a comparison between themselves and another class, nor upon a sanction of approval from them. Rather, the *felt happiness*

higher class *"felt* themselves to be 'happy'; they did not have to establish their happiness artificially by examining their enemies, or to persuade themselves, *deceive* themselves, that they were happy (as all men of *ressentiment* are in the habit of doing)."[83]

If, on the aristocratic scale of values, "happiness" is directly tied to action, the slave's set of values is characterized by an entirely passive sense of happiness. The latter kind of happiness—that of slave morality—is, he says, "essentially narcotic, drug, rest, peace, *sabbath*, slackening of tension and relaxing of limbs, in short, *passivity.*"[84] His happiness essentially consists in a withdrawal from all potentially harmful, dangerous, or painful stimuli whatsoever: effectively, then, it amounts to a flight, a withdrawal, from reality itself. Such a passively construed sense of happiness testifies dramatically to the slave's *lack* of independence, power, and pride—egoistic values that would otherwise serve as a stimulus for the aristocratic equation. As creatively "inverted," or "negated," and forged under the impress of slavish *ressentiment*, the negative value standard of slave morality—dependence, weakness, humility, and pity— thus testifies to both the slave's *inability* to find happiness in action as well as to his effective renunciation of all real agency, independence, autonomy, or self-sovereignty whatsoever.

With the abdication of real agency, the slave is necessarily submissive, compliant—a position that alone remains the sole source of pleasure, now negatively construed as passivity, avoidance of distress, of reality. This whole process of abdication and withdrawal results in a sort of abject dependency and reliance upon what is not one's own to serve as the basis of self-value and value in general. Since the slave—or utilitarian—scale of values is now constructed according to a nonegoistic standard, precisely according to the "herd" morality, the value of the self, the ego, is necessarily inverted and devalued. In such circumstances, morally "correct" behavior, action for "the good," is necessarily inimical to one's own best interests. No longer acting for oneself by drawing upon one's own cultivated and trained resources, one can no longer attain any *real* sense of happiness. Since they are *prescribed* by the herd morality, one's own moral actions effectively *proscribe* one's own happiness. For Nietzsche, this is a terrible mistake. One of the "great errors" of mankind, Nietzsche would recall in the *Twilight of the Idols* (1888), is the belief that happiness, even of such a low form, can be ordained from without, that it can be achieved by passive submission to a set of prescribed rules or "ideals," that is, by compliantly reacting to their imperative nature:

[handwritten marginalia: "happiness causes virtue" and "not v.v."]

The most general formula on which every religion and morality is founded is: "Do this and that, refrain from this and that—then you will be happy! Otherwise. . . ." Every morality, every religion, *is* this imperative; I call it the great original sin of reason, the *immortal unreason*. In my mouth, this formula is changed into its opposite—first example of my "revaluation of all values": a well-turned-out human being, a "happy one," *must* perform certain actions and shrinks instinctively from other actions; he carries the order, which he represents physiologically, into his relations with other human beings and things. In a formula: his virtue is the *effect* of his happiness.[85]

Fatally condemned to perpetuating his own unhappiness, out of inability, weakness, and fear, the slave's own impotence eventually becomes fully delusional: by means of his imaginary value "inversion," he reinterprets his own misery and suffering into exemplary cases of virtue itself, and this is precisely what constitutes his moral-psychological "victory" over the now-despised aristocratic values. As Nietzsche would elaborate this "counterfeiting" of *ressentiment* values:

> The oppressed, downtrodden, [and] outraged exhort one another with the vengeful cunning of impotence: "let us be different from the evil, namely good! And he is good who does not outrage, who harms nobody, who does not attack, who does not requite, who leaves revenge to God, who keeps himself hidden as we do, who avoids evil and desires little from life, like us, the patient, humble, and just."[86]

The pent-up hatred toward the overlord can now be discharged in the denunciation of his "evil" enemy, and the slave can take a refreshing pleasure in this release of his vengeance, an emotional release that effectively serves to anesthetize the sufferer. Orchestrating the discharge of this hatred against the "evil" and "ungodly," the priestly class also propagates the "counterfeiting" of *ressentiment* "ideals." In section 14, Nietzsche offers a veritable catalogue of these moral misnomers of *ressentiment*:

> Weakness is lied into something meritorious . . . and impotence which does not requite into "goodness of heart"; anxious lowliness into "humility"; subjection to those one hates into "obedience" (that is, to one of whom they say he commands this subjection—they call him God). The inoffensiveness of the weak man, even the cowardice of which he has so much . . . acquire flattering names, such as "patience," and are even called virtue itself; his inability for revenge is called unwillingness to revenge, perhaps even forgiveness. . . . Vengefulness and hatred? . . . [This is now termed] "the triumph of *justice*"; what they hate is not their enemy, no! they hate "injustice," they hate "godlessness"; what they believe in

and hope for is not the hope of revenge . . . but the victory of God, of the *just* God, over the godless.[87]

Under the direction of the priestly class, the further dissemination of these nonegoistic values serves to consolidate and to preserve the "herd," or the "flock" of "followers," and at the same time, these values do yield up some lesser sense of pleasure to the "followers"—if only by obtaining the praise of others—a secondary kind of pleasure, that of feeling "good" by doing good deeds for "others." It is in this sense that Nietzsche remarks, in the third essay, that the priest has an enormous utility: "if one wanted to express the value of the priestly existence in the briefest formula it would be: the priest *alters the direction of ressentiment.*"[88] *the value of the priest* ✗

In essays 2 and 3 of the *Genealogy*, Nietzsche will address the "psychology of the priest" at length, claiming that it is the priests themselves who invent the concept of original sin, thereby placing the initial cause of human suffering in the very hands of those who suffer, namely, the sufferers themselves. By the same token, the priest is the only one who can absolve the sinner of his or her suffering. In this case, the priest will redirect the sufferer's *ressentiment* back upon the sufferer in the form of a set of self-inflicted ascetic practices, for example, of self-lacerating atonement, of desperate prayers and tearful lamentations, to be employed by the sinful sufferer, in order to seek the priest's absolution of sin and the promise of grace and redemption. In the first essay of the *Genealogy*, however, Nietzsche asserts that such redemption from suffering is to be found in the promise of heavenly bliss itself, namely, with the advent of the "Last Judgment," "the victory of God" over the sinners, over the unjust and the godless: such would be their heaven, "the coming of *their* Kingdom, of the 'Kingdom of God.'"[89]

In testimony to the "forging" or "counterfeiting" of *ressentiment* values, Nietzsche proposes that Dante himself should stand corrected on his view of the Christian afterlife. Rather than just placing "above the gateway of his hell the inscription 'I too was created by eternal love,'" he should have placed as a motto over the gates of the Christian Paradise "and its 'eternal bliss' the inscription 'I too was created by eternal hate'—provided a truth may be placed above the gateway to a lie!"[90]

It is perhaps the consistency of its willful misrepresentation of the real that Nietzsche finds so disturbing, so reprehensible, about the *ressentiment*-laden individual. Having inverted and devalued the aristocratic nobility of strength, and thus having compensated its own impotent hatred with the crown of an eternal, heavenly afterlife, the Christian morality of *ressentiment* then goes on to *indict* the active nobility of strength precisely for its *not being weak*. Seizing upon the "seduction of language" that supposes a "doer" behind the "deed," a hidden "cause" behind the real "effect"—a "lightning" behind the "flash"— slave morality "doubles the deed" and posits the belief in an independent "subject" behind, underlying, the living, human being, an independent subject who is allegedly free in turn to elect the very nature of "its" own being, "its" own reality, of course, in accordance with the passive and reactive values of *ressentiment*. But for Nietzsche, the "subject" in question here is merely the mystification of the *linguistic subject* itself, the first person singular, *impersonal pronoun*, "it." In terms of articulating objective reality, this would be the linguistic subject of predication, the indeterminate substratum, or indexical, which is descriptively accounted for in terms of its observable properties or determinate predications, in space-time. Nietzsche explicitly equates this underlying subject of linguistic predication with Kant's thing-in-itself. In terms of subjective, human existence, Nietzsche further equates this linguistic "subject" with the pronominal subject, the first person singular, *personal pronoun*, "I." What is thus the linguistic subject of a spoken or written sentence, the pronoun "I," becomes—"owing to the seduction of language"⁹¹—misinterpreted *metaphysically* as an immaterial and immortal "soul," one possessed of the miracle of free will.

While Nietzsche would explicitly criticize such metaphysical notions as "the immortal soul," "free will," and "the Kingdom of Heaven," elsewhere— especially in *The Gay Science*, *Beyond Good and Evil*, *Twilight of the Idols*, and *The Antichrist*—he argues, here, in the *Genealogy*, that the notion of an immortal soul possessed of free will is devised by the Christian morality of *ressentiment* so as to make the master morality *accountable* for its actions and therefore to render them guilty, that is, <u>sinful, for *not acting*</u> out of weakness, <u>passivity, impotence.</u>

> Just as the popular mind separates the lightning from its flash and takes the latter for an *action*, for the operation of a subject called lightning, so popular morality also separates strength from expressions of strength, as if there were a neutral substratum behind the strong man, which was *free* to express strength or not to do so. But there is no such substratum; there is no "being" behind doing, effecting, becoming; "the doer" is merely a fiction added to the deed—the deed is everything. The popular mind in fact doubles the deed: it posits the same event first as cause and then a second time as its effect. . . . [Thus,] under the misleading influence of language . . . no wonder if the submerged, darkly glowering

emotions of vengefulness and hatred exploit this belief for their own ends and in fact maintain no belief more ardently than the belief that *the strong man is free to be weak and the bird of prey to be a lamb*—for thus they gain the right to make the bird of prey *accountable* for being a bird of prey.[92]

Judged morally guilty and reprehensible precisely for not being who they really are—strong and active people of respect, who rightly requite good for good, bad for bad—such noble aristocrats are then said to deserve the "just punishment" of damnation and eternal suffering in hell. Vengeance shall belong to the Lord, and the faithful shall delight in the punishment of the damned. As Nietzsche quotes the preeminent spiritual authority of the church, St. Thomas Aquinas—seemingly from memory—"The blessed in the kingdom of heaven will see the punishments of the damned, *in order that their bliss be more delightful for them.*"[93]

The development of this entire eschatology of bliss—from the inversion of noble values to the eternity of a punitive afterlife—is the consequence, the legacy, of *ressentiment* morality and its transfiguration of the empirically real into the metaphysically ideal: its fundamental misinterpretation of weakness for strength.

Unable to assert themselves in the first place, unable to will themselves out of their state of inert passivity, the weak call their own *incapacity* an act of *free will* and then condemn the proud and powerful for not giving up their pride and power. Nietzsche adds—as if they could? As if a fundamental pride, nobility, and strength of character could be stripped from people like so many garters or corsets. Motivated by a profound sense of *ressentiment*, slave morality thereby *misinterprets* its very weakness for strength. It designates its inability to act, its own powerlessness, as a miraculous affirmation of self-restraint, self-possession, and control: namely, as the masterful exercise of *free will* over and upon itself. Nietzsche would draw a poignant portrait of such an individual in section 10, the "man of *ressentiment*":

> He is neither upright nor naive nor honest and straightforward with himself. His soul *squints*; his spirit loves hiding places, secret paths and back doors, everything *covert* entices him as *his* world, *his* security, *his* refreshment; he understands *how to keep silent*, how *not to forget*, how to *wait*, how to be provisionally self-deprecating, and humble. A race of such men of *ressentiment* is bound to become eventually *cleverer* than any noble race; it will also honor cleverness to a greater degree.[94]

Clearly, a *society* of this kind will discourage the exceptional person, the creative and assertive artist, thinker, politician, or poet. Interestingly enough,

the social dimension

the *social phenomenon* of *ressentiment* only appears after the Judeo-Christian tradition had managed to consolidate its hold upon the political structures of Europe. The great subversion there, of course, was the implied egalitarianism of Christianity. The medieval feudal order fell precisely to democratic claims. It is at this stage of political development, *within* the democratic state, that one often finds the greatest expression of *ressentiment* and where *ressentiment* reaches its highest pitch. This occurs when social equality is claimed and professed as a veritable birthright, yet where inequality in fact takes place. The difference between the *is* and the *ought*, between what presently takes place as a matter of course and what *should* be, what *ought* to be, is perhaps the greatest occasion for the impotent will to revolt, to thrash about, and to self-righteously demand redress for all its grievances, real or imaginary. It is altogether possible that many modern forms of bigotry and racism find their origin here as well.[95]

To be generous, Nietzsche's argument about a "slave revolt" in morality is hardly meant to be an accurate historical portrait. Indeed, he tells us in section 16 that this key value inversion is only a "symbol" of the "struggle" between different moral evaluations that occur "across all human history.[96] Rather, as he later claimed in *Ecce Homo*, the *Genealogy* is the attempt by a "psychologist" to understand the deeper processes of social-historical formation that underlie our seemingly "instinctive" moral behavior, as well as the values that are attested to by such behavior. If Nietzsche's genealogical analysis of "good and bad, good and evil" indicate two broadly differing systems of moral evaluation roughly equivalent to the ancient Greco-Roman "master" morality and a modern Judeo-Christian or utilitarian "slave" morality, his principal point is to illustrate how the complex variety of moral evaluations <u>coexist</u> even in our own culture, and certainly, in our own person.

> Let us conclude. The two *opposing* values "good and bad," "good and evil" have been engaged in a fearful struggle on earth for thousands of years; and though the latter value has certainly been on top for a long time, there are still places where the struggle is as yet undecided. One might even say that it has risen ever higher and thus become more and more profound and spiritual: so that today there is perhaps no more decisive mark of a *"higher nature,"* a more spiritual nature, than that of being divided in this sense and a genuine battleground of these opposed values.[97]

That our complex set of moral "sentiments" and moral "concepts" can be clearly articulated and detailed upon the background of a general sense of their complex and still evolving historical provenance is testimony to the value of genealogical analysis itself. But their presentation, the illustration of the "perspectives" they yield—together with an understanding of the psychological dynamics they entail—is only preparation for what Nietzsche views as the greater task. He concludes the first essay by reformulating his initial task of a "critique of value," or the question as to the "value of value": "The question: what is the *value* of this or that table of values and 'morals'? should be viewed from the most divers perspectives; for the problem 'value *for what*?' cannot be examined too subtly."[98]

If Nietzsche's genealogical analysis—with its reliance upon historical, linguistic, and etymological research—succeeds to the extent of raising this task as a question, Nietzsche suggests that other disciplines must be called upon for *resolving* the "problem" of the "value *for what*?" Much in the spirit of his earlier essay, "History in the Service and Disservice *of Life*,"[99] Nietzsche concludes that further analysis of value formation and critical moral evaluation would likewise benefit from drawing upon the modern life sciences themselves—psychology, medicine, and physiology—and this would be "the most amicable and fruitful exchange" with philosophy.[100] With the assistance of the modern life sciences, the philosopher could in turn begin to achieve his *true calling*, what Nietzsche had characterized in an unfinished essay dating back to the spring of 1873, "The Philosopher as Cultural Physician." The philosopher, joined by researchers from the variety of modern scientific disciplines, would then attempt to analyze the organic and material (in addition to the psychological) conditions underlying, or entailed by, "every table of values . . . known to history or ethnology."[101] These philosopher-physicians would be enjoined to relate the results of their extensive, comparative analyses and evaluations to the broader human concerns of community, of personal health and well-being, of biological and social adaptation to changing conditions—ultimately, to enhance our capacities so as to ensure a future strength of human character and to promote an even greater degree of personal autonomy and cultural development:

> *All* the sciences have from now on to prepare the way for the future task of the philosophers: this task understood as the solution of the *problem of value*, the determination of the *order of rank among values*.[102]

CONSCIENCE

If, in the first essay of *On the Genealogy of Morals*, Nietzsche described *ressentiment* and slave morality according to the psychological dynamics of a repressed and inverted will—where human suffering has to be compensated for and this compensation has to be expressed or exteriorized; in this case, as the projection of a set of revalued values—in the second essay, he employs the same model to account for the emergence of one's own *conscience*.[103] It is on this basis that Nietzsche goes on to explain the moral phenomenon of *bad conscience*, of what he calls *guilt*, or—in a religious sense—*sin*.

where does conscience come from?

What we ordinarily understand as the psychological state of our own personal *conscience*, Nietzsche argues, first arises out of a trained memory and a sense of responsibility, two functions that are strictly required and needed by the individual if he or she is to have the practical assurance of his or her own future existence—one of coexistence—within political or civil society. Specifically, *memory* and *responsibility* are forcibly involved in ordering the acts of economic exchange, of trade and barter.[104] They are relied upon to ensure the possibility of sustained commerce and of contractual dealings in general.

To say that I shall incur an obligation means that I must pay back the particular *debt* I have assumed. I must settle the terms of the contract. Quite simply, I answer for, I am *responsible* for, the obligation I have incurred. Or else—or else!—I shall have to suffer the consequences for my breach of contract. Second, I *remember* all too well what these consequences can be, because *fear* has impressed this into my *memory*.

Thus, for Nietzsche, conscience is really a kind of memory that is inspired by fear: fear of what painful suffering might result if one fails to be responsible to the terms of an obligation or if one fails to carry out the terms of a contract. In an early section of *The Gay Science*, Nietzsche had drawn attention to the close relation between the fear of pain, the power to inflict pain, and our memory of this conjunction:

> Benefiting and hurting others are [two] ways of exercising one's power upon others; that is all one desires in such cases. One hurts those whom one wants to feel one's power, for pain is a much more efficient means to that end than pleasure; pain always raises the question about its origin while pleasure is inclined to stop with itself, without looking back.[105]

Now, underlying my fear as a debtor, Nietzsche suggests that a parallel emotion occurs on the side of the other party, on the side of the creditor. If, as a debtor, I fail to live up to the precise terms of the contract, if I fail to pay back the stipulated commodity (whether this be money, manufactured articles, agricultural produce, or other goods) or if I fail to pay back some other commodity of equal value (such as rendering over any assets or valuables I might possess, or even bartering my labor or my skills), then, in the end, I can only repay the debt by gratifying the creditor's basest desires—by gratifying his pleasure in cruelty. I give him the only thing left to me—my freedom or my body—for him to enjoy or to abuse, in whatever manner gives him the most pleasure. This, then, is performed in lieu of monetary repayment of the debt.

Unable to recover his monetary loss, the creditor invariably punishes me, the debtor. But why should the creditor take pleasure in the exercise of punishment (i.e., in punishing me)? Nietzsche argues that the creditor does this for the sole reason of seeing me suffer. Ultimately, this means he can exercise his power over me, and he enjoys the pleasurable feeling he takes in actively exercising his cruelty. My pain thus serves to repay my debt. It serves as a particularly intense form of entertainment for him, indeed, as a spectacle, as a feast for his cruelty.

We note, in this case, the mechanism of what is at work here, a pattern very similar to the case given in Nietzsche's first essay concerning the revaluation of values, what he called "the slave revolt in morals." Here, the debtor's abasement (i.e., his lowering, his humiliation, his lack of respect, his diminished importance) elevates the creditor's importance, his perceived sense of self-respect, self-importance, his vanity and pride. It is only because the debtor now grovels about in embarrassment and pain, it is only because of his demonstrable weakness and humiliation, that the creditor in his turn feels more important, more powerful. Doubtless, it is precisely for the same reason that victorious armies and propaganda ministers of all ages invariably display their defeated victims, publicly, in the worst possible state of submission, in the extremes of humiliation: the captured enemy soldiers are filed by in tattered rags, emaciated; tin cups in their hands, with blood-stained shards of fabric wrapped around their wounds. Inevitably the refugees come, begging, pleading, imploring for a few grains of rice, a coin perhaps, or a crust of bread—from *you*, you victorious allies and superhuman gods.[106]

Conscience, then, is the fearful memory of what happens when the debtor fails to complete the terms of his contract with the creditor. Pangs of conscience, according to this account, are no more than pangs of fear for self-preservation, in the extreme, for preservation of one's life, home, family, and self-respect. Nietzsche would remark at considerable length on this most human of human processes:

> Let us be clear as to the logic of this form of compensation, for it is strange enough. An equivalence is provided by the creditor's receiving—in place of a

the pleasure of doing evil

literal compensation for an injury (thus, in place of money, land, possessions of any kind)—a recompense in the form of a kind of *pleasure*—the pleasure of being allowed to vent his power freely upon one who is powerless, *the voluptuous pleasure of doing evil for the pleasure of doing it*, the enjoyment of violation.[107]

See Augustine

At this point in his account, Nietzsche proceeds to broaden the scope of his analysis, extending it to the order of social stratification. Here, the member of the lower social class, motivated in part by his ongoing *ressentiment*, will seek to exact a long-deferred vengeance upon the representative of the upper class:

> This enjoyment will be the greater, the lower the creditor stands in the social order, and can easily appear to him as a foretaste of higher rank. In punishing the debtor, the creditor participates in *a right of the masters*; at last, he, too, may experience for once the exalted sensation of being allowed to despise and mistreat someone else as "beneath" him—or, at least, if the actual power and administration of punishment has already passed on to the "authorities," to *see* him despised and mistreated. The compensation, then, consists in a warrant for and title to cruelty. To what extent can suffering balance debts or guilt? To the extent that to *make* suffer was in the highest degree pleasurable, to the extent that the injured party [the creditor] exchanged for the loss he sustained, including the displeasure caused by the loss, an extraordinary counterbalancing pleasure; that of *making suffer*—a genuine *festival*, something which, as aforesaid, was prized the more highly the more violently it contrasted with the rank and social standing of the creditor.[108]

When Nietzsche raises the issue of punishment in the context of his developing argument about the origin of conscience, what his discussion reveals is that punishment is central to the making of a memory—a "mnemotechnics," as he says—of fear. This fear-inspired memory serves to structure our responsibility in our lawful and conscientious contractual dealings. In what amounts to a particularly strident definition of negative reinforcement, he would remark, "If something is to stay in the memory it must be burned in: only that which never ceases to *hurt* stays in the memory."[109] And after citing a blood-curdling list of tortures that were traditionally inflicted as punishment upon wrongdoers—stoning, breaking on the wheel, piercing with stakes, quartering, boiling in oil, flaying alive, smearing the criminal with honey and leaving him in the sun for the flies—he then concludes:

> With the aid of such images and procedures one finally remembers five or six "I will not's," in regard to which one had given one's *promise* so as to participate in the advantages of society—and it was indeed with the aid of this kind of memory

that one at last came "to reason"! Ah, reason, seriousness, mastery over the affects, the whole somber thing called reflection, all these prerogatives and show-
pieces of man: how dearly they have been bought! how much blood and cruelty
lie at the bottom of all "good things"!110

What Nietzsche does not want to argue is the more traditional claim that
punishment is at the origin of "bad conscience" (i.e., guilt). He wants to take
the argument to a much deeper level, both culturally and psychologically. Ad-
vocates of retributive justice would claim that punishment is a function of justice in that it balances the wrongs committed against us. The punishment
inflicted on the wrongdoer serves as repayment or retribution for the initial
injustice, the original violation. They would then claim that such punishment
is itself instrumental in bringing about a sense of guilt and would therefore
serve as a detriment to future misconduct, thus being of great social utility. But
Nietzsche disagrees on both counts.

As for the former position, Nietzsche suggests two reasons why the case is
more complicated. On the one hand, he argues against the position of Eugen
Dühring, who claimed that justice is simply to be understood as retribution or
revenge with a fair name.111 But, for Nietzsche, such a position does not really
explain anything: it begs the question of why one takes pleasure in the cruel
punishment of the wrongdoer. Also, justice conceived on the basis of revenge
or resentment remains reactive, and its purported sense of "fairness" would be
overwhelmed in the encounter with the truly active, powerful drives and affects
manifested by the opposing wrongdoer, such as his "lust for power, avarice,"
and his heightened display of unreflective egoism. Confronted with such
strong, opposing states, any claim to "fairness" or "justice" grounded in the
reactive feelings would lose all pretense of objectivity and would devolve into
"deadly enmity and prejudice," thus ridiculing any sense of impartial justice.
Simply stated, revenge amounts to no more than revenge, it cannot claim to be
the origin of justice.

> As for Dühring's specific proposition that the home of justice is to be sought in
> the sphere of reactive feelings, one is obliged for truth's sake to counter it with a
> blunt antithesis: the *last* sphere to be conquered by the spirit of justice is the
> sphere of the reactive feelings! When it really happens that the just man remains
> just even toward those who have harmed him (and not merely cold, temperate,
> remote, indifferent: being just is always a *positive* attitude), when the exalted,
> clear objectivity, as penetrating as it is mild, of the eye of justice and *judging* is
> not dimmed even under the assault of personal injury, derision, and calumny, this

is a piece of perfection and supreme mastery on earth—something it would be prudent not to expect or to *believe* in too readily.[112]

Ultimately, Nietzsche argues that "justice" is entirely conventional—not natural, not the expression of some unegoistic, natural sentiment or instinct— and that it exists only in function of the institution of law. In the absence of law there is neither justice nor injustice, merely the opposition and conflict that belong to the "basic functions" of organic life: "injury, assault, exploitation."[113]

A broader consideration that Nietzsche addresses in the course of his analysis is the conventional feeling that there is a particular purpose behind punishment. Nietzsche attributes this sentiment—as he had attributed the "moral feeling," in the first essay of the *Genealogy*—to the English psychologists. In this case, he points to the work of the neo-Darwinian philosopher Herbert Spencer, for whom the purpose behind punishment would be social adaptation.[114] Nietzsche's approach is markedly different in kind: he argues that punishment is itself *overdetermined* in meaning, and that it has *multiple* and often *conflicting* interpretations, according to the myriad details of history, culture, the level and type of social development attained, and various other contextual specifications.[115] Thus, for Nietzsche, punishment itself preexisted any single determinate "purpose" or "meaning," and most likely emerged in primitive society as a positive, unfettered, and explosive impulse of anger and dissatisfaction: as such, punishment was not initially tied to retribution. Any clearly retributive sense of justice postulates a sense of accountability, of responsibility, on the part of the individual, and this, in turn, supposes an exercise of control over one's own will, a "free will." According to this position, one holds the wrongdoer accountable for his or her actions or unjust behavior, and thus deserving of punishment. Or, as Nietzsche summarizes this view, "The criminal deserves punishment *because* he could have acted differently."[116]

But such a view is distinctly modern, and it entails a rather complexly developed sense of intellectual and legal sophistication, as well as a highly cultivated psychological maturity, all maintained and enforced by the "straightjacket" of social conformity to the instituted "herd morality." From a genealogical point of view—informed by the "historical sense"—Nietzsche rather traces the impulse to punish to a more primitive, archaic psychology, where one's affects and drives were not governed by prudence or calculation, nor were they constrained by the authority of law. In such a state—one more of nature than convention—the individual acted straightforwardly, without emotional reserve, repression, reflection, or sublimation:

Throughout the greater part of human history punishment was *not* imposed *because* one held the wrongdoer responsible for his deed, thus *not* on the presupposition that only the guilty one should be punished: rather, as parents still punish their children, from anger at some harm or injury, vented on the one who caused it.[117]

f In Cold Blood T. Capote

As for the alleged causal relation between punishment and guilt, Nietzsche charges that if punishment were successful in inducing guilt, then surely, those who were most frequently punished—criminals, prisoners, convicts, and so forth—would feel most guilty and, hence, would be *least* likely to pursue a course of illegal misconduct or criminality. But, as he observes in this regard:

Punishment is supposed to possess the value of awakening the *feeling of guilt* in the guilty person; one seeks in it the actual *instrumentum* of that psychical reaction called "bad conscience," "sting of conscience." . . . [But] it is precisely among criminals and convicts that the sting of conscience is extremely rare; prisons and penitentiaries are *not* the kind of hotbed in which this species of gnawing worm is likely to flourish. . . . Generally speaking, punishment makes men hard and cold; it concentrates; it sharpens the feeling of alienation; it strengthens the power of resistance. . . .

If we consider those millennia *before* the history of man, we may unhesitatingly assert that it was precisely through punishment that the development of the feeling of guilt was most powerfully *hindered*—at least in the victims upon whom the punitive force was vented. For we must not underrate the extent to which the sight of the judicial and executive procedures prevents the criminal from considering his deed, the type of his action *as such*, reprehensible: for he sees exactly the same kind of actions practiced in the service of justice and approved of and practiced with a good conscience: spying, deception, bribery, setting traps, the whole cunning and underhanded art of police and prosecution, plus robbery, violence, defamation, imprisonment, torture, murder, practiced as a matter of principle and without even emotion to excuse them, which are pronounced characteristics of the various forms of punishment—all of them therefore actions which his judges in no way condemn and repudiate as such, but only when they are applied and directed to particular ends.[118]

Thus, while the threat of punishment is central to the construction of "conscience"—the fear of retribution for failure to repay an obligation—Nietzsche claims that punishment is itself too overdetermined in nature and meaning to serve as the origin of "bad conscience" or guilt. As he remarks, the "form" of punishment is relatively enduring, that is, "the custom, the act, the 'drama,' and a certain strict sequence of procedures" involved in punishment, but the "meaning" of punishment is far more fluid:

The concept [of] "punishment" possesses in fact not *one* meaning but a whole synthesis of "meanings": the previous history of punishment in general, the history of its employment for the most various purposes, finally crystallizes into a kind of unity that is hard to disentangle, hard to analyze and, as must be emphasized especially, totally *indefinable.* Today it is impossible to say for certain *why* people are really punished.[119]

Furthermore, if "punishment" seemed to emerge initially as an archaic and unreflective expression of powerful instincts and affects, of, for example, anger, then there would seem to be no specific purpose or meaning to it, such as the purported adaptation to social conditions. This is why Nietzsche argues that for punishment to acquire any specific determination, such as the balancing of wrongs or serving as a rectification of harm, or as retribution for injuries committed against us, then it would have to be understood to follow the institution of commerce and law. Thus, a relatively stable society first has to be imposed upon the earlier "natural" state of humanity, and only in function of the subsequent and secondary institutions of law, commerce, and rule governance can deeds and acts be measured, apportioned, and valued—and thus enter into exchange relations, such as would be required by the notion of retributive justice.[120] Effectively, anger has to be held in check by the primitive state, so as to provide the necessary conditions of stability that would allow for the conduct of commerce, trade, and civil existence. Only when these conditions are met can there be any sense of "justice."[121] It is thereby in consequence of a shared sense of justice that the very notion of "guilt" or bad conscience arises, and not out of punishment or revenge. Rather, it arises out of the individual debtor-creditor relationship and becomes transferred to a more general social-political context.

BAD CONSCIENCE, GUILT, OR SIN

Nietzsche claims that the first condition for guilt, or "bad conscience," stems from our earliest ancestor's being forced to live under a primitive tyrannical rule—in other words, by being forced to live in a political or civil state, a coherent primitive society governed by rules, by law, and enforced by the power of a common authority. In first describing this primitive civil or political order, Nietzsche calls upon his earlier debtor-creditor model to explain the dynamics that bind or subject the individual to this common authority. Effectively, the community as a whole stands as a creditor to the individual members, who are

debt to
society

*Rain's Rhinoceros
T. Merton
on solitude
see*

indebted, indeed obligated, to the community for their personal protection, security, peace, and the wide range of civilized advantages only the greater community—the state—can provide. Each member is in turn pledged to protect and preserve the community through personal compliance to its laws and through his or her cooperative efforts to maintain civil stability and well-being in the face of enmity, conflict, and external hostilities. This is the cost of membership in the community. Should an individual member transgress his or her civil bond of obligation to the community at large through criminal or civil misconduct, not only will this individual have incurred the demand for retribution from the individuals he or she may have injured, but more importantly, the individual has broken his or her initial pledge to the community as a whole. Such a case of criminal transgression, as Nietzsche would remark in section 9 of the *Genealogy*, not only illustrates what civil society is worth to the individual but also dramatically highlights the opposition between membership in such a community and the reversion to barbarism, to a state of precivil existence.

> The community, the disappointed creditor, will get what repayment it can, one may depend on that. The direct harm caused by the culprit is here a minor matter; quite apart from this, the lawbreaker is above all a "breaker," a breaker of his contract and his word *with the whole* in respect to all the benefits and comforts of communal life of which he has hitherto had a share. The lawbreaker is a debtor who has not merely failed to make good the advantages and advance payments bestowed upon him but has actually attacked his creditor: therefore he is not only deprived henceforth of all these advantages and benefits, as is fair—he is also reminded *what these benefits are really worth.* The wrath of the disappointed creditor, the community, throws him back again into the savage and outlaw state against which he has hitherto been protected: it thrusts him away—and now every kind of hostility may be vented upon him.[122]

Such is the violence of the state. Itself instituted by violence, "civil" society will use every coercive means at its disposal to prevent its disaggregation, namely, the reversion of its members to their former condition, to the state of "nature" (i.e., the prepolitical or apolitical state), which is now termed the condition of savagery and barbarism.[123] At stake for the state, then, is its very condition—civilization itself—however "bathed in blood" its own origins may well have been. But by stressing what is at stake in the opposition between civil society and its antecedent condition, Nietzsche wishes to emphasize just how *how* transformed the nature of the individual has become, precisely by his subjection to even the earliest forms of civilization. By this—his enforced socialization—the individual's pain and suffering *increase* immeasurably. He is no *the individual transformed* longer able to freely vent his anger, passions, or joyful exuberance, as he could in a state of nature. His freedom to outwardly discharge his instinctual energy, emotions, or life force is *inhibited* the moment he enters into civil society:

> Enclosed within the walls of society and of peace, . . . suddenly all their instincts were disvalued and "suspended." . . . A dreadful heaviness lay upon them. They felt unable to cope with the simplest undertakings; in this new world they no longer possessed their former guides, their regulating, unconscious and infallible drives. . . . I believe there has never been such a feeling of misery on earth, such a leaden discomfort—and at the same time the old instincts had not suddenly ceased to make their usual demands! Only it was hardly or rarely possible to humor them.[124]

The individual's freedom to live—however he sees fit—is henceforth subject to regulation by the state and is thus suppressed, "forcibly made latent," by the state. Indeed, it is precisely the function of the state to employ every "judicial and executive procedure" up to and including "robbery, violence, defamation, imprisonment, torture, [and] murder, practiced as a matter of principle," to ensure the individual's subjection.[125] *see Freud*

But if the individual is denied this external outlet of expression, his or her vitality must inevitably be channeled elsewhere. In civil society, this urge to express one's passions, to exteriorize one's emotions, instinctual desires, or aggressions must be subverted and be directed inward.[126] So, instead of striking outward, the individual attacks him- or herself. The instinctual energy becomes inner-directed, or rather, self-inflicted: quite simply, one comes to war with oneself. Nietzsche would describe this blockage, redirection, and subsequent "internalization" of instincts as the very origin of "bad conscience":

> All instincts that do not discharge themselves outwardly *turn inward*—this is what I call the *internalization* of man; thus it was that man first developed what was later called his "soul." The entire inner world, originally as thin as if it were stretched between two membranes, expanded and extended itself, acquired depth, breadth, and height, in the same measure as outward discharge was *inhibited*. Those fearful bulwarks with which the political organization protected itself against the old instincts of freedom—punishments belong among these bulwarks—brought about that all those instincts of wild, free, prowling man turned backward against man himself. Hostility, cruelty, joy in persecuting, in attacking, in change, in destruction—all this turned against the possessors of such instincts: *that* is the origin of the "bad conscience."[127]

If the individual's own instinctual self-expression now becomes a kind of repression (Freud would later call this "primary repression"),[128] he or she in

R.D Laing
The Divided Self

turn becomes tamed, divided, and immobilized. Divided against oneself, an inner world of conflict opens up. At once, this becomes a place of psychological hesitation and caution, where one must painstakingly reflect upon the efficacy and propriety of one's actions—ever fearful of incurring punishment by committing some thoughtless expression of instinctual, and thus potentially violent and transgressive, behavior. Instinctual drives, formerly unbound and capricious, now have to become controlled, mastered, and this calls for entirely new psychological resources to be forged from the former instincts, precisely in view of now having to control them. The newfound abilities of "thinking, inferring, reckoning, co-ordinating cause and effect" will force conscious reflection and self-conscious behavior onto the newly socialized individual.[129]

What Nietzsche finds so striking here is that the production of this inner world of conscious reflection and self-control—"the soul"—now becomes the very site of human suffering: self-suffering. In the absence of external enemies and pleasurable external outlets for aggression, the socialized individual, "forcibly confined to the oppressive narrowness and punctiliousness of custom," is now obliged to redirect his instinctual energies *against himself*, precisely so as to "tame" himself. It is this new practice of taming oneself, training oneself to accommodate oneself to the strictures of civil society, that takes a terrifying toll upon the individual's former well-being. Even if this process creates an entirely new kind of human being—civilized, thoughtful, reflective, self-controlled—it is nonetheless the origin of an intense suffering, since it is brought about *civilizing* through a violent mistreatment directed against oneself, a process of self-laceration and self-punishment. Ultimately, Nietzsche will describe the civilizing *guilt* process of guilt, of the bad conscience—"something so new, profound, unheard of, enigmatic, contradictory, *and pregnant with a future* that the aspect of the earth was essentially altered"[130]—as *the distinctively human illness*:   *NhB*

This animal that rubbed itself raw against the bars of its cage as one tried to "tame" it; this deprived creature, racked with homesickness for the wild, who had to turn himself into an adventure, a torture chamber, an uncertain and dangerous *the* wilderness—this fool, this yearning and desperate prisoner became the inventor *sick* of the "bad conscience." But thus began the gravest and uncanniest illness, from *animal* which humanity has not yet recovered, man's suffering *of man, of himself*—the result of a forcible sundering from his animal past, as it were a leap and plunge into new surroundings and conditions of existence, a declaration of war against the old instincts upon which his strength, joy, and terribleness had rested hitherto.[131]

Remarkably, with this self-infliction of bad conscience, where the "instinct for *freedom* [is] pushed back and repressed, incarcerated within, and finally able to discharge and vent itself only on itself,"[132] an element of the earlier, archaic instincts is retained—at least, this is what Nietzsche advances as a hypothesis—namely, one's ancestral pleasure in cruelty. But with the "internalization" of these instincts, they are turned against the subject himself, producing the paradoxical result that one takes pleasure in one's own cruelty to oneself. This happens at the very moment when the subject is crafting his or her newly socialized self, a self being tamed and trained according to the new model or new "ideal" of the "unegoistic," socially conforming member of the herd morality. One hurts oneself—and takes pleasure in it—by fashioning oneself, by literally sacrificing oneself, to the new ego ideal of the "selfless individual," the morally responsible, self-sacrificing, humble citizen. Nietzsche goes on to liken this self-transformation to the process of artistic creation, whereby the artist imposes an enormous task or burden upon him- or herself—along with the rigid determination and self-discipline this creative task involves—in order to attain an ideal of beauty: the artist suffers in his or her painful struggle to create, and at the same time, delights in this suffering as a foretaste of attaining his or her ideal of perfection, beauty itself. In this delight, in this "secret self-ravishment, this artist's cruelty, this delight in imposing a form upon oneself as a hard, recalcitrant, suffering material," the artist willfully drives him- or herself ever harder—agonizingly so—to further create in turn.[133] This artist's "self-ravishment," which consists in redirecting the archaic impulse of cruelty back upon oneself, yielding pleasure in the very suffering of pain, is the "hint" that Nietzsche offers as to how the "unegoistic" emotions came to be valued on the basis of the "bad conscience":

> This hint will at least make less enigmatic the enigma of how contradictory concepts such as *selflessness, self-denial, self-sacrifice* can suggest an ideal, a kind of beauty; and one thing we know henceforth—I have no doubt of it—and that is the nature of the *delight* that the selfless man, the self-denier, the self-sacrificer feels from the first: this delight is tied to cruelty.[134]

Briefly restated, the first condition for guilt or bad conscience is the generalized increase in suffering brought about in civil society by the internalization of the instincts and drives. One can no longer strike out at will, neither against someone else nor even in an unconventional way, against something else, such as property. Convention, that is, social or rule-governed, behavior becomes our "second nature," and the cost of this transformation is enormous: life itself becomes a species of crippling frustration behavior, from which we continually suffer, yet, in which, we find a perverse pleasure.[135]

The second general condition for guilt or bad conscience arises out of our need to interpret the suffering brought about by our insertion into civil society, to make some sense out of it, to find meaning in our suffering. The ancient lament of the prophet Job is heard even today, in some quarters: "Why do we suffer?" "What does this suffering mean?" "What is the reason for it?" and—perhaps, most significantly, "Why does it have to happen to me?" At this stage of his extended analysis, Nietzsche briefly recalls the classical explanation of man. He points out that ancient cultures distinguished humankind from the brutes, from the animals, precisely because of its distinctive ability to reason, to explain, to judge, to place value on things. Thus, for the Greeks, man was defined, essentially, as the "living, thinking being": Plato calls him the zõon logon échon. Nietzsche points out that in ancient Sanskrit, the words for man and mind (men and mon) share a common etymology. In Old High German and in Gothic German, this relation still carried, in the terms man and mana— again, man and mind. Perhaps we could even carry out Nietzsche's earlier metaphor of rumination and say that this is a peculiar way we humans have of ingesting or digesting things; we compel ourselves, as humans, to place an order on them, so as to deal with them wholly, coherently, effectively.[136] We have to make sense of things: this is our distinctively human inheritance, our human nature, as it were.

These first two conditions for bad conscience or guilt—the increase of human suffering that results from the institution of civil society, and the need to interpret that suffering—combine on the level of cultural interpretation. Nietzsche locates the origin of this interpretation in a specific application of the debtor-creditor relationship, namely, the traditional recognition between generations that there exists a "juridical duty toward earlier generations" on the part of the later generations.[137] In this instance, the cultural formulation of guilt becomes the following: we, as a collective body, owe our ancestors a debt of gratitude for making our present society prosperous, at least to the extent that it continues to exist, and we with it. Thus ancestor worship evolves, with its elaborate rituals of celebration, whereby the ancient deeds performed by the ancestors, together with the prosperity that derives from those deeds, are repaid by the succeeding generations. Offerings, sacrifices, and so forth are given in thanks, in homage, as respectful repayment to the founders of the society. Nietzsche goes on, however, to note a remarkable fact here: insofar as the society grows more powerful and prosperous, so does the feeling of indebtedness and the need of paying back that debt to the spiritual forebears. The sentiment of compensation and obligation persists across the ages: "Perhaps *this* festival will satisfy them!" Perhaps the debt can finally be settled by establishing a temple or by having an annual sacrifice, celebration, or feast. But, Nietzsche continues, "In the end, the ancestor must necessarily be transformed into a *god*"[138]—precisely because of the magnitude and duration of the prosperity bequeathed us. The spiritual presence of the ancestors eventually becomes overpowering and they become gods of every pale and hue. It suffices to think of Greek mythology and the status attributed to its ancient heroes: in the afterworld, they people the Elysian Fields as demigods and can intervene effectively in the affairs of man. Or of Norse mythology, where the heroes and warriors of past ages rule the present from the drinking halls of Valhalla. Christian beatification as well as political enshrinement only testify to the enduring persuasiveness of this transformation.

Once the ancestor has been retroactively transformed into a god, there is no end to the consequences. With the advent of institutionalized religion, guilt or bad conscience becomes transferred from the order of civil, or human, law to that of divine law, divine ordinance—and for Nietzsche, this is what constitutes *the moralization of guilt*, "more precisely, the involvement of the bad conscience with the concept of god."[139] Thus, duty and guilt become religious presuppositions of conscience, such that divine commandment effectively governs human behavior. With this development, a higher stage is reached. Our guilt and indebtedness becomes *sin* for the Judeo-Christian God. Since the feeling of indebtedness or guilt increases proportionally with the power of the culture's god (reflected in the duration and success of his peoples), then, as Nietzsche claims, "the Christian God, as the maximum god attained so far, was therefore accompanied by the maximum feeling of guilty indebtedness on earth."[140] With the advent of the Judeo-Christian Creator God and the moralization of guilt, the individual becomes literally indebted to God for the universe itself: guilt becomes *infinitized*, or as Nietzsche remarks, the debt is finally judged to be "irredeemable." Once this admission is made, however, a remarkable awareness takes place. Since the indebtedness (i.e., the traditional sentiment of fully discharging the original obligation) is now seen to be *impossible*—how can one plausibly *repay* the infinite source of creation itself?—the *opposite* sentiment arises, namely, that one *denies the very possibility of discharge*, and consequently, that penance is also "irredeemable." Hence, one assumes the "debt" upon oneself:

The *aim* now is to turn back the concepts "guilt" and "duty," back against whom? There can be no doubt: against the "debtor" first of all, in whom from now on the bad conscience is firmly rooted, eating into him and spreading within him like a polyp.[141]

At such a stage of reflection in the development of the religious sentiment, Nietzsche claims that the believer is placed in a completely hopeless situation. He is confronted with the prospect of *"eternal* punishment," arising from the recognition that the indebtedness can never be repaid, the debt can never be discharged. Seeking to disburden himself from the prospect of an irredeemable debt that he has taken upon himself, the believer now attempts to *project* the initial *cause* of this impossible guilt, this bad conscience, *elsewhere: either* upon the primal ancestor himself, "who is from now on burdened with a curse ('Adam,' original sin, 'unfreedom of the will')," *or* upon nature as a primordial source of evil, *or* upon "existence in general," as being patently worthless.[142] Of course, for Nietzsche, all these expedients of projecting the *cause* of the initial indebtedness—which bad conscience had already "burned in" to our souls—outward, upon the past and upon the world at large, paints an earthly existence of unremitting nihilism, suffering, and despair. Human consolation for such an insufferable existence would, as Nietzsche suggests, at best amount to a Buddhistic withdrawal into "nothingness": abdication and suicidal flight into a state of complete resignation.

Faced with this extreme-most situation of the religiomoral interpretation, one need not dispense with "the conception of gods *in itself*," Nietzsche counsels.[143] Given the reality of human suffering and the demand of human reason to explain this suffering, even *within* the context of a religious worldview, other solutions than the "bad conscience" are indeed possible. The Greeks, for example, as Nietzsche relates it, had a remarkably generous solution to this problem: their gods acknowledged themselves to be the source, the cause, of evil, so *they assumed* the burden of guilt.[144] If suffering—as punishment—was visited by the gods upon humanity, perhaps so as to provide them with an entertaining spectacle of cruelty, then quite simply, *they* were to blame; thereby, exonerating mankind of guilt.[145] By the same token, if the gods themselves were the source of evil, then, by comparison, the gravity of mankind's occasional transgressions was lessened in turn and attributed to ordinary human frailty and folly. As Nietzsche remarks, in discussing the classical Greek resolution to the theologically understood problem of evil and human suffering, their solution was to *vindicate humanity* by frankly admitting human imperfection, thereby avoiding the self-laceration of an impossible human guilt:

These Greeks used their gods precisely so as to ward off the "bad conscience" so as to be able to rejoice in their freedom of soul. . . . In this way the gods served to justify man to a certain extent even in his wickedness, they served as the originators of evil—in those days they took upon themselves, not the punishment but, what is *nobler*, the guilt.[146]

For Christianity, however—and Nietzsche never ceases to lament this final development—the solution was exactly opposite to that of the pre-Socratic Greeks. The Christian theological resolution, which Nietzsche terms "a paradoxical and horrifying expedient" that seemed to provide a "temporary relief" for the suffering of its members, was to have God himself assume the suffering: by sacrificing himself. Through Jesus' crucifixion—a "stroke of genius"—God intervened on behalf of the debtor, to relieve the human suffering borne *from guilt*, from our original indebtedness. While such a solution seemed to *alleviate suffering*, by having God assume it himself—his self-consumption in suffering—out of *love* for the sinners, what is remarkable, paradoxical, and horrifying to the Christian solution is precisely the fact that it *compounds* human *guilt*. Now, mankind intensifies the *cause* of his suffering by *adding* the guilt for God's own sacrifice, Jesus' crucifixion, to his own earlier situation of an already infinitized guilt. An infinite guilt becomes augmented and compounded precisely because Jesus died on the cross for *our* sins—hence, we are responsible for *his* death—his death for us, Nietzsche ironically adds, out of his love for us: a love freely given, and hence, a gift of love that by nature cannot be conditional upon reciprocity,[147] otherwise, it would not be a freely given love, nor would it be a gift at all. For Nietzsche, in any case, the crucial fiction of the crucifixion is that it eliminates human suffering. By his account, however, even if the image of the crucifixion temporarily serves to assuage the burden of suffering, it rather—in the longer run—*increases* the sum of human suffering by intensifying and multiplying the cause of the suffering, namely, guilt itself.

Burdened with guilt and indebted by sin, the priest's role is henceforth to *explain* our suffering as *punishment*, as the painful consequence of our violating or transgressing the divine will. Ranging in severity from Adam's original sin—eating fruit from the tree of the knowledge of good and evil—to one's minor moral lapses, humanity itself has sinned: it has effectively broken the covenant, the divine contract, as it were. We are thereby held responsible to ourselves, in the face of the infinite creator, for our own suffering. Our fall is one into sin! Expelled from the Garden of Eden and its "tree of life," humankind is henceforth enjoined by God to suffer an utterly ignominious existence:

To the woman he [i.e., God] said; "I will intensify the pangs of your childbearing; in pain shall you bring forth children." . . . To the man he said: "Cursed be the ground because of you! In toil shall you eat its yield all the days of your life. . . . For you are dirt and to dirt you shall return." (Genesis 3:16, 17, 19)

Humanity thus accuses itself for its pain: in failing to fully conform to his divine prescriptions, in being *ungodlike*, we have incurred his wrath. Consequently, we must suffer eternal perdition or seek to gain, to curry, his favor. For Christian theology, one attempts to gain grace and redemption: in general, one atones or makes restitution for one's transgressive deeds. In this fashion, we lash out against all that is natural in us, against everything within us that is *not* godlike. We impose an unnatural ideal upon ourselves, one that is Godlike; an idealized existence of faultless moral virtue, guided by the truth of divine ordinance, a religious and moral ideal according to which we attempt to conform our lives. Beset by this ideal, we lacerate ourselves out of guilt, we deny our very human flesh (for it is tainted by Adam's sin), we deny the passions (what is called "the unholy beast within"), and through the practice of moral asceticism, we seek to remove ourselves from this world, this real and material world—the "merely" material world, the "world of illusion," of "delusion, lust, and turmoil." As Nietzsche would say, "Here is sickness, beyond any doubt, the most terrible sickness that has ever raged in man." He would remark at length:

> You will have guessed what has really happened here, *beneath* all this: that will to self-tormenting, that repressed cruelty of the animal-man made inward and scared back into himself, the creature imprisoned in the "state" so as to be tamed, who invented bad conscience in order to hurt himself after the *more natural* vent for this desire to hurt had been blocked—this man of the bad conscience has seized upon the presupposition of religion so as to drive his self-torture to its most gruesome pitch of severity and rigor. Guilt before *God*: this thought becomes an instrument of torture to him. He apprehends in "God" the ultimate antithesis of his own ineluctable animal instincts; he reinterprets these animal instincts themselves as a form of guilt before God (as hostility, rebellion, insurrection against the "lord," the "father," the primal ancestor and origin of the world): he ejects from himself all his denial of himself, of his nature, naturalness, and actuality, in the form of an affirmation, as something existent, corporeal, real, as God, as the holiness of God, as God the Judge, as God the hangman, as the beyond, as eternity, as torment without end, as hell, as the immeasurability of punishment and guilt.[148]

As if this veritable catalogue of infamies wasn't already enough, Nietzsche continues:

In this mental cruelty there resides a madness of the will which is absolutely unexampled; the *will* of man to find himself guilty and reprehensible to a degree that can never be atoned for; his *will* to think himself punished without any possibility of the punishment becoming equal to the guilt; his *will* to infect and poison the fundamental ground of things with the problem of punishment and guilt, . . . his *will* to erect an ideal—that of the "holy God"—and in the face of it to feel the palpable certainty of his own absolute unworthiness. Oh this insane, pathetic beast—man! What ideas he has, what unnaturalness, what paroxysms of nonsense, what *bestiality of thought* erupts as soon as he is prevented just a little from being a *beast in deed*![149]

Even more peculiar is the fact that with the increase in suffering, man's ancestral *cruelty* is itself internalized to a fever pitch. Due to his insertion into civil society, and with the moralization of guilt, he gains pleasure in his own self-cruelty. The more he tortures himself under the cloak of religious or moral self-righteousness, the happier—and the more virtuous—he becomes. Thanks to the religiomoral teachings of the priestly morality, and the entire range of "repentance and redemption *training*,"[150] *human suffering now has meaning*. Because suffering *has* meaning, mankind can endure it. Not only can he endure it, but he can inflict this misery upon himself, he can bathe in his love of cruelty to himself and find in this the means to redemption as well.

But—and perhaps what is most striking in Nietzsche's account—even aside from the trappings of religious redemption, man's own *cruelty* eventually proves to be his salvation. By venting those pent-up emotions and passions, anger, aggression, and cruelty, upon *himself*, he nonetheless *releases them*, he effectively discharges them. And, this release of tension produces a kind of anesthesia. He counteracts the pain of suffering, even if he only hurts himself in turn, but at least that calms the spirit.

For every sufferer instinctively seeks a cause for his suffering; more exactly, an agent; still more specifically, a *guilty* agent who is susceptible to suffering—in short, some living thing upon which he can, on some pretext or other, vent his affects, actually or in effigy: for the venting of his affects represents the greatest attempt on the part of the suffering to win relief, *anesthesia*—the narcotic he cannot help desiring to deaden pain of any kind . . . a desire to *deaden pain by means of affects* . . . to *deaden*, by means of a more violent emotion of any kind, a tormenting, secret pain that is becoming unendurable, and to drive it out of consciousness at least for the moment: for that one requires an affect, as savage an affect as possible, and in order to excite that, any pretext at all. "Someone or other must be to blame for my feeling ill"—this kind of reasoning is common to all the sick.[151]

The self-torture of guilt for the sufferer is thus like a purge, a catharsis, an emetic. Moreover, it gratifies the very human desire to explain suffering by finding meaning in it. In this way, Nietzsche argues that the priest—or the administrator, the civil servant, the agent of bureaucracy: in short, any authority—has a great function. His function is *to alter the direction of ressentiment* and to turn it *back upon* the suffering masses.

> "I suffer: someone must be to blame for it"—thus thinks every sickly sheep. But his shepherd, the ascetic priest, tells him: "Quite so, my sheep! someone must be to blame for it: but you yourself are this someone, you alone are to blame for it—*you alone are to blame for yourself!*"—This is brazen and false enough: but one thing at least is achieved by it, the direction of *ressentiment* is *altered.*[152]

The tour de force accompanies this redirection of suffering: this impotent striking back upon themselves, in the form of the guilty conscience, gives them pleasure! It redeems suffering with meaning. Furthermore, and this is an extremely important consequence, this generally distributed guilt among the mass of citizens makes the state itself more stable. The suffering multitudes take their misfortunes out upon themselves and are thus less likely to engage in a civil revolt.[153] The anesthesia of self-suffering (a true sadomasochism if there ever was one) drains them of energy and renders them exhausted, docile, harmless; in its most fully achieved state, "the supreme state, *redemption* itself," this feeling of exhaustion, of narcotic alleviation, effectively becomes a "hypnotic muting of all sensitivity, of the capacity to feel pain."[154]

There are indeed other ways of directing the flow of *ressentiment* in making *work* a virtue. Thus, work itself, *labor*, becomes a means of virtuously alleviating suffering.

> It is beyond doubt that this regimen [of *mechanical activity*] alleviates an existence of suffering to a not inconsiderable degree: this fact is today called, somewhat dishonestly, "the blessings of work." The alleviation consists in this, that the interest of the sufferer is directed entirely away from his suffering—that activity, and nothing but activity, enters consciousness, and there is consequently little room left in it for suffering. . . . Mechanical activity and what goes with it, . . . how subtly the ascetic priest has known how to employ them in the struggle against pain! When he was dealing with sufferers of the lower classes . . . he required hardly more than a little ingenuity in name-changing and rebaptizing to make them see benefits and a relative happiness in things they formerly hated.[155]

Another expedient the priest employs in altering the direction of suffering and *ressentiment* is to train people in the habit of doing "good deeds"—the act of *"giving* pleasure," through charity, helping, praising, and so forth—which gives the sufferer a feeling of pleasure and superiority as the doer, as the giver: "The happiness of 'slight superiority,' involved in all doing good, being useful, helpful, and rewarding, is the most effective means of consolation for the physiologically inhibited."[156]

In any case, one suffers because one is guilty. The guilt must therefore be answered for: it must be expiated or at least atoned for, *even if* this increases one's own suffering. Here is a madness which, if not strictly generated *by* the state, nonetheless serves to *perpetuate* the state. Whether this be in terms of a civil or an ecclesiastical office, Nietzsche concludes that the chief task of the priest lies in "the exploitation of the *sense of guilt*."[157]

THE ASCETIC IDEAL

The extremely problematic and complex issues of guilt, sin, suffering, discipline, cruelty, and self-cruelty—and the great variety of different valuations attached to them—are discussed at length and in detail in the third essay of the *Genealogy*. The title of the third essay is "What Is the Meaning of Ascetic Ideals?" and it is explicitly an attempt to interpret the various meanings and valuations associated with or implied by the diversity of ascetic practices. In this respect, Nietzsche brings the richness of his genealogical method to bear on the issue of asceticism in the same way he raised the question, in the preface, as to "the *value* of morality."[158] The first two essays constituted his interpretation, or "exegesis," of traditional values, and he tells us in the preface that a similar exegesis is the task in the third essay:[159]

> An aphorism, properly stamped and molded, has not been "deciphered" when it has simply been read; rather, one has then to begin its *exegesis*, for which is required an art of exegesis. I have offered in the third essay of the present book an example of what I regard as an "exegesis" in such a case—an aphorism is prefixed to the essay, the essay itself is a commentary on it.[160]

The aphorism in question is section 1 itself, which begins with the sentence that lends itself as the title to the whole essay: "What Is the Meaning of Ascetic Ideals?"[161] The section continues by illustrating the great number of instances that could be adduced as exemplary, yet markedly differing, cases of asceticism, as found in, for example, the lives and practices of artists, philosophers, scholars, women, the physically impaired, and the mentally challenged, as well as priests and saints. Toward the end of the section, he sums up these markedly different cases with the remark, "*That* the ascetic ideal has meant so many things," it has tested the very limits of the human imagination in trying to grasp or interpret it. But, like his earlier examination of "revenge," "asceticism" has no strict conceptual unity; it is rather on the order of what Nietzsche terms a "pocket" word:

> The word "revenge" is said so quickly it almost seems as if it could contain no more than one conceptual and perceptional root. And so one continues to strive to discover it: just as our economists have not yet wearied of scenting a similar unity in the word "value" and of searching after the original root-concept of the word. As if every word were not a pocket into which now this, now that, now several things at once have been put.[162]

Likewise, the complexity of "asceticism" is comparable to that of "punishment," which Nietzsche had analyzed in section 13 of the second essay and about which he said that it "possesses in fact not one meaning but a whole synthesis of 'meanings,'" indeed, that it was "totally *indefinable*," because "all concepts in which an entire process is semiotically concentrated elude definition; only that which has no history is definable."[163] While, in a traditional sense, "asceticism" and "ascetic ideals" usually signify the practice of living in conformity to the divine will, most ordinarily this translates into the practices of personal self-denial, abstinence, and a morally rigorous self-discipline. Or, as Nietzsche would sum up this traditional view, "The three great slogans of the ascetic ideal are familiar: poverty, humility, chastity."[164]

However familiar such slogans about the ascetic ideal may be, Nietzsche already begins a preliminary inquiry into their *meaning* in the first section, such that any significant *unity* in the *practices* of asceticism is all but excluded. Thus, for the "artist," ascetic ideals may have no meaning at all, or alternatively, they may mean "too much." For philosophers, scholars, or scientists, ascetic ideals may signify an "instinct" of spirituality and may well be the foretaste of a higher human freedom. For "women," they may be employed instrumentally to attain a desirable or seductive "charm." For the ill-constituted or disturbed, the ascetic ideal may provide an illusory compensation for the unpleasant realities of an existence filled with suffering—such that they could "see themselves as 'too good' for this world." In the case of the "priest," the practice of ascetic ideals yields an immense degree of temporal, political, and spiritual "power," a veritable "license for power" over others. For the "saints," these ascetic ideals might serve as a "pretext for hibernation," a lust for "glory," or a supreme redemption from sensibility itself, in their self-abandonment to the bliss of mystically ecstatic states of religious consciousness, "their form of madness."[165]

Given this diversity of meaning to ascetic ideals, Nietzsche concludes section 1 by invoking the strange power of the human intellect that he saw as a central agency in his account of the "bad conscience," namely, our human need to find meaning, to impose meaning, even where there is none, even at the very heart of meaningless human suffering. Asceticism thus will find its unity not from a collection of its multiple and diverse practices, but precisely from the human need to *understand*, and ultimately, to *interpret*: in other words, *a significant goal or purpose must be found for*, or *established upon*, the various practices and experiences themselves, even upon the most painful. Concluding the aphorism in section 1, he remarks:

> *That* the ascetic ideal has meant so many things to man, however, is an expression of the basic fact of the human will, its *horror of a vacuum. It needs a goal*—and it will rather will *nothingness* than *not* will.—Am I understood? . . . Have I been understood? *"Not at all, my dear sir!"*—Then let us start again, from the beginning.[166]

The ensuing third essay is thus Nietzsche's extended exegetical analysis of the various terms and practices given in the "aphorism," which is section 1 and which itself issues from the earlier analysis of "guilt" or "bad conscience," the "womb" of ascetic ideals, given in the second essay.

Ultimately, when Nietzsche comes to speak of *the* ascetic ideal in the singular, he means the systematic unity of *interpretation* that the tradition of "moral metaphysics" has imposed upon the world of human concerns. This tradition stems from the earlier period of Platonic metaphysics and extends right through the modern Judeo-Christian religious and moral teaching, a tradition that posits a divine, transcendent source for all intelligibility, value, and truth. In the human need to find meaning throughout the whole of material and spiritual existence, the ascetic ideal has given unity and purpose to the world: it has *given meaning* to the world and to the individual who suffers from that world.

In its most recognizable historical formulation, Nietzsche terms the ascetic ideal "the religious neurosis" and finds it a positively *harmful* instrument to humanity in general:

> When such a system is chiefly applied to the sick, distressed, and depressed, it invariably makes them *sicker*, even if it does "improve" them; one need only ask psychiatrists what happens to patients who are methodically subjected to the

torments of repentance, states of contrition, and fits of redemption. One should also consult history: wherever the ascetic priest has prevailed with this treatment, sickness has spread in depth and breadth with astonishing speed. What has always constituted its "success"? A shattered nervous system added to any existing illness. . . . In the wake of repentance and redemption *training* we find tremendous epileptic epidemics . . . terrible paralyses and protracted states of depression . . . witch-hunt hysteria . . . death-seeking mass deliria. . . . Broadly speaking, the ascetic ideal and its sublimely moral cult, this most ingenious, unscrupulous, and dangerous systematization of all the means for producing orgies of feeling under the cover of holy intentions, has inscribed itself in a fearful and unforgettable way in the entire history of man—and unfortunately *not only* in his history.[167]

Yet precisely this recognition of its *comprehensiveness*, a moralized worldview that gathers the immense plurality of individual events, personal experiences, even political states and nature itself, under one all-inclusive, systematic *interpretation*—one that, at the same time, excludes all alternative interpretations—this is what constitutes the extraordinary *power* of the ascetic ideal.

What is the meaning of the *power* of this ideal, the monstrous nature of its power? Why has it been allowed to flourish to this extent? . . . The ascetic ideal has a *goal*—this goal is so universal that all the other interests of human existence seem, when compared with it, petty and narrow; it interprets epochs, nations, and men inexorably with a view to this one goal; it permits no other interpretation, no *truth* other goal; it rejects, denies, affirms, and sanctions solely from the point of view of *its* interpretation. . . . it believes that [there is] no power on earth that does not first have to receive a meaning, a right to exist, a value, as a tool of the ascetic ideal, as a way and means to *its* goal, to *one* goal.[168]

Most simply stated, this *one goal* of the ascetic ideal is *truth*, absolute truth. It is the function of "moral metaphysics" to lend *meaning* to all things insofar as they can be valued and rendered intelligible according to the standards of this "absolute truth"—which is ultimately coextensive with the divine being itself. In this sense, for the ascetic ideal, God *is* truth, as well as being the *source* of all meaning and value. But however comprehensive and powerful this system of interpretation has proven to be—disseminated as it has been through the Western tradition, dating back at least to the period of Platonic thought—Nietzsche wishes to impress upon us that it is only *one* of many possible systems of interpretation.[169] We should recall the itinerary of Nietzsche's own interpretation of how this comprehensive, traditional view—the ascetic ideal—emerged: namely, from suffering itself, from the reflex of cruelty directed back against oneself, within the confines of primitive civil society.[170]

Effectively, the religiomoral tradition *interprets* our original suffering, of "bad conscience," as *sin*; it interprets the *cause* of the suffering as *guilt* and the *meaning* of our suffering as *punishment*—as divine retribution for our transgression of divine will and authority, that is, for our sins—from which we suffer, and for which we inflict additional suffering upon ourselves in atonement, in our ascetic pursuit of redemption.[171]

It was precisely due to its uniquely divine prerogative, however, that the ascetic ideal triumphed: it was the only ideal consistently at work in the West. Moreover, in claiming to be the very source of truth and meaning, not only were alternative hypotheses excluded from the start but it also *rendered* everything meaningful and truth-functional. It thereby satisfied the basic human demand that things make sense: even humanity itself, even its deepest despair in suffering.

> Man, the bravest of animals, and the one most accustomed to suffering, does *not* repudiate suffering as such; he *desires* it, he even seeks it out, provided he is shown a *meaning* for it, a *purpose* of suffering. The meaninglessness of suffering, *not* suffering itself, was the curse that lay over mankind so far—*and the ascetic ideal offered man meaning!* It was the only meaning offered so far. . . . In it, suffering was *interpreted*; the tremendous void seemed to have been filled; the door was closed to any kind of suicidal nihilism. This interpretation—there is no doubt of it—brought fresh suffering with it, deeper, more inward, more poisonous, more life-destructive suffering; it placed all suffering under the perspective of *guilt*.
>
> But all this notwithstanding—man was *saved* thereby, he possessed a meaning, he was no longer like a leaf in the wind, a plaything of nonsense—the "senseless"—he could now *will* something; no matter at first to what end, and why; with what he willed *the will itself was saved*.
>
> We can no longer conceal from ourselves what is expressed by all that willing which has taken its direction from the ascetic ideal; this hatred of the human, and even more of the animal, and more still of the material, this horror of the senses, of reason itself, this fear of happiness and beauty, this longing to get away from all appearance, change, becoming, death, wishing, from longing itself—all this means—let us dare to grasp it—*a will to nothingness*, an aversion to life; but it is and remains a *will!* And to repeat in conclusion what I said at the beginning: man would rather will *nothingness* than *not* will.[172]

Given such a statement of the ascetic ideal at the very conclusion of his final essay, in what sense could it be said that Nietzsche articulates a positive account of value in the *Genealogy of Morals*? What is the role of science or

science

philosophy in its capacity to explain, and thus furnish, the possibility of some one moral truth?[173] For Nietzsche, both science and philosophy ultimately tend to share the same ideal as that of traditional religion—the ascetic ideal—which aims to negate the sinful body and the pleasures of the flesh and which further aims to attain absolute truth, moral purity, and salvation in a heaven of the intellect: graciously free from the delusions of finite, material existence.[174] In its extreme case then, for Nietzsche, the will to absolute moral truth equals the will to absolute purity, equals the will to God, equals the will to nothingness. But what of ordinary human life and its value? Here, Nietzsche offers the spectacle of life as a whole, together with its pains and joys, instead of an illusory escape into a transcendent, divine afterworld. On the contrary, Nietzsche finds such an explanation as the traditional Christian view, which posits sin as the source of human suffering, all the while lending meaning to that suffering, so antithetical to ordinary human life as to be positively fictitious. Indeed, in one of his very last written works, *The Antichrist*, he would make a veritable indictment against this tradition, a tradition that forcefully contributes to the *increase* in human suffering.[175]

Throughout the entire course of his writings, Nietzsche suggests that we embrace life with a completeness and intensity of will. This is especially the case in the face of those moments that are painful, that cause suffering, even though those moments are themselves meaningless and without any purpose whatsoever. To do this, we must be strong enough and proud enough of what and who we *really are* in fact. Value, then, will derive from the exercise and dominion of our own life and not from the authority of the state, its priests and administrators, and surely not from some otherworldly source. But Nietzsche feels that this is a hard truth, a difficult one to explain, much less, to embrace.

Given Nietzsche's critique of the tradition, especially of its claim to have metaphysically grounded the entirety of material and social reality in the moral and religious teachings of a transcendent order that lends meaning and purpose to our lives, what remains? Precisely—as if we had forgotten—the whole of the natural order, with its continual processes of change and mutation: all of this underlying our human, social, and historical existence. With neither a divine "creation" nor a final resolution of sin, suffering, or anything else, the world simply goes on, transforming itself out of itself—as an endless process of natural metamorphosis, basically following the first law of thermodynamics: the general conservation of matter and energy. Nietzsche terms such a natural world—without an absolute font of divine truth, without sin, without transcendent moral purpose, without divine salvation, where matter and energy conserve themselves in endless cycles of natural exchange and recurrence—"the eternal return of all things." He expresses this notion in terms of a parable, one that forces the question of value—and the interpretation of that value—back upon the individual, as the individual's own creative task of rendering life significant, important, worthy of his or her own respect and joyful exuberance. The parable is given in his earlier work, *The Gay Science* (section 341), and its title is somewhat dramatic, foreboding—it is called "the greatest weight" or "the heaviest burden":

> What, if some day or night a demon were to steal after you into your loneliest loneliness and say to you, "This life as you now live it and have lived it, you will have to live once more and innumerable times more; and there will be nothing new in it, but every pain and every joy and every thought and sigh and everything unutterably small or great in your life will have to return to you, all in the same succession and sequence—even this spider and this moonlight between the trees, and even this moment and I myself. The eternal hourglass of existence is turned upside down again and again, and you with it, speck of dust!"
>
> Would you not throw yourself down and gnash your teeth and curse the demon who spoke thus? Or, did you once experience a tremendous moment when you would have answered him, "You are a god and never have I heard anything more divine." If this thought gained possession of you, it would change you as you are or perhaps crush you. The question in each and every thing, "Do you desire this once more and innumerable times more?" would weigh upon your actions as the greatest weight. Or [on the contrary] how well disposed would you have to become to yourself and to life [so as] to crave *nothing more fervently* than this ultimate, eternal, confirmation and seal?[176]

What is principally involved in this parable is the call to reexamine, and perhaps to change, our fundamental, evaluative attitudes. The parable of the "eternal return of all things" ends on just this note: "How you would have to become so favorably inclined to yourself and to life, so as to crave nothing more fervently than this ultimate eternal confirmation and seal."

In reference to the final paragraph, at the end of the third essay, we see that the last sentences in the *Genealogy* answer two questions: (1) They refer back to the initial preface of the work—to "we who are unknown to ourselves." Thus, the very subtitle of the book as a whole is confirmed—it is "a polemic," that is, a controversial argument or debate against received opinion, and not a positive account. As he describes the *Genealogy* in his later work, *Ecce Homo*, "The three inquiries which constitute this *Genealogy* are perhaps uncannier than anything else written so far."[177] Uncanny: the German word is *unheimlich*, which derives from the old German word for home, *Heimat* and its derivative *Heimlich*, homely, comfortable, at ease in familiar surroundings. Uncanny, or *unheimlich*, thus means strange, weird, without a home. There is neither a dwelling nor a resting place, no sure place to sleep and to dream of good and evil, much less to celebrate their homecoming. (2) "Man would rather will nothingness than not will"; in other words, the will itself *is* saved. But this, like the parable of the eternal return of all things, is cast in the *conditional*. "*How you would have to become so favorably inclined?* . . ." On the Genealogy of Morals, then, is only that—an inquiry into the historical conditions of what has been created and repeatedly transformed so far: namely, the all-too-human values, good and bad, good and evil.

NOTES

The following abbreviations are used throughout the notes:

BGE *Beyond Good and Evil*
BT *The Birth of Tragedy*
CW *The Case of Wagner*
EH *Ecce Homo*
GM *On the Genealogy of Morals*
GS *The Gay Science*
HAH *Human, All Too Human*
KSA *Samtliche Werke: Kritische Studienausgabe*
PTAG *Philosophy in the Tragic Age of the Greeks*
WP *The Will to Power*
Z *Thus Spoke Zarathustra*

PREFACE

1. Letter to Franz Overbeck of August 5, 1886, in *Selected Letters of Friedrich Nietzsche*, ed. and trans. Christopher Middleton (Chicago: University of Chicago Press, 1969), p. 254.
2. Letter to Peter Gast of July 18, 1887, in *Selected Letters*, p. 269.
3. Letter to Franz Overbeck of March 24, 1887, in *Selected Letters*, p. 266.
4. Letter to Gast, *Selected Letters*, p. 269.

INTRODUCTION

1. The obituary notice in the *London Times* of August 27, 1900, for example, remarked that "Nietzsche's philosophy, being revolutionary and altogether unpractical, obtained a certain number of followers in this country, as any violent view of life, violently expressed, always will." The *New York Times* obituary, speaking of the very same man, observed, "He was one of the most prominent modern German philosophers, and is considered the apostle of extreme modern rationalism . . . [a philosopher] whose

ideas have had such a profound influence on the growth of political and social life throughout the civilized world" (August 26, 1900).

2. For an extensive account of Nietzsche's relationship with his sister, and the problems to which this relationship gave rise, see H. F. Peters, *Zarathustra's Sister* (New York: Crown, 1977). While there are some interpretive difficulties with this text, it contains a wealth of biographical material. The definitive biography remains Curt Paul Janz's *Friedrich Nietzsche: Biographie* (Munich: Carl Hanser, 1978).

3. On this, see especially Nietzsche's letter to his friend of long standing, Malwida von Meysenbug (June 1884), where he bitterly relates both his sister's "despicable and undignified behavior" toward Lou Salomé and her involvement with Förster's schemes in Paraguay. Elisabeth subsequently suppressed two-thirds of the letter and forged a flattering adaptation of the rest, addressing it to herself. The letter is to be found in Karl Schlechta's edition of Nietzsche's *Werke in drei Bänden*, vol. 3 (Munich: Carl Hanser, 1954–56), pp. 1420–22, and in Christopher Middleton's *Selected Letters of Friedrich Nietzsche* (Chicago: University of Chicago Press, 1969), pp. 226–29.

4. On Elisabeth Förster-Nietzsche's manipulation of the manuscript material, see Schlechta's discussion in his edition of Nietzsche's *Werke*, vol. 3, pp. 1408–23. See also, Erich Podach's *Friedrich Nietzsches Werke der Zusammenbruchs* (Heidelberg: Wolfgang Rothe, 1961) and his *Ein Blick in Notizbücher Nietzsches: Ewige Wiederkunft, Wille zur Macht, Ariadne; Eine schaffensanalytische Studie mit 4 Abbildungen* (Heidelberg: Wolfgang Rothe, 1963). For some perspective on this continuing controversy, the reader should also examine Walter Kaufmann's analysis in his essay "Nietzsche in the Light of his Suppressed Manuscripts," *Journal of the History of Philosophy* 2 (October 1964), pp. 205–25. This has been revised and added as an appendix to the third and fourth editions of his *Nietzsche: Philosopher, Psychologist, Antichrist* (Princeton: Princeton University Press, 1968, 1974).

5. For a thorough discussion of Elisabeth's handling of the posthumous writings, see R. J. Hollingdale, *Nietzsche: The Man and His Philosophy* (Baton Rouge: Louisiana State University Press, 1965), esp. pp. 289–305.

6. To be sure, many writers have done a great service in rectifying this extremely distorted view of Nietzsche. Unfortunately, however, the very terms of the debate and the rhetoric with which even the most sincere defense is pursued can often exacerbate the entire issue. Walter Kaufmann, for instance, in his timely *Nietzsche: Philosopher* (first published in 1950), despite his laudable intention to "dissociate" Nietzsche from "the Nazis," could almost be said to have extended the debate due to his excessive preoccupation with it.

7. Heinrich Wisser, one of Nietzsche's fellow students at the time, remarked that "Ritschl . . . had exercised such attraction on young academicians that the number of philologists in Leipzig suddenly soared from forty to one hundred and forty." Cf. Sander L. Gilman, ed., *Conversations with Nietzsche: A Life in the Words of His Contemporaries*, trans. David J. Parent (Oxford: Oxford University Press, 1987), p. 27.

8. Letter to Elisabeth Nietzsche, June 11, 1865, in *Selected Letters*, p. 7.

9. These works are to be found in F. Nietzsche, *Historische-kritische Gesamtausgabe. Werke*, 5 vols. (Munich: C. H. Beck, 1934–40), reedited by C. Koch and K. Schlechta as F. Nietzsche, *Frühe Schriften*, 5 vols. (Munich: C. H. Beck, 1994).

10. Ritschl's recommendation is to be found in Johannes Stroux's *Nietzsches Professeur in Basel* (Jena: Frommannsche Buchhandlung, 1925), pp. 32ff. Excerpts from the letter are cited in *The Portable Nietzsche*, ed. and trans. W. Kaufmann (New York: Viking, 1954), pp. 7–8.

11. The lectures would later be published as the *History of Greek Culture*, trans. P. Hilty (New York: Frederick Ungar, 1963).

12. Letter to Rohde, November 9, 1868, in *Selected Letters*, p. 39.

13. The question of Nietzsche's illness still remains a matter of some speculation. Two postmortem analyses failed to disclose any syphilitic infection, but the course and development of his symptoms seemed to indicate the likelihood of such an illness. The issue is discussed at length in Kurt Hildebrandt, *Gesundheit und Krankheit in Nietzsches Leben und Werk* (Berlin: Karger, 1926). See also Erich Podach, *Nietzsches Zusammenbruch: Beiträge zu einer Biographie auf Grund unveröffentlichter Dokumente* (Heidelberg: Kampmann, 1930). This work has been translated into English by F. A. Voit as *The Madness of Nietzsche* (New York: Putnam, 1931). The most definitive account of Nietzsche's health—with a wealth of documentation—is Pia Daniella Volz's *Nietzsche im Labyrinth seiner Krankheit: Eine medizinisch-biographische Untersuchung* (Würzburg: Königschausen and Neumann, 1990). See also Peters, *Zarathustra's Sister*, pp. 183–85; D. Allison, "Nietzsche's Identity," in *The Fate of the New Nietzsche*, ed. Keith Ansell-Pearson and Howard Caygill (Aldershot: Avebury, 1993), pp. 15–42; and David Krell, *Infectious Nietzsche* (Bloomington: Indiana University Press, 1996), esp. pp. 197–212.

14. Ulrich von Wilamowitz-Moellendorf, *Zukuntsphilologie! Eine Erwiderung auf Friedrich Nietzsches Geburt der Tragödie* (Berlin, 1872). Reprinted in Karlfried Gründer, ed., *Der Streit um Nietzsches "Geburt der Tragödie"* (Hildesheim: Georg Olms, 1969), pp. 27–55. English translation by Gertrude Postl, "Future-Philology! A Reply to Friedrich Nietzsche's *Birth of Tragedy*," in *New Nietzsche Studies* 4, no. 1–2 (Spring–Summer 2000), pp. 1–32.

15. Letter to Wagner, mid-November 1872, in *Selected Letters*, pp. 110–12.

16. Letter to Von Meysenbug, November 7, 1872, in *Selected Letters*, p. 108.

CHAPTER I

1. These early texts are to be found in the German critical edition of Nietzsche's works, Friedrich Nietzsche, *Samtliche Werke: Kritische Studienausgabe*, ed. G. Colli and M. Montinari (Berlin: Deutcher Taschenbuch Verlag/de Gruyter, 1980), henceforth referred to as *KSA*. "The Greek Musical Drama," *KSA* 1: 515–32; "Socrates and Tragedy," *KSA* 1: 533–49; "The Dionysian Worldview," *KSA* 1: 553–77 (trans. Ronald Speirs, in *The Birth of Tragedy and Other Writings*, ed. Raymond Geuss and Ronald Speirs [Cambridge: Cambridge University Press, 1999], pp. 117–38); "The Birth of Tragic Thought," *KSA* 1: 581–99 (trans. Ursula Bernis, in the *Graduate Faculty Philosophy Journal* 9, no. 2 [Fall 1983], pp. 3–15); "Socrates and Greek Tragedy," *KSA* 1: 604–40; "On Music and Words," *KSA* 7: 359–69, 185–90, trans. Walter Kaufmann, in Carl Dahlhaus, *Between Romanticism and Modernism: Four Studies in the Music of the Later 19th Century* (Berkeley: University of California Press, 1980), pp. 106–19.

2. Two of Nietzsche's last works discuss the problematic nature of his relations with Wagner, *The Case of Wagner* and *Nietzsche contra Wagner*, both written in 1888.

3. From *Selected Letters of Friedrich Nietzsche*, ed. and trans. Christopher Middleton (Chicago: University of Chicago Press, 1969), p. 84. Erwin Rohde was one of Nietzsche's closest friends during their period of university studies in Leipzig. He later taught philology at the Universities of Kiel and Leipzig and is most remembered for his

major work, *Psyche* (1891, 1894), which dealt with the Greek religious cults of the soul and their beliefs in immortality.

4. Nietzsche's personal correspondence with Wagner lost none of its effusive praise, however: "May my book be at least in some degree adequate to the interest which you have till now shown in its genesis—an interest which really puts me to shame. And if I myself think that, in the fundamentals, I am right, then that means only that *you*, with *your art*, must be eternally right. On every page you will find that I am only trying to thank you for everything you have given me; only doubt overcomes me as to whether I have always correctly received what you gave. Later, perhaps, I shall be able to do some things better; and by 'later,' I mean here the time of 'fulfillment,' the Bayreuth cultural period. Meanwhile, I feel proud that I have now marked myself out and that people will now always link my name with yours" (letter to Wagner, January 2, 1872, in *Selected Letters*, p. 91). For a balanced and detailed view of Nietzsche's relations with Wagner—personal, philosophical, and musical—see George Liébert's most informative *Nietzsche et la musique* (Paris: Presses Universitaires de France, 1995).

5. Indeed, quite literally: Nietzsche had the printer model the book's design on one of Wagner's own pamphlets, "The Object of Opera." Cf. for example, Nietzsche's letter to von Gersdorff, of November 18, 1871, in *Selected Letters*, p. 84.

6. Ulrich von Wilamowitz-Moellendorf had, like Nietzsche, been a student at Pforta and Bonn. Unlike Nietzsche, Wilamowitz chose to remain at Bonn with Otto Jahn to complete his doctorate rather than to follow Ritschl to Leipzig. In his later years Wilamowitz said that Nietzsche's rather derisive comment about Jahn's musical insensitivity in section 19 of *The Birth of Tragedy* "had excited my moral indignation" and thus had provoked him to write the pamphlet ("Philology of the Future! A Reply to Friedrich Nietzsche's *Birth of Tragedy*"). The German title *"Zukunftsphilologie"* was at once a transparently sarcastic jibe at Nietzsche's unconventional (thus, nonprofessional) style of composition and his embrace of Wagner. Wagner, after all, was the preeminent representative of the new, indeed revolutionary, style of musical composition—highly chromatic and programmatic—which was then being literally heralded as the "music of the future," or *"Zukunftsmusik."* He conceded that he was put up to write the piece by a senior colleague of his at the University of Berlin, Rudolph Schöll, as well, it seems, as having been encouraged to do so by the historian Theodor Mommsen. Nonetheless, Wilamowitz basically challenged every aspect of Nietzsche's work: its attempt to grasp classical Greek culture in distinctly modern terms (invoking Schopenhauer and Wagner), its lack of scientific methodology, a seeming disregard for any secondary scholarship whatsoever, its flamboyant, rhetorical style of composition, its embrace of mystical intuition, its paucity of logical and historiographical argumentation, and its flagrant metaphysical presumptions. While Wilamowitz would go on to become one of Germany's greatest classical scholars, it seems that, at the age of twenty-four, when he attacked Nietzsche, he perhaps suffered some sense of pique or academic jealousy toward Nietzsche, stemming from their earlier Pforta days and from his sense that Nietzsche was unduly helped by Ritschl's nomination of him to the Basel teaching post (without the doctorate!). An excellent and detailed discussion of these issues is to be found in M. S. Silk and J. P. Stern's comprehensive work, *Nietzsche on Tragedy* (Cambridge: Cambridge University Press, 1981), esp. pp. 90–131. A most complete dossier of correspondence, articles, manifestos, and reviews concerning the Nietzsche-Wilamowitz dispute is given in *Querelle autour de* La Naissance de la tragédie: *Nietzsche, Ritschl, Rohde, Wilamowitz, Wagner*, ed. Monique Dixaut (Paris: Vrin, 1995). For a remarkably insightful analysis of Nietzsche's historical and philological methodolo-

gies—and the complex welter of problems they give rise to in his attempt to render a coherent portrait of ancient Greek culture—see James A. Porter, *The Invention of Dionysus* (Stanford: Stanford University Press, 2000).

7. F. Nietzsche, *The Birth of Tragedy*, "Attempt at a Self-Criticism," sec. 3, in The Birth of Tragedy *and* The Case of Wagner, trans. W. Kaufmann (New York: Random House, 1967), p. 19. All references to Nietzsche's *The Birth of Tragedy* and *The Case of Wagner* refer to this source and will be abbreviated as *BT* and *CW*, respectively, hereafter.

8. *BT*, "Attempt at a Self-Criticism," Sec. 6, p. 24.

9. *CW*, "Epilogue," p. 191.

10. *BT*, "Attempt at a Self-Criticism," Sec. 5, p. 23.

11. *BT*, "Attempt at a Self-Criticism," Sec. 5, p. 23.

12. *BT*, "Attempt at a Self-Criticism," Sec. 5, p. 23.

13. This is perhaps the definitive sense in which Apollo and Dionysus should be termed "art deities"—as symbolizing distinctive attitudinal formations characteristic of the broader culture. That Apollo would come to be the "patron deity" of the visual arts and Dionysus the "patron deity" of music, is Nietzsche's interpretive attribution, strictly speaking, of what he saw as archetypal social, mythical, and artistic motifs in classical Greek culture.

14. Emile Durkheim would term this "collective effervescence" and describe it at length in his extremely important work of 1912, *The Elementary Forms of the Religious Life* (New York: Free Press, 1965), esp. book 2, chap. 7, "Origin of the Idea of the Totemic Principle or Mana," pp. 235–72. For a recent discussion of the political implications of such frenzied, collective celebrations, see Michèle Richman, "The Sacred Group: A Durkheimian Perspective of the Collège de Sociologie (1937–39)," in *Bataille: Writing the Sacred*, ed. Carolyn Bailey Gill (New York: Routledge, 1995), pp. 58–75.

15. Cf. F. Nietzsche, *The Will to Power*, ed. and trans. W. Kaufmann and R. J. Hollingdale (New York: Vintage, 1968), secs. 800, 842, and 1024. Further references to *The Will to Power* will be to this volume and cited *WP*.

16. *BT*, "Attempt at a Self-Criticism," Sec. 5, p. 24.

17. F. Nietzsche, *Twilight of the Idols*, "What I Owe to the Ancients," sec. 4, in *The Portable Nietzsche*, trans. and ed. W. Kaufmann (New York: Viking, 1954), pp. 561–62. For an extended discussion of the morality of bitterness and resentment—or, as Nietzsche usually terms this, according to French usage, *ressentiment*—the reader should refer to his work of 1887, *On the Genealogy of Morals*, 1st essay: "Good and Evil, Good and Bad," esp. sec. 10–17, in *On the Genealogy of Morals* and *Ecce Homo*, trans. W. Kaufmann and R. J. Hollingdale (New York: Vintage, 1969), pp. 36–56. (Hereafter all cites for *On the Genealogy of Morals* are from this volume and will be cited as *GM*.)

18. Nietzsche, *Twilight of the Idols*, "Morality as Anti-Nature," sec. 1, p. 487.

19. For an analysis of Dionysus and the Dionysian tradition, see especially C. Kerenyi, *Dionysus: Archetypal Image of Indestructible Life*, trans. Ralph Manheim (Princeton: Princeton University Press); E. R. Dodds, *The Greeks and the Irrational* (Berkeley: University of California Press, 1951); P. Slater, *The Glory of Hera: Greek Mythology and the Greek Family* (Boston: Beacon, 1968); W. F. Otto, *Dionysus: Myth and Cult*, trans. Robert B. Palmer (Bloomington: Indiana University Press, 1965); M. P. Nilsson, *The Dionysiac Mysteries of the Hellenistic and Roman Age* (Lund, Sweden: Svenska Institute i Athen, 1957); W. K. C. Guthrie, *The Greeks and Their Gods* (Boston: Beacon, 1955); G. E. Mylonas, *Elusis and the Elusinian Mysteries* (Princeton: Princeton

University Press, 1961); E. Tripp, *Crowell's Handbook of Classical Mythology* (New York: Meridian, 1974). Since recent archaeological studies have revealed references to Dionysus in Linear B tablets, dating from the Mycenaean age (i.e., back to the second millennium B.C.), Silk and Stern argue for an earlier, and hence "domestic," Dionysus of the pre-Homeric period: "Unlike the 'Hellenic' Apollo, then, the 'foreign' Dionysus has a secure place in pre-Homeric Greece" (Silk and Stern, *Nietzsche on Tragedy*, pp. 171ff.). Effectively, they identify this Mycenaean period of Dionysus with what Nietzsche would term the "age of the Titans," by which he generally means the early archaic period—and while such evidence may well indicate a domestic provenance for Dionysus, it may equally suggest an earlier date of visitation by this peregrinating deity. In any case, Nietzsche himself repeatedly made the claim that the Greece of the classical period had a far more ancient and troubled history than most nineteenth-century scholars would concede.

✓   20. K. J. Dover gives a particularly detailed historical account of archaic and classical Greek morality in his *Greek Popular Morality in the Time of Plato and Aristotle* (Oxford: Blackwell, 1974).

21. See H. D. F. Kitto's account of this transitional period in his *The Greeks* (Baltimore: Penguin, 1960).

22. For an extended reflection on the effects of the Persian Wars upon Greek culture, see Nietzsche's text of 1875, "The Struggle between Science and Wisdom," in F. Nietzsche, *Philosophy and Truth: Selections from Nietzsche's Notebooks of the Early 1870s*, ed. and trans. Daniel Breazeale (New York: Humanities Press International, 1990), pp. 127–46. See also *KSA* 8: 97–120. On the important role of Themistocles and the dramatic aftereffects of the Battle of Salamis for classical Greek culture, see D. Allison, "Recipes for Ruin," in *International Studies in Philosophy* 23, no. 2 (1991), pp. 36–54.

23. Nietzsche's discussion of Socrates extends from his earliest lecture courses at Basel—indeed, even at Pforta, he claimed his favorite book was Plato's *Symposium*—through his final writings. In the course of Nietzsche's lifelong reflection, he depicts a tension between Socrates' genuine philosophic brilliance, his personal courage and independence of spirit, his institution of the rational discipline of science in the quest for truth, and what Nietzsche sees as Socrates' inability to achieve a balanced life of emotional maturity and complexity, a strong antisensualistic tendency, an indifference toward the arts and toward the rich cultural and mythical traditions of Greece. This ambivalent view of Socrates is already clear in sections 12–15 of *BT*, and it is fairly well continued through such works as *Human, All Too Human* (cf. vol. 2, part 2, sec. 86), *The Gay Science* (cf. secs. 32, 328, 340, 372), and *Beyond Good and Evil* (cf. sec. 190). (Cites from *Human, All Too Human* are from F. Nietzsche, *Human, All Too Human: A Book for the Free Spirits*, trans. R. J. Hollingdale [Cambridge: Cambridge University Press, 1986], hereafter cited as *HAH*; cites from *The Gay Science* are from F. Nietzsche, *The Gay Science*, trans. W. Kaufmann [New York: Vintage, 1974], hereafter cited as *GS*; cites from *Beyond Good and Evil* are from *Beyond Good and Evil: Prelude to a Philosophy of the Future*, trans. W. Kaufmann [New York: Vintage, 1966], hereafter cited as *BGE*), But toward the final period, Nietzsche becomes far more strident in his criticism of Socrates' extravagant moralizing, his stress of an extreme and isolating kind of individualism, and what he understood to be Socrates' overidealization of reason, truth, and reality. These themes converge most forcefully in the 1888 work *The Twilight of the Idols*, in the section entitled "The Problem of Socrates." Walter Kaufmann gives a balanced view of Nietzsche's assessment of Socrates in his *Nietzsche: Philosopher, Psychologist, Antichrist*, 4th ed. (Princeton: Princeton University Press, 1974), chap.

13, pp. 391–411. For an extended discussion on this, see also Victor Tejera, *Nietzsche and Greek Thought* (Dordrecht: Kluwer, 1987), esp. chaps. 5 and 6, pp. 71–113.

24. F. Nietzsche, *Ecce Homo*, "The Birth of Tragedy," sec. 1, in *On the Genealogy of Morals and* Ecce Homo, trans. W. Kaufmann and R. J. Hollingdale (New York: Vintage, 1969), p. 271. (Hereafter all cites to *Ecce Homo* are taken from this volume and cited as *EH*.)

25. "Greek antiquity provides the classical set of examples for the interpretation of our entire culture and its development. It is a means *for understanding ourselves*, a means for regulating our age—and thereby a means for overcoming it" (Nietzsche, *Philosophy and Truth*, p. 127).

26. For an extended discussion of nihilism—its origins, dynamics, and effects—see his posthumously edited work (assembled from his notebooks, dating from 1883 to 1888) *The Will to Power*, particularly book 1, entitled "European Nihilism," in *WP*, pp. 7–82. A most comprehensive account of nihilism is given by Stanley Rosen in his *Nihilism: A Philosophical Essay* (New Haven: Yale University Press, 1969); cf. also Michael Allen Gillespie, *Nihilism before Nietzsche* (Chicago: University of Chicago Press, 1995).

27. *EH*, sec. 4, p. 274.

28. Nietzsche, *Twilight of the Idols*, "What I Owe to the Ancients," sec. 5.

29. "In the doctrine of the [Dionysian] mysteries, *pain* is pronounced holy: the pangs of the woman giving birth hallow all pain; all becoming and growing—all that guarantees a future—involves pain. . . . The psychology of the orgiastic as an overflowing feeling of life and strength, where even pain still has the effect of a stimulus, gave me the key to the concept of *tragic* feeling, which had been misunderstood by Aristotle and, quite especially, by our modern pessimists [i.e., Schopenhauer]" (Nietzsche, *Twilight of the Idols*, pp. 561–62). Cf. also sec. 4 of the 1886 preface to *BT*.

30. Certainly, one of the most crucial accounts of pain is his treatment of it in the second essay of the *Genealogy of Morals*, where Nietzsche associates the individual's memory with the fearful anticipation of pain in his account of the origin of *conscience* (arising out of the debtor-creditor relation) and its development into *guilt* and *sin*. This leads to an analysis of the ideological manipulation of guilt and sin, so as to induce absolution through atonement, which increases human suffering in turn—and in consequence, lends meaning and purpose to suffering, making it and life bearable (through the agency that lends it meaning: the metaphysical morality of the church or state).

31. Cf. Nietzsche's discussion concerning the origins of law, in *The Antichrist*, sec. 57, in Kaufmann's *The Portable Nietzsche*, pp. 643–44.

32. See especially Michel Foucault's discussion of this ("Nietzsche, Freud, Marx") in D. Ormiston and A. Schrift, eds., *Transforming the Hermeneutic Context* (Albany: SUNY Press, 1990).

33. Arguing against the persistent "classical stereotype," in his *The Glory of Hera,* ✔ Philip Slater writes that the period of classical Greek civilization cannot be "reduced to the ethereal land of sunshine to which all too many classicists have consigned it—a stereotype which seems to me a far more profound derogation. When Murray tells us that 'Greek thought, always sincere and daring, was seldom brutal, seldom ruthless or cruel'; or Nilsson feels obliged to apologize for rejecting the preposterous notion that the Greeks were not superstitious; or Rose tells us piously that 'the Greeks were in general a people of clean life,' they are asking us to share a vision which is not only false but emasculated and bloodless. To recreate Greece in the image of Plato is to reduce a rich and vibrant society to its most arteriosclerotic by-product. . . . The idealizing attitude gives rise to many absurdities in description and interpretation. Kitto repeatedly

asks how it happens that the Greeks, who were never childish or stupid or vulgar or irrational or superstitious, could ever have done all the childish, stupid, vulgar, irrational, and superstitious things they did, and contrives many ingenious explanations without ever questioning his postulate. His explicit assumption, which he shares with many others, is that beautiful architecture, sculpture, literature, and so forth, is somehow incompatible with ordinary human folly (he is apparently unacquainted with any creative people)" (pp. xxii–xxiv).

34. Philip Slater singles out the work of H. J. Rose (*A Handbook of Greek Mythology* [New York: Dutton, 1959]) as a prime example of this idealizing tendency. Quoting Rose: "The Greeks at their best were sane, high-spirited, clear-headed, beauty-loving optimists, and not in the least other-worldly. Hence their legends are almost without exception free from the cloudiness, the wild grotesques, and the horrible features which beset the popular traditions of less gifted and happy peoples. Even their monsters are not very ugly or uncouth, nor their ghosts and demons paralyzingly dreadful. Their heroes, as a rule, may sorrow, but are not broken-hearted; on occasion they are struck down by an adverse fate, but not weakly overwhelmed; they meet with extraordinary adventures, but there is a certain tone of reasonableness running through their most improbable exploits. As for the gods and their supernatural characters, they are . . . on the whole neither irrational nor grossly unfair in their dealings" (Rose, p. 14). Slater comments: "One is surprised to find this statement followed by a relatively uncensored presentation of the Greek myths, in dazzling contradiction to each of his remarks. Indeed, few mythologies show us more madness, more weak, depressed, uncouth, and suffering heroes, more grotesque and terrifying monsters, more vicious and vindictive deities" (*Glory of Hera*, pp. xxiv–xxv).

35. F. Nietzsche, *Unmodern Observations*, ed. William Arrowsmith, trans. Gary Brown (New Haven: Yale University Press, 1990), pp. 87–145. This translation of *Vom Nutzen und Nachteil der Historie für das Leben* complements an equally excellent translation by R. J. Hollingdale, *On the Uses and Disadvantages of History for Life*, in his edition and translation of Nietzsche's *Unzeitgemäße Betrachtungen* (*Untimely Meditations*) (Cambridge: Cambridge University Press, 1983), pp. 57–123.

36. For a discussion of this issue, see especially A. Lesky, *A History of Greek Literature* (New York: Crowell, 1966), pp. 232–33, and Silk and Stern, *Nietzsche on Tragedy*, esp. chaps. 6–7, pp. 132–224.

37. While the terms Apollonian and Dionysian had been used earlier by such figures as Winckelmann, Schelling, Schopenhauer, A. Feuerbach, Michelet, and Genelli, it was Nietzsche who formulated them in a far deeper and consequential way, giving them what is now recognized as their definitive cast. In section 1 of *The Birth of Tragedy*, Nietzsche simply states, "The terms Dionysian and Apollonian we borrow from the Greeks, who disclose to the discerning mind the profound mysteries of their view of art, not to be sure in concepts, but in the intensely clear figures of their gods" (p. 33). An excellent account of the Apollonian-Dionysian dynamic is given by Dieter Jähnig in his "Liberating the Knowledge of Art from Metaphysics in Neitzsche's *Birth of Tragedy*," trans. B. Babich and H. Schmid, *New Nietzsche Studies* 4, no. 1/2 (Summer 2000): 77–121.

38. These concerns would be discussed at length in Nietzsche's very next work (of 1873), "David Strauss, the Confessor and the Writer," the first of his *Untimely Meditations*, trans. Herbert Golder, in Nietzsche, *Unmodern Observations*, pp. 15–72.

39. In response to the traditional view—advanced by Wilamowitz in his pamphlet—Nietzsche would remark to Rohde, "If only people would stop this soft talk of the

Homeric world as a youthful one, the springtime of the Greeks, and so on. In the sense in which it is maintained, the idea is false. That a tremendous, wild conflict, emerging from dark crudity and cruelty, precedes the Homeric era, that Homer stands as victor at the end of this long and desolate period—this is one of my most certain convictions. The Greeks are much older than people think. One can speak of spring as long as one has a winter to precede it, but this world of purity and beauty did not drop from the sky." Letter to Rohde, July 16, 1872, in *Selected Letters*, pp. 96–97.

40. "Homer's Contest," in F. Nietzsche, *Nietzscheana*, trans. Christa D. Acampora, no. 5 (Urbana, Ill.: North American Nietzsche Society, 1996), p. 2. This very important early essay, "Homers Wettkampf," has also been translated by Carol Diethe as "Homer on Competition," to be found in F. Nietzsche, *On the Genealogy of Morality*, ed. K. Ansell-Pearson, trans. Carol Diethe (Cambridge: Cambridge University Press), pp. 187–94. These translations replace the earlier English translation of "Homer's Contest," by Maximilian A. Mügge, in Oscar Levy, ed., *The Complete Works of Friedrich Nietzsche*, vol. 2, *Early Greek Philosophy and Other Essays* (London: Foulis, 1911), pp. 52–53. An abridged translation by Walter Kaufmann appears in his *The Portable Nietzsche*, pp. 32–39.

41. "Homer's Contest," in *Nietzscheana*, p. 2.

42. "Homer's Contest," in *Nietzscheana*, pp. 2–3.

43. In the "Homer's Contest" essay, Nietzsche quotes Hesiod's formulation (from the *Works and Days*, lines 11–26) that there are two Goddesses of Strife (*eris*): a bad Strife who encourages war and cruelty, which leads to annihilation, and a good Strife who drives mankind to productive action—to work, to labor in the fields, and to acquire wealth. The good Strife incites a praiseworthy kind of envy (even resentment and jealousy) in the individual, which provokes a positive sense of competitiveness, a motivational drive to excel and to perform honorable acts. In *HAH*, vol. 2, part 2, sec. 39, he rephrases his observations concerning Strife made in "Homer's Contest," such that bad Strife leads mankind to bring others down below a common level, and good Strife raises the individual to a level higher than the norm. In *Philosophy in the Tragic Age of the Greeks*, Nietzsche remarks that Heraclitus extended the notion of competition to the level of a cosmological doctrine, whereby reality itself consists in the play, the continual strife and resolution, of opposites, resulting in a dynamic world of *becoming*—a world of constant change and transformation (not a static world of *being*). On this basis, the very balance of opposing forces constitutes justice (*dike*): "The strife of the opposites gives birth to all of becoming; the definite qualities which look permanent to us express but the momentary ascendancy of one partner. But this by no means signifies the end of the war; the contest endures in all eternity. Everything that happens, happens in accordance with this strife, and it is just in the strife that eternal justice is revealed. It is a wonderful idea, welling up from the purest springs of Hellenism, the idea that strife embodies the everlasting sovereignty of strict justice, bound to everlasting laws. Only a Greek was capable of finding such an idea to be the fundament of a cosmology; it is Hesiod's good *Eris* transformed into the cosmic principle; it is the contest-idea of the Greek individual and the Greek state, taken from the artist's *agon*, from the contest between political parties and between cities—all transformed into universal application so that now the wheels of the cosmos turn on it" (Nietzsche, *Philosophy in the Tragic Age of the Greeks* [hereafter *PTAG*], trans., Marianne Cowan [Chicago: Regnery, 1962], sec. 5, p. 55; also in *KSA* 1: 825).

In notes from the same period (esp. *KSA* 7: 393–410), Nietzsche speculates that the *agon* itself stemmed from war—effectively, the good Strife being engendered by the bad Strife (in Hesiod, both would have been children of Night). Indeed, he remarks that the competition or contest between city-states can easily revert to war. With regard to the Apollonian victory over the previous age of barbarism (i.e., the Homeric triumph over the pre-Homeric age), the struggle for existence is overcome by the struggle for glory: "The poet overcomes the struggle for existence in that he idealizes it into a free competition. Here, the existence for which one still struggles is existence through praise, in posthumous glory" (*KSA* 7: 398).

Instead of city-states waging war for the entertainment of the gods, individual participants of equal stature would henceforth compete—in the theater, in the gymnasium, in the Olympian games, in the court of law, or, indeed, in the marketplace—for victory, glory, and honor before the Greek public itself.

44. *BT*, sec. 3, pp. 41, 43.

45. *BT*, sec. 3, p. 43.

46. *BT*, sec. 3, p. 42.

47. Sir David Ross, ed. and trans., *The Works of Aristotle*, vol. 12 (London: Oxford University Press, 1952), fragment 6, pp. 18–19.

48. *WP*, sec. 1067; cf. also secs. 1048–52. Nietzsche will also later identify Dionysus with the figure of Zarathustra (and he will equate Dionysian wisdom with Zarathustra's teaching of the eternal return), the epic-dithyrambic character from his work of the same name, published in 1883–85: cf. *EH*, "Thus Spoke Zarathustra," secs. 6–8, pp. 304–9; *EH*, "The Birth of Tragedy," secs. 3–4, pp. 273–75. Also, Nietzsche, *Twilight of the Idols*, "What I Owe to the Ancients," sec. 5, pp. 562–63.

49. *BT*, sec. 3, p. 44.

50. This is one of the principal misunderstandings found in certain recent interpretations of *BT* (e.g., that of Paul de Man, in his *Allegories of Reading: Figural Language in Rousseau, Nietzsche, Rilke, and Proust* [New Haven: Yale University Press, 1979]). For an extended discussion of the Apollonian and Dionysian, especially with regard to the supposed "metaphysical priority" of the Dionysian, cf. D. Allison, "Nietzsche Knows No Noumenon" in D. O'Hara, *Why Nietzsche Now?* (Bloomington: Indiana University Press, 1985), pp. 295–310.

51. A particularly insightful—invaluable—view of the Dionysian state is given by Georges Bataille in the introduction and the first two chapters of his *Eroticism*, trans. Mary Dalwood (London: Calder, 1962), pp. 11–48. Bataille develops his account through the notions of "continuity" and "discontinuity." See also his *Inner Experience*, trans. Leslie A. Boldt (Albany: SUNY Press, 1988).

52. This duality of motivation that underlies the Dionysian and Apollonian attitudes is derived—ultimately—from the classic opposition that Socrates drew concerning the parentage of Love, in his *Symposium* (203 b1ff.), that is, the opposition between *Poros*, or plenty, and *Penia*, or want. The opposition recurs frequently in Nietzsche's work, including his critique of romanticism, his distinction between aristocratic and slave morality, the psychology of asceticism and *ressentiment*, of health and decadence, and the general dynamics of strength and weakness, of active forces and reactive forces—in art as in life. For an excellent account of Diotima's speech, see Stanley Rosen, *Plato's Symposium* (New Haven: Yale University Press, 1968), esp. chap. 7, pp. 197–277. This general opposition forms the analytical core of Gilles Deleuze's interpretation of Nietzsche in his work, *Nietzsche and Philosophy*, trans. Hugh Tomlinson (New York: Columbia University Press, 1983).

53. "Individuation knows but one law—the individual, i.e., the delimiting of the boundaries of the individual, *measure* in the Hellenic sense. Apollo, as ethical deity,

exacts measure of his disciples, and, to be able to maintain it, he requires self-knowledge. And, so, side by side with the aesthetic necessity for beauty, there occur the demands 'know thyself' and 'nothing in excess'; consequently overweening pride and excess are regarded as the truly hostile demons of the non-Apollonian sphere, hence as characteristics of the pre-Apollonian age—that of the Titans; and of the extra-Apollonian world—that of the barbarians" (*BT*, sec. 4, p. 46). On the Greek incomprehension of this barbarity, see Gilles Deleuze's "Nomad Thought," in *The New Nietzsche*, ed. D. Allison (Cambridge: MIT Press, 1985), pp. 142–49.

54. *BT*, sec. 2, p. 39.

55. Euripides, *Bacchae*, lines 1122–46, trans. Henry Birkhead, in *Ten Greek Plays*, ed. L. R. Lind (Boston: Houghton Mifflin, 1957), pp. 356–57.

56. *BT*, sec. 4, p. 46.

57. The individual's own particularity, that is, what determines him or her as a unique and distinctive subject, is thus the effect of the structuring and acculturating elements in the society at large: its collective set of values, norms, habits, laws, institutions, myths, ideals, and so forth.

58. *BT*, sec. 4, p. 47. See also Kitto, *The Greeks*, pp. 84–89.

59. *BT*, sec. 5, p. 48. See also Lesky, *History of Greek Literature*, pp. 110–14. Silk and Stern indicate the unlikelihood of any such double portrait of Homer and Archilochus prior to the fourth century B.C. Silk and Stern, *Nietzsche on Tragedy*, pp. 401ff., n. 9.

60. *BT*, sec. 8, p. 61.

61. *BT*, sec. 24, p. 141.

62. *BT*, sec. 21, p. 126; sec. 22, p. 130. See also secs. 23 and 24 for an extended discussion of the musical mood of the aesthetic spectator. The relevance of this to tragedy is clearly stated by Nietzsche: "Now transfer this phenomenon of the aesthetic spectator into an analogous process in the tragic artist, and you will have understood the genesis of the tragic myth" (*BT*, sec. 24, p. 140).

63. *WP*, para. 1067, pp. 549–50.

64. The intoxicating effects of these instruments on the Greek populace is sufficiently witnessed by Aristotle's strenuous rejection of them in *The Politics*. For Aristotle, the flute, especially (as well as the zither, sackbut, and heptagon), serves only the "vulgar pleasure" of the audience: "It does not express a state of character, but rather a mood of religious excitement; and it should therefore be used on those occasions when the effect to be produced on the audience is the release of emotion, and not instruction." Significantly, "Flute playing prevents the player from using the voice." He continues, citing an ancient myth: "Athena, it tells us, invented the flute—and then threw it away." Aristotle's explanation? "She threw it away because the study of flute-playing has nothing to do with the mind." *The Politics of Aristotle*, book 8, 6, trans. E. Barker (New York: Oxford University Press, 1962), pp. 348–49.

65. *BT*, sec. 21, p. 124.

66. *BT*, sec. 8, p. 64.

67. *BT*, sec. 8, p. 64.

68. *BT*, sec. 8, pp. 64–65.

69. It is traditionally held that the poet Arion of Methymna (on the island of Lesbos), a gifted singer, composer, and cithara player, was the first figure to have publicly staged the dithyramb—in the city of Corinth, toward the end of the seventh century B.C. Herodotus discusses Arion in his *Histories*, 1: 23, 24 (trans. R. Waterfield [Oxford:

Oxford University Press, 1998], pp. 11–12). See also Silk and Stern, *Nietzsche on Tragedy*, pp. 142–59.

70. Traditionally, this was attributed to the Greek playwright and actor Thespis, who was said to have first introduced the speaking part at the Athens Dionysia festival in 535 B.C.

71. *BT*, sec. 8, p. 66.

72. *BT*, sec. 8, p. 66.

73. *BT*, sec. 8, p. 67.

74. *BT*, sec. 10, p. 74.

75. *BT*, sec. 9, p. 71. For an extended discussion of these dynamics, see also Edmund Leach, "Structuralism in Social Anthropology," in *Structuralism*, ed. D. Robey (Oxford: Oxford University Press, 1973), pp. 37–56.

76. *BT*, sec. 9, p. 69.

77. *WP*, sec. 851, p. 449.

78. *BT*, sec. 24, p. 140.

79. *BT*, sec. 16, p. 104. This sentiment will find striking expression in Nietzsche's later development of such themes as the Eternal Recurrence, especially in *The Gay Science* and *Zarathustra*.

80. *BT*, sec. 25, p. 144.

81. *BT*, sec. 21, p. 130.

82. *BT*, sec. 21, p. 130.

83. *BT*, sec. 17, p. 105.

84. *BT*, sec. 11, pp. 80–81 [emphasis added]; sec. 12, p. 86.

85. *BT*, sec. 12, p. 82.

86. For a discussion of this affinity of interpretation, see Leo Strauss's introduction in his *Socrates and Aristophanes* (New York: Basic Books, 1966).

87. *BT*, sec. 14, p. 91.

88. *BT*, sec. 17, p. 107.

89. *BT*, sec. 14, p. 92.

90. *BT*, sec. 15, pp. 95, 96.

91. On the role of the icon (*eikon, eikasia*) and veridical representation in Plato and Nietzsche, see D. Allison, "Iconologies: Reading *Simulations* with Plato and Nietzsche," in *Recherches Sémiotiques/Semiotic Inquiry* 16, nos. 1–2 (1996), pp. 89–111.

92. *BT*, sec. 10, p. 75.

93. "Strife, for Schopenhauer, is a proof of the internal self-dissociation of the Will to Live, which is seen as a self-consuming, menacing and gloomy drive, a thoroughly frightful and by no means blessed phenomenon" (*PTAG*, p. 56).

94. *BT*, sec. 25, p. 143.

95. *BT*, sec. 25, p. 143.

96. *BT*, sec. 18, p. 112.

97. *BT*, sec. 15, p. 97.

98. For a definitive discussion of Nietzsche's understanding and judgment of science, see Babette Babich, *Nietzsche's Philosophy of Science* (Albany: SUNY Press, 1994). For a remarkably comprehensive range of contemporary views concerning Nietzsche and science, see Babette Babich, ed., *Nietzsche, Epistemology, and Philosophy of Science: Nietzsche and the Sciences*, 2 vols. (Dordrecht: Kluwer, 1999).

99. *BT*, sec. 15, pp. 95–97.

100. *BT*, sec. 13, pp. 87–88.

101. Nietzsche's own position on metaphysics at the time generally accords with this.

In formulating his account of Heraclitus (Nietzsche taught a course on the pre-Socratics in the summer semester of 1872), one gets a fair sense of his emerging views: "Heraclitus . . . denied the duality of totally diverse worlds. . . . He no longer distinguished a physical world from a metaphysical one, a realm of definite qualities from an undefinable 'indefinite' [as had his predecessor, Anaximander]. And after this first step, nothing could hold him back from a second, far bolder negation: he altogether denied being. For this one world which he retained—supported by eternal unwritten laws, flowing upward and downward in brazen rhythmic beat—nowhere shows a tarying, an indestructibility, a bulwark in the stream. Louder than Anaximander, Heraclitus proclaimed: 'I see nothing other than becoming. . . .' Heraclitus' regal possession is his extraordinary power to think intuitively. . . . But intuitive thinking embraces two things: one, the present many-colored and changing world that crowds in upon us in all our experiences, and two, the conditions which alone make any experience of this world possible: time and space. . . . And that space is just like time, and that everything which coexists in space and time has but a relative existence, that each thing exists through and for another like it, which is to say through and for an equally relative one.—This is a truth of the greatest immediate self-evidence for everyone, and the one which for this reason is extremely difficult to reach by way of concept or reason. But whoever finds himself directly looking at it must at once move on to the Heraclitan conclusion and say that the whole nature of reality [*Wirklichkeit*] lies simply in its acts [*Wirken*] and that for it there exists no other sort of being" (*PTAG*, sec. 5, pp. 51–53).

Looking back at *The Birth of Tragedy* several years later, Nietzsche would remark, "The antithesis of a real and an apparent world is lacking here: there is only *one* world, and this is false, cruel, contradictory, seductive, without meaning—A world thus constituted is the real world. *We have need of lies* in order to conquer this reality, this 'truth,' that is, in order to *live*—That lies are necessary in order to live is itself a part of the terrifying and questionable character of existence. Metaphysics, morality, religion, science—in this book these things merit consideration only as various forms of lies: with their help one can have *faith* in life. . . . In this way, this book is even anti-pessimistic: that is, in the sense that it teaches something that is stronger than pessimism, 'more divine' than truth: *art*" (*WP*, sec. 853, pp. 451–53). This is precisely why Nietzsche would say in sec. 18 of *BT* that the Socratic, the artistic, and the tragic cultures are "three stages of illusion . . . [that] are actually designed only for the more nobly formed natures, who actually feel profoundly the weight and burden of existence, and must be deluded by exquisite stimulants into forgetfulness of their displeasure. All that we call culture is made up of these stimulants" (pp. 109–10). With regard to the association of the noumenal or World-Will with the domain of the unconditioned, Nietzsche remarks in *Human, All Too Human,* "As against this, more rigorous logicians, having clearly identified the concept of the metaphysical as that of the unconditioned, consequently also unconditioning, have disputed any connection between the unconditioned (the metaphysical world) and the world we know" (*HAH*, vol. 1, sec. 16, "Appearance and Thing in Itself," pp. 19–20).

102. In a later reflection on this problem, he would note, "I began with a metaphysical hypothesis about the sense of music: but at bottom, there was a *psychological experience* for which I didn't know how to give a sufficient *historical* explanation. The transfer of music into the metaphysical was an act of veneration and gratitude; in the end all religious people have done the same thing with their own experience.—Then, there was the other side of the coin: the indisputably harmful and destructive action this revered music [i.e., Wagner's music] had upon me—and by the same token, the end of

my religious veneration. It was then that I opened my eyes to the modern need *for* music (which appears historically at the same time as the growing need for narcotics)" (*KSA* 12: 123).

103. *BT*, sec. 24, p. 141.

104. Marghanita Laski, *Ecstasy: A Study of Some Secular and Religious Experiences* (Bloomington: Indiana University Press, 1961), p. 16.

105. Laski, *Ecstasy*, esp. appendices A–J, pp. 375–533. In appendix A Laski gives an interesting analysis of Nietzsche's remarks on musical ecstasy in sec. 1 of *CW* (pp. 405 ff.).

106. See note 1.

107. In Martin Heidegger's *Being and Time* (trans. John Macquarrie and Edward Robinson [New York: Harper and Row, 1962], part 1, div. 1, chap. 5, secs. 29–30, pp. 172–82), he gives an exemplary account of "Stimmung," borrowing in large part from Nietzsche's own reflection.

108. See, e.g. "On Music and Words," *KSA* 7: 364; or Dahlhaus, *Between Romanticism and Modernism*, p. 111.

109. See Nietzsche, *Twilight of the Idols*, sec. 8, "Toward a Psychology of the Artist," in *The Portable Nietzsche*, pp. 519–20.

110. "On Music and Words," *KSA* 7: 362–63; or Dahlhaus, *Between Romanticism and Modernism*, p. 109. Music is indeed a "sanctuary" in that it is its own world—it is a constructed, artificial world, which is immediately experienced as a completely controlled environment, engaging the emotions and structuring the reception of temporality and movement: it resolves an enormity of elements and anticipations into perfect form and beauty.

111. When Nietzsche returns to *The Birth of Tragedy*, with his preface of 1886, he is specific in characterizing the Apollonian and Dionysian as psychological "drives" (*Triebe*: Kaufmann translates this as "tendencies") in the very first paragraph of the first section, and he goes on to say that they find expression in dreams, in mystical-ecstatic dancing (he mentions St. John's and St. Vitus's dance), and in licentious orgies.

112. *KSA* 7: 23.

113. In his recent volume, *Music, the Brain, and Ecstasy: How Music Captures Our Imagination* (New York: William Morrow, 1997), Robert Jourdain specifies three kinds of dissonance to be resolved by the listener: auditory critical band frequency interference and synchronicity of sound beat—both of which are complemented by overtone interactions—as well as the more complex structural element, harmonic dissonance, involving chord movement. Cf., esp., pp. 100–105.

114. Jourdain, *Music, the Brain, and Ecstasy*, pp. 302–3.

115. Jourdain, *Music, the Brain, and Ecstasy*, pp. 312–13. In a note from early 1888, Nietzsche himself makes a remarkably similar observation: "If the essence of 'pleasure' has been correctly described as a feeling of more power (hence as a feeling of difference, presupposing a comparison), this does not yet furnish a definition of 'displeasure.' The false opposites in which the people, and *consequently* language, believes, have always been dangerous hindrances to the advance of truth. There are even cases in which a kind of pleasure is conditioned by a certain *rhythmic sequence* of little unpleasurable stimuli: in this way a very rapid increase of the feeling of power, the feeling of pleasure, is achieved. This is the case, e.g., in tickling, also the sexual tickling in the act of coitus: here we see displeasure at work as an ingredient of pleasure. It seems, a little hindrance that is overcome and immediately followed by another little hindrance that is again overcome—this game of resistance and victory arouses most strongly that gen-

eral feeling of superabundant, excessive power that constitutes the essence of pleasure" (*WP*, sec. 699, p. 371).

116. While the auditory cortex is densely connected to the temporal and frontal lobes of the brain, it is not so connected with the motor cortex or the somatosensory cortex (and this would seem to block the automatic engagement of the kinesthetic-motor system by the auditory system). Rather, we seem to use our muscular system to represent musical patterns of tension, anticipation, impetus, movement, trajectory, contour, and so forth, so as to serve as a system of notation to inscribe and remember musical patterns as they transpire temporally, and thus to amplify our experience of its complexity and the satisfaction this yields. Thus, musical patterns are replicated in the motor system as well as in the auditory system. In this sense, our kinesthetic system becomes a kind of resonator, and our body literally permits itself to become an instrument, to be played by the music. More simply stated, perhaps, this is exactly how we "go with the flow," how we "get into" musical rhythms and harmonic cadences. It is at this level of bodily representation that the neurons within the kinesthetic-motor system are excited and begin to discharge endorphins, further enhancing the sense of pleasure—in this case, delight, ecstasy—in our experience of music. And we become transformed (cf. Jourdain, *Music, the Brain, and Ecstasy*, pp. 324–26).

117. Aristophanes portrayed Socrates, in *The Clouds*, as teaching the criminal doctrine that "Zeus is not." In a note from the period of *The Birth of Tragedy*, Nietzsche also remarked, it "is a very ancient Germanic idea" that "all the old Gods must die . . . Sigurd, Odin, Balder" (*KSA* 7: 107).

118. *BT*, sec. 23, p. 137.

119. Aristotle, *Nichomachean Ethics*, trans., Martin Oswald (Indianapolis: Bobbs-Merrill, 1962), line 1095b, p. 7.

120. For a supplementary discussion about how he viewed the modern crisis in culture during this period, see Nietzsche's work of 1873, "History in the Service and Disservice of Life," esp. chap. 4, in *Unmodern Observations*.

CHAPTER 2

1. Letter of September, 1882, in *Selected Letters of Friedrich Nietzsche*, Christopher Middleton (Chicago: University of Chicago Press), p. 193. Of the four books, or chapters, that comprise the first edition, book 4 was the only one to receive a title, "Sanctus Januarius," so named after Saint Januarius—San Gennaro—whose blood, it is said, miraculously came back to life every year. That Nietzsche should choose this name is understandable, since following a particularly painful bout of his recurring illness, he likewise felt miraculously revivified. Indeed, the prescription for regaining his health, he remarked, was precisely to write *The Gay Science* itself: "Nobody should be annoyed with me for having a good opinion of my medicine. *Mihi ipsi scripsi* [I have written for myself] . . . I was in all respects my own doctor. . . . Admittedly, others might perish by using the same remedies; that is why I exert everything in warning others against me. Especially this latest book, which is called *The Gay Science*, will scare many people away from me—you too perhaps" (letter to Erwin Rohde, July 15, 1882; *Selected Letters*, p. 187).

2. *GS*, sec. 324, p. 255.

3. In brief, Nietzsche views this as an affirmative understanding of the world and

as a positive practical teaching for the conduct of one's life—an understanding that would enable the individual to attain a fulfillment of his or her own capacities and to secure a sense of autonomy and freedom from the pettiness and shame that Nietzsche held derived from the "herd morality," generally imposed upon us by the sanctions of traditional religion. Such a "gay science" would also contrast with the character of the conventional academic formation of his time, which Nietzsche viewed as excessively abstract and unrelated to the complex life concerns of the developing individual. Even more strongly, Nietzsche maintained that the conventional education and learning were a disservice to the individual in that they enforced a restrictive conformity upon the subject, such that the individual was valued only in terms of his service—indeed, the individual's submission—to the state, that is, as a "herd" member.

4. Letter to Reinhart von Seydlitz, February 12, 1888, in *Selected Letters*, p. 284.

5. *GS*, sec. 359, pp. 314–15.

6. *EH*, "The Gay Science" ("la gaya scienza"), p. 294.

7. Letter to Heinrich von Stein, December 1882, in *Selected Letters*, p. 197. That Nietzsche himself would have wished to be disburdened of some of his own heartbreak at the time is also clear. December 1882 marked the irrevocable break in his relations with Lou Salomé, the only woman he ever truly loved in his life. Invited to Rome in the early spring of 1882 by Paul Rée to meet Lou Salomé, Nietzsche not only fell achingly, wholeheartedly in love with her—proposing marriage some three times—but he thought by his truest intuition that Lou would become his foremost follower and disciple of his philosophy. Nietzsche's infatuation with Lou was complete, but unfortunately, it proved to be largely unrequited (if not largely delusional). Rée, who introduced the two, was also impassioned for Lou, and Lou—recognizing Nietzsche's oftentimes difficult and demanding personality, as well as his virtual penury—ultimately left Nietzsche for Rée in the fall of that same year. Rée, who seemed far more emotionally tractable than Nietzsche, and whose family held extensive financial and land holdings in West Prussia and Pomerania, would be a far more suitable companion for the young Lou, even if she was reluctant to marry him. In any case, Lou's abandonment of Nietzsche and Rée's betrayal of personal trust, as Nietzsche saw it, left him personally wounded and emotionally eviscerated. Quite simply, what had at first promised to be a casual relation of friendship and intellectual companionship among the three had proven to become a complete disaster for Nietzsche.

8. F. Nietzsche, *Thus Spoke Zarathustra*, part 1, in *The Portable Nietzsche*, ed. and trans. W. Kaufmann (New York: Viking Press, 1968), p. 152. (Hereafter all references to *Thus Spoke Zarathustra* will be from this volume and cited as Z.)

9. All natural processes—organic and inorganic—are thus active transformations, and for Nietzsche, this means that nature (and life, especially) is fundamentally affirmative in character. In developing his notion of "will to power," Nietzsche's understanding of physical theory was very much influenced by his reading the eighteenth-century Jesuit mathematician Joseph Ruggiero Boscovitch's work, *A Theory of Natural Philosophy Reduced to a Single Law of the Actions Existing in Nature* (1758). Boscovitch maintained that the atom was not a solid particle, but rather, a nonmaterial center of "force." This *force* is the sole constituent of reality itself, or as Nietzsche would prefer to term it, stressing the innate "activity" of the natural order, "actuality." In a letter to Peter Gast (March 20, 1882), he says, for Boscovitch, "there is no 'matter' anymore—except as a source of popular belief. The *force of gravity* is, like the *vis inertiae*, certainly a manifestation of force, simply because force is all there is! . . . But if one goes along with [Robert] Mayer [*Mechanics of Heat*] in still believing in matter and in solid corpo-

real atoms, then one cannot decree that there is only *one* force. . . . Ultimately even Mayer has a second force in the background, the *primum mobile*, God,—besides motion itself. And he certainly needs God" (*Selected Letters*, pp. 182–83). From a draft written in the late 1880s, he would continue this line of thought (already clearly present in *GS*, sec. 109): "The mechanistic world is imagined in terms of a world as presented to eye and touch (as a world 'in motion'), in such a way that it can be calculated, in such a way that causing units are supposed, 'things,' 'atoms,' whose effect remains constant (the false concept of the subject carried across into the concept of the atom). . . . If we eliminate all these trimmings, no things remain but dynamic quanta, in a relation of tension to other dynamic quanta, whose essence consists in their being related to all other quanta, in their 'effect' on these" (*Selected Letters*, p. 182). These views would be more clearly stated in *Beyond Good and Evil* (sec. 36), when he effectively defines what he means by the "will to power": "Suppose all organic functions could be traced back to this will to power and one could also find in it the solution of the problem of procreation and nourishment—it is *one* problem—then one would have gained the right to determine *all* efficient force univocally as—*will to power*. The world viewed from inside, the world defined and determined according to its 'intelligible character'—it would be 'will to power' and nothing else" (p. 48).

10. *GS*, sec. 310, pp. 247–48. Nietzsche composed this section while he was spending the winter and spring of 1881–82 on the Ligurian coast of Italy. He recounts the visit and the importance it would have in inspiring his later *Zarathustra*, in *Ecce Homo* ("Thus Spoke Zarathustra," sec 1): "The following winter I stayed in that charming quiet bay of Rapallo which, not far from Genoa, is cut out between Chiavari and the foothills of Portofino. My health could have been better . . . my small *albergo* [was] situated right at the sea so that the high sea made it impossible to sleep at night. . . . In spite of this it was this winter and under these unfavorable circumstances that my *Zarathustra* came into being. Mornings I would walk in a southerly direction on the splendid road to Zoagli, going up past pines with a magnificent view of the sea; in the afternoon, whenever my health permitted it, I walked around the whole bay from Santa Margherita all the way to Portofino" (p. 297).

11. "The aphorism, the apothegm, in which I am the first among the Germans to be a master are the forms of *eternity*; it is my ambition to say in ten sentences what everyone else says in a book—what everyone else does *not* say in a book." *Twilight of the Idols*, "Skirmishes," sec. 51, in Kaufmann's *The Portable Nietzsche*, pp. 555–56.

12. Such an understanding dramatically anticipates what, for contemporary usage, is generally taken to be "nonessentialist" ways of thinking.

13. *GS*, secs. 110–13, pp. 169–73.

14. "On Truth and Lie in an Extra-Moral Sense," in Kaufmann's *The Portable Nietzsche*, pp. 46–47. The complete text (*KSA* 1: 873–90) is to be found in F. Nietzsche, *Philosophy and Truth: Selections from Nietzsche's Notebooks of the Early 1870s*, ed. and trans. Daniel Breazeale (Atlantic Highlands, N.J.: Humanities Press, 1979), pp. 78–97. The "leaf" example is an instructive way of showing how we come to *construct* what were traditionally held to be "essential forms" or "conceptual identities." The point is that through a *movement* of thought (i.e., by comparing and contrasting examples, through abstracting away differences), we arrive at what *seems* to be, and what, practically speaking, serves us *as*, a stable identity—or essence, or form. Thus, identity for Nietzsche, is derived from (and is "constructed" out of) a preceding, initial set of differences. Otherwise stated, the metaphorical precedes the literal, and the consequence is, for Nietzsche, that truth itself becomes problematic. On the multiple senses

of "truth" in Nietzsche, see John Wilcox, *Truth and Value in Nietzsche: A Study of His Metaethics and Epistemology* (Ann Arbor: University of Michigan Press, 1974).

The "leaf" example is also an ironic observation by Nietzsche on Goethe's pathetic attempts to actually find such an ideal form, so as to further his own scientific investigations and to serve as a source of poetic inspiration. In his case, he was seeking to find the archetypal "essence" of all plants (i.e., the "primal plant") in, of all places, the Public Gardens of Palermo: "Early this morning I went alone to the Public Gardens . . . but, before I knew it, another spirit seized me. . . . Seeing such a variety of new and renewed forms, my old fancy suddenly came back to mind: Among this multitude [of plants], might I not discover the Primal Plant? There certainly must be one. Otherwise, how could I recognize that this or that form *was* a plant if all were not built upon the same model? . . . With this model and the key to it, it will be possible to go on forever inventing plants and know that their existence is logical; that is to say, if they do not actually exist, they could, for they are not the shadowy phantoms of a vain imagination, but possess an inner necessity and truth. The same law will be applicable to all other living organisms" (J. W. Goethe, *Italian Journey*, trans. W. H. Auden and Elizabeth Mayer [London: Penguin, 1962], pp. 258–59, 310–11).

15. In a letter to the Danish literary critic and historian, Georg Brandes (December 2, 1887), Nietzsche remarks, "A few readers whom one personally knows, and no other readers—that is really one of my wishes. . . . You see what posthumous thoughts I live among. But a philosophy like mine is like a grave—one does not live with others any more. *Bene vixit qui bene latuit* [he lives well who hides himself well]—that is what is written on Descartes' tombstone—an epitaph if ever there was one!" *Selected Letters*, pp. 278–80. Descartes assumed this motto (from Ovid, *Tristia* III. iv. 25) under the threat of persecution from the Inquisition, when he was about to publish his early treatise, *The World*. He mentions the circumstances of his caution, his decision not to publish the work, in a letter to Father Mersenne (March 1636): "Doubtless you know that Galileo was recently censured by the Inquisitors of the Faith, and that his views about the movement of the earth were condemned as heretical. I must tell you that all the things I explained in my treatise, which included the doctrine of the movement of the earth, were so interdependent that it is enough to discover that one of them is false to know that all the arguments I was using are unsound. Though I thought they were based on very certain and evident proofs, I would not wish, for anything in the world, to maintain them against the authority of the Church. I know that it might be said that not everything which the Roman Inquisitors decide is automatically an article of faith, before it is decided upon by a General Council. But I am not so fond of my own opinions as to want to use such quibbles to be able to maintain them. I desire to live in peace and to continue the life I have begun under the motto *Bene vixit, bene qui latuit*. And so I am more happy to be delivered from the fear of my work's making unwanted acquaintances than I am unhappy at having lost the time and trouble which I spent on its composition." *Descartes: Philosophical Letters*, ed. and trans. Anthony Kenny (Oxford: Clarendon Press, 1970), pp. 25–26.

16. This was one of the important issues Nietzsche raised in his earlier work, *The Birth of Tragedy*, when the "Apollonian vision" of the traditional gods and heroes was set forth as a protective myth or "illusion" to shroud the Greeks from the painful and destructive "truth" that reality itself is meaningless, painful, and pointless.

17. It is perhaps in this sense that one should interpret the sense of the subtitle Nietzsche joins to *Thus Spoke Zarathustra*, namely, "A Book for Everyone and No One."

18. Nietzsche met Malwida von Meysenbug in Bayreuth in 1872 at the Wagner household. She had sympathized with the popular uprising during the 1848 revolution in Germany and moved to London, where she lived for years in political exile. A close friend of Russian émigré Alexander Herzen, she would later adopt his daughter, Olga, upon his death. She became a very close friend and trusted confidant of Nietzsche as well as of the Wagners and was a friend of other such notable figures as Mazzini, Garibaldi, Renan, Michelet, Baudelaire, and Berlioz. Malwida was regarded as one of the foremost proponents of equal rights for women and worked tirelessly for their advancement in education and politics. Her major work of three volumes, *Memoirs of an Idealist*, addresses these and many other related issues in detail. Together with Paul Rée and one of his former students, Albert Brenner, Nietzsche would pass the winter of 1876 through the spring of 1877 in Sorrento with Malwida trying to recover from a particularly serious recurrence of his illness. In fact, this would be his second leave of absence from the University of Basel due to reasons of extremely poor health. Later, Malwida would establish her permanent residence in Rome, where she conducted a regular gathering of visiting friends, intellectuals, artists, and musicians. It would be through her circle of friends that she would bring Nietzsche and Lou Salomé together in 1882.

19. Letter to Malwida von Meysenbug, May 1887, in *Selected Letters*, p. 266. Recall that Nietzsche himself died in 1900. As he remarked in *The Gay Science*, "We, too, do what all prudent masks do. . . . But there are also other ways and tricks when it comes to associating with or passing among men—for example, as a ghost, which is altogether advisable if one wants to get rid of them quickly and make them afraid. Example: One reaches out for us but gets no hold of us. That is frightening. Or we enter through a closed door. Or after all lights have been extinguished. Or after we have died. The last is the trick of *posthumous* people par excellence . . . it is only after death that we shall enter *our* life and become alive, oh, very much alive, we posthumous people" (sec. 365, p. 321).

20. "Formation" should be understood in the broadly construed German sense of *Bildung*, that is, the "education" of the individual, predicated upon his or her own abilities, experiences, and goals. Thus, formal educational instruction, as well social and cultural formation, all enter into the "education" of the individual, in an ongoing personal itinerary of maturation and development. Nietzsche's concern with the individual's educational and cultural formation is consistently stressed throughout the course of his work, from the early essays ("Schopenhauer as Educator," "On the Uses and Disadvantages of History for Life" in his *Unmodern Observations*) right through his final *Ecce Homo*. A satisfactory formation, for Nietzsche, would, at the very least, demand the cultivation of a sense of personal autonomy, the capacity to critically understand one's contemporary culture and its historical antecedents, as well as the responsibility to formulate one's own well-considered set of values and judgments. Understandably, then, Nietzsche's audience is at once conceived to be "multiple" and never "just anybody." The objectives, strategies, and tactics employed by the author in the composition of his text will inevitably be met with corresponding, though different, considerations and interests on the part of each reader. It is precisely in deference to and out of respect for the latter that Nietzsche writes as he does: rarely in a universal mode of address, never with the sense that a purely formal and abstract argument should (or, in fact, could) compel assent indifferently, to the always real concerns of an individual's life.

21. In a letter to Reinhart von Seydlitz of the same year (February 12, 1888), Nietz-

sche would say: "My formula for this is the 'transvaluation of all values.'" *Selected Letters*, p. 283.

22. For a discussion of this topic in Nietzsche, see Michel Foucault, "A Preface to Transgression," in his *Language, Counter-Memory, Practice* (Ithaca: Cornell University Press, 1977), pp. 29–52. In any case, we should be clear here that this entire system is part of what Nietzsche means by *God*, taken in the *broader sense*: the whole tradition-ally justified order of the social symbolic—its rules, laws, reasons, codes of value, and behavior. The *death of God* will thus be, in part, a de-legitimizing of this whole order, a withdrawal of our assent to its presumed absolute authority. This poses a particularly difficult problem for Nietzsche, however, in that we can only "know ourselves" in the terms afforded us by the language, concepts, and codes of our social symbolic order: hence, in section 354 of *GS*, he will say that it is only as a social, or "herd," animal that we can self-consciously come to "know" ourselves—and this will necessarily be an "average" understanding. While all our *actions* are personal and unique, as soon as we translate them into the meaningful, linguistic terms of a "knowing consciousness," they no longer seem to be. Rather than following Socrates' injunction to "know thyself," Nietzsche will rather follow Pindar's advice to "become what you are." That is, to deter-mine one's own values, apart from the "herd," to cultivate one's own singular "inter-ests," and to discipline one's own habits and "instincts."

23. Gilles Deleuze, "Nomad Thought," in *The New Nietzsche*, ed. D. Allison (Cam-bridge: MIT Press, 1985), p. 143.

24. For an extended discussion of this, see part 1 of Nietzsche's *Beyond Good and Evil*, trans. W. Kaufmann (New York: Vintage, 1966), "On the Prejudices of Philoso-phers," esp. sec. 2, pp. 9–11, and sec. 20, pp. 27–28.

25. The empirical claim for such a totalized system is one of the enduring charms of traditional thought: from Jorge Luis Borges's "Great Library of China," preceded by Leibniz's encyclopedia of compossibilities, back through St. Augustine's somewhat leaden expression of the divine comprehension of all possibles: "The fact is that God, whose knowledge is simple in its multiplicity, and one in its diversity, comprehends all incomprehensible things with an incomprehensible comprehension" (St. Augustine, *City of God*, trans. G. Walsh, D. Zema, G. Monahan, and D. Honan, ed. V. Bourke [New York: Image Books, 1958], book 12, chap. 19).

26. *GS*, sec. 110, "Origin of Knowledge," pp. 169–71.

27. Surely, this was one of Nietzsche's principal concerns in analyzing the Dionysian and Apollonian motifs in *The Birth of Tragedy*. In fact, he saw these two motifs as typical responses Greek culture took to ensure its own survival, responses to the basic motivational concerns of life: precisely to "the question mark concerning existence," in Schopenhauer's terms. Nietzsche discusses this insight at length in *GS*, sec. 357, pp. 304–10.

28. Note from *KSA* 7: 109. The text of *The Gay Science* literally foams with exam-ples of ad hominem argumentation; e.g., his frequent discussions of various philosophi-cal positions advanced by Wagner, Schopenhauer, Spinoza, Kant, Plato, "the English moralists"—Hume, Mill, Spencer—and so forth almost invariably turn on some per-sonal bias, prejudice, or on some perceived human fault on their part.

29. A typical example of this claim is given at length in section 2 of the introduction to *GS*, pp. 33–35.

30. Cf. Hobbes, *Leviathan* (Chicago: Henry Regnery, 1956), part 1, chap. 11, e.g., p. 94: "Fear of oppression, disposes a man to anticipate or to seek aid by society: for there is no other way by which a man can secure his life and liberty."

31. Doubtless, Nietzsche's understanding was also tempered by his reading of Ludwig Feuerbach, especially his *On the Essence of Christianity* (1841), which stresses the anthropological origins of religion, as well as by the traditional texts of Niccolò Machiavelli and, especially, the Roman philosopher-poet Lucretius. In fact, Nietzsche had written one of his earliest essays on this very subject, "On Christianity," toward the end of April 1862, clearly indicating Feuerbach's influence. The text is to be found in *Nietzsches Werke, Historisch-Kritisch Gesamtausgabe* (Munich: C. H. Beck, 1934–40), vol. 2, p. 63.

32. *GS*, sec. 127, p. 183. Cf. also *WP*, secs. 135–216, pp. 85–127.

33. *GS*, sec. 135, pp. 187–88.

34. *GS*, sec. 112, pp. 172–73; sec. 370, pp. 327–31.

35. Perhaps this is nowhere more directly stated than in St. Thomas Aquinas's doctrine "On the Various Kinds of Law," in his *Summa Theologica*, I–II, qq. 91–95: (1) Eternal law: "Law is nothing else but a dictate of practical reason emanating from the ruler who governs a perfect community. Now it is evident, granted that the world is ruled by divine providence . . . that the whole community of the universe is governed by the divine reason. Therefore the very notion of the government of things in God, the ruler of the universe, has the nature of a law. And since the divine reason's conception of things is not subject to time, but is eternal . . . therefore it is that this kind of law must be called eternal." Thomas goes on to specify that (2) "natural law" is man's participation in the "eternal law." (3) "From the precepts of the natural law . . . human reason needs to proceed to the more particular determination of certain matters. These particular determinations, devised by human reason, are called human laws." (4) "Since man is ordained to an end of eternal happiness which exceeds man's natural ability . . . therefore it was necessary that, in addition to the natural and the human law, man should be directed to his end by a law given by God. . . . It was necessary for this purpose that a divine law [i.e., the eternal law, as *revealed* in the Holy Scriptures] should supervene. . . . In order, therefore, that no evil might remain unforbidden and unpunished, it was necessary for the divine law to supervene, whereby all sins are forbidden." *Introduction to St. Thomas Aquinas*, ed. and trans. Anton Pegis (New York: Random House, 1948), pp. 616–22.

36. See esp. *GM*, essay 2, sec. 7, pp. 67–69; essay 3, sec. 28, pp. 162–63.

37. A recent Gallup poll indicates the depth and strength of contemporary American piety. In a book by George Gallup and James Castelli, *The People's Religion: American Faith in the '90s* (New York: Macmillan, 1990), the poll shows that nine out of ten Americans say they have never doubted the existence of God. Eight of ten Americans say they believe in a Judgment Day. Seven out of ten say they believe in life after death, and 37 percent of Americans say they believe in the Devil.

38. *GS*, sec. 51, p. 115; sec. 319, p. 253; sec. 324, p. 255.

39. *GS*, sec. 353, pp. 296–97.

40. In Kaufmann's *The Portable Nietzsche*, pp. 42–43.

41. *GS*, secs. 109–14, pp. 167–75; sec. 121, p. 178.

42. This recalls the prophet Job's own lament (Job 23:3, 6, 8; 29:2–3): "Oh, that today I might find him . . . would that he himself might heed me! . . . But if I go to the east, he is not there; or to the west, I cannot perceive him: where the north enfolds him, I behold him not; by the south he is veiled, and I see him not. . . . Oh, that I were as in the months past! As in the days when God watched over me, while he kept his lamp shining above my head, and by his light I walked through darkness." (All scripture cites in this book are taken from the New American Bible.) One is also reminded of

Diogenes the cynic, who wandered about other marketplaces with a lantern, looking for an "honest" man.

43. *GS*, sec. 125, pp. 181–82.

44. On the traditional doctrines of causality, see Aristotle's *Physics*, book 2. For their relation to the Thomistic proofs of God's existence, see St. Thomas Aquinas, *Summa Theologica* I, q. 2, art. 3., in Pegis, *Introduction to St. Thomas Aquinas*.

45. On this matter, the reader should consult, especially, Martin Heidegger's 1957 essay, "The Onto-Theo-Logical Constitution of Metaphysics," in *Identity and Difference*, trans. Joan Stambaugh (New York: Harper and Row, 1969), pp. 42–76. For an excellent account of Nietzsche's relation to the metaphysical tradition, see Michel Harr, *Nietzsche and Metaphysics*, trans. M. Gendre (Albany: SUNY Press, 1996).

46. For one of the earliest, and most thorough, doctrinal elaborations of this, see St. Augustine, *De Trinitate* and *De Libero Arbitrio*.

47. *GS*, sec. 343, pp. 279–80.

48. *GS*, sec. 358, pp. 310–12.

49. *GS*, sec. 357, p. 307.

50. Traditionally, the "truths" of faith were "higher" than the "truths" of reason. This is what St. Thomas would call the "double canon" of truth, whereby philosophy would be ancillary—a handmaiden—to theology. Practical understanding of such higher truths could be perplexing indeed, however, for the ordinary individual. St. Thomas, for example, would address the seeming contradictions between reason and faith that frequently arise in the course of our experience and seek to resolve them: "Now a thing is said to be self-evident in two ways: first, in itself; secondly, in relation to us. . . . But some propositions are self-evident only to the wise, who understand the meaning of the terms of such propositions. Thus to one who understands that an angel is not a body, it is self-evident that an angel is not circumscriptively in a place. But this is not evident to the unlearned, for they cannot grasp it. . . . I Kings ii. 6: *The Lord killeth and maketh alive*. Consequently, by the command of God, death can be inflicted on any man, guilty or innocent, without any injustice whatsoever. In like manner, adultery is intercourse with another's wife; who is allotted to him by the law emanating from God. Consequently, intercourse with any woman, by the command of God, is neither adultery nor fornication.—The same applies to theft" (*Summa Theologica* I–II, q. 94, in Pegis, *Introduction to St. Thomas Aquinas*, pp. 636, 644).

51. On the crucial doctrine of analogy—which Thomas gave in his *De Veritate*, II, 11—see the account by the late–fifteenth- to early sixteenth-century Neo-Thomist thinker and prelate, Cardinal Thomas de Vio, called Cajetan, *The Analogy of Names* (*De Nominum Analogia*).

52. On Cusa, see esp. Ernst Cassirer, *The Individual and the Cosmos in Renaissance Philosophy*, trans. M. Domandi (New York: Harper and Row, 1963), pp. 7–22; and Alexander Koyré, *From the Closed World to the Infinite Universe* (New York: Harper and Row, 1958), pp. 5–27.

53. Nietzsche's 1888 work *The Antichrist* pursues these issues in a strikingly astringent tone and in unsparing detail. His critique of Christianity—as purely fictional—is perhaps best summarized in section 15: "In Christianity neither morality nor religion has even a single point of contact with reality. Nothing but imaginary *causes* ('God,' 'soul,' 'ego,' 'spirit,' 'free will'—for that matter, 'unfree will'), nothing but imaginary *effects* ('sin,' 'redemption,' 'grace,' 'punishment,' 'forgiveness of sins'). Intercourse between imaginary *beings* ('God,' 'spirits,' 'souls'); an imaginary *natural* science (anthropocentric; no trace of any concept of natural causes); an imaginary *psychology* (nothing

but self-misunderstandings, interpretations of agreeable or disagreeable general feelings—for example, of the states of the *nervus sympathicus*—with the aid of the sign language of the religio-moral idiosyncrasy: 'repentance,' 'pangs of conscience,' 'temptation by the devil,' 'the presence of God'); an imaginary *teleology* ('the kingdom of God,' 'the Last Judgment,' 'eternal life').

"This *world of pure fiction* is vastly inferior to the world of dreams insofar as the latter *mirrors* reality, whereas the former falsifies, devalues, and negates reality. Once the concept of 'nature' had been invented as the opposite of 'God,' 'natural' had to become a synonym of 'reprehensible': this whole world of fiction is rooted in *hatred* of the natural (of reality!); it is the expression of a profound vexation at the sight of reality.

"But this *explains everything*. Who alone has good reason to lie his way out of reality? He who suffers from it. But to suffer from reality is to be a piece of reality that has come to grief. The preponderance of feelings of displeasure over feelings of pleasure is the cause of this fictitious morality and religion; but such a preponderance provides the very formula for decadence" (in *The Portable Nietzsche*, pp. 581–82).

As Freud would later say, it is precisely due to this lack of contact with reality that many religious beliefs are not merely errors, or illusions, but delusions: "In the case of delusions we emphasize as essential their being in contradiction with reality" (*The Future of an Illusion*, in *The Standard Edition of the Complete Psychological Works of Sigmund Freud*, vol. 21, trans. James Strachey [London: Hogarth Press, 1961], p. 31). The "technique" of religion, Freud would remark, "consists in depressing the value of life and distorting the picture of the real world in a delusional manner—which presupposes an intimidation of the intelligence. At this price, by forcibly fixing them in a state of psychical infantilism and by drawing them into a mass-delusion, religion succeeds in sparing many people an individual neurosis. But hardly anything more" (*Civilization and Its Discontents*, in *Standard Edition of Freud*, vol. 21, pp. 84–85).

54. *GS*, sec. 343, p. 279.

55. *GS*, sec. 347, pp. 287–90.

56. *GS*, sec. 343, pp. 279–80.

57. *GS*, sec. 377, p. 338. Perhaps influenced in part by his appreciation of the German poet Hölderlin (especially the latter's "Homecoming" and "Evening Fantasy"), Nietzsche had already composed a poem on much the same theme in August 1859 (i.e., at the age of fourteen), "Without a Homeland," in which he remarks, "And whoever knows me calls me / The homeless man" (pp. 12–13, in Philip Grundlehner's *The Poetry of Friedrich Nietzsche* [New York: Oxford University Press, 1986], which is an excellent discussion and analysis of Nietzsche's poetic works, extensive indeed). By the time this passage was written for book 5 of *The Gay Science*, Nietzsche's own passport would bear this title (*heimatlos*: stateless, without a home)—Swiss citizenship requiring an uninterrupted residence of eight years within a particular canton.

58. *GS*, sec. 108, p. 167.

59. *GS*, sec. 109, p. 168.

60. *GS*, sec. 380, p. 342.

61. *GS*, sec. 347, pp. 289–90.

62. "Who are we anyway? If we simply called ourselves, using an old expression, godless, or unbelievers, or perhaps immoralists, we do not believe that this would even come close to designating us. . . . Ours is no longer the bitterness and passion of the person who has torn himself away and still feels compelled to turn his unbelief into a new belief, a purpose, a martyrdom" (*GS*, sec. 346, p. 286).

63. The reference is to the celebrated "Defenestration of Prague" in 1618. Two

Roman Catholic emissaries from the Prince of Bavaria tried to impose religious orthodoxy on the citizens of Prague, who were largely followers of the Protestant reformer
Zwingli. The crowd at the Prague town hall became so incensed with the Catholic
emissaries that they proceeded to throw both of them out the second-story window.
Their fall was broken by a huge pile of manure, heaped against the back wall of the
town hall, which thus saved the two Catholics from injury. While the Catholic represen-
tatives saw this as divine intervention on their behalf, the Protestants in attendance
tended to regard it as just a heap of rubbish. This simple event served to trigger the
Thirty Years' War. Interestingly, see Nietzsche's remarks on "Religious Wars," *GS*, sec.
144, pp. 192–93.

64. This is one of the many insights Nietzsche draws from Ralph Waldo Emerson.
In the fall of 1881, Nietzsche composed a small notebook of epigrams and citations
directly taken from the 1858 German edition of Emerson's *Essays*. Emerson's influence
on Nietzsche is discussed at length by E. Baumgarten in his *Das Vorbild Emersons in
Werke und Leben Nietzsches* (Heidelberg, 1957); see also George Stack, *Nietzsche and
Emerson: An Elective Affinity* (Columbus: Ohio State University Press, 1992).

65. *GS*, sec. 93, p. 146.

66. *GS*, sec. 377, p. 340.

67. *GS*, sec. 377, p. 339.

68. *GS*, sec. 347, p. 288.

69. *GS*, sec. 344, pp. 281–83. Two recent volumes explore Nietzsche's highly complex reflections on the scientific issues of his day, at length and in detail: *Nietzsche,
Theories of Knowledge, and Critical Theory: Nietzsche and the Sciences I*, and *Nietzsche, Epistemology, and Philosophy of Science: Nietzsche and the Sciences II*, ed. B.
Babich and R. Cohen (Dordrecht: Kluwer, 1999). These are volumes 203 and 204,
respectively, of the much acclaimed Boston Studies in the Philosophy of Science series.

70. "We are not nearly 'German' enough, in the sense in which the word 'German'
is constantly being used nowadays, to advocate nationalism and race hatred and to be
able to take pleasure in the national scabies of the heart and blood poisoning that now
leads the nations of Europe to delimit and barricade themselves against each other as
if it were a matter of quarantine" (*GS*, sec. 377, p. 339).

71. *GS*, sec. 109, pp. 168–69.

72. Philosophy itself has done this from the very beginning, for example, with the
concept of "being"—as Nietzsche points out in his essay "Philosophy in the Tragic Age
of the Greeks": " 'Being must be given to us somehow, must be somehow attainable; if
it were not we could not have the concept' (Beneke). The concept of being! As though
it did not show its low empirical origin in its very etymology! For *esse* basically means
'to breathe.' And if man uses it of all things other than himself as well, he projects his
conviction that he himself breathes and lives by means of a metaphor, (i.e., a non-logical
process, upon all other things). He comprehends their existence as a 'breathing' by
analogy with his own. The original meaning of the word was soon blurred, but enough
remains to make it obvious that man imagines the existence of other things by analogy
with his own existence, in other words anthropomorphically and in any event, with non-
logical projection. But even for man—quite aside from his projection—the proposition
'I breathe, therefore being exists' is wholly insufficient" (trans. Marianne Cowan [Chi-
cago: Gateway, 1962], sec. 11, p. 84).

73. Nietzsche states his strongest assertions against this anthropomorphizing tendency by the natural sciences as such: "We say it is 'explanation'; but it is only in 'description' that we are in advance of the older stages of knowledge and science. We

describe better—we explain just as little as our predecessors. . . . How could we ever explain! We operate only with things which do *not* exist, with lines, surfaces, bodies, atoms, divisible times, divisible spaces—how can explanation ever be possible when we first make everything a *conception, our* conception! It is sufficient to regard science as the exactest humanizing of things that is possible; we always learn to describe ourselves more accurately by describing things and their successions. Cause and effect: there is probably never any such duality; in fact, there is a *continuum* before us, from which we isolate a few portions;—just as we always observe a motion as isolated points, and therefore do not properly see it, but infer it" (*GS*, sec. 112, pp. 172–73).

This is a striking commentary on the very foundation of modern physics, as articulated by Descartes in his *Rules for the Direction of the Mind* and the *Discourse on Method*, where he tries to establish his claim for a universally objective science (i.e., the celebrated *mathesis universalis*). In the fourth *Rule*, Descartes advances his hypothesis: "When I considered the matter more closely, I came to see that *the exclusive concern of mathematics is with questions of order or measure*, and that it is *irrelevant* whether the measure in question involves *numbers*, figures, stars, sounds, *or any other object whatever*. This made me realize that there must be a general science which explains all the points that can be raised concerning order and measure *irrespective of the subject-matter*, and that this science should be termed *mathesis universalis*—a venerable term . . . that *entitles* [all the] other sciences to be called branches of *mathematics*. How superior it is to these subordinate sciences both in utility and simplicity is clear from the fact that it covers all they deal with, and more besides" (R. Descartes, *Rules for the Direction of the Mind*, in *The Philosophical Writings of Descartes*, trans. J. Cottingham, R. Stoothoff, and D. Murdoch [Cambridge: Cambridge University Press, 1985], vol. 1, p. 19). As to the *origin* of this order, which will serve to render the sciences *universal and objective*, Descartes quite candidly admits that this order (mathematical quantifiability, which permits the analysis from simple to complex—whether in proportions, lines, figures, and so forth, and their subsequent geometrical and algebraic symbolization) is *merely supposed*: "The third [precept of method is] to direct my thoughts in an orderly manner, by *beginning* with the simplest and *most easily known* objects in order to ascend little by little, as by degrees, to knowledge of the most complex, and *by supposing some order even among objects that have no natural order of precedence*" (*Discourse on Method*, in *Philosophical Writings of Descartes*, vol. 1, p. 120, emphasis added).

74. *GS*, sec. 346, p. 286.

75. Nietzsche had discussed this issue at some length in his earlier essay on historiography of 1873, "History in the Service and Disservice of Life," effectively disputing the very distinction made by Rousseau that there was a basic and noble "human nature"—a "first nature"—that became overlaid with "culture," the corrupting influence of a "second nature." Nietzsche would maintain throughout his work that the human subject must be understood in a radically finite, historical sense, and in doing so, one could continually transform oneself, drawing upon the resources of the past and present, always in view of overcoming present faults and weaknesses—what he would characterize as the task of Zarathustra's "overman." The task of "overcoming" the so deeply enracinated effects of tradition in *The Gay Science*, to free oneself from the shadows of the "old God," is stated clearly, and more generally, in this earlier essay: "For since we happen to be the products of earlier generations, we are also the products of their blunders, passions, and misunderstandings, indeed, of their crimes; it is impossible to free ourselves completely from this chain. If we condemn those blunders and exempt

ourselves of guilt for them, we cannot ignore the fact that our existence is rooted in them. At best we create a conflict between our inherited, ancestral nature and our knowledge, and perhaps even a revolt of a strict new discipline against what was long ago inbred and inborn. We plant in ourselves a new habit, a new instinct, a second nature, so that the first nature withers. It is an attempt to give ourselves a past *a posteriori*, as it were, a past from which we prefer to be descended, as opposed to the past from which we did descend—always a risky task since it is so difficult to set limits to this rejection of the past, and because second natures are generally weaker than first natures. Too often we know the good but fail to do it because we also know the better but are incapable of doing it. But now and then a victory does occur, and for those who struggle, for those who use critical history in the service of life, there is a significant consolation in knowing that even this first nature was once a second nature, and that every victorious second nature will become a first" (F. Nietzsche, *Unmodern Observations*, ed. William Arrowsmith, trans. of "History in the Service and Disservice of Life" by G. Brown [New Haven: Yale University Press, 1990], p. 103).

76. *GS*, sec. 343, p. 279.

77. We find this sentiment quite clearly articulated by Nietzsche already by the age of seventeen: "How often the entire history of philosophy has seemed to me a tower of Babel. . . . An infinite confusion of ideas among the people is the desolate result. And major upheavals are imminent once the masses realize that the entire fabric of Christianity is grounded in assumptions: the existence of God, immortality, Biblical authority, inspiration, and yet other doctrines will forever remain problems. I have attempted to deny everything! Oh! tearing down is easy! But building up again! And even tearing down seems easier than it really is" ("Fate and History: Thoughts" [1862], in *Young Nietzsche and Philosophy: Three Juvenile Essays*, trans. R. Perkins [Mt. Pleasant, Mich.: Enigma Press, n.d.], p. 5). The text corresponds to *Historisch-Kritisch Gesamtausgabe*, vol. 2, pp. 54–59. Cf. also, *GS*, sec. 301, pp. 241–42; sec. 307, pp. 245–46.

78. *GS*, sec. 341, pp. 273–74.

79. In a note from 1881, when Nietzsche was developing his notion of the eternal return, he remarks, "Let us imprint the image of eternity upon *our* life. This thought contains far more than all those religions which hold our present lives in contempt as being ephemeral, and which have taught us to raise our sights towards some dubious, *other* life" (*KSA* 9: 503).

80. It is precisely the eternal cycle, the "cyclical movement" of the given total "quantity of forces," and this stands as a "primordial law, without exception or transgression" (*KSA* 11: 502). See below, chapter 3, on *Thus Spoke Zarathustra*, for a more comprehensive discussion of the will to power and its general importance to Nietzsche's thought.

81. *GS*, sec. 337, pp. 268–69. Nietzsche borrows this often repeated image of the golden sea from Pindar's eulogy "To Thrasybulus of Acragas: A Song for the End of a Feast." See *The Odes of Pindar*, trans. Sir John Sandys (Cambridge: Harvard University Press, 1919), p. 587.

82. *GS*, sec. 349, pp. 291–92.

CHAPTER 3

1. Letter to Carl von Gersdorff, June 28, 1883, in *Selected Letters of Friedrich Nietzsche*, ed. and trans. Christopher Middleton (Chicago: University of Chicago Press, 1969), p. 213.

2. Letter to Peter Gast, August 1883, in *Selected Letters*, p. 218.

3. Letter to Gast, September 2, 1884, in *Selected Letters*, p. 230. See also, *EH*, chap. 3, sec. 1, p. 259 where, only four years later, von Stein is said not to have understood a single word of *Zarathustra*. Remarkably, von Stein was one of only three people whom Nietzsche considered to be his intellectual peers, the other two being Wagner and Rohde.

4. Zarathustra tells the readers in part 4 ("On the Higher Man") that "I stood in the marketplace. And as I spoke to all, I spoke to none" (*Z*, p. 398). This is clearly meant to recall the earlier passage in *The Gay Science* (sec. 125), where "the madman" announced the death of God in the marketplace and was met with complete incomprehension by the people there.

5. Letter to Rée of March 21, 1882, in Lou Salomé, *Friedrich Nietzsche: The Man in His Works*, ed. and trans. Siegfried Mandel (Redding Ridge, Conn.: Black Swan, 1988), p. xliv.

6. Salomé, *Friedrich Nietzsche*, p. xliv.

7. In her later work of 1951, *Lebensrückblick*, Lou Salomé recalled that at the time, "I had to live on my mother's military pension, and that if I were to marry I would lose the small portion of that pension I received as the only daughter of a Russian nobleman" (Lou Andreas-Salomé, *Looking Back: Memoirs*, ed. Ernst Pfeiffer, trans. Breon Mitchel [New York: Paragon House, 1991], p. 47).

8. Sacro Monte rises behind the village of Orta San Giulio to an altitude of some 1,300 feet. It was dedicated to St. Francis of Assisi and has a path starting from the gateway at the Church of the Assumption that is flanked by a series of some twenty early Renaissance chapels, some of which contain figures illustrating the life of the saint, as well as having frescos by Giovanni Battista, Giovanni Mauro delle Rovere, Antonio Maria Crespi, and Giulio Cesare Procaccini.

9. In her Tautenburg journal from August 14, 1882, Lou would write of Nietzsche, "We often recall our time together in Italy, and when we climbed the . . . [and here, Lou had later excised material from her journal entry] narrow path, he said quietly, 'Sacro Monte—I thank you for the most exquisite dream of my life'" (Andreas-Salomé, *Looking Back*, p. 167).

10. Salomé, *Friedrich Nietzsche*, p. 54.

11. Curt Paul Janz, *Friedrich Nietzsche: Biographie in drei Bänden* (Munich: Carl Hanser Verlag, 1978), vol. 2, p. 148.

12. During her visit to the Bayreuth festival, Elisabeth had written to Nietzsche expressing her outrage about Lou's socially "scandalous" flirtations with the young men of the Wagner circle, especially the Russian painter (and set designer for *Parsifal*) Count Joukouski, and that she was soliciting and rejecting a host of marriage offers in function of this unspeakable behavior. Furthermore, Elisabeth wrote that Lou publicly claimed to be the most intimate of Nietzsche's friends—Nietzsche the apostate!—that she was initiated into his most secret philosophy, and that in many respects she was even more adept at dealing with his philosophical problems than Nietzsche himself. Granted that Lou had done little more than socialize with her Russian counterpart, the fact that she (rather than Elisabeth!) was taken into the very heart of the elite circle of Wagner's friends, even though Lou admitted she was virtually tone-deaf, outraged the fiercely jealous and petit bourgeois-indignant Elisabeth. What access she had to a cultural life at all beyond the provincial gloom of Naumburg (and the prospect of remaining there as a spinster for the rest of her life) was simply due to her brother. The prospect of

losing this access—and Nietzsche himself—to the wiles of a coquettish Russian girl of twenty-one simply augmented her fury.

Upon receipt of Elisabeth's flagrant accusations against Lou, Nietzsche then wrote to Lou, admonishing her to behave properly and discreetly, thus angering Lou (who had on the very same day written Nietzsche to tell him how devoted she was to Elisabeth and how Elisabeth had been "such a great help to her") in turn. Offended by the letter, Lou wrote back to Nietzsche, reprimanding him for his reproaches and put off her departure so as to rebuke Nietzsche, as well as to enjoy the festival atmosphere at Bayreuth for a few more days. Nietzsche wrote back on August 4 in an attempt to smooth out their relations a bit, explaining that it was pointless for both of them to suffer any more over the matter. Meanwhile, word of the "scandal" had spread to Paul Rée, who was staying at his family's estate in Stibbe, setting him into a fit of impassioned jealousy.

When Elisabeth and Lou regrouped in Jena on August 7 in preparation for the visit to Nietzsche, in Tautenburg at the home of Professor Gelzer, Elisabeth once again exploded in fury and venomous rage against Lou. Lou, in turn, lashed out against Elisabeth, sarcastically ridiculing Elisabeth's idealized picture of Nietzsche as a model of saintly virtue and morality. Apparently, Lou had been apprised by Paul Rée about certain sexual indiscretions Nietzsche had earlier enjoyed with a young peasant girl during the period of their Sorrento visit in 1877, as well as Rée's mentioning Nietzsche's earlier letter about a brief, trial marriage of "two years"(i.e., his inclination for a "free union" of concubinage or hetaera), not unlike Wagner's early relation with Cosima. During the Tautenburg visit, in any case, Elisabeth was virtually excluded from any significant participation between the two. Indeed, for the rest of her life Elisabeth would continue to impugn Lou on virtually every occasion she could.

For an extended discussion of Nietzsche's relation to Lou Salomé, see esp. Janz, *Friedrich Nietzsche*, vol. 2, chap. 3, pp. 110–58; and Andreas-Salomé, *Looking Back*, chap. 5, pp. 44–56.

13. A month later, in mid-December, still reeling from the loss of Lou and still furious over his sister's machinations in the whole affair, Nietzsche would write (and of this letter, only the following fragment remains):

My dears, Lou and Rée,
Do not be upset by the outbreaks of my "megalomania" or of my "injured vanity"—and even if I should happen one day to take my life because of some passion or other, there would not be much to grieve about. What do my fantasies matter to you? (Even my truths mattered nothing to you till now.) Consider me, the two of you, as a semilunatic with a sore head who has been totally bewildered by long solitude.
To this, I think, *sensible* insight into the state of things I have come after taking a huge dose of opium—in desperation. But instead of losing my reason as a result, I seem at last to have *come* to reason. Incidentally, I was really ill for several weeks; and if I tell you that I have had twenty days of Orta weather here, I need say no more.
Friend Rée, ask Lou to forgive me everything—she will give me an opportunity to forgive her too. For till now I have not forgiven her.
It is harder to forgive one's friends than one's enemies.
Lou's "justification" occurs to me . . . (*Selected Letters*, p. 198)

Some four years later, Paul Rée would in turn leave Lou when she decided to accept a marriage proposal by an older professor of oriental languages and philology,

Friedrich Carl Andreas (who, to get Lou's consent to marry him, stabbed himself in the chest, nearly killing himself). Lou would pursue her studies in psychoanalysis, and later, become a close collaborator of Freud. She would go on to write extensively her own memoirs, a novel, as well as several works on psychoanalysis, in addition to her studies of Nietzsche, Freud, Rilke, and Ibsen. After leaving Lou, Rée obtained a degree in medicine and went on to establish his practice in a small village in the Upper Engadine. He died from a fall, while hiking, in 1901.

14. *Selected Letters*, pp. 198–99.

15. As the founder of classical Zoroastrianism, the prophet Zoroaster is traditionally thought to have lived somewhat prior to the emergence of the Achaemenian empire in Persia, in the seventh century B.C. He was said to have been the author of Zoroastrianism's principal text, the *Zend Avesta*, of which only fragments remain from the earliest version.

16. *EH*, "Destiny;" sec. 3, pp. 327–28.

17. *GS*, book 5, sec. 357, p. 307.

18. Z, part 1, "Zarathustra's Prologue," sec. 3, p. 124.

19. Nietzsche himself seems to admit this at a later date, when he looks back on the composition of *Zarathustra* from the perspective of *Ecce Homo*: "Here man has been overcome at every moment; the concept of the 'overman' has here become the greatest reality" (*EH*, p. 305).

20. For an excellent and detailed account of Nietzsche's relative familiarity with Buddhist and Hindu thought, see G. M. C. Sprung, "Nietzsche's Interest in and Knowledge of Indian Thought," in *The Great Year of Zarathustra (1881–1981)*, ed. David Goicoechea (Lanham, Md.: University Press of America, 1983), pp. 166–80. Cf. also Graham Parkes, ed., *Nietzsche and Asian Thought* (Chicago: University of Chicago Press, 1991). Nietzsche was familiar with Hermann Oldenberg's biographical study of Buddhism (*Buddha. Sein Leben, seine Lehre, seine Gemeinde* [Berlin, 1881]), Jacob Wagernagel's work on Brahmin thought (*Über den Ursprung des Brahmanismus* [Basel, 1877]), Otto Böthlink's *Indische Sprüche* (Petersburg, 1870–73), and several texts from the Pali canon, as well as the excellent book by his friend, Paul Deussen, *Das System des Vedânta nach den Brama-Sûtra's des Bâdarâyana und dem Kommentare des Çankara über dieselben* (Leipzig: Brockhaus, 1883). Probably most important to the concerns of *Zarathustra*, however, was Nietzsche's reading of Friedrich Creuzer's work, *Symbolik und Mythologie der alten Völker* (Leipzig: Heyer and Lesre, 1820; 3rd ed., 1836–43), which he used in preparation for his coursework in the winter semester of 1875–76, and again in 1877–78, concerning the ancient Greek religious cults. Creuzer discusses the Persian religions and the *Zend Avesta*, in particular, at great length in his work, drawing on ancient Greek and Latin sources that were also familiar to Nietzsche.

21. This variety of personal characteristics found in the dramatic portrayal of Zarathustra is set forth severally in Nietzsche's almost reverential descriptions of the pre-Socratic philosophers, in his work of 1873, *Philosophy in the Tragic Age of the Greeks*—as, for example, in his comparison between Heraclitus and Empedocles: "Never, for example, could one imagine such pride as that of Heraclitus, simply as an idle possibility. Looked at from a general point of view, all striving for insight seems, by its very nature, dissatisfied and unsatisfactory. No one will believe, therefore, in such regal self-esteem and calm conviction that he is the only rewarded wooer of truth, except by the instruction of history that such a man did once exist. Such men live inside their own solar system; only there can we look for them. A Pythagoras, an Empedocles too, treated himself with an almost super-human esteem, almost with religious reverence, but the

great conviction of metempsychosis and of the unity of all life led him back to other human beings, for their salvation and redemption. The feeling of solitude, however, that pierced the Ephesian hermit of the temple of Artemis [i.e., Heraclitus], we can intuit only when we are freezing on wild desolate mountains of our own. No all-powerful feeling of compassionate emotions, no desire to help, to heal, to save, stream forth from Heraclitus. He is a star devoid of atmosphere. His eye, flaming toward its inward center, looks outward dead and icy, but with the semblance of sight. All around him, to the very edge of the fortress of his pride beat the waves of illusion and of wrongness. Nauseated, he turns from them. . . . He was thinking of the game of the great world-child Zeus. He did not need human beings, not even those who would benefit from his insights" (trans. Marianne Cowan [Chicago: Gateway, 1962], pp. 66–67).

22. "It is neither proper not intelligent to anticipate the least of the reader's objections. It is altogether advisable and *very astute* to let the reader *himself* express the quintessence of our philosophy" (*KSA* 9: 39).

23. For a more detailed account of Nietzsche's use of this rhetorical device, see D. Allison, "A Diet of Worms: Aposiopetic Rhetoric in *Beyond Good and Evil*," in *Nietzsche Studien, Internationales Jarbuch für die Nietzsche-Forschung 1990* (Berlin: de Gruyter, 1989), vol. 19, pp. 43–58.

24. Z, part 4, "On the Higher Man," sec. 2, p. 399.

25. Z, part 3, p. 310.

26. In his writings immediately prior to *Zarathustra*, namely, *The Gay Science*, parts 1–4, Nietzsche clearly states that he himself has personally attained this disposition of complete affirmation of all that exists—of his own life, of the history and humanity that has preceded him—even granting those disagreeable or painful components that are necessarily constitutive of human existence: "Today everybody permits himself the expression of his wish and his dearest thought; hence I, too, shall say what it is that I wish from myself today, and what was the first thought to run across my heart this year—what thought shall be for me the reason, warranty, and sweetness of my life henceforth. I want to learn more and more to see as beautiful what is necessary in things; then I shall be one of those who make things beautiful. *Amor fati* [love of fate]: let that be my love henceforth! I do not want to accuse; I do not even want to accuse those who accuse. *Looking away* shall be my only negation. And all in all and on the whole: some day I wish to be only a Yes-sayer. . . . For it is only now that the idea of a personal providence confronts us with the most penetrating force, and the best advocate, the evidence of our eyes, speaks for it—now that we can see how palpably always everything that happens to us turns out for the best. Every day and every hour, life seems to have no other wish than to prove this proposition again and again. Whatever it is, bad weather or good, the loss of a friend, sickness, slander, the failure of some letter to arrive, the spraining of an ankle, a glance into a shop, a counter-argument, the opening of a book, a dream, a fraud—either immediately or very soon after, it proves to be something that 'must not be missing'; it has a profound significance for *us*. Is there any more dangerous seduction that might tempt one to renounce one's faith in the gods of Epicurus who have no care and are unknown. . . . Indeed, now and then someone plays with us—good old chance; now and then chance guides our hand, and the wisest providence could not think up a more beautiful music than that which our foolish hand produces then" (*GS*, part 4, secs. 276–77, pp. 223–24). It should be noted that Nietzsche was rewriting and editing the final draft of *The Gay Science*, parts 1–4, at the very moment he was enjoying Lou Salomé's companionship, in August 1882 in Tautenberg, thinking it would continue and flourish.

27. "The word 'overman' . . . has been understood almost everywhere with the utmost innocence in the sense of those very values whose opposite Zarathustra was meant to represent—that is, as an 'idealistic' type of a higher kind of man, half 'saint,' half 'genius'" (*EH*, vol. 3, sec. 1, p. 261).

28. *BGE*, part 1, sec. 36, p. 48.

29. In one of Nietzsche's earliest formulations of this, he attributes the precise return of all things to the teachings of the Pythagoreans in his essay of 1873, "History in the Service and Disservice of Life": "In point of fact, what was once possible could be possible again only if the Pythagoreans were right in their conviction that, given the same configurations of heavenly bodies, earthly events must be repeated down to the minutest detail—so that every time the stars resume a certain pattern, a Stoic will conspire with an Epicurean and murder Caesar, and every time they reach another position, Columbus will discover America. Only if the earth always began its drama anew after the fifth act; only if it were certain that the same tangle of motives, the same deus ex machina, the same catastrophe would recur at fixed intervals." He then qualifies this by remarking, "which is improbable unless astronomers become astrologers once more." In *Unmodern Observations*, ed. William Arrowsmith, trans. Gary Brown (New Haven: Yale University Press, 1990), p. 97.

30. *The Zend Avesta*, part 1, "The Vendidad," trans. James Darmesteter (Delhi: Motilal Banarsidass, 1988), esp. chap. 19, sec. 2, 29–34, pp. 212–14.

31. Bernd Magnus discusses this issue at length in his analysis of the eternal return. See his *Nietzsche's Existential Imperative* (Bloomington: Indiana University Press, 1978), esp. chaps. 4–6.

32. The point is central to Pierre Klossowski's highly original reading of the eternal return, in his *Nietzsche and the Vicious Circle*, trans. D. Smith (Chicago: University of Chicago Press, 1998). Perhaps a more conventionally empirical argument against such an identical reaggregation of the "returned" human subject would *begin* with the rather sobering admission that each single human being is roughly composed of 10^{13} bodily cells and is host to 10^{14} more bacterial cells: a biological composite, then, of 1.1×10^{14} cells. Even given the persistence—or "recurrence" of the "same" cells, on a *biological* level, they would have, properly speaking, only *one* precise aggregation or arrangement out of 10^{28} possibilities—and this, at just one moment of one individual's life.

33. *GS*, sec. 341, pp. 273–74.

34. In one of his more dramatic accounts in support of the "scientific" validity of the eternal return, Nietzsche actually invokes the thermodynamic theories of William Thompson, First Baron Kelvin. See, for example, *WP*, sec. 1066.

35. *KSA* 10: 115.

36. *KSA* 10: 521.

37. "I have come across this idea in earlier thinkers: every time it was determined by other ulterior considerations (—mostly theological, in favor of the *creator spiritus*)" (*WP*, sec. 1066, p. 548). One such figure he has in mind is Plato, specifically the account of the world's nature and creation as presented in the *Timaeus*: "Now the creation took up the whole of each of the four elements, for the creator compounded the world out of all the fire and all the water and all the air and all the earth. . . . Of design . . . [the world] was created thus—his own waste providing his own food" (Plato, *Timaeus*, 32C5–33C9, trans. B. Jowett, in *Plato: The Collected Dialogues*, ed. Edith Hamilton and Huntington Cairns [Princeton: Princeton University Press, 1963], p. 1164). Nietzsche's paraphrase in *The Will to Power*: "The new world-conception.—The world exists . . . but it has never begun to become and never ceased from passing away—it maintains

itself in both.—It lives on itself: its excrements are its food" (sec. 1066, p. 548). Nietzsche immediately gives a qualification of the *Timaeus* account: "We need not worry for a moment about the hypothesis of a *created* world. The concept 'create' is today completely indefinable."

38. As Nietzsche had succinctly expressed this in section 109 of *The Gay Science*, "There is nobody who commands, nobody who obeys, nobody who trespasses. . . . There are no purposes" (p. 168).

39. For Nietzsche, sensible reality alone serves as the basis for all life and for all understanding of one's life. As he would remark in *Beyond Good and Evil*, "All credibility, all good conscience, all evidence of truth come only from the senses" (sec. 134, p. 88).

40. Zarathustra cannot even converse about the religious and metaphysical errors of the old saint in the forest in section 2 of "Zarathustra's Prologue." When he asks the saint about his own religious concerns, Zarathustra is answered with a barely intelligible salad of words: "I make songs and sing them; and when I make songs, I laugh, cry, and hum: thus I praise God. With singing, crying, laughing, and humming, I praise the god who is my god." Given these ravings, Zarathustra's only response is to walk away: "When Zarathustra had heard these words he bade the saint farewell and said: 'What could I have to give you?' " (p. 124).

41. For an extended discussion of "the death of God" and, for Nietzsche, the enormity of its consequences, see chapter 2 above.

42. Z, part 1, sec. 3, "Zarathustra's Prologue," p. 124.

43. Z, part 1, sec. 3, "Zarathustra's Prologue," p. 125.

44. As Nietzsche remarked in section 109 of *The Gay Science*, "When will all these shadows of God cease to darken our minds? When will we complete our de-deification of nature? When may we begin to '*naturalize*' humanity in terms of a pure, newly discovered, newly redeemed nature?" (pp. 168–69).

45. *EH*, chap. 4, sec. 3, p. 328.

46. The Zarathustra who begins his descent from the mountain at the start of section 2 of the prologue is met by an old man—the Saint—in the forest who recalls an earlier encounter with him, "years ago": "But he has changed. At that time you carried your ashes to the mountains: would you carry your fire to the valleys?" (p. 122). The earlier account would suggest Zoroaster's account of the soul being led up above the sacred mountain, Hara-berezaiti, leaving the decaying world for the permanent realm of paradise (*Zend Avesta*, p. 213). But this encounter is clearly with a reborn Zarathustra who has abjured all "otherworlds," declaring that God is dead. The old man remarks to Zarathustra that his new teaching may well be inflammatory: "Do you fear to be punished as an arsonist?" (Z, part 1, p. 122).

This phoenix-like rebirth at the start of *Zarathustra* also seems to point to a personal event in Nietzsche's life, when he claimed "a sudden and profoundly decisive change in my taste, especially in music." He claimed to be "reborn" at the time: a "phoenix of music flew past" himself and his friend and associate, Peter Gast, while visiting the spa town of Recoaro, Italy, in the spring of 1881. In fact, Nietzsche dates the initial conception of *Zarathustra* part 1 from that very moment, and its conclusion in February 1883 at the very moment Wagner died, in Venice—"eighteen months for the pregnancy." He discusses this in the first section of his chapter on *Zarathustra* in *Ecce Homo* (p. 294) and refers us to the very last lines of the last section of *Zarathustra*, part 1, which he reprints in the preface to *Ecce Homo*, and which dramatically states his own newfound personal and intellectual independence.

47. *Z*, part 2, "On Self-Overcoming," p. 225.

48. Cf. Luke 3:23. To sharpen the parallel with Jesus, Nietzsche rewrites the opening passage of "Zarathustra's Prologue," which had previously appeared as section 342 in *The Gay Science*, specifically omitting the reference he earlier had made to Lake Urmi, or Urmia—in the northwestern mountains of what is presently Iran—the region where the historical Zoroaster was believed to have lived in the mid-seventh century B.C. The lessening of references to the historical Zoroaster—after the prologue—is made further evident by Nietzsche's frequent paraphrasing of the Gospels, as well as by many allusions to the Old and New Testaments. Far more relevant to engage the Bible than the *Zend Avesta*, Nietzsche's critique of the metaphysical moralization of nature thus falls directly on the tradition of Christian—rather than Zoroastrian— doctrine. While Nietzsche had claimed, in *Ecce Homo*, that Zoroaster should be the first to recognize the error of this metaphysical teaching, he effectively shifts this acknowledgment to the figure of Jesus in part 4 of *Zarathustra*. After repeatedly having characterized the traditional Christian morality as a sad and gloomy affair, a doctrine that burdens one down with "the spirit of gravity," so that "the greatest sin here on earth" seems to have been *laughter* (*Z*, part 4, sec. 16, p. 405), Nietzsche paraphrases Jesus' Sermon on the Plain (Luke 6:25): "Woe unto those who laugh here." Nietzsche concludes part 4 by having the lion (Christ is "the Lion of Judah" in the New Testament) shake his head in amazement and burst out into roaring laughter.

49. For a remarkably fascinating revisit to this mythically charged place—and age— see Roberto Calasso, *The Marriage of Cadmus and Harmony*, trans. T. Parks (New York: Knopf, 1993).

50. For an account of *The Bacchae*, see above, chapter 1. Thebes, incidentally, was held to be the birthplace of Dionysus himself—his mother Semele, being one of the daughters of King Cadmus and the goddess Harmonia.

51. Given Nietzsche's repeated insistence on the highly personal nature of *Zarathustra*, and how it expressed his own state of mind at the time, there appear to be two additional personal allusions to Zarathustra's "mountain." On the one hand, it suggests the Grail mountain (Monsalvat), as expressed, for example, in Wagner's *Parsifal*—and in this respect, Zarathustra ironically refers to the figure of Amfortas, who due to his wounds, is unable to bear children, and who is incapable of death. The Zoroaster legend, however, suggests that he will bear children, and—absent the Grail and spear—will be followed by a reign of millennia (precisely, through his children). Likewise, Zarathustra will mimic Parsifal's quest for retrieving the spear (which killed Jesus on the cross and had wounded Amfortas), by leaving the mountain. Zarathustra, however, will descend to *give* his gift, rather than to *receive* a mystical offering of redemption. (Indeed, Nietzsche would be most explicit on this opposition between himself and Wagner in *The Case of Wagner, Nietzsche contra Wagner, Ecce Homo*, and the celebrated section 1052 from *The Will to Power* notes.) Thus, Zarathustra will conduct a life of tragic affirmation, in opposition to Wagner's romantic quest of Christian redemption.

What further complicates the allusiveness of Zarathustra's mountain is that—with Mount Cithaeron as a guiding motif—it also carries with it the meaning of perhaps Nietzsche's most personally erotic adventure, his presumed seduction of Lou Salomé in the spring of 1882 on Sacro Monte, in the northern lake district of Italy. One can only say "presumed" because Lou destroyed the pages of her diary concerning their visit to the mountain. Nonetheless, both would refer to the afternoon spent on the gentle slopes of Sacro Monte—having escaped the presence of Lou's mother (as chaperone) and Paul Rée (who was vying with Nietzsche for Lou's favors)—as "the miracle of Sacro Monte."

52. Mark 1:14–15.

53. Matthew 5:22.

54. *GS*, book 3, sec. 116, p. 174.

55. See *GM*, part 1, sec. 10, pp. 36ff.

56. Much of the irony and humor in Nietzsche's caricature of its residents derives from his reading of Sebastian Brant's *The Ship of Fools* (*Das Narrenschiff*), first published in Basel in 1494. The book is composed of 112 sections in rhymed prose. Highly aphoristic in character, each section—much like *Zarathustra* itself—is captioned with an admonition or injunction concerning human customs, follies, and foibles. The book was extremely popular at the time and was widely translated. Incidentally, it was the first published piece of literature to mention the discovery of America by Christopher Columbus—a figure with whom Nietzsche readily identified himself. Brant studied philosophy, especially the work of Aristotle, at the University of Basel, and then went on to receive doctorates in canon and civil law, which he taught (in addition to humanities) at the University of Basel. Later, he became the municipal chancellor of Strasbourg and a devoted friend of Erasmus. Nietzsche doubtless discussed *The Ship of Fools* with his close friend and colleague Wilhelm Vischer, professor of history at the University of Basel and author of *The History of the University of Basel from 1460–1529*, who wrote extensively on Brant. In section 13 of Brant's work, "Of Amours" (*Von Buolschafft*), Brant mentions the medieval legend of Aristotle's being seduced by Phyllis—the lover of Philip of Macedon's son, young Alexander—into having him play "pony" with Phyllis riding on his back, wielding a "whip" of flowering branches (see the photos on page 156). The section begins with Venus's injunction, "My rope pulls many fools about; Ape, cuckold, ass, and silly lout; Whom I seduce, deceive, and flout." The imagery will surface in *Zarathustra*, book 1, "On Little Old and Young Women," when the little old woman tells Zarathustra, "You are going to women? Do not forget the whip!" (p. 179; see also *BGE*, sec. 147, p. 89).

57. Creuzer's *Symbolik und Mythologie der Alten Völker* had mistakenly given alternate etymologies for "Zoraster," namely, "Zeretoschtro-Zeratuscht," which he translated as "Golden Star"—"Star of Light," or "Shining Gold." Cf. Janz, *Friedrich Nietzsche*, vol. 2, p. 230.

58. Z, part 1, "Zarathustra's Prologue," sec. 1, p. 122.

59. Cf. Matthew 8:1; John 3:31.

60. *Republic* 327Aff., 354A. On Bendis, see Strabo, *Geography*, X.466.

61. *Republic*, 507C7.

62. Z, part 2, "On Priests," p. 205.

63. See Z, part 2, "On Priests," p. 203: "He whom they call Redeemer has put them in fetters: in fetters of false values and delusive words. Would that someone would yet redeem them from their Redeemer. . . . They would have to sing better songs for me to learn to have faith in their Redeemer." Zarathustra's remark sarcastically reverses the final chorus of Wagner's *Parsifal*, first produced in the early summer of 1882 at Bayreuth. In the last scene, Parsifal, who has reunited the spear of Longinus with the Holy Grail, out of pity for the suffering Amfortas (himself an emblem of Jesus' suffering for humanity on the cross: the name "Amfortas" derives from the Latin *infirmitas*, or "weakness," the weakness or infirmity of human suffering, which can only be redeemed by pity), ascends the stairs to the altar in the church of the Grail Castle, grasps the Grail itself, and then falls prostrate into silent prayer. Surrounded by the squires, youths, and

knights of the Grail, the voice of an angelic choir descends from above the altar's cross, announcing: "Highest miracle of Salvation! Redemption to the Redeemer." With an added touch of irony, given the fact that the spear initially drew Christ's blood on the cross, then caused the bleeding wound of Amfortas, and that the Grail itself caught the blood of Jesus, Zarathustra would go on to say, "folly taught that with blood one proved truth. But blood is the worst witness of truth; blood poisons even the purest doctrine and turns it into delusion and hatred of the heart. And if a man goes through fire for his doctrine—what does that prove?" (Z, pp. 204–5).

In his preface to the second volume of *Human, All Too Human*, written in 1886, Nietzsche reflected back on his shock and sense of loss and betrayal in what he saw as Wagner's complete abdication to the forces of reaction—to a pietistic Christianity, to a rabid German nationalism and anti-Semitism, and to a sentimental and deluded form of cultural romanticism at the very moment Europe needed more than ever to have confidence in its future and to have its intellectual forces awakened to the profound challenges posed by modernity itself. He would remark, "At that time [July1882] it was indeed high time *to say farewell*: and I immediately received a confirmation of the fact. Richard Wagner, seemingly the all-conquering, actually a decaying, despairing romantic, suddenly sank down helpless and shattered before the Christian cross. . . . Was there no German with eyes in his head, empathy in his conscience, for this dreadful spectacle? Was I the only one who—suffered from it? Enough, this unexpected event illumined for me like a flash of lightning the place I had left—and likewise gave me those subsequent horrors that he feels who has passed through a terrible peril unawares. As I went on alone, I trembled; not long afterwards I was sick, more than sick, I was weary of the unending disappointment with everything we modern men have left to inspire us, of the energy, labour, hope, youth, love everywhere *dissipated*; weary with disgust at the femininity and ill-bred rapturousness of this romanticism, weary of the whole idealist pack of lies and softening of conscience that had here once again carried off the victory over one of the bravest; weary, last but not least, with the bitterness of a suspicion—that, after this disappointment, I was condemned to mistrust more profoundly, despise more profoundly, to be more profoundly alone than ever before. My *task*—where had it gone?" (*HAH*, vol. 2, preface, sec. 3, pp. 210–12).

64. Z, part 1, "Zarathustra's Prologue," sec. 4, p. 127.
65. Letter to Erwin Rohde, February 22, 1884, in *Selected Letters*, pp. 220–21.
66. Letter to Malwida von Meysenbug, first week of June 1884, in *KSA, Sämtliche Briefe*, vol. 6, pp. 509–10.
67. Letter to Heinrich von Stein, December 1882, in *Selected Letters*, p. 197.
68. Letter to Paul Deussen, September 14, 1888, in *Selected Letters*, p. 311. Nietzsche would reaffirm this task in the penultimate section of *Ecce Homo*: "Have I been understood?—I have not said one word here that I did not say five years ago through the mouth of Zarathustra.

"The uncovering of Christian morality is an event without parallel, a real catastrophe. He that is enlightened about that, is a *force majeure*, a destiny—he breaks the history of mankind in two" (*EH*, "Why I am a Destiny," sec. 8, p. 333).

69. GS, book 5, sec. 343, p. 279.
70. GM, book 1, sec. 7, p. 34.
71. EH, "Destiny," sec. 1, p. 327. For an extremely insightful discussion of Nietzsche's engagement with the political, see Michel Haar, "The Institution and Destitution of the Political According to Nietzsche," trans. M. Sanders, in *New Nietzsche Studies* 2, no. 1/2 (Fall/Winter 1997), pp. 1–36. See also Tracy Strong, *Friedrich Nietzsche and*

the Politics of Transfiguration (Berkeley: University of California Press, 1975); and Law-rence Hatab, *A Nietzschean Defense of Democracy: An Experiment in Postmodern Poli-tics* (Chicago: Open Court, 1995).

72. F. Nietzsche, *Daybreak: Thoughts on the Prejudices of Morality*, trans. R. J. Hollingdale (Cambridge: Cambridge University Press, 1982), book 4, sec. 330, p. 162.

73. The rhetoric of Zarathustra's opposition to conventional values is remarkably strident, even hyperbolic, in tone. He fancies himself a "robber," a "destroyer," a "law-breaker," a "despiser." But, as Nietzsche explained the use of this excessive rhetoric in *Ecce Homo*, he called himself an "immoralist" because "I needed a word that had the meaning of a provocation for everybody" (*EH*, "Destiny," sec. 7, p. 332).

74. Z, part 1, "Prologue," sec. 6, pp. 131–32.

75. Cf. Matthew 13.

76. Z, part 1, "Prologue," sec. 5, p. 129.

77. Z, part 1, sec. 5, p. 128. "The Stammerer" would plausibly refer to either Jesus or St. Paul. Cf. *KSA* 13: 337; and *Daybreak*, book 1, sec. 68.

78. Matthew 13:42.

79. Z, part 1, "Prologue," sec. 9, p. 135.

80. Otherwise, one risks confusing the publicly voiced opinions held about moral values with the effective or performative reality of the values themselves, thus rendering their critique inadequate. Nietzsche is careful to make this distinction in *GS*, book 5, sec. 345.

81. It will be the task of *On the Genealogy of Morals* to undertake this "critique" of moral values at length and in detail.

82. Exodus 20.

83. Matthew 5.

84. "Draw up a list of the various propensities and virtues of the philosopher—his bent to doubt, his bent to deny, his bent to suspend judgment (his 'ephectic' bent), his bent to analyze, his bent to investigate, seek, dare, his bent to compare and balance, his will to neutrality and objectivity. . . . Is it not clear that for the longest time all of them contravened the basic demands of morality and conscience (not to speak of reason quite generally, which Luther liked to call 'Mistress Clever, the clever whore'). . . . Our attitude toward *ourselves* is *hubris*, for we experiment with ourselves in a way we would never permit ourselves to experiment with animals and, carried away by curiosity, we cheerfully vivisect our souls: what is 'salvation' of the soul to us today? Afterward we cure ourselves. . . . We violate ourselves nowadays, no doubt of it . . . ever questioning and questionable . . . and thus we are bound to grow day-by-day more questionable, *worthier* of asking questions; perhaps also worthier—of living?" (*GM*, book 3, sec. 9, pp. 112–13).

85. Z, part 1, "On the Teachers of Virtue," p. 142. The scriptural references are, for example, to Psalms 4:8 ("In peace I shall both lie down and sleep, for you alone, Lord, make me secure"), Proverbs 3:24 ("When you lie down, you need not be afraid, when you rest, your sleep will be sweet"), and Ecclesiastes 5:12 ("Sleep is sweet to the laboring man").

86. Or "backworlds": *Hinterwelten*. The term not only signifies a world "beyond" or "behind," but it suggests that such views amount to a "backward" kind of teaching, one that is simply outmoded, retrograde.

87. Z, part 1, "On the Afterworldly," pp. 142–43.

88. Z, part 1, p. 143.

89. *Z*, part 1, p. 143. For an extended discussion of Nietzsche's anthropomorphic account of the divine, see above, chapter 2.

90. *Z*, part 1, p. 143.

91. *Z*, part 1, p. 144.

92. *Z*, part 1, "On the Despisers of the Body," p. 147.

93. As Nietzsche would remark in section 16 of the second essay of *On the Genealogy of Morals*, primitive individuals, "enclosed within the walls of society and of peace . . . [and who were previously] well adapted to the wilderness, to war, to prowling . . . suddenly all their instincts were disvalued and 'suspended' . . . a dreadful heaviness lay upon them. They felt unable to cope with the simplest undertakings; in this new world they no longer possessed their former guides, their regulating, unconscious and infallible drives: they were reduced to thinking, inferring, reckoning, co-ordinating cause and effect, these unfortunate creatures; they were reduced to their 'consciousness,' their weakest and most fallible organ! . . . and at the same time the old instincts had not suddenly ceased to make their usual demands! Only it was hardly or rarely possible to humor them. . . . All instincts that do not discharge themselves outwardly *turn inward*— this is what I call the *internalization* of man: thus it was that man first developed what was later called his 'soul.' The entire inner world, originally as thin as if it were stretched between two membranes, expanded and extended itself, acquired depth, breadth, and height, in the same measure as outward discharge was *inhibited*." Nietzsche would go on to remark that while this internalization, or repression and sublimation, of primitive instinctual life brought an enormous amount of pain and suffering with it—and this is his characterization of "guilt" or "bad conscience"—nonetheless, this process of forced "internalization" virtually gave rise to the human species itself: "The existence on earth of an animal soul turned against itself, taking sides against itself, was something so new, profound, unheard of, enigmatic, contradictory, *and pregnant with a future* that the aspect of the earth was essentially altered. Indeed, divine spectators were needed to do justice to the spectacle that thus began and the end of which is not yet in sight" (*GM*, book 2, sec. 16, pp. 85–86).

94. "As the most endangered animal, he *needed* help and protection, he needed his peers, he had to learn to express his distress and to make himself understood; and for all of this he needed 'consciousness' first of all, he needed to 'know' himself what distressed him, he needed to 'know' how he felt, he needed to 'know' what he thought. For, to say it once more: Man, like every living being, thinks continually without knowing it; the thinking that rises to *consciousness* is only the smallest part of all this—the most superficial and worst part—for only this conscious thinking *takes the form of words, which is to say signs of communication*, and this fact uncovers the origin of consciousness. . . . The human being inventing signs is at the same time the human being who becomes ever more keenly conscious of himself. It was only as a social animal that man acquired self-consciousness—which he is still in the process of doing, more and more.

"My idea is, as you see, that consciousness does not really belong to man's individual existence but rather to his social or herd nature; that, as follows for this, it has developed subtlety only insofar as this is required by social or herd utility" (*GS*, book 5, sec. 354, pp. 298–99).

95. "Christian morality—the most malignant form of the will to lie . . . *corrupted* humanity. . . . It is *not* error as error that horrifies me at this sight . . . it is the lack of nature, it is the utterly gruesome fact that *antinature* itself received the highest honor as morality and was fixed over humanity as law and categorical imperative.—To blunder

to such an extent, not as individuals, not as a people, but as humanity!—That one taught men to despise the very first instincts of life; that one mendaciously invented a 'soul,' a 'spirit,' to ruin the body; that one taught men to experience the presupposition of life, sexuality, as something unclean; that one looks for the evil principle in what is most profoundly necessary for growth, in *severe* self-love" (*EH*, "Destiny," sec. 7, p. 332).

96. *Z*, part 1, "Despisers," p. 146.

97. *GS*, book 5, sec. 354, p. 299.

98. René Descartes, *Discourse on Method*, in *The Philosophical Writings of Descartes*, trans. J. Cottingham, R. Stoothoff, and D. Murdoch (Cambridge: Cambridge University Press, 1985), vol. 1, part 1, pp. 112–13.

99. Indeed, Descartes's remarks about the discipline of philosophy are radically reaffirmed by Nietzsche, in *Thus Spoke Zarathustra*, part 2, sec. 16, "On Scholars." Descartes observes "that philosophy gives us the means of speaking plausibly about any subject and of winning the admiration of the less learned . . . [but unfortunately] it has been cultivated for many centuries by the most excellent minds and yet there is still no point in which it is not disputed and hence dubious" (*Discourse on Method*, pp. 113–15). His remarks about traditional moral theory are almost a presentiment of Nietzsche's own views: "I compared the moral writings of the ancient pagans to very proud and magnificent palaces built only on sand and mud. They extol the virtues, and make them appear more estimable than anything else in the world; but they do not adequately explain how to recognize a virtue, and often what they call by this fine name is nothing but a case of insensibility, or pride, or despair, or parricide" (Descartes, *Discourse on Method*, p. 114, trans. modified).

100. Descartes, *Discourse on Method*, p. 112.

101. *Z*, part 1, prologue, sec. 9, p. 136.

102. Descartes, *Discourse on Method*, p. 113.

103. Letter to Gast, September 2, 1884, in *Selected Letters*, p. 230.

104. Letter to von Gersdorff, June 28, 1882, in *Selected Letters*, p. 213.

105. *Z*, part 4, "On the Higher Man," sec. 1, p. 398.

106. Indeed, Nietzsche would inscribe a dedication in his gift of *Zarathustra* to Resa von Schirnhofer by quoting from the first line of Ovid's *Metamorphoses*: "I propose to talk of the body's metamorphoses into new forms."

107. In the section "On the Thousand and One Goals," Zarathustra discusses the harnessing of the collective will—its will to power—to create new values, new meaning and estimations. But the individual self must first overcome the limitations of his own people and create still higher human values out of himself; to create egoistic values out of his self-love and love for new goals.

108. *Z*, part 1, "On the Three Metamorphoses," p. 137.

109. *Z*, part 1, p. 138.

110. *KSA* 10: 180.

111. *Z*, part 1, "Metamorphoses," p. 138.

112. *GS*, book 4, sec. 341, pp. 273–74.

113. *GM*, book 3, secs. 7–8, p. 108.

114. *GM*, book 3, sec. 8, p. 111.

115. *GM*, book 3, sec. 7, p. 107.

116. *GM*, book 3, sec. 8, p. 109.

117. *GM*, book 3, sec. 8, p. 109.

118. *Z*, part 1, p. 138. In keeping with the motif of the flight into the "desert," Zarathustra recalls Moses' flight from Egypt, and from Egyptian servitude; but to re-

ceive the new law, the Ten Commandments—the "thou shalts"—Moses must first descend from the mountain and destroy the symbol of the reigning values, namely, the Golden Calf. Cf. Exodus 32.

119. Nietzsche would on occasion recall St. Thomas Aquinas's etymology of the term "law": namely, that in the Latin, *lex* (law) derives from *ligare* (to bind). For a more extensive discussion of law, see *HAH*, vol. 1, "The Religious Life"; *Daybreak*, book 1, sec. 68; *GM*, book 2, sec. 9; and F. Nietzsche, *The Antichrist*, in *The Portable Nietzsche*, trans. and ed. W. Kaufmann (New York: Viking, 1954), sec. 57.

120. *Z*, part 1, "Metamorphoses," p. 139.

121. *Daybreak*, book 1, sec. 9, "Concept of Morality of Custom," pp. 8–9.

122. *Daybreak*, book 1, sec. 9, "Concept of Morality of Custom," p. 9.

123. *HAH*, vol. 2, "The Wanderer and His Shadow," sec. 43, p. 321.

124. *Daybreak*, book 1, sec. 19, p. 19.

125. *Antichrist*, secs. 11–12, pp. 577–79. These sections are particularly devoted to a critique of Kantian moral philosophy, although their import is indeed far broader. For a striking criticism of the imperative quality of morality and religion, see F Nietzsche, *Twilight of the Idols*, "The Four Great Errors," sec. 2, in Kaufmann's *The Portable Nietzsche*, pp. 493–94. An excellent discussion of these issues is to be found in Richard White, *Nietzsche and the Problem of Sovereignty* (Urbana: University of Illinois Press, 1997).

126. *HAH*, vol. 2, part 2, "The Wanderer and His Shadow," sec. 41, p. 320.

127. *HAH*, vol. 2, part 2, "The Wanderer and His Shadow," sec. 41, p. 320.

128. *Daybreak*, book 1, sec. 35, p. 25.

129. "Whenever an evil chance event—a sudden storm or a crop failure or a plague—strikes a community, the suspicion is aroused that custom has been offended in some way or that new practices now have to be devised to propitiate a new demonic power and caprice. This species of suspicion and reflection is thus a direct avoidance of any investigation of the real natural causes of the phenomenon: it takes the demonic cause for granted. This is one spring of the perversity of the human intellect which we have inherited: and the other spring arises close beside it, in that the real natural *consequences* of an action are, equally on principle, accorded far less attention than the supernatural (the so-called punishments and mercies administered by the divinity). Certain ablutions are, for example, prescribed at certain times: one bathes, not so as to get clean, but because it is prescribed. One learns to avoid, not the real consequences of uncleanliness, but the supposed displeasure of the gods at the neglect of an ablution. Under the pressure of superstitious fear one suspects there must be very much more to this washing away of uncleanliness, one interprets a second and third meaning into it, one spoils one's sense for reality and one's pleasure in it, and in the end accords reality a value *only insofar as it is capable of being a symbol*. Thus, under the spell of the morality of custom, man despises first the causes, secondly the consequences, thirdly reality, and weaves all his higher feelings (of reverence, of sublimity, of pride, of gratitude, of love) into an *imaginary world*: the so-called higher world" (*Daybreak*, book 1, sec. 33, p. 24).

130. *HAH*, vol. 1, "The Religious Life," secs. 133, 135, pp. 72–73.

131. *Z*, part 1, "Metamorphoses," p. 139.

132. *HAH*, vol. 1, "The Religious Life," sec. 133, p. 72.

133. *HAH*, vol. 1, sec. 134, pp. 72–73.

134. Or, as Zarathustra would announce, "He once loved 'thou shalt' as most sacred: now he must find illusion and caprice even in the most sacred, that freedom from his

love may become his prey: the lion is needed for such prey" (Z, part 1, "Metamorpho-ses," p. 139).

135. *HAH*, vol. 1, "The Religious Life," sec. 133, p. 73.

136. *HAH*, vol. 1, "The Religious Life," sec. 133, p. 72.

137. In the Sixth Meditation, e.g., Descartes would remark, "If nature is considered in its general aspect, then I understand by the term nothing other than God himself, or the ordered system of created things established by God." René Descartes, *Meditations on First Philosophy*, in *Philosophical Writings of Descartes*, vol. 2, p. 56.

138. Z, part 1, "Metamorphoses," p. 139.

139. Cf. chap. 2 for a detailed examination of this metaphysical/moral/theological unity, which constitutes the very foundation of Western thought and value.

140. Especially worthy of note, in this regard, would be his essays "David Strauss: Writer and Confessor," "History in the Service and Disservice of Life," and "Schopen-hauer as Educator," in his *Unmodern Observations*; also, *Daybreak, Human, All Too Human, On the Genealogy of Morals, The Antichrist*, and several extensive selections in *The Will to Power* notes.

141. "To the psychologists first of all, presuming they would like to study *ressenti-ment* close up for once, I would say: this plant blooms best today among anarchists and anti-Semites . . . [who attempt] to sanctify *revenge* under the heading of *justice*—as if justice were at bottom merely a further development of the feeling of being aggrieved—and to rehabilitate not only revenge but all *reactive* affects in general. . . . As for Dühr-ing's specific proposition that the home of justice is to be sought in the sphere of the reactive feelings, one is obliged for truth's sake to counter it with a blunt antithesis: the *last* sphere to be conquered by the spirit of justice is the sphere of the reactive feelings! When it really happens that the just man remains just even toward those who have harmed him . . . and *judging* is not dimmed even under the assault of personal injury, derision, and calumny, this is a piece of perfection and supreme mastery on earth" (*GM*, book 2, sec. 11, p. 74).

142. *HAH*, vol. 1, "The Religious Life," sec. 138, p. 74.

143. Cf. Plato's *Symposium*, 191A3–192A2.

144. *GS*, book 4, sec. 290, p. 233.

145. It is in much the same terms as these that Nietzsche first sketches out the notion of the eternal return in *The Gay Science*, sec. 341.

146. *GS*, book 4, secs. 276–77, pp. 223–24.

147. *EH*, "Thus Spoke Zarathustra," sec. 4, p. 301.

148. *EH*, "Thus Spoke Zarathustra," sec. 4, p. 302.

149. *EH*, "Thus Spoke Zarathustra," sec. 7, p. 307.

150. *EH*, "Thus Spoke Zarathustra," sec. 7, p. 306.

151. Z, part 1, p. 179.

152. Years later, in her posthumously published autobiography, Lou would recall the episode: "[Nietzsche] arranged a photograph of the three of us, in spite of strong objec-tions on the part of Paul Rée, who suffered throughout his life from a pathological aversion to the reproduction of his features. Nietzsche, who was in a playful mood, not only insisted on the photo, but took a personal hand in the details—for example the little (far too little!) cart, and even the touch of kitsch with the sprig of lilacs on the whip, etc" (Andreas-Salomé, *Looking Back*, p. 48).

153. Some of the earliest main versions of the tale come down in the rhymed verse of the minstrel Henry D'Andeley, in the sermons of Jacques de Vitry and Berthold von Regensburg, and in the songs of Minnesänger Frauenlob, and it is also invoked in

section 13 of Sebastian Brant's *The Ship of Fools* (*Das Narrenschiff*), titled "Of Loves," which begins with Venus's injunction, "My rope pulls many fools about; Ape, cuckold, ass, and silly lout; Whom I seduce, deceive, and flout." The tale later gets incorporated into a carnival play by Hans Sachs (the sixteenth-century "Meistersinger" of Nurem-burg), and it is the subject of a 1513 Hans Baldung Grien engraving, "Aristotle and Phyllis." A tapestry depicting the tale, dating back to 1320, is still exhibited in the Augustinermuseum in Freiburg im Bresgau. For a detailed account of the tapestry, see Ingeborg Krummer-Schroth, "L'image d'Aristote sur une tapisserie médiéval," in *L'endurance de la pensée: Pour saluer Jean Beaufret*, ed. René Char (Paris: Editions Plon, 1968), pp. 331–38.

154. The tradition probably derived from the "ship-wagons" used in the Dionysian festival of Anthesteria, among others, the wagon being used especially in various ancient fertility rites. In medieval times, the wagons (L. *carrus navalis*) carried carnival revelers, whose duty and pleasure it was to make ribald comments and scurrilous jokes to those in attendance. That Nietzsche had this image in mind seems to be reflected in the title of a book he was just then beginning to take notes on, in the spring of 1882, which he proposed to call "The Book of Fools" (*Narren-Buch* [*KSA* 9: 680]), whose first entry reads, "Whoever is full of pride hates the very horse who pulls his wagon" (*KSA* 9: 673).

155. Some commentators hold that the "whip" scene in "Little Old and Young Women" itself constitutes a kind of imaginary revenge against Lou for wielding the "whip." L. D. Derkson writes, "Apparently Nietzsche felt powerless against Lou Sa-lomé; hence the fantasy of turning the situation around, a fantasy in which the male is in control" (*Dialogues on Women: Images of Women in the History of Philosophy* [Amsterdam: VU University Press, 1996], p. 119). The only problem with this interpre-tation is that it was Nietzsche himself who orchestrated the photograph in the first place (even choosing as a backdrop for the pose a picture of the Jungfrau!), and he was hardly flogged into doing that. For an extended discussion of the scene, and of Nietzsche's relations with Lou Salomé and other women, see Carole Diethe, *Nietzsche's Women: Beyond the Whip* (Berlin: de Gruyter, 1996).

156. Making such a *split* in the character of Zarathustra—elevating the part that was rich, creative, and destined to fulfill his enormous task, and finally dismissing the painful and burdensome part—would mirror Nietzsche's own way of coming to terms with the person of Wagner by being able, finally, to separate out a "good" from a "bad" Wagner. He would remain faithful to and respectful of the former, but sarcastically dismissive of the latter. In his letter to Gast, just after hearing of Wagner's death in Venice (February 13, 1883), he would write, "This winter was the worst in my life; and I regard myself as the victim of a disturbance in *nature*. . . . I was *violently* ill for several days, and my landlord and his wife were most concerned. Now I am all right again, and even think Wagner's death brought me the greatest relief I could have had. It was hard to be for six years the opponent of a man whom one has admired above all others, and I am not built coarsely enough for *that*. Eventually, it was the old Wagner against whom I had to defend myself; as for the real Wagner, I shall be in good measure his heir (as I often used to tell Malwida). Last summer I felt that he had taken away from me all the people in Germany worth influencing, and that he was beginning to draw them into the confused and desolate malignancy of his old age" (*Selected Letters*, pp. 207–8).

157. "All men incapable of wielding some kind of weapon or other—mouth and pen included as weapons—become servile" (*HAH*, vol. 1, chap. 3, sec. 115, p. 66).

158. The modern city of Agrigento, near Mt. Etna, where Empedocles is alleged by some to have committed suicide attempting to find truth in the bowels of the earth, or

to make a self-sacrifice and to prove he had become a god. The account by Heraclides Ponticus has Pantheia comatose for thirty days, and Galen claimed her to have been dead for seven days. Cf. *The Poem of Empedocles*, trans. Brad Inwood (Toronto: University of Toronto Press, 1992), p. 151; and *Empedocles: The Extant Fragments*, trans. M. R. Wright (Indianapolis: Hackett, 1995), pp. 12–13.

159. John Sallis cites one of the more typical examples of Nietzsche's sketches for the Empedocles tragedy in his excellent book, *Crossings: Nietzsche and the Space of Tragedy* (Chicago: University of Chicago Press, 1991), pp. 108–9:

"Empedocles, driven through all the stages, religion, art, science, turns the latter against itself, dissolving it.

"Departure from religion, through the insight that it is deception.

"Now joy in artistic shining, driven from it through the recognized sufferings of the world. Woman as nature.

"Now he observes the sufferings of the world like an anatomist, becomes *tyrannos*, uses religion and art, becomes steadily harder. He resolves to annihilate his people, because he has seen that they cannot be healed. The people are gathered about the crater: he becomes mad and before he vanishes proclaims the truth of rebirth. A friend dies with him" (*KSA* 7: 126).

See also David Krell's most insightful *Postponements: Woman, Sensuality, and Death in Nietzsche* (Bloomington: Indiana University Press, 1986), esp. chap. 2; likewise, see Clémence Ramnoux's detailed analyses of the drafts in his " 'Les fragments d'un Empédocle' de Fr. Nietzsche," in *Revue de Métaphysique et de Morale*, no. 1 (January–March 1965), pp. 199–212.

160. *EH*, sec. 7, p. 307.

161. In Italian, *panna* is the term for "cream," from which one of the traditional "virgin" spring waters derives its commercial name—for its smooth, sweet taste.

162. Although not specifically termed Pantheia, as was the case with the historical figure and Hölderlin's Pantheia, in *The Birth of Tragedy* drafts, she is provisionally called "Corinna," the name of a young poetess, who was a friend of the Greek poet Pindar—perhaps Nietzsche's favorite ancient poet. She is variously referred to as a "young girl," a "woman," "Corrina and her old and noble mother," and "Corrina and her daughter Lesbia" (*KSA* 7: 235–36, 269–70).

163. *KSA* 7: 125, 234.

164. *KSA* 10: 443.

165. *KSA* 10: 443.

166. *KSA* 10: 446.

167. *KSA* 10: 446–47.

168. *KSA* 10: 512.

169. *KSA* 10: 513.

170. *KSA* 10: 593–94.

171. *Z*, part 2, "On Redemption," p. 252.

172. It might well be said that this is also our profoundly human "contradiction," which is also the contradiction of modernity itself—generally, the "absurd" condition of modernity.

173. *GS*, book 5, sec. 370, pp. 328–30. Two causal chains lead to this situation: Zoroaster's historical encoding of a metaphysically grounded moral order, as well as the ontogenesis of a near-universal human suffering. Greek rationality and Christian myth become the immediate vehicles of its modern appearance.

174. This is to be contrasted with the conventional, moralizing "pity" of self-

righteous sentimentality: a kind of pity that effectively denigrates the person who is the object of one's pity by lowering the other's self-esteem, resulting in the other's shame. Moreover, this debasement of the other occurs in due proportion to the elevation of one's own concealed pride in being able to look at the other as "beneath" oneself. Thus, for Nietzsche, what initially appears to be a virtuous moral action, indeed, a "selfless" or "nonegoistic" act, is oftentimes simply an unacknowledged form of hypocrisy, and a shameful one at that. Cf. *GS*, book 3, secs. 271–75; book 4, sec. 338.

175. *Z*, part 3, "The Convalescent," sec. 2, p. 330.

176. *Z*, part 3, "On the Vision and the Riddle," sec. 2, p. 271.

177. See, e.g., *Twilight of the Idols*, "The Four Great Errors," sec. 8, p. 501; *WP*, sec. 552, p. 299; *WP*, sec. 765, pp. 402–3; *WP*, sec. 787, p. 416; *KSA* 9: 496; *KSA* 10: 237–38, 245, 514; *KSA* 11: 553.

178. See *Antichrist*, sec. 26, p. 596.

179. *Z*, part 3, "Vision," sec. 2, p. 271.

180. *Z*, part 3, "The Convalescent," sec. 2, p. 330.

181. *EH*, "Destiny," sec. 3, pp. 327–28.

182. "The Cure of a Demoniac" in Mark 1:21–28; Luke 4:31–37.

183. Revelation 10:9.

184. *Z*, part 4, "Honey," p. 351.

185. Nietzsche is quite clear about Zarathustra's inability to grasp and express the thought of the eternal return in his notes of the period. For example, in reviewing the third section of *Zarathustra*, he remarks, "N.B. The thought itself is not expressed in the third part: it is only a preparation" (*KSA* 10: 520). Sometimes it seems as if the thought itself is too strong: "The fear of the doctrine's consequences: perhaps the best people will be destroyed by it? and that the worst will adopt it?" (*KSA* 10: 521) Sometimes it seems as if Zarathustra himself is simply too weak to grasp the teaching: "Not saying *the least thing* paralyzes all his energy: he feels that up till now he has *avoided* a thought, and this is what attacks him with all its force? It is a struggle: which of the two will be strong enough: Zarathustra or the thought?" (*KSA* 10: 521) At the close of *Zarathustra* part 2, a demand is posed to him in a dream: "You know it, Zarathustra, but you do not say it!" In response, he remarks, "Yes, I know it, but I do not want to say it! . . . Alas, I would like to, but how can I? Let me off from this! It is beyond my strength!" (Z, part 2, "The Stillest Hour," p. 257).

186. *Z*, part 4, "The Honey Sacrifice," p. 352.

187. Jonah 2:1–9.

188. Kaufmann, *The Portable Nietzsche*, p. 75. See *KSA* 9: 207.

189. *Z*, part 4, "The Honey Sacrifice," p. 350.

190. *The Bacchae* (710–13), trans. H. Birkhead, in *Ten Greek Plays*, ed. L. R. Lind (Boston: Houghton Mifflin, 1957), p. 347. Empedocles, likewise, has his worshipers of Aphrodite "dashing onto the ground libations of yellow honey" (DK 128, in Wright, *Empedocles*, p. 259).

191. Here, as in the very first section of "Zarathustra's Prologue," Nietzsche places himself in patent opposition to Christ's teaching, in Revelation 22:17–20, where Christ himself is said to be the "gift" of life-giving water: " 'Come.' Let the one who thirsts come forward, and the one who wants it receive the gift of life-giving water. I warn everyone who hears the prophetic words in this book: if anyone adds to them God will add to him the plagues described in this book, and if anyone takes away from the words in this prophetic book, God will take away his share in the tree of life and in the holy

city described in this book. The one who gives this testimony says 'Yes, I am coming soon.' Amen! Come, Lord Jesus."

In "Zarathustra's Prologue," he remarks that he has gathered up "too much honey; I need hands outstretched to receive it. . . . Bless the cup that wants to overflow, that the water may flow from it golden and carry everywhere the reflection of your [the sun's] delight" (Z, part 1, p. 122). To compound this correction to the book of Revelation, Zarathustra assumes the guise, not only of Jesus, as "the fisher of men," but "as the most sarcastic of all who fish for men" (Z, part 1, p. 351), he casts himself as the fisher king of Wagner's *Parsifal*. The fisher king was the projection of Amfortas, king of the Grail Castle, the treasure castle on the Grail Mountain, which contained the Holy Grail itself, whose secret was the promise of eternal life. Nietzsche's sarcasm derives from the fact that Amfortas himself could not have children because (i.e., according to the original *Parzival*, written toward the end of the twelfth century by Wolfram von Eschenbach) his testicles were wounded by the spear of Longinus. It was Wagner's *Parsifal*, with its reversion to Christian-mystical imagery of chastity and redemption that infuriated Nietzsche, signaling the final impossibility of any future positive relations. Since one element of the break in their relations was Wagner's insistence that Nietzsche seek medical assistance for what he thought to be Nietzsche's onanism, the sarcasm of "The Honey Sacrifice" would finally lay the ghost of Wagner to rest—completely inverting the role of the "fisher king" to Zarathustra himself, a "squanderer" of honey "with a thousand hands" (Z, p. 350). Nietzsche first mentions this insulting accusation by Wagner, obliquely, in a letter to Overbeck written during the period of *Zarathustra*'s composition (February 22, 1883), saying "a deadly offence came between us; and something terrible could have happened if he lived longer" (*Selected Letters*, p. 209). The offense specifically involved a letter Wagner wrote to Nietzsche's physician, Dr. Otto Eiser, commenting on what he thought to be the cause of Nietzsche's eye troubles and migraines: "I have been thinking for some time, in connection with Nietzsche's malady, of similar cases I have observed among talented young intellectuals. I watched these young men go to rack and ruin, and realized only too painfully that such symptoms were the result of masturbation." When Nietzsche had his next consultation with Dr. Eiser—who was also the founder of the Frankfurt Wagner Circle—Eiser informed Nietzsche that he had been in correspondence with Wagner about his illness. He must have informed Nietzsche about the content of Wagner's letter because, as Eiser later recalled, Nietzsche practically exploded: "He began to rant and rave. He was beside himself and I dare not repeat the words he uttered about Wagner" (cited in Joachim Köhler, *Nietzsche & Wagner: A Lesson in Subjugation*, trans. R. Taylor [New Haven: Yale University Press, 1998], pp. 146–47, 156). The incident with Dr. Eiser dates back to April 4, 1878, and it forced Nietzsche into a humiliating double bind. As Köhler so aptly describes the poisonous dynamics of the situation, "After this outburst . . . Nietzsche fell silent. He had no alternative, for as the law of denunciation works, by defending himself, a man makes a rod for his own back. Yet if he fails to produce arguments in his defence, he loses everything" (Köhler, *Nietzsche & Wagner*, p. 156). Curt Paul Janz also discusses the significance of this incident at length in his *Friedrich Nietzsche*, vol. 1, "Dr. med. Otto Eiser," pp. 785–90.

Nietzsche nonetheless finds occasion to hurl some excoriating invective at Wagner—even if it is beyond the grave (Z, part 4, "The Magician"): "'You may have deceived people subtler than I,' Zarathustra said harshly. 'I do not guard against deceivers; I have to be without caution; thus my lot wants it. You, however, have to deceive: that far I know you. . . . You wicked counterfeiter, how could you do otherwise? You would rouge even your disease when you show yourself naked to your doctor. In the same way you have just now rouged your lie when you said to me, "I did all this *only* as a game." . . . I solve your riddle: your magic has enchanted everybody, but no lie or cunning is left to you to use against yourself: you are disenchanted for yourself. You have harvested nausea as your one truth. Not a word of yours is genuine any more, except your mouth—namely, the nausea that sticks to your mouth' " (pp. 368–69). See also, Dietrich Fischer-Dieskau, *Wagner & Nietzsche*, trans. J. Neugroschel (New York: Seabury, 1976), pp. 159ff.; Martin Gregor-Dellin, *Richard Wagner: His Life, His Work, His Century*, trans. J. Brownjohn (New York: Harcourt Brace Jovanovich, 1983), pp. 451–58; "Wagner and Nietzsche," trans. M. Tanner, in *Wagner Handbook* (Cambridge: Harvard University Press, 1992), pp. 327–42; and Siegfried Mandel, *Nietzsche & the Jews* (Amherst, Mass.: Prometheus Books, 1998), pp. 118–20.

192. See especially, *BGE*, part 1, pp. 9–32; and "On Truth and Lie in an Extra-Moral Sense," in *The Portable Nietzsche*, pp. 42–47.

193. His inversion of "the best cursed things in the world" to the most "humanly good" things is a particularly clear articulation of this overcoming. In the section "On the Three Evils," Nietzsche emphasizes sex, the lust to rule and the "self-enjoying" virtue of a "healthy" selfishness as the transformed values that the "sword of judgment" will bring about, at the moment of "the great noon"—when the shadowing clouds, the spirit of gravity, of the old order finally dissipates (Z, part 3, secs. 1–2, pp. 298–303). Alluding to Descartes's famous "dream" of November 10–11, 1619, when he claimed to have been revealed the new ordering principle of nature, his "universal mathematics," Nietzsche would remark, in favor of his new world of "will to power," "Thus my dream found the world . . . 'where there is force, *number* will become mistress: she has more force' " (Z, part 3, p. 299).

194. Z, part 4, "The Honey Sacrifice," p. 352. The phrase itself seems to have been borrowed from Ernest Renan's work of 1863, *The Life of Jesus*.

195. See *HAH*, vol. 1, chap. 3, "The Religious Life," esp. sec. 111, "Origin of the Religious Cult," pp. 63–65.

196. In a letter to Franz Overbeck from August 1883, Nietzsche would write: "I enclose . . . the first public statement on *Zarathustra I*; strange to relate, the letter was written in a prison. What pleases me is to see that this first reader has at once felt what it is all about: the long-promised Antichrist. There has not been since Voltaire such an outrageous attack on Christianity. *Ecrasez l'infame!*" (*Selected Letters*, p. 219).

197. See *WP*, sec. 797, p. 419.

198. This humorously rejoins the *Zend Avesta*'s account of Zoroaster's spilling of his seed: "Three times [Zoroaster] came near unto his wife Hrôgvi, and three times the seed fell upon the ground." Following this, the angel Neryosangh retrieves the seed, which is then entrusted to Ardvisusr, a water divinity, and is guarded by 99,999 Fravashi spirits—protecting it from fiends. "A maid bathing in the lake Kasava will conceive by it and bring forth the victorious Saoshyant [Zarathustra's sons], who will come from the region of the dawn to free the world from death and decay, from corruption and rottenness" (*Zend Avesta*, p. lxxix). Tradition has it that the three sons, born at intervals of a thousand years, will be named Hoshedar, Hoshedar-mah, and Soshyos, and their respective virginal mothers are purported to be Shemik-abu, Shapir-abu, and Gobakabu (in Dhalla, M. N., *History of Zorvastrianism* [New York: AMS Press, 1977], pp. 423–29).

199. "Scorn," in "Joke, Cunning, and Revenge," *GS*, p. 45.

200. "From High Mountains," *BGE*, p. 241.

201. Z, part 4, sec. 1, "The Ass Festival," p. 426.

202. In "The Stillest Hour," a voiceless dream speaks out to Zarathustra in his sleep: "You must yet become as a child and without shame. The pride of youth is still upon you; you have become young late; but whoever would become as a child must overcome his youth too. . . . O Zarathustra, your fruit is ripe, but you are not ripe for your fruit. Thus you must return to your solitude again; for you must yet become mellow" (Z, part 2, p. 259).

203. Indeed, quite literally. Recall Nietzsche's remark, in *Human, All Too Human*, that heaven and the gods are themselves products of dreams: "*Misunderstanding of the Dream*.—The man of the ages of barbarous primordial culture believed that in the dream he was getting to know a *second real world*: here is the origin of all metaphysics. Without the dream one would have had no occasion to divide the world into two. The dissection into soul and body is also connected with the oldest idea of the dream, likewise the postulation of a life of the soul, thus the origin of all belief in spirits, and probably also the belief in gods. 'The dead live on, *for* they appear to the living in dreams': that was the conclusion one formerly drew, throughout many millennia" (*HAH*, vol. 1, sec. 5, p. 14).

204. Z, part 3, sec. 2, "On Old and New Tablets," p. 308.

205. On occasion, this might not be such a bad thing—especially when one has had quite enough of one's own travails. Nietzsche would discuss the virtues of sleep in his earlier *Daybreak*: "What can one do to arouse oneself when one is tired and has had enough of oneself? One person recommends the casino, another Christianity, a third electricity. The best thing, however, my melancholy friend, is plenty of sleep, real and metaphorical! Thus one will again awake to a new morning! The art in the wisdom of life lies in knowing how to fall asleep in either sense at the proper time" (*Daybreak*, book 4, sec. 376, p. 383).

206. On a corrected page proof for *Ecce Homo*, "Why I Am So Wise," sec. 3, that was received by the printer but held for further clarification—and later destroyed by Nietzsche's sister, Elisabeth—Nietzsche raises one enduring objection to the eternal return (a copy was later found in Peter Gast's literary estate and is included in the recent critical edition. See M. Montinari, "Ein neuer Abschnitt in Nietzsches Ecce Homo"—"A new Paragraph in N's EH"—in *Nietzsche-Studien* I, 1972, pp. 380–418): "When I look for my profoundest opposite, the incalculable pettiness of the instincts, I always find my mother and my sister—to be related to such *canaille* would be a blasphemy against my divine nature. . . . I confess that the deepest objection to the 'Eternal Recurrence', my real idea from the abyss, is always my mother and my sister" (in *EH*, pp. 41–42; *KSA* 6: 268).

207. Z, part 4, "The Drunken Song," sec. 12, p. 436.

208. Z, part 4, "At Noon," p. 389

209. Z, part 4, "The Cry of Distress," p. 355.

210. "Every action performed by a human being becomes in some way the cause of other actions, decisions, thoughts, that everything that happens is inextricably knotted to everything that will happen, one comes to recognize the existence of an actual *immortality*, that of motion: what has once moved is enclosed and eternalized in the total union of all being like an insect in amber" (*HAH*, vol. 1, part 4, sec. 208, p. 97).

211. Z, part 4, p. 439.

212. Nietzsche sums up his personal situation at the time, in a letter to his sister, Elisabeth. He writes the letter in lieu of attending Elisabeth's wedding—something he absolutely refused to do, given her choice of a spouse—and in hopes of at least appear-

ing to lend a note of reconciliation to their longstanding animosity over the Lou affair. He also realizes that he may not see her for some time, since she and Förster had long planned to leave for Paraguay following the wedding. He writes, "On the decisive day in your life . . . I must draw up a sort of account of my life. . . . So that you may in the future have a kind of indication as to how far your brother's judgment will require from you much prudence and perhaps also forbearance, I am describing for you today, as a sign of great affection, the bad and difficult nature of my situation. I have found until now, from the earliest childhood, *nobody* who had the same needs of heart and conscience as myself. This compels me still today, as at all times, to present myself, as best I can, and often with a lot of bad feeling, among one or another of the sorts of human being who are permitted and understandable nowadays. But that one can only really grow among people of *like mind* and like will is for me an axiom of belief. . . . that I have no such person is my misfortune. My university existence was a wearisome attempt to adapt to a false milieu; my approach to Wagner was the same—only in the opposite direction. Almost all my human relations have resulted from attacks of a feeling of isolation: Overbeck, as well as Rée and Malwida—I have been ridiculously happy if ever I found, or thought I had found, in someone a little patch or corner of common concern. My mind is burdened with a thousand shaming memories of such weak moments, in which I absolutely could not endure solitude any more. Not omitting my illness, which always discourages me in the most horrifying way; I have not been so profoundly ill for nothing, and am ill on the average now still—that is, depressed—as I say, simply because I was lacking the right milieu and I always had to playact somewhat instead of refreshing myself in people. I do not for that reason consider myself in the least a secret or furtive or mistrustful person; quite the reverse! *If I was that, I would not suffer so much!* But one cannot just simply communicate, however much one wants to; one has to find the person to whom communication can be made. The feeling that there is about me something very remote and alien, that my words have other colors than the same words from other people . . . precisely this feeling, of which testimony has lately been reaching me from various sides, is nevertheless the subtlest degree of 'understanding' that I have till now found. . . . Do not therefore think me mad, my dear Lama, and especially forgive me for not coming to your wedding" (letter of May 5, 1885, in *Selected Letters*, pp. 240–41).

213. *BGE*, book 9, sec. 269, pp. 217–18.
214. Letter to Gast, July 23, 1885, in *Selected Letters*, p. 243.
215. *BGE*, book 9, sec. 269, p. 219.
216. *BGE*, book 9, sec. 269, p. 219.
217. *BGE*, book 9, sec. 269, p. 219.
218. *BGE*, book 9, sec. 269, p. 220.
219. *Z*, part 3, "On Old and New Tablets," sec. 2, p. 309.
220. *Z*, part 3, sec. 16, p. 318.
221. *Z*, part 3, sec. 21, p. 321.
222. *Z*, part 3, sec. 21, p. 321.
223. *Z*, part 3, sec. 4, p. 311.
224. *HAH*, vol. 1, preface, secs. 1–8, pp. 5–10; *HAH*, vol. 2, preface, secs. 1–7, pp. 209–14.
225. *GS*, book 5, sec. 380, pp. 342–43.
226. *Meditations*, in *Philosophical Writings of Descartes*, vol. 2, Med. I, p. 15.
227. *HAH*, vol. 1, preface, sec. 2, p. 6. In the preface to part 2 of *Human, All Too Human*, he reformulates this "invention" of another "free spirit" and, less dramatically,

says that, "As a solitary I spoke without witnesses," thus internalizing the discussion as an "inner" dialogue (*HAH*, vol. 2, preface, sec. 5, p. 212).

228. *HAH*, vol. 1, preface, sec. 3, pp. 6–7.

229. *HAH*, vol. 1, preface, sec. 3, p. 7.

230. Even if this involves an initial period of studied affectation or pretense, such that by repetition, one could induce oneself to acquire in person those attitudes one initially feigns: "It was then I learned the art of *appearing* cheerful, objective, inquisitive, above all healthy and malicious . . . here a sufferer and self-denier speaks as though he were *not* a sufferer and self-denier. Here there is a *determination* to preserve an equilibrium and composure in the face of life and even a sense of gratitude towards it, here there rules a vigorous, proud, constantly watchful and sensitive will that has set itself the task of defending life against pain and of striking down all those inferences that pain, disappointment, ill-humor, solitude, and other swampgrounds usually cause to flourish like poisonous fungi" (*HAH*, vol. 2, preface, sec. 5, p. 212).

231. *GS*, book 5, sec. 382, p. 346.

232. *HAH*, vol. 1, sec. 292, p. 134.

233. *HAH*, vol. 1, preface, sec. 3, p. 7.

234. *HAH*, vol. 1, secs. 5–6, pp. 8–9.

235. *HAH*, vol. 1, sec. 5, p. 8.

236. Nietzsche would call this "the pathos of distance" in *BGE*, book 9, sec. 257, pp. 201–2. Cf. also *BGE*, book 2, secs. 43–44, pp. 53–56; and *EH*, "The Untimely Ones," sec. 3, p. 281.

237. *HAH*, vol. 1, preface, sec. 5, p. 8.

238. *HAH*, vol. 1, preface, sec. 6, p. 9.

239. *HAH*, vol. 1, part 5, sec. 292, p. 135.

240. *HAH*, vol. 1, preface, sec. 6, p. 9.

CHAPTER 4

1. Letter to Franz Overbeck, Summer 1886, *Selected Letters of Friedrich Nietzsche*, ed. and trans. Christopher Middleton (Chicago: University of Chicago Press, 1969), p. 254.

2. Cf. F. Nietzsche, *Kritische Studien Ausgabe*, vol. 8, *Nachgelassene Fragmente 1875–1879* (Berlin: De Gruyter, 1988), pp. 86–87 ("On Religion"), and pp. 176–78 ("The Transcendent Satisfaction of Vengeance").

3. Letter to Franz Overbeck, August 5, 1886, in *Selected Letters*, pp. 254–55.

4. Letter to Jakob Burckhardt, September 22, 1886, in *Selected Letters*, p. 255.

5. Cf. Curt Paul Janz, *Friedrich Nietzsche: Biographie in drei Bänden* (Munich: Carl Hanser Verlag, 1978), vol. 2, p. 562. Resa von Schirnhofer, a young friend of Nietzsche's at the time, relates an anecdote about one of Nietzsche's longtime summer acquaintances at Sils-Maria, an elderly "intelligent Englishwoman, Mrs. Fynn, a believing Catholic, for whom Nietzsche had a sincere respect. When I got to know her personally in Geneva, she told me how Nietzsche had, with tears in his eyes, asked her not to read his books, since 'there was so much in them that was bound to hurt her feelings' " (in Sander L. Gilman, *Conversations with Nietzsche*, trans. David J. Parent [New York: Oxford University Press, 1987], p. 195).

6. Letter to Franz Overbeck, March 24, 1887, in *Selected Letters*, p. 264.

7. Letter to Malwida von Meysenbug, May 12, 1887, in *Selected Letters*, p. 266.

8. Ibid.

9. Letter to Hippolyte Taine, July 4, 1887, in *Selected Letters*, p. 268. Taine was a celebrated French historian and literary critic. Nietzsche held Taine in high regard and had sent him an unsolicited copy of *Beyond Good and Evil*. Taine wrote back in October 1886 that he thought well of the volume, and Nietzsche responded—nine months later!—with this note of thanks.

10. Letter to Nietzsche from Jakob Burckhardt, September 26, 1886, in Janz, *Friedrich Nietzsche*, vol. 3 p. 495.

11. The review appeared in the September 16–17, 1886, issue of *Der Bund* and is reprinted in Janz, *Friedrich Nietzsche*, vol. 2, pp. 257–64. Cf. Widmann's "Nietzsche's Dangerous Book," trans. Tim Hyde and Lysane Fauvel, in *New Nietzsche Studies* 4, no. 1–2 (Spring/Summer 2000), pp. 191–97.

12. Letter to Malwida von Meysenbug, September 24, 1886, in *Selected Letters*, p. 257.

13. Machiavelli's celebrated position reversing this teaching is one of the most dramatic testimonies of early modernity. Cf. his *The Prince*, chap. 25, "How Much Fortune Can Do in Human Affairs and How It May Be Opposed": "Fortune [i.e., "fate," or "divine providence"] is a woman, and it is necessary, if you wish to master her, to conquer her by force; and it can be seen that she lets herself be overcome by the bold rather than by those who proceed coldly. And therefore, like a woman, she is always a friend to the young, because they are less cautious, fiercer, and master her with greater audacity" (The Prince *and* The Discourses, trans. L. Ricci [New York: Random House, 1940], p. 94).

14. Letter to Franz Overbeck, January 9, 1887, in *Selected Letters*, p. 258.

15. At the time, Nietzsche would write, "Thanks to my long-suffering disposition, I have clinched my teeth and endured agony upon agony during the last few years, and at times it seems as if I had been born into the world for this and nothing else. I have paid tribute in the fullest measure to the philosophy that teaches this long-suffering. My neuralgia goes to work as thoroughly and scientifically as if it were trying to probe and find out just what degree of pain I am able to endure, and thirty hours is required for each of these tests. I must count on a repetition of this research work every four or eight days. . . . But now the time has come when I can no longer endure it, and either I wish to live on in good health or not at all! A complete rest, mild air, long walks, darkened rooms—all this I expect to find in Italy" (letter to Richard Wagner, September 27, 1876, in *The Nietzsche-Wagner Correspondence*, ed. Elisabeth Förster-Nietzsche, trans. Caroline Kerr [New York: Liveright, 1949], p. 288).

16. This proved unsuccessful. Nietzsche saw Wagner for the last time in Sorrento, on October 4. In the course of their final evening's walk, as Nietzsche's sister Elisabeth relates the incident, "Wagner began to speak of his religious feelings and experiences in a tone of the deepest repentance, and to confess a leaning towards the Christian dogmas. For example, he spoke of the delight he took in the celebration of the Holy Communion" (*Nietzsche-Wagner Correspondence*, p. 294). Nietzsche found this at once hypocritical—Wagner was a life-long atheist—and as pandering to the pious sensibilities of German Christians, hoping to find additional financial support for his Bayreuth musical festival, which had run up a deficit of some 160,000 marks. With this final encounter, Nietzsche had lost all respect for Wagner's personal integrity, sincerity, and candor. The appearance of *Parsifal* would only serve to confirm Nietzsche's judgment that Wagner

had abdicated his once highly valued creative qualities to become a Catholic-Romantic mystagogue and apologist.

17. On the topic of Nietzsche's hoped-for community of intellectuals, see Hubert Treiber, "Nietzsche's Monastery for Freer Spirits and Weber's Sect," in H. Lenmann and G. Roth, *Weber's Protestant Ethic: Origins, Evidence, Contents* (Cambridge: Cambridge University Press, 1987), pp. 133–60.

18. For an informed discussion of the relations between Nietzsche and Rée during this period, see Paul-Laurent Assoun's essay, "Nietzsche et le Réelism," which serves as an introduction to the French edition of Rée's *Origin: De l'origine des sentiments moraux*, ed. P.-L. Assoun, Fr. trans. Michel-François Demet (Paris: Presses Universitaires de France, 1982), pp. 5–68.

19. *HAH*, vol. 1, chap. 2, "On the History of the Moral Sensations," sec. 37, pp. 32–33.

20. *HAH*, vol. 1, chap. 2, "On the History of the Moral Sensations," sec. 37, p. 33. The passage cited from Rée is to be found in his *Der Ursprung der moralischen Empfindungen* (Chemnitz: Schmeitzner, 1877), p. viii.

21. *HAH*, vol. 1, chap. 2, "On the History of the Moral Sensations," sec. 37, p. 13.

22. On Lou Salomé and her relations with Nietzsche and Rée, see above, chapter 2, note 7, and the discussion in chapter 3. A recent interpretive analysis is given by Jean-Pierre Faye, *Nietzsche et Salomé: La philosophie dangereuse* (Paris: Grasset, 2000).

23. On Overbeck's friendship with Nietzsche and his strictly historical and academic understanding of theology, cf. "Der neue Lebensgefährte (Overbeck)," in Janz, *Friedrich Nietzsche*, vol. 1, pp. 358–63.

24. Interestingly, the protagonist in question, Kuno (a parson's son), is strongly modeled on the person of Nietzsche himself. The characterization is reiterated in Lou's biography of Nietzsche as well, in her *Friedrich Nietzsche in seinen Werken* (Vienna: Konegen, 1894), translated as *Friedrich Nietzsche: The Man in His Works*, trans. and ed. Siegfried Mandel (Redding Ridge, Conn.: Black Swan, 1988). Lou herself used a pseudonym, Henri Lou, in publishing the work. It has often been suggested that the pseudonym refers back to Hendrick (Henri) Gillot, since she writes extensively of him elsewhere, and because it was he who assigned her the name "Lou," thereby replacing her given Christian name, Louise.

25. *GM*, preface, sec. 4, p. 18.

26. *GM*, preface, sec. 7, p. 21.

27. Rarely does Nietzsche express this kind of bitterness, even rancor, toward anyone, much less toward a friend of longstanding, like Rée. Personally, Nietzsche felt completely abandoned by Lou—the only person he truly loved in his entire life—when she left for Berlin with Rée. Likewise, he felt betrayed by Rée for the very same reason. All the same, Nietzsche's denunciation of Rée testified to substantive philosophical differences. Already by the time of the first volume of *Human, All Too Human* (1878), Nietzsche had opposed his "history" to Rée's "origin" of "the moral sentiments," and his subsequent works testify to the deep cultural and historical indebtedness of what appear to be straightforward value or truth claims concerning "origins" (much less, those supposed "origins" in "human nature" of a disinterested, utilitarian morality, as advanced by Rée). The very notion that interpretation—and thus, philosophical explanation—can *stop* at some purported origin, at some *terminus ad quem* of investigation, and that such a "ground" or "origin" would itself be meaningful, from a current perspective, becomes an increasingly important preoccupation of Nietzsche's growing criticism. By 1881, he would claim in *Daybreak: Thoughts on the Prejudices of Morality*,

"Why is it that this thought comes back to me again and again in ever more varied colors?—that *formerly*, when investigators of knowledge sought out the origin of things they always believed they would discover something of incalculable significance for all later action and judgment, that they always *presupposed*, indeed, that the *salvation* of man must depend on *insight into the origin of things*: but that now, on the contrary, the more we advance towards origins, the more our interest diminishes; indeed, that all the evaluations and 'interestedness' we have implanted into things begin to lose their meaning the further we go back and the closer we approach the things themselves. *The more insight we possess into an origin the less significant does the origin appear*: while *what is nearest to us*, what is around us and in us, gradually begins to display colors and beauties and enigmas and riches of significance of which earlier mankind had not an inkling" (*Daybreak*, trans. R. J. Hollingdale [Cambridge: Cambridge University Press, 1982], book 1, "Origin and Significance," sec. 44, pp. 30–31). This growing "suspicion" of origins would continue to be pursued throughout *The Gay Science*, *Thus Spoke Zarathustra*, and *Beyond Good and Evil*, finally to emerge as the developed methodology of "genealogical" analysis in the second essay of the *Genealogy*—where even the claim of an accurate historical analysis would be superseded by a genealogical or semiological analysis: "The cause of the origin of a thing and its eventual utility, its actual employment and place in a system of purposes lie worlds apart: whatever exists, having somehow come into being, is again and again reinterpreted to new ends, taken over, transformed and redirected by some power superior to it. [This] . . . involves a fresh interpretation, an adaptation through which any previous 'meaning' and 'purpose' are necessarily obscured or even obliterated. . . . The entire history of a 'thing,' an organ, a custom can in this way be a continuous sign-chain of ever new interpretations and adaptations" (*GM*, book 2, sec. 12, p. 77).

28. In a draft for section 3 of "Why I Write Such Good Books," in *Ecce Homo*, Nietzsche remarks, "My writings are difficult; I hope this is not considered an objection? To understand the most *abbreviated* language ever spoken by a philosopher . . . one must follow the *opposite* procedure of that generally required by philosophical literature. Usually, one must *condense*, or upset one's digestion; I have to be diluted, liquefied, mixed with water, else one upsets one's digestion. . . . I am *brief*; my readers themselves must become long and comprehensive in order to bring up and together all that I have thought, and thought deep down. On the other hand, there are prerequisites for 'understanding' here, which very few can satisfy: one must be able to see a problem in its proper place—that is, in the context of the other problems *that belong with it*" (appendix 2 to *EH*, p. 340).

29. *GM*, preface, sec. 1, p. 15.

30. Z, part 3, "On Old and New Tablets," sec. 2, p. 308.

31. "In fact, the problem of the origin of evil pursued me even as a boy of thirteen: at an age in which you have 'half childish trifles, half God in your heart,' I devoted to it my first childish literary trifle, my first philosophical effort—and as for the 'solution' of the problem I posed at that time, well, I gave the honor to God, as was only fair. . . . Fortunately I learned early to separate theological prejudice from moral prejudice and ceased to look for the origin of evil *behind* the world" (*GM*, preface, sec. 3, pp. 16–17). The early essay Nietzsche here refers to is most likely his sketch of April 1862, "Über das Christentum On Christianity," in F. Nietzsche, *Historisch-kritisch Gesamtausgabe. Werke* (Munich: C. H. Beck, 1933–40), vol. 2, p. 63.

32. *GM*, preface, sec. 3, p. 17.

33. Cf. also *BGE*, parts 8 ("Peoples and Fatherlands") and 9 ("What Is Noble"),

and *WP*, book 4 ("Discipline and Breeding"), for an extensive clarification of these issues.

34. "Let us articulate this *new demand*: we need a *critique* of moral values, *the value of these values themselves must first be called into question*—and for that there is needed a knowledge of the conditions and circumstances in which they grew, under which they evolved and changed" (*GM*, preface, sec. 6, p. 20).

35. Nietzsche had projected a second volume of the *Genealogy*—again, a polemic— whose essays would be titled "The Gregarious Instinct in Morality," "The History of Morality as the Work of Denaturing," and "Among the Moralists and the Philosophers of Morality." In a programmatic note to this projected work, he added, "Morality—I've already had occasion to say it—has been up until now the Circe of philosophers. Post-face. Settling accounts with morality. It is at the origin of pessimism and nihilism. It gives them their highest formal expression" (Janz, *Friedrich Nietzsche*, vol. 2, p. 562). For a critical elaboration of Nietzsche's moral theory, see Keith Ansell-Pearson, *Nietzsche contra Rousseau: A Study of Nietzsche's Moral and Political Thought* (Cambridge: Cambridge University Press, 1991).

36. *GM*, preface, sec. 5, p. 19.

37. "In every teacher and preacher of what is *new* we encounter the same 'wickedness' that makes conquerors notorious, even if its expression is subtler. . . . What is new, however, is always *evil*, being that which wants to conquer and overthrow the old boundary markers and the old pieties; and only what is old is good" (*GS*, book 1, sec. 4, p. 79). Nietzsche here makes a clear allusion to Machiavelli's *Prince*, chapter 6: "It must be considered that there is nothing more difficult to carry out, nor more doubtful of success, nor more dangerous to handle, than to initiate a new order of things. For the reformer has enemies in all those who profit by the old order, and only lukewarm defenders in all those who would profit by the new order, this lukewarmness arising partly from fear of their adversaries, who have the laws in their favor; and partly from the incredulity of mankind, who do not truly believe in anything new until they have had actual experience of it. Thus it arises that on every opportunity for attacking the reformer, his opponents do so with the zeal of partisans, the others only defend him half-heartedly, so that between them he runs great danger" (*The Prince*, in Ricci, The Prince *and* The Discourses, pp. 21–22).

38. Recall, in *The Birth of Tragedy* and in the texts of the early 1870s, the rich insights Nietzsche derived about classical Greek culture from his examination of the role played by the *agon*, the struggle or conflict, as a defining motif of the tragic period. For Nietzsche, the *agon* seemed to constitute the great health, the distinctively affirmative character, of classical Greek culture in general. Cf. the discussion in chapter 1.

39. Nietzsche had succinctly expressed his views on this in his earlier work, *The Gay Science*, esp. book 3, sec. 116: "*Herd Instinct.*—Wherever we encounter a morality, we also encounter valuations and an order of rank of human impulses and actions. These valuations and orders of rank are always expressions of the needs of a community and herd: whatever benefits it most—and second most, and third most—that is also considered the first standard for the value of all individuals. Morality trains the individual to be a function of the herd and to ascribe value to himself only as a function. The conditions for the preservation of different communities were very different; hence there were very different moralities. Considering essential changes in the forms of future herds and communities, states and societies, we can prophesy that there will yet be very divergent moralities. Morality is herd instinct in the individual" (pp. 174–75).

40. *GS*, book 1, sec. 21, pp. 93–94.

41. H. Marcuse, *One-Dimensional Man* (Boston: Beacon Press, 1964). Cf. esp. chap. 3, "The Conquest of the Unhappy Consciousness: Repressive Desublimation," pp. 56–83. See also, *GS*, book 1, sec. 24, pp. 96–99.

42. By the same token, and on the surface, Nietzsche himself could hardly take issue with the requisite civilities of humane treatment and the sympathetic deference toward others that one comes to expect in ordinary society. Rather, what is at issue is something other than the often concealed and distorted motivations that subtend our ordeals of civility.

43. *GM*, preface, sec. 6, p. 20.

44. *GM*, preface, sec. 7, p. 21.

45. *Twilight of the Idols*, in *The Portable Nietzsche*, ed. and trans. W. Kaufmann (New York: Viking Press, 1968), p. 501.

46. *The Antichrist*, in *The Portable Nietzsche*, pp. 581–82.

47. *GM*, book 1, sec. 1, p. 24.

48. *GS*, book 4, sec. 335, pp. 263–64.

49. *GM*, book 1, secs. 1–2, p. 25.

50. For Nietzsche's extensive reflections on history and historiography, see the second essay, "History in the Service and Disservice of Life," of his *Unmodern Observations*, ed. William Arrowsmith, trans. Gary Brown, (New Haven: Yale University Press, 1990), pp. 73–145. While the notion of a "genealogy" is first introduced in section 1 as a concern for a historical inquiry into the origins of morality, in section 4 Nietzsche introduces the discipline of linguistics, and specifically the practice of etymological analysis, as a more useful and more significant model of genealogy. For an extended discussion of the concept, see Michel Foucault, "Nietzsche, Genealogy, History," trans. Donald Bouchard and Sherry Simon, in *The Foucault Reader*, ed. Paul Rabinow (New York: Pantheon Books, 1984), pp. 76–100.

51. *HAH*, vol. 2, part 1, sec. 89, p. 232.

52. *HAH*, vol. 2, part 2, sec. 52, p. 323.

53. *Daybreak*, book 1, sec. 34, p. 25.

54. *GM*, book 1, sec. 2, p. 25. Nietzsche's paraphrase, here, of the so-called English psychologists is actually drawn from chapter 1 of Paul Rée's *The Origin of the Moral Sensations*, "The Origin of the Concepts 'Good' and 'Evil' "—the very first sentence of which declares, "Two instincts [*Triebe*] are united in everyone, namely, the egoistic and the unegoistic"(Rée, *Der Ursprung der moralischen Empfindungen*, p. 1). Suffice it to say that Nietzsche took issue with this position from the outset, and that the first essay of the *Genealogy* constitutes in large part his response to it. Rée's own position was strongly influenced by Sir John Lubbock's then-popular book on anthropology, *Prehistoric Times* (1865), as well as by the works of Bain, Tylor, Darwin, Mill, Hume, Helvetius, Hutcheson, and Locke.

55. In the first essay, Nietzsche generally calls this historical transformation a "revaluation" (*Umwerthung*) or an "inversion" (*Umkehrung*) of values. Looking back on the *Genealogy* the very next year (1888) in *Ecce Homo*, he would term the work as a whole "three decisive preliminary studies by a psychologist for a revaluation of all values" (*EH*, p. 313). By the fall of 1888, he would see the radicalization and extension of this "revaluation" or "inversion" of traditional moral values as his own singular task, "an immeasurably difficult and decisive task, which, *when it is understood*, will split humanity into two halves. Its aim and meaning is, in four words: the *transvaluation* [*Umwertung*] *of all values*" (*Selected Letters*, p. 311).

56. *GM*, book 1, sec. 4, pp. 27–28.

57. Hence, for Nietzsche, when discussing moral terms especially, one must always

raise the subsequent question "*Who* asks?" about these terms, these evaluative positions and issues, since their meaning will vary according to the social position—and the distinctive character associated with that position—of the person who affirms (or denies) them. Thus, "how different these words 'bad' and 'evil' are, although they are both apparently the opposite of the same concept 'good.' But it is *not* the same concept 'good': one should ask rather precisely *who* is 'evil' in the sense of the morality of *ressentiment* [i.e., of the lower class]. The answer, in all strictness is: *precisely* the 'good man' of the other morality, precisely the noble, powerful man, the ruler, but dyed in another color, interpreted in another fashion, seen in another way by the venomous eye of *ressentiment*" (*GM*, book 1, sec. 11, p. 40).

58. *GM*, book 1, sec. 5, p. 31.

59. *GM*, book 1, secs. 5, 6, pp. 31–33.

60. *GM*, book 1, sec. 7, p. 33. Nietzsche had earlier discussed a similar transformation of value with the emergence of Socratic value, at the eclipse of the classical period, in *The Birth of Tragedy*.

61. While resentment as such may assume many forms, Nietzsche distinguished two principal kinds in his "The Wanderer and His Shadow" (1879): an immediate sort and one that is deferred. In the former case, one must "distinguish first of all that defensive return blow which one delivers even against lifeless objects (moving machinery, for example) which have hurt us: the sense of our counter-action is to put a stop to the injury by putting a stop to the machine. To achieve this the violence of the counter-blow sometimes has to be so great as to shatter the machine. . . . One behaves in a similar way towards people who have harmed us when we feel the injury directly; if one wants to call this an act of revenge, all well and good; only let it be considered that *self-preservation* alone has here set its clockwork of reason in motion, and that one has fundamentally been thinking, not of the person who caused the injury, but only of oneself: we act thus *without* wanting to do harm in return, but only so as *to get out* with life and limb." As for the second kind of revenge, Nietzsche continues, "One needs time if one is to transfer one's thoughts from oneself to one's opponent and to ask oneself how he can be hit at most grievously. This happens in the second species of revenge: its presupposition is a reflection over the other's vulnerability and capacity for suffering: one wants to hurt." In both cases of revenge, then, *action is exacted against the opponent*, the person who initially inflicted the pain or suffering. In the first instance one is motivated by the desire to avoid future harm to oneself, and in the second, one wishes to hurt the other so as to restore one's loss or, more commonly, to restore one's sense of honor. In the latter case, the type of revenge will differ as to whether the initial offense to one's honor or dignity was public or private. Nietzsche goes on to further remark, "His revenge will be the more incensed or the more moderate according to how deeply or weakly he can think his way into the soul of the perpetrator and the witnesses of his injury; if he is wholly lacking in this kind of imagination he will not think of revenge at all, since the feeling of 'honor' will not be present in him and thus cannot be wounded. He will likewise not think of revenge if he *despises* the perpetrator and the witnesses: because, as people he despises, they cannot accord him any honor and consequently cannot take any honor away from him either" (*HAH*, vol. 2, part 2, sec. 33, pp. 316–18).

62. Max Scheler, *Ressentiment*, trans. William Holdheim (New York: Free Press, 1961), pp. 45–46.

63. Nietzsche's discussion of *requital* owes much to his reading of Hobbes's *Levia-*

than (Chicago: Henry Regnery, 1956), part 1, chap. 11, "Of the Difference of Manners."

64. Freud would describe this psychological mechanism as a "substitutive satisfaction," in his *Moses and Monotheism*, part 2, sect. F, "The Return of the Repressed," in *The Standard Edition of the Complete Psychological Works of Sigmund Freud*, trans. James Strachey (London: Hogarth Press, 1961), vol. 23, pp. 124–27.

65. *HAH*, vol. 1, sec. 45, pp. 36–37.

66. *HAH*, vol. 1, sec. 45, p. 37.

67. Scheler, *Ressentiment*, pp. 48, 58.

68. Freud's reflections on this strikingly corroborate Nietzsche's own views. See, especially, "Moses and Monotheism," in *Standard Edition of Sigmund Freud*, vol. 23, part 1, sec. D, pp. 80–92; vol. 23, part 2, sec. C, pp. 111–15; and vol. 23, part 2, sec, H, pp. 132–37.

69. *BGE*, sec. 225. In his very last work, *Ecce Homo*, Nietzsche applies this analysis to his own person. Cf. esp. chap. 1, "Why I Am So Wise," secs. 2–6, pp. 222–31.

70. *Daybreak*, book 1, sec. 38, p. 27.

71. *BGE*, sec. 52. Nietzsche rewrites this passage somewhat, and it figures as part of section 22, from the third essay of the *Genealogy*. There he remarks, "I do not like the "New Testament," that should be plain. . . . The *Old* Testament—that is something else again: all honor to the Old Testament! I find in it great human beings, a heroic landscape, and something of the very rarest quality in the world, the incomparable naiveté of the strong heart; what is more, I find a people. In the New one, on the other hand, I find nothing but petty sectarianism, mere rococo of the soul" (p. 144).

72. *Daybreak*, book 3, sec. 205, pp. 124–25. Nietzsche's discussion here finds a striking echo in Jean-Paul Sartre's account of the Jews' "authentic response" to the historical "situation" imposed upon them by the anti-Semite, in his *Anti-Semite and Jew*, trans. George Becker (New York: Schocken Books, 1965), pp. 136–41.

73. Cf. G. W. F. Hegel, *The Phenomenology of Mind*, trans. J. B. Baillie (London: George Allen & Unwin, 1949), sec. B, "Self-Consciousness," chap. 4, part A, "Independence and Dependence of Self-Consciousness: Lordship and Bondage," pp. 228–40.

74. *GM*, book 1, sec. 7, p. 34.

75. "One should not imagine it [i.e., this Christian love] grew up as the denial of that thirst for revenge, as the opposite of Jewish hatred! No, the reverse is true! That love grew out of it as its crown, as its triumphant crown spreading itself farther and farther into the purest brightness and sunlight, driven as it were into the domain of light and the heights in pursuit of the goals of that hatred—victory, spoil, and seduction—by the same impulse that drove the roots of that hatred deeper and deeper and more and more covetously into all that was profound and evil" (*GM*, book 1, sec. 8, p. 35). Thus, as Nietzsche had argued in *Daybreak*, "Of the people of Israel," the specifically Jewish revenge took the form of "scorning being scorned," rather than of *ressentiment* as such: "they have known how to create for themselves a feeling of power and of eternal revenge out of the very occupations left to them (or to which they were left); one has to say in extenuation even of their usury [and it should be recalled that the church traditionally enjoined Christians not to handle money as a profession. Who would be better suited to do this than the Jews, who were generally forbidden to own land?] that without this occasional pleasant and useful torturing of those who despised them it would have been difficult for them to have preserved their own self-respect for so long. For our respect for ourselves is tied to our being able to practice requital. At the same time, however, their revenge does not easily go too far; for they all possess the

liberality, including liberality of soul, to which frequent changes of residence, of climate, of the customs of one's neighbors and oppressors educates men" (book 3, sec. 205, pp. 124–25).

76. *GM*, book 1, sec. 7, p. 34. Since *ressentiment* is initially understood as a psychological means of defense and compensation, its extension to a group, a nation-state, or even an entire civilization is problematic. But Nietzsche would argue, precisely by means of a genealogical analysis, that such "sentiments" are already encoded in our own social-symbolic order—as are the feelings of "guilt," or of "romantic love," much less something like the linguistic structures of rationality itself. Hence, for Nietzsche, there arises the always difficult problem of *really* being able to "know oneself." By the same token, the breadth of extensional application for such notions as *ressentiment* enables him to shift his discussion *from* the individual *to* a people and their broader culture. This *shift* in reference often produces striking historical lacunae and other discontinuities of argumentation, which often appear as inconsistencies or contradictions, if one disregards, for example, Nietzsche's concern for rhetorical stress, stylistic considerations, context, and so forth.

77. *GM*, book 1, sec. 10, pp. 36–37.

78. *GS*, book 1, sec. 13, pp. 87–88.

79. Again, "bad" originally designated the common, ordinary, or plebian—those not possessed of high position and the virtues associated with them. The transformation of "bad" as a character designation for the lower classes parallels the designation "good" for the noble class, but the term originally carries "no inculpatory implication" with it: "The most convincing example of [this] . . . is the German word *schlecht* [bad] itself: which is identical with *schlicht* [plain, simple]—compare *schlechtweg* [plainly], *schlechterdings* [simply]—and originally designated the plain, the common man, as yet with no inculpatory implication and simply in contradistinction to the nobility. About the time of the Thirty Years' War, late enough, therefore, this meaning changed into the one now customary" (*GM*, book 1, sec. 4, p. 28). With this change, Nietzsche draws attention to what he sees as the moral fragility and arrogance of his own contemporaries—precisely those people from whom he had chosen to absent himself: "*Of German virtue.*—How degenerate in its taste, how slavish before dignitaries, classes, decorations, pomp and splendor, must a people have been when it evaluated the *Schlichte* [the simple] as the *Schlechte* [the bad], the simple man as the bad man! The moral arrogance of the Germans should always be confronted with this little word '*schlecht*': nothing further is needed" (*Daybreak*, book 4, sec. 231, p. 138).

80. Cf. Freud, in *Standard Edition of Sigmund Freud*, vol. 12, *Totem and Taboo*, esp. chap. 4, sec. 2, p. 125, and sec. 5, pp. 140–46; also, vol. 21, *Civilization and Its Discontents*, chap. 5, pp. 108–16.

81. *GM*, book 1, sec. 10, p. 38. The reference is to Aristotle's use of *eu pratein* in the *Ethics*, esp. 1095A14ff.: "To resume the discussion: since all knowledge and every choice is directed towards some good, let us discuss what is in our view the aim of politics, i.e., the highest good attainable by action. As far as its name is concerned, most people would probably agree: for both the common run of people and cultivated men call it happiness, and understand by 'being happy' the same as 'living well' and 'doing well' [*eu pratein*]. . . . Thus, if there is some one end for all that we do, this would be the good attainable by action; if there are several ends, they will be the goods attainable by action" (Aristotle, *Nicomachean Ethics*, trans. Martin Ostwald [Indianapolis: Bobbs-Merrill, 1962], pp. 6, 14).

82. Perhaps Aristotle's most detailed account of human happiness and its constit-

uent parts is to be found in his *Rhetoric*, 1360B8–1362A14: "We may define happiness as prosperity combined with excellence; or as independence of life; or as the secure enjoyment of the maximum of pleasure; or as a good condition of property and body, together with the power of guarding one's property and body and making use of them. That happiness is one or more of these things, pretty well everybody agrees.

"From this definition of happiness it follows that its constituent parts are: good birth, plenty of friends, wealth, good children, plenty of children, a happy old age, also such bodily excellences as health, beauty, strength, large stature, athletic powers, together with fame, honour, good luck, and excellence. A man cannot fail to be completely independent if he possesses these internal and these external goods; for besides these there are no others to have. (Goods of the soul and of the body are internal. Good birth, friends, money, and honour are external)" (*Rhetoric*, trans. W. Rhys Roberts, in *The Complete Works of Aristotle*, ed. Jonathan Barnes [Princeton: Princeton University Press, 1984], vol. 2, p. 2163).

83. *GM*, book 1, sec. 10, p. 38.
84. *GM*, book 1, sec. 10, p. 38.
85. *Twilight of the Idols*, sec. 2, in Kaufmann, *The Portable Nietzsche*, p. 493.
86. *GM*, book 1, sec. 13, p. 46.
87. *GM*, book 1, sec. 14, pp. 47–48.
88. *GM*, book 3, sec. 15, p. 127.
89. *GM*, book 1, sec. 14, p. 48.
90. *GM*, book 1, sec. 15, p. 49.
91. *GM*, book 1, sec. 13, p. 45.
92. *GM*, book 1, sec. 13, p. 45.
93. *GM*, book 1, sec. 15, p. 49.
94. *GM*, book 1, sec. 10, p. 38.
95. Jean-Paul Sartre's portrait of the anti-Semite, in his *Anti-Semite and Jew*, provides many illustrations of this. Likewise, Max Scheler's extended analysis of *ressentiment* in his book of the same title, serves to dramatically confirm Nietzsche's analysis.
96. *GM*, book 1, sec. 16, p. 52. Nietzsche mentions other possible historical examples of a "slave revolt" against the "classical ideal," such as the Protestant Reformation as an uprising against the Renaissance, and the French Revolution as an attack against French aristocratic culture of the sixteenth and seventeenth centuries. It would be fair to say that precisely the lack of historical detail in Nietzsche's account of these events— and of the "slave revolt" in general—is sufficient witness to their "symbolic" or "psychological" value.
97. *GM*, book 1, sec. 16, p. 52.
98. *GM*, book 1, sec. 17, p. 55.
99. In *Unmodern Observations*, pp. 73–145.
100. *GM*, book 1, sec. 17, p. 55.
101. *GM*, book 1, sec. 17, p. 55.
102. *GM*, book 1, sec. 17, p. 56.
103. As with most occurrences of the term, Nietzsche's use of "will" is extremely general. He sometimes means by this personal motives, particular intentions or desire-formations, as well as the general range of emotions, drives, and affects that serve to make up one's character.
104. Here, Nietzsche draws upon Aristotle's etymological observation that acts of commercial exchange bear the mark of law or convention, the very ordering principles of society. Money (*numis*) or currency (*nomisma*) derives its value (to proportionally

measure commodities) from law or convention (*nomos*). Money thus permits regulated and ordered acts of exchange (thus reciprocally satisfying the demands or needs of the buyer and seller) that are necessary to the stability of human association (i.e., to the state). The common etymological root for money and the conventions of law (specifically, the "inherited" and oftentimes "unwritten" laws of convention, prescribed by long usage), *numis* and *nomos*, respectively, is *nem*, which basically means "apportioning" or "assigning" a place, a position, and stipulating its boundaries. See Aristotle's *Ethics*, book 5, chap. 5, and his *Politics*, book 1, chap. 9, for an extensive discussion of this relation.

105. *GS*, book 1, sec. 13, p. 86.

106. Nietzsche elaborates this feeling of the triumphant power of the victor and his merciless desire to inflict cruelty and punishment on the defeated, in the case of warfare, in *GM*, book 2, secs. 9 and 13. For an extensive discussion of this subject, see Elaine Scarry, *The Body in Pain* (Oxford: Oxford University Press, 1985), esp. part 1, chap. 2, "The Structure of War: *The Juxtaposition of Injured Bodies and Unanchored Issues*." Nietzsche gives a clear and concise account of his own "warlike nature" and how this colors the style (and serves to explain the often bellicose rhetoric) of his philosophical critique in *EH*, "Why I Am So Wise," sec. 6, pp. 229–31.

107. *GM*, book 2, sec. 5, pp. 64–65. This pleasure of violation, of transgression, is effectively the pleasure that stems from the pure exercise of solipsistic power—with neither reason (it is not instrumental to anything else) nor constraint (it is precisely the constraint of the other in general that is destroyed through this extreme exercise of one's own power) to provoke or to impede it. Hence, in addition to the feeling of pleasure taken in feeling superior to someone else, Nietzsche characterizes this pleasure of violation itself as "voluptuous": it is the full and incommensurable gratification taken in the exercise of one's extreme most sensual and instinctual expression. Nietzsche's description faithfully—and ironically—recalls St. Augustine's own experience of "sin," when, as a young man, he stole a neighbor's pears: "All my enjoyment was in the theft itself and in the sin. . . . Our real pleasure was simply in doing something that was not allowed. Such was my heart . . . that I became evil for nothing, with no reason for wrongdoing except the wrongdoing itself. The evil was foul, and I loved it; . . . I loved my sin—not the thing for which I had committed the sin, but the sin itself" (*Confessions*, trans. Rex Warner [New York: New American Library, 1963], book 2, p. 45). Nietzsche discusses this "pleasure of doing evil for the pleasure of doing it" in *HAH*, vol. 2, sec. 50, in the context of his argument against pity—invoking Plato, La Rochefoucauld, and Prosper Merimée as witnesses to the universality of this pleasurable feeling. On both occasions, he cites the phrase in French (taken from Prosper Merimée's *Lettres à une inconnue*, 1874).

108. *GM*, book 2, secs. 5, 6, pp. 64–65.

109. *GM*, book 2, sec. 3, p. 61.

110. *GM*, book 2, sec. 3, p. 62. Nietzsche's discussion of punishment and torture derives in large part from his close reading of A. H. Post, especially his *Baustein für eine allgemeine Rechtswissenschaft auf vergleichend-ethnologischer Basis*, 2 vols. (Oldenburg, 1880–81).

111. Cf. *GM*, book 2, sec. 11, pp. 73–76.

112. *GM*, book 2, sec. 11, p. 74.

113. *GM*, book 2, sec. 11, p. 76. A corollary to this would be that the "equality" of subjects would also be a legal consideration, a status granted—like "rights"—by the state. There is neither "justice" nor "equality," nor "rights" by nature or in nature.

These will be seen to derive from the subsequent "moralization" of nature, as introduced by the teachings of religion and metaphysics.

114. *GM*, book 2, sec. 12, pp. 76–79.

115. "To give at least an idea of how uncertain, how supplemental, how accidental 'the meaning' of punishment is, and how one and the same procedure can be employed, interpreted, adapted to ends that differ fundamentally, I set down here the pattern that has emerged from consideration of relatively few chance instances I have noted. Punishment *as* a means of rendering harmless, of preventing further harm. Punishment *as* recompense to the injured party for the harm done, rendered in any form (even in that of a compensating affect). Punishment *as* the isolation of a disturbance of equilibrium, so as to guard against any further spread of the disturbance. Punishment *as* a means of inspiring fear of those who determine and execute the punishment. Punishment *as* a kind of repayment for the advantages the criminal has enjoyed hitherto (for example, when he is employed as a slave in the mines). Punishment *as* the expulsion of a degenerate element (in some cases, of an entire branch, *as* in Chinese law: thus *as* a means of preserving the purity of a race or maintaining a social type). Punishment *as* a festival, namely *as* the rape and mockery of a finally defeated enemy. Punishment *as* the making of a memory, whether for him who suffers the punishment—so called 'improvement'—*or* for those who witness its execution. Punishment *as* payment of a fee stipulated by the power that protects the wrongdoer from the excess of revenge. Punishment *as* a compromise with revenge in its natural state when the latter is still maintained and claimed *as* a privilege by powerful clans. Punishment *as* a declaration of war and a war measure against an enemy of peace, of the law, of order, of the authorities, whom, *as* a danger to the community, *as* one who has broken the contract that defines the conditions under which it exists, *as* a rebel, a traitor, and breaker of the peace, one opposes with the means of war" (*GM*, book 2, sec. 13, pp. 80–81; emphasis added). Michel Foucault pursues this subject of seeing punishment as a complex social function, one involving a highly developed set of methods in the state's exercise of power and transformative techniques, in his *Discipline and Punish*, trans. Alan Sheridan (New York: Vintage, 1979). Indeed, acknowledging his debt to Nietzsche, he proposes to undertake "a genealogy of the present scientifico-legal complex from which the power to punish derives its bases, justifications and rules, from which it extends its effects and by which it masks its exorbitant singularity" (p. 23).

116. *GM*, book 2, sec. 4, p. 63.

117. *GM*, book 2, sec. 4, p. 63.

118. *GM*, book 2, sec. 15, pp. 81–82. Cf. also Foucault, *Discipline and Punish*, part 3, chap. 2, "Illegalities and delinquency," pp. 257–92, and part 3, chap. 3, "The Carceral," pp. 293–308.

119. *GM*, book 2, sec. 13, pp. 79–80.

120. *GM*, book 2, sec. 4, p. 63.

121. *GM*, book 2, sec. 11, pp. 75–76.

122. *GM*, book 2, sec. 9, p. 71.

123. As Nietzsche would describe this institutional and ongoing condition of state violence in section 17, "that the welding of a hitherto unchecked and shapeless populace into a firm form was not only instituted by an act of violence but also carried to its conclusion by nothing but acts of violence—that the oldest 'state' thus appeared as a fearful tyranny, as an oppressive and remorseless machine, and went on working until this raw material of people and semi-animals was at last not only thoroughly kneaded and pliant but also *formed*" (*GM*, book 2, sec. 17, p. 86).

124. *GM*, book 2, sec. 16, p. 84.

125. *GM*, book 2, sec. 14, p. 82. As Freud would remark in *The Future of an Illusion*, "One would think that a re-ordering of human relations should be possible, which would remove the sources of dissatisfaction with civilization by renouncing coercion and the suppression of the instincts. . . . It seems rather that every civilization must be built up on coercion and renunciation of instinct; it does not even seem certain that if coercion were to cease the majority of human beings would be prepared to undertake to perform the work necessary for acquiring new wealth. . . . It is just as impossible to do without control of the mass by a minority as it is to dispense with coercion in the work of civilization. For masses are lazy and unintelligent; they have no love for instinctual renunciation, and they are not to be convinced by argument of its inevitability; and the individuals composing them support one another in giving free rein to their indiscipline. . . . To put it briefly, there are two widespread human characteristics which are responsible for the fact that the regulations of civilization can only be maintained by a certain degree of coercion—namely, that men are not spontaneously fond of work and that arguments are of no avail against their passions" (*Standard Edition of Sigmund Freud*, vol. 21, pp. 7–8).

126. Again, Freud's account is in striking accord with that of Nietzsche: "It is in keeping with the course of human development that external coercion gradually becomes internalized; for a special mental agency, man's super-ego, takes it over and includes it among its commandments. . . . As regards the earliest cultural demands, which I have mentioned, the internalization seems to have been very extensively achieved" (*Standard Edition of Sigmund Freud*, vol. 21, p. 11). Of course, for Freud, the super-ego serves to function in much the same way that Nietzsche's notion of bad conscience does: it internalizes an ideal of rule and authority, and it operates as a judge and moral censor upon the individual, imposing "ideals" for behavior and is ever-watchful over the propriety of one's actions.

127. *GM*, book 2, sec. 16, pp. 84–85.

128. See, especially, Freud, "Inhibitions, Symptoms and Anxiety," in *Standard Edition of Sigmund Freud*, vol. 20, p. 94.

129. *GM*, book 2, sec. 16, p. 84.

130. *GM*, book 2, sec. 16, p. 85.

131. *GM*, book 2, sec. 16, p. 85.

132. *GM*, book 2, sec. 17, p. 87.

133. *GM*, book 2, sec. 18, p. 87. Nietzsche further develops the artist's "ascetic ideal" at length in the third essay of the *Genealogy*, especially in sections 2–4, which are devoted to the analysis of one artist, Richard Wagner.

134. *GM*, book 2, sec. 18, p. 88.

135. Freud would later agree with Nietzsche that the kind of suffering brought about by our subjection to the order of civil society is perhaps the most painful of all: "We are threatened with suffering from three directions: from our own body, which is doomed to decay and dissolution and which cannot even do without pain and anxiety as warning signals; from the external world, which may rage against us with overwhelming and merciless forces of destruction; and finally from our relations to other men. The suffering which comes from this last source is perhaps more painful to us than any other" (*Standard Edition of Sigmund Freud*, vol. 21, p. 77).

136. Cf. also *BGE*, part 7, sec. 230, p. 160.

137. *GM*, book 2, sec. 19, p. 88.

138. *GM*, book 2, sec. 19, p. 89.

139. *GM*, book 2, sec. 20, p. 91.

140. *GM*, book 2, sec. 20, p. 90.

141. *GM*, book 2, sec. 21, p. 91.

142. *GM*, book 2, sec. 21, p. 92.

143. *GM*, book 2, sec. 23, p. 93.

144. This would be the pre-Socratic, or Homeric-Hesiodic, understanding. Plato's account is highly critical of this and it anticipates the later Christian account. In the "Myth of Er" (*Republic*, X, 614Bff.), Socrates would have the individual assume the full responsibility for his transgressions and injustices, at the cost of his eternal soul "being dropped into Tartarus" (616A5). Poetic accounts of the gods intervening to determine man's fate—much less, that the gods might themselves be the cause of evil—would be strictly proscribed in an ideal "republic." Cf., especially, Plato's excoriation of Homer and Hesiod, in connection with educating the young guardians, in the *Republic*, II, 376E–III, 398C.

145. *GM*, book 2, sec. 7, p. 69.

146. *GM*, book 2, sec. 7, pp. 93–94.

147. "God himself makes payment to himself, God as the only being who can redeem man from what has become unredeemable for man himself—the creditor sacrifices himself for his debtor, out of *love* (can one credit that?), out of love for his debtor!" (*GM*, book 2, sec. 21, p. 92). For an extended discussion of Nietzsche's understanding of love and gifts, see Gary Schapiro, *Alcyone: Nietzsche on Gifts, Noise, and Women* (Albany: SUNY Press, 1991).

148. *GM*, book 2, sec. 22, p. 92

149. *GM*, book 2, sec. 22, p. 93.

150. *GM*, book 3, sec. 21, p. 142.

151. *GM*, book 3, sec. 15, p. 127.

152. *GM*, book 3, sec. 15, p. 128.

153. Cf. Freud, "The Future of an Illusion," in *Standard Edition of Sigmund Freud*, vol. 21, chap. 2.

154. *GM*, book 3, sec. 17, p. 132; sec. 18, p. 134.

155. *GM*, book 3, sec. 18, p. 134.

156. *GM*, book 3, sec. 18, p. 135.

157. *GM*, book 3, sec. 20, p. 141.

158. *GM*, preface, sec. 5, p. 19. Nietzsche would go on to remark, "It is my purpose here to bring to light . . . what [the ascetic ideal] *means*; what it indicates; what lies hidden behind it, beneath it, in it; of what it is the provisional, indistinct expression, overlaid with question marks and misunderstandings" (*GM*, book 3, sec. 23, p. 145).

159. Indeed, the third essay is prefaced by a brief motto from the section entitled "On Reading and Writing," from part 1 of *Zarathustra*, where Nietzsche instructs the reader how to interpret his aphoristic style of writing in terms of *his own personal values*: namely, in terms of a courageous love of life, tempered by laughter.

160. *GM*, preface, sec. 8, p. 23.

161. *GM*, book 3, sec. 1, p. 97.

162. *HAH*, vol. 2, part 2, p. 316.

163. *GM*, book 2, sec. 13, p. 80.

164. *GM*, book 3, sec. 8, p. 108.

165. *GM*, book 3, sec. 1, p. 97.

166. *GM*, book 3, sec. 1, pp. 97–98.

167. *GM*, book 3, sec. 21, pp. 142–43. Nietzsche discusses "priestly asceticism"—

recall that several generations of Nietzsche's ancestors were Lutheran pastors—at length in sections 11–22. In section 19, he distinguishes two general types of ascetic practices, or "means," by which the priest deals with people's suffering: a relatively "innocent" sort—he summarizes these in the first paragraph—and a "guilty" sort, which consists in the employment of the "great affects" ("anger, fear, voluptuousness, revenge, hope, triumph, despair, cruelty") to unleash "orgies of feeling" in the suffering individual, so as to divert them from their "dull pain and lingering misery" (pp. 139–40). In neither set of ascetic practices, however, does the priest "cure" the suffering. In fact, Nietzsche claims, the widespread harm inflicted upon the population of Europe by the practice of priestly asceticism is only exceeded by that brought about by the Germans and by syphilis.

168. *GM*, book 3, sec. 23, p. 146.

169. If the ascetic ideal has served as the preeminent model of interpretation for Western thought, Nietzsche nonetheless sees it as practically antithetical to ordinary common sense, positing as it does such "conceptual fictions" as a "pure, will-less, painless, timeless, knowing subject," or even such "contradictory concepts" as "pure reason," "absolute spirituality," or "knowledge in itself" (references, in this case to the German metaphysical idealism of Schopenhauer and Kant). But Nietzsche goes on to maintain that such antithetical views are themselves helpful, even if they only serve as limited "perspectives" in enabling us to attain a broader sense of "objectivity"— precisely "so that one knows how to employ a *variety* of perspectives and affective interpretations in the service of knowledge" (*GM*, book 3, sec. 12, p. 119). In the end, since Nietzsche claims that there is no absolute truth "in itself," no "disinterested" knowing or experiencing, we must *reverse* the traditional imperative—maintained by the ascetic ideal—that there is only *one* truth, or *one* perspective, and that all others must be excluded. Rather, since all knowledge or experience is itself contextually situated, historically oriented, and given to a particular, complex subject, we should cultivate as many perspectives as possible in our search for a more objective understanding of things: "There is *only* a perspective seeing, *only* a perspective 'knowing'; and the *more* affects we allow to speak about one thing, the *more* eyes, different eyes, we can use to observe one thing, the more complete will our 'concept' of this thing, our 'objectivity' be" (*GM*, book 3, sec. 12, p. 119). Most importantly, however, it is only from the distance afforded to us by such "perspectives," that we can begin to "interpret," and thus "evaluate," what was formerly taken as an indisputable goal or end "in itself," such as the ascetic ideal's notion of an unquestioned—and unquestionable—metaphysical "truth." Hence, Nietzsche's continuing preoccupation with the *value of*, for example, "morality," "truth," "life," "value," "punishment," and so forth, estimations that are always subject to further reflection, revision, and qualification (i.e., to further interpretation). For an excellent account of Nietzsche's "perspectivism," see Alan Schrift, *Nietzsche and the Question of Interpretation* (New York: Routledge, 1990), esp. chaps. 6 and 7.

170. To recapitulate Nietzsche's earlier account, somewhat, he claimed that it was due to the increase in suffering, as well as to the sense of indebtedness to one's ancestors, that primitive humanity internalized the set of enforced social prohibitions required to maintain civil order and society (i.e., herd morality). With the repression of one's own egoistic instincts, one acted for, or in the name of, the community. As that community prospered, so did the sense of indebtedness to its ancestors. As the sense of indebtedness increased, so did the spiritual power of the ancestors, until they became retroactively transformed into divinities—ultimately attaining the greatest of power, the monotheistic creator God of the Judeo-Christian tradition. Not only are the believers

felt to be indebted to the traditional God for the world itself, but they are further obligated by his absolute spiritual authority and moral law, as revealed in scripture. This obligation is impossibly compounded with the advent of the crucifixion, Nietzsche claims, and the believers' sense of indebtedness becomes the burden of an impossible sin.

171. Nietzsche's rejoinder to this traditional account of "sin" is relatively straightforward: "Man's 'sinfulness' is not a fact, but merely the interpretation of a fact, namely of physiological depression [or inhibition]—the latter viewed in a religio-moral perspective that is no longer binding on us.—That someone *feels* 'guilty' or 'sinful' is no proof that he is right, any more than a man is healthy merely because he feels healthy" (*GM*, book 3, sec. 16, p. 129). Rather, Nietzsche goes on to explain, in section 17, the real causes for such suffering, depression, or inhibition are multiple: organic, physiological, emotional, dietary, and so forth. Hence, the priest can at best provide consolation and temporary alleviation for the sufferer by attending to his discomfiture, but he can give no lasting "cure," because he has misinterpreted its real cause.

172. *GM*, book 3, sec. 16, pp. 162–63.

173. The problem with science, for Nietzsche, is not that it lacks sincere, devoted practitioners, or that in its ordinary employment or theoretical development, it is not successful and rigorous. Rather, Nietzsche claims that it lacks an ideal of value; its present goal is "truth," but this is generally not regarded as problematic by science. Much as the religiomoral teaching, and indeed, like the traditional philosophical teaching, the objective of "truth" stands as an uncritical goal, that is, truth itself is held to be beyond criticism, inestimable, unquestionable in its value. In this respect, truth as the ascetic ideal appears as a metaphysically charged "ultimate reality"—truth "in itself," as it were. Hence, Nietzsche will often speak of the scientist's "faith," or of the philosopher's "faith," in *truth*, precisely, as "beyond" question, reason, and appeal. For Nietzsche, such a "truth" must itself be subject to interpretation and criticism as to its application, its various extensions, its preconditions and implicit objectives, its human and contextual relevance, and so forth. In short, truth itself must be understood as a functional element within a system of interpretation, of signs, and not as being transcendent to it. In doing this, Nietzsche poses the problem of value or normativity, as a problem, to the conduct of the sciences. For an extended and exceptionally well-informed discussion of these issues, see Babette Babich, *Nietzsche's Philosophy of Science* (Albany: SUNY Press, 1994), esp. chaps. 4 and 5.

174. "Suppose such an incarnate will to contradiction and antinaturalness is induced to *philosophize*: upon what will it vent its innermost contrariness? Upon what is felt most certainly to be real and actual: it will look for error precisely where the instinct of life most unconditionally posits truth. It will, for example, . . . downgrade physicality to an illusion; likewise pain, multiplicity, the entire conceptual antithesis 'subject' and 'object'—errors, nothing but errors! To renounce belief in one's ego, to deny one's own 'reality'—what a triumph! . . . [This] reaches its height when the ascetic self-contempt and self-mockery of reason declares: '*there is* a realm of truth and being, but reason is *excluded* from it!' " (*GM*, book 3, sec. 12, p. 118).

175. Cf. esp. *The Antichrist*, sec. 15, pp. 581–82, and *Twilight of the Idols*, "Morality as Anti-Nature," pp. 486–92.

176. *GS*, book 4, sec. 341, p. 273.

177. *EH*, "Genealogy of Morals," p. 312.

INDEX

Aeschylus, 53, 56, 59
agon, 33, 60
Alexander the Great, 155, 156, 157; and
    Phyllis, 155, 156
amor fati, 278n26
Andreas-Salomé, Lou, 2, 112–15, 140,
    154, 155, 157, 158, 189, 190, 264n7,
    267n18, 275n7, 275n12, 276n13,
    282n51, 289n152, 299n27
aphorism, 76, 240, 265n11
Apollo, Apollonian, 18, 19, 20–25, 26, 31–
    39, 40, 42, 51, 56, 60, 161
aposiopesis and Nietzsche's style, 118,
    278n23
a priori values, 193
Aquinas, Thomas, Saint, 95, 219, 269n35,
    270n50
Archilochus, 45, 46, 50
Aristotle, 30, 38, 54, 155, 156, 187, 214,
    259n64, 305n82, 306n104
asceticism, 141; ascetic ideal, xv, 240–47,
    311n169; priestly asceticism, 310n167

Babich, Babette, 260n98, 312n173
Bauer, Bruno, 184
Beatitudes, 135
Binswanger, Otto, 12
Borges, Jorge Luis, 268n25
Boscovitch, Joseph Ruggiero, 264n9
Brahms, Johannes, 184
Brandes, Georg, 266n15
Brant, Sebastian, 157, 282n56, 289n153

"Buddhism." *See* nihilism
Burckhardt, Jacob, 7, 8, 183

Cadmus, 128
catharsis, 54
Christ, 167, 173, 236, 283n63
Christianity, xv, 5, 20, 86, 93, 94, 99, 117,
    122, 129, 135, 145, 148, 166, 197, 210,
    211, 217, 220, 234, 236, 271, 281n48,
    304n75
conscience, 221–40; bad conscience, 225,
    228–40, 242, 309n126; origin of, 224.
    See also guilt; sin
creditor, 223, 224, 229
Critias, 46
cruelty, 232, 238

D'Andeley, Henry, 289n153
death of God, viii, 68, 72, 73, 88, 90–109,
    118, 125, 127, 131, 133, 150, 268n22
debt–debtor relationship, xiv, 222, 233,
    234, 235
Defenestration of Prague, 272n63
Deleuze, Gilles, 82
Delphi, oracle at, 24
Descartes, René, 138, 149, 175, 273n73,
    286n99, 288n137
Deussen, Paul, 131
de Vitry, Jacques, 289n153
Dionysus, Dionysian, 18, 19, 20–25, 26,
    31, 37, 39–57, 129, 161, 254n21,
    254n37; Dionysian play, 55; intoxica-
    tion, 41, 66; and music drama, 60–67;

ABOUT THE AUTHOR

David B. Allison is professor of philosophy at the State University of New York at Stony Brook. He is the editor of the groundbreaking anthology *The New Nietzsche*.